THE BIRTH OF THE ARAB CITIZEN
AND THE CHANGING MIDDLE EAST

THE BIRTH OF THE ARAB CITIZEN AND THE CHANGING MIDDLE EAST

EDITED BY
STUART SCHAAR
AND
MOHSINE EL AHMADI

OLIVE
BRANCH
PRESS

An imprint of Interlink Publishing Group, Inc.
www.interlinkbooks.com

First published in 2016 by

OLIVE BRANCH PRESS
An imprint of Interlink Publishing Group, Inc.
46 Crosby Street, Northampton, Massachusetts 01060
www.interlinkbooks.com

Library of Congress Cataloging-in-Publication Data available
978-1-56656-973-6

Cover image © Joel Carillet

Printed and bound in the United States of America

To request our complete 48-page, full-color catalog, please call us toll free
at 1-800-238-LINK, visit our website at www.interlinkbooks.com or write
Interlink Publishing, 46 Crosby Street, Northampton, MA 01060
e-mail: info@interlinkbooks.com

Stuart dedicates this book to his friend
Eqbal Ahmad (1933–1999)
and to the exciting times we shared.

Mohsine dedicates this book to his children,
Aladin and Shahrazad,
and his wife Nadia, the magic lamp.

||||||||||||||||||||||||||||||||||||||||||||||||||||||||||||||||||||||||||||||||

ACKNOWLEDGMENTS

We thank, first of all, Wolfgang Meissner, former director of the Goethe Institute in Rabat, Morocco, for financial assistance in organizing this book. Thanks too to Michel Moushabeck for his interest in the project and for backing it up with the resources of Interlink Publishing.

We wish also to thank the contributors to the book, who donated their chapters because they understood the worth of the project. Through Dr. Marion Berghahn, her publisher at Berghahn Books, Dr. Renate Bridenthal found us Bernard Heise, a fine German translator in New Zealand. Thanks also to Kirsten Bauer and Radia Ben Abbou for doing other translations. Dr. James Miller, head of the Moroccan-American Commission for Educational and Cultural Exchange (MACECE), the Fulbright Program in Rabat, suggested contributors, as did Dr. Tom DeGeorges formerly of the American University of Sharjah (United Arab Emirates); Abbas Shiblak, Director of Shaml, the Palestine Refugee and Diaspora Center (Ramallah); Dr. Sari Hanafi, Chairperson, Department of Sociology and Media Studies, American University of Beirut; and Dr. Ella Shohat and Alex Winder (both of New York University). Heidi Frieder of Art Head donated her time to help with graphics.

||||||||||||||||||||||||||||||||||||||||||||||||||||||||||||||||||||||||||||||||

NOTE ON TRANSLITERATION AND SPELLING

Throughout this book we have omitted the Arabic *'ayan* (') and *'hamza* ('). We avoid most Arabic plurals and add an *s* to the singular form of the word, placing the plural at the first usage of a word, if necessary. We also adopt English usage of Arabic words, such as "ulema," as they appear in standard English-language dictionaries. Place names and people's names are referred to as per standard English spellings in most cases—e.g. "Mohamed" vs "Muhammad"—or, in those cases where there is no commonly accepted spelling, as referred to locally. Place names in Arabic have not been italicized. The same is true for Arabic and French personal names. All British spellings have been changed to US format.

CONTENTS

II

INTRODUCTION
DIRECTIONS AND DEFINITIONS
STUART SCHAAR

The failure of all of the Arab revolts, except for the one in Tunisia, can be explained largely by the lack of theoreticians of revolution in the Middle East and North Africa who might have provided a blueprint for how to overturn local dictatorial regimes and keep them overturned. In most of the Arab world, old reactionary forces retook or remained in power after the revolts ran their course. Most of the young people who initially fomented the uprisings in the Middle East and North Africa (the MENA region) had neither the interest nor the theoretical backgrounds to formulate plans for revolutionary transformations. They headed revolts, not revolutions.

Recall that in the great historic revolutions that had previously taken place in the previous century, such as the Russian and Chinese upheavals, leading figures like Vladimir Lenin and Mao Zedong provided theoretical analysis of how to overthrow the old regimes and replace them with revolutionary states. In both cases, communist cadres infiltrated the old regimes' armies and, after civil wars, captured and held onto their respective states. We know from the ground-breaking research of Orlando Figes how precarious communist power was in the first year after the Russian revolution. It was a miracle, Figes concludes, that the communist party succeeded in remaining in control of the state.[1]

In the 1960s Sayyid Qutb, head of the Muslim Brotherhood in Egypt, advocated infiltrating the Egyptian army as part of his plan to overthrow the state. President Gamal Abdel Nasser responded by having him killed. In order to accede to power, the Muslim Brotherhood in the twenty-first century had to renounce the use of all forms of violence before it could participate in post revolt elections. Ultimately, for the revolt to have succeeded and taken root, the power of the Egyptian army—after the army had initially sided with the crowd—would have had to whittle away. The opposite happened.

I

In Iran, Ayatollah Ruhollah Khomeini captured the state after returning to his country from French exile in 1979. Using the clerical infrastructure in place for centuries—comprising experienced clergy who had organized mass religious demonstrations and ceremonies flawlessly for centuries—he had a ready-made base for establishing his control. He added to that force a revolutionary guard composed of 250,000 formerly unemployed youth whom he armed with Israeli Uzi machine guns left over from the Shah's regime, and stationed groups of them in every mosque throughout the country. These young men were given the power to intervene at will in people's homes to arrest dissidents and enforce conformity. The new regime also purged the army. The long war against Iraq that followed the revolution allowed the clerical regime to consolidate its power. It also helped that each ayatollah had an automatic mass following that venerated its chosen clerical leaders. Khomeini's adepts contributed an estimated $40 million yearly for good works, and he and his clerical followers organized revolutionary propaganda as well.

The lack of revolutionary theory and a blind faith in democratic institutions, such as free elections, sidelined the young people who initially organized the revolts. Mosques and traditional mobilizing tools—landlord-peasant relations and patronage systems, clan structures, patrilineal relationships, and intact remnants of old party structures—largely determined election results. Old political parties organized by overthrown dictators proved more resilient than anyone could have imagined, and served as mobilizing tools for elections. Money secretly spread about by local billionaires and rulers of the Gulf states as well as behind-the-scenes machinations of the great powers influenced outcomes and counterrevolutions.

Counterrevolutions came faster in the Middle East and North Africa than anyone imagined possible. Riding the crest of a popular revolt against the Muslim Brotherhood in Egypt, the army staged a coup d'état and overthrew the elected government led by Mohamed Morsi on July 3, 2013. One of the richest men in Egypt, the billionaire Copt cell phone magnate Naguib Sawiris, clandestinely financed the movement opposing the Brotherhood, without demonstrators necessarily knowing where the money came from. The military strongman who became president, General and Field Marshall Abdel Fattah el-Sisi, led the charge against the Brotherhood, and the army killed about 1,000 people who protested these changes, while Egyptian judges meted out significant numbers of death sentences to Brotherhood leaders and militants. Any opposition to the military state from any quarter has been crushed.

To give the appearance of evenhandedness, the state arrested leading secular figures who had led the April 6 Youth Movement that first began the revolt. Ahmad Maher (1980–), Mohamed Adel (1988–), and Ahmad Douma

(1985–) are now serving prison terms. Others escaped into exile. Some major liberal figures, such as Saad Eddin Ibrahim, surprised some of their followers and supported the military coup.[2] The message is clear: the army is in control and will not tolerate any political activity whatsoever. Thousands have been arrested and hundreds have been given long prison sentences, making the present Egyptian regime even worse in this respect than that of Hosni Mubarek.

The irony of the new order is that the Egyptian military now completely dominates the country's economy. Modern capitalists such as Gamal Mubarek (the ex-president's son) and his friends have been removed, arrested, and sentenced to prison, losing their significant investments in a myriad of projects. The army, using free or cheap conscript labor, is enriching itself as it has done since the days of President Nasser.

The US role in this transition remains murky. The Obama administration has unfrozen money that is earmarked for Egypt since the late 1960s to maintain peace with Israel. No significant protests were registered in Washington over the overthrow of a democratically elected government and the US is now conducting business as usual with Cairo, while once more encouraging Egyptian involvement as intermediaries in the Palestinian-Israeli conflict.

During July and August 2014, Israeli troops invaded Gaza and destroyed scores of tunnels that previously gave Hamas access to Israeli territory. Missiles and bombs flew in all directions, destroying large swaths of Gaza's buildings and killing more than 2,000 Palestinians, including many civilians. Israel's Iron Dome defense system supplied by the United States kept damage to a minimum in the Jewish state as Hamas and Islamic Jihad lobbed hundreds of missiles into Israel. An uneasy truce has been arranged by the Egyptians, but the warring parties stand poised to renew hostilities. Israel demanded that the Palestinians abide by previous agreements and demilitarize Gaza, a position Hamas rejects.

With democracy rejected by the Egyptian military, the Syrian, Yemeni, and Libyan regimes imploding, the Israeli-Palestinian crisis unresolved, Iraq facing increased sectarian conflicts between its Shia and Sunni populations, and an encroaching Islamic State winning lightning victories, coupled with greater external interference, extremists have found the space to expand their control of large swaths of the MENA region. For four years the Syrian regime led by Bashar al-Assad has assaulted its own population ferociously in order to stay in power. Support for Assad has been forthcoming from Iran, Russia, and the Lebanese Hezbollah, giving the Syrian regime significant staying power. Radical jihadist movements have also flourished, and Islamic State (ISIS) has captured large swaths of territory in Syria and Iraq, allowing it to set up a Caliphate, causing panic among fleeing civilians, especially among Christian,

Shia, and other sectarian communities, whose members fear captivity and death. Massacres of both mainstream Muslims and minorities has made life impossible for many, not least those belonging to marginal communities, who have made it known that they want to migrate out of the Middle East after having lived there for thousands of years. More than three million Syrians have been forced to flee their homes, fearful of the extremists; many of the non-Muslims caught in Islamic State's conquered territory either have to pay the minority tax (*jizyah*) or convert to the radicals' brand of Islam.

Status quo world powers such as the United States, Russia, and China, and joined by Israel and the oil rich Gulf states, will seek to keep change at bay and will shore up new dictatorships. It still remains easier for the great powers and their conservative surrogates to deal with oligarchies and military elites than back participant, loosely organized mass movements or poorly organized youth in the face of a new, ferocious enemy reminiscent of the terroristic Mongols of past centuries.

Altruism also has become an enemy in post revolt states. The Islamist-dominated Muslim Brotherhood in Egypt and the Ennahda Movement in Tunisia predictably favored their own and shut out of political processes and economic participation militants from other groupings, who sacrificed to get rid of the old regimes. The basic ingredients of democracy, the give and take and sharing of the pie, was not accepted by the electoral victors immediately after the revolts. The Muslim Brotherhood's political wing in Egypt won the presidential elections with the slightest majority, yet ruled as if it had swept to power in a landslide. In Tunis, Ennahda, having gained 37 percent of the parliamentary vote, had to ally with two secular parties to govern the country, yet made decisions as if it alone ruled. Both Islamist-dominated parties tolerated the reactionary Salafists (extremely conservative Muslims), whom the Saudis generously funded in both Egypt and Tunisia, and thereby antagonized the many Muslims in those two countries who had increasingly distanced themselves from extremists. Attempts by the Islamist parties to enshrine sharia law in the new constitutions of Egypt and Tunisia met with stiff opposition in both countries, and contributed to the mass rebellion against Brotherhood rule and the army coup, and forced Ennahda to give up power in favor of a caretaker government of technicians.

Neither party took into consideration that the majority of citizens voted for them in compensation for their past victimization, as a payback for the Islamic-generated charity they had dispensed, and also because they represented forces for change away from the old dictatorships. Some voters also thought that the Gulf sheikhdoms would support these Islamists and underwrite massive loans through Islamic banking and spark an economic boom.

That never happened. The majority of the electorates in both countries did not vote for the establishment of new dictatorships.[3]

THE SYRIAN AND IRAQI NIGHTMARES

Despite all the conflicts that have cropped up throughout the region, the Syrian Civil War became a festering problem with no end in sight, counting 210,000 deaths by April 2015, one third of that representing civilians.[4] Four million refugees, mostly women and children, who have fled the country into neighboring states, creating havoc both in Syria and in bordering areas by early July 2015. More than eleven million Syrians have been forced out of their homes, while more than one-third of housing has been damaged or destroyed. Nearly 40 percent of hospitals have been obliterated and about two million children have stopped going to school. At the beginning of 2015, with the war estimated to have cost $202 billion, some 2.5 million Syrians living in battle zones faced hunger and some quarter of a million imminent starvation.[5] Thirty percent of the Syrian population now lives in abject poverty.

Initially President Barack Obama threatened to intervene militarily in Syria, unilaterally if necessary, in the face of Russian and Chinese vetoes in the United Nations Security Council opposing military action. The British Parliament voted against any such action and US polls demonstrated that 65 percent of Americans opposed doing so. With US troops in Afghanistan drawing down and with fresh memories of President George W. Bush's catastrophic invasion of Iraq to overthrow Saddam Hussein, and the ensuing development of sectarian conflicts there, the US public had no taste for more military intervention in the volatile Middle East. President Obama welcomed a Russian proposal calling on Syria to dismantle its chemical weapons (originally stockpiled as a reaction to Israel's atomic arsenal, but now hopelessly outdated because of new effective Israeli defense shields).

Competition between Qataris and Saudis for influence over Syrian rebel factions and the Wahhabi Saudis' long-standing opposition to the Muslim Brotherhood and all its offshoots in and out of Syria complicated US policy in Syria and elsewhere in the region. The US could not control the flow of Gulf money and arms flowing into battle zones, sowing trouble for all but the recipients. The situation in Syria and neighboring Iraq is extremely complex. Thousands of battle-tested foreign jihadist fighters have infiltrated into both countries across bordering states, carrying sophisticated weapons or capturing government arms and vehicles, seizing oil fields and refineries, selling petroleum at cut-rate prices, and stealing money from captured banks. The BBC in May 2015 estimated that ISIS's war chest amounted to some two billion dollars.

ISIS leaders have made it clear that they intend to redraw the map of the Muslim world and create a new caliphate out of conquered Syrian and Iraqi territory. In addition, Boko Haram in northern Nigeria, militia elements in Libya, and some of the Afghan Taliban have joined Islamic State. Meanwhile massacres of minorities and Shiites who refuse to convert to hard-line Sunni Islam has caused havoc in those areas conquered by ISIS. The US finally intervened with air strikes against these radical elements in August 2014 under the pretext of saving minority communities of Yazidis and Christians. The Obama administration also began bombing ISIS strongholds in Syria, after the Assad regime in August 2014 welcomed foreign intervention to weaken and destroy the radicals.

The Iraqi army, trained and equipped by the US, continues to melt away, leaving behind sophisticated military equipment ISIS confiscates as it has expanded its control of territory. Some Iraqi Sunni officers and troops who fought in Saddam Hussein's army have joined forces with ISIS, as have many tribal Sunni Iraqis, who were marginalized by the Shiite-dominated government of Nouri al-Maliki in Baghdad. An open question remained whether a new Iraqi government formed in late August and early September 2014 could ally with Sunni fighters and tribesmen to turn back ISIS and rule in the name of a large coalition. Their use of Shiite militias at the end of May 2015 to substitute for crumbling military forces can only antagonize sectarian cleavages and cause greater problems over the long run.

The non–al-Qaeda Syrian opposition concluded that the presence of those extremists could only strengthen their enemies in the region, including Israel and the Assad regime. The latter used the terrorism card to sow confusion among its Western opponents. A pattern emerged demonstrating that the Syrian government, in its massive bombing campaigns against civilians, did not attack known al-Qaeda bases in the north of Syria, and reports flowed that Damascus was indirectly purchasing petroleum from ISIS elements that controlled some Syrian oil wells.

Russia has pushed Assad to negotiate a ceasefire in the war, but did not nudge him into relinquishing power, a demand of the united opposition.[6] As we went to press, a resolution of the Syrian crisis seemed as elusive as ever.

Other MENA countries face their own immediate problems. Libya, for example, has succumbed to warlordism, adding further to the country's chronic statelessness. A danger exists that Libya could implode and, if lucky, be reconstituted as four separate states, representing remnants of Ottoman provinces in pre-European colonial times. Bahrain, under Saudi military occupation, has been locked down. In Yemen, weakened by regionalism and tribalism, Shiite Houthi rebels, backed by Iran, and military forces loyal to the country's former president, Ali Abdullah Saleh, initiated a civil war. The Saudis, as defenders of Sunni orthodoxy and fearful of Yemen's civil war spreading to the Arabian Peninsula, initiated an air campaign to strike what some commentators believe are Iranian-backed Houthi targets. Tunisia, meanwhile, despite its remarkable achievement of forging a new liberal constitution by consensus, faces major economic difficulties. Women everywhere in the region face increased restrictions on their liberty of action and by intensified male chauvinism.

THE NEED FOR A LONG VIEW APPROACH

Recall that history is filled with revolution and counterrevolution. In nineteenth-century Europe, Napolean I, Metternich, Bismarck, all were counterrvolutionaries. Ultimately, however, upheavals, including two monumental twentieth-century wars, created a strong democratic movement throughout Europe, and economic growth markedly improved the lives of millions of people, while the unshackling of capitalism created pervasive poverty besides untold riches.

On the whole, the world is certainly a better place because of the French, Russian, and Chinese revolutions, although people living through them and immediately afterward could not have imagined what would emerge in their wake. It took time to appreciate fully the legacies of these and other revolutions, giving the long *durée* approach to history special meaning for all mass revolts and upheavals. In other words, we cannot judge outcomes of such mass movements in terms of immediate results, but rather we have to view their long-term outcomes. What has developed in the immediate wake of the Arab revolts, does not necessarily define what the final outcome will be.[7]

A new category of Arab citizen is emerging, mostly fearless in defending her or his rights.[8] Even when intimidated by some of the new forces released by the revolts, such as revitalized Salafists in multiple guises, and in some countries armed bands taking the law into their own hands, or political parties and militaries rooted in the past, the proliferation of new civil society associations and of a new freedom of thought and expression, especially among young people, gives some hope that all is not lost and that a new, better society may come into being throughout the region over time. This will not happen immediately or automatically by itself, but rather those who cherish universal rights, transparency, the limitation of corruption, and widened opportunities will have to keep their guard up, organize fearlessly, and not give up hope that their actions can help change their world for the better. Past struggles elsewhere demonstrate that expanding rights and opportunities entails constant struggle that must go on continuously, often in the face of fearful opposition.

There seem to be enough people in the MENA region who are ready for the challenges ahead and have the stamina to sustain long-term commitments.

Social movements in the region have benefited from the revolts, not only by freeing people's minds and tongues, but also by demonstrating the advantage of collective action. Young people have creatively transformed their online social networks and digital gadgets into platforms for organizing new channels of communication in ways undreamed of before the revolts began.

Nevertheless, some MENA intellectuals have allowed pessimism to get the better of them, as they see conservative forces, abetted by widespread illiteracy and poverty, winning mass elections. The Syrian quagmire and uncertainty over the future of Palestine have cast a pall over the MENA region. But space has opened that did not exist before to organize, make collective demands, and hold responsible those holding the reigns of power. The weakening of some states as a result of the revolts may even allow new civil forces to form and strengthen themselves free of strong central controls.

THE VOCABULARY OF REVOLT

Many commentators have expressed their dissatisfaction with the term "Arab Spring" to describe the series of events that have marked the region since the end of 2010.[9] The term evokes the memory of the Prague Spring of 1968, marking the revolt of Czechoslavaks in the face of preponderant Soviet power. The USSR, at the height of its influence, easily crushed the movement and postponed the liberation of Eastern Europe until the Soviet empire imploded at the end of 1991. By citing parallels with this aborted Eastern European movement, those who coined the term "Arab Spring" left themselves open to pessimism and despair as new realities took shape that called into question the notion of liberation. Several books, in fact, have appeared referring to "the Arab winter," implying a failure of the revolts.[10] The terms "revolt" or "uprising" may be preferable to describe those momentous political events that have taken place in the Arab world over the past few years.

The word "revolution" implies monumental change in institutions, as well as class struggles; in short, significant social upheaval. So far in the MENA region, entrenched military forces and some old political parties (sometimes in reconstructed forms) have taken power. Such was the case in Tunisia with Nidaa Tounes or "Call of Tunisia," headed by Béji Caïd Essebsi, who has grouped together moderate members of the Destour Party and the Constitutional Democratic Rally (RCD, as per its French initials) through which presidents Habib Bourguiba and Zine al-Abdine Ben Ali had ruled.

Likewise, dominant classes remain intact, stymieing those who would like to foment revolutions. Many individuals who had collaborated with the old regimes have been attempting to reinvent themselves as Islamists, defenders of barricades, or democrats, depending on their co-citizens' short memories, and their own experience in government and business to help kick-start the new economies and political processes in place since the revolts. However, voters, with great sophistication, have tended to reject these imposters, but new media in place since the revolts have given such people platforms to reestablish their presence in print, on the air waves, and within politics.

THE REVOLTS IN THE CONTEXT OF THE NEW INFORMATION AGE

As a historian I understand the weight of the past on the present. I cannot, however, argue, as many of my prominent colleagues in the field of MENA studies have done, that what we have witnessed in the region since December 2010—mass revolts, the overthrow of dictators, and the empowerment of millions who lost their fear of challenging the rotten regimes that ruled over their lives for decades—is just one more manifestation of popular uprisings that have marked the region periodically since the late-nineteenth century and even before that.[11]

What we are living through is not just more of the same. Sometimes we need to acknowledge that times change dramatically, that great historical breaks do occur, and that we are living in a new epoch known as the Information Age, as significant in its transformative power as what happened in the 1750s, when parts of the world began moving from the agricultural to the industrial age.[12] This new age is certainly just beginning but already has altered our lives dramatically. That does not mean that all parts of the world are caught up equally in this transformation, but it does signify that many millions of people around the globe have entered the digital age, including those in the MENA region. However, as Omar Foda points out in Chapter 3 on Egypt, most rural people who voted in post revolt elections fell back on old means of mobilization, and the Internet had little or no effect on their electoral choices. This helps explain why the Muslim Brotherhood's Mohamed Morsi and the old-guard political leader Ahmad Shafik ended up sweeping the first stage of presidential elections: their old electoral machines still functioned efficiently enough to pull out votes. Christopher Davidson (Chapter 7) contrarily points out that digital technology has invaded all levels of life in the Gulf States, making it much more difficult for local rulers to control content. Ubiquitous cell phones, mini-computers containing still and movie cameras, new tablets, satellite technology with new, 24/7 news channels, and social media sites have transformed the way that Arab urbanites (the majority of MENA's population) communicate, get their news, organize their lives, and bring crowds together to face down dictators. That is not to say that the old methods of communication and organizing by word of mouth, in many places where people congregate such as mosques, markets, and schools do not continue to play a vital role in mass mobilization, but something new has been added, facilitating urban revolts and crowd formation and giving people courage to eradicate their fear. Women, especially, as Sahar Khamis argues in Chapter 11, have been liberated even in the most conservative countries such as Yemen, and have used social networks to organize their participation. The massification of access to digital communication devices means that poor and rich, women as well as men, can access information and organize using new technology. Internet cafés have opened in urban slums and some, but by no means all, rural zones, beginning a process that one day in the near future may fully democratize participation. Satellite antennas have sprung up in tin-can shantytowns, and portable ones are sometimes fitted on nomads' tents. You no longer need a personal computer to participate in the World Wide Web. Manifold alternatives exist, giving even the most deprived urbanites and some rural dwellers access.

OUT OF CONFUSION AND CHAOS A NEW WORLD MAY EMERGE
WHY ANOTHER BOOK ON THE SUBJECT?

More than sixty books have appeared in English already on the subject of the "Arab Spring."[14] More than a score have been published in French, several of which are conspiratorial, viewing the US as a major manipulator of events surrounding the Arab revolts.[15] A few French titles attempt to describe what happened, but most books take a short term view, not seeing the long *durée*, and are therefore pessimistic regarding the present and near future.[16] There are, of course, an untold number of books in Arabic.[17] Paula Gondolfi also produced an excellent one in Italian on art and the Arab revolts.[18]

Why have Mohsine El Ahmadi and I added to this long list? Our book offers a unique blend of political analysis, by prominent scholars of the MENA region, with chapters on culture and political economy, including Viola Shakir's contribution on cinema in Egypt and Tunisia before and after the revolts (Chapter 15), Carol Solomon's richly illustrated chapter on street art in the Tunisian uprising (Chapter 16), Farid El Asri on popular music in the Arab revolts (Chapter 17), Stuart Schaar on Tunisian cyber activists (Chapter 14), Alex Winder on rumors and conspiracy theories in Egypt's Tahrir Square (Chapter 19), and Farhad Khosrokhavar on the Arab revolt and self-immo-lation (Chapter 17). Sahar Khamis has written an essay on women's activism during the uprisings (Chapter 10) while Clement Henry analyzes MENA's political economy (Chapter 11), and Eve Sandberg and Seth Binder examine Morocco's King Mohammed VI's economic policies (Chapter 13).

Following Mouin Rabbani's opening chapter on Islamic State, our country and regional studies begin with Stuart Schaar's personal witness on Tunisian realities (Chapter 2), and Omar Foda, a member of the Tahrir Documents collective, provides a poignant analysis of Egypt's revolt and its aftermath (Chapter 3). Curtis R. Ryan delves into the reactions of the Hashemite Kingdom of Jordan to the wider revolts (Chapter 4), while Joshua Landis examines the lasting power of Bashar al-Assad's regime in Syria (Chapter 5). Abaher El-Sakka shares with us (Chapter 6) his interviews with Palestinian youth involved in nonviolent resistance to Israeli occupation and control on the West Bank and in Gaza. Christopher Davidson views the Arab revolts from the perspective of the Persian/ Arabian Gulf (Chapter 7), while Prashant Bhatt, a medical doctor from the Indian subcontinent, working in a Libyan hospital in Tripoli, shares his insights into expatriate and local reactions to events in the country's former capital (Chapter 8). Mohsine El Ahmadi and Aziz Radi dissect Moroccan reactions, especially that of the February 20 Movement (Chapter 9), while Karim Amellal seeks to answer the question of why Algerians did not foment their own revolt (Chapter 10).

Finally, Simon Louvish examines reactions in Israel and the wider Arab world within the framework of identity politics (Chapter 20) and John L. Hammond shows how events in the MENA region stimulated the US Occupy Wall Street movement (Chapter 21).

SPEND, SPEND, AND SPEND

No part of the MENA region escaped the effects of the Arab revolt. The Saudis promised to spend $100 billion to upgrade housing and provide a better life for some of the poorest people living in their very rich kingdom. The other monarchies and republics followed the Saudi lead, promising to leave subsidies intact on food and other staples, despite pressures coming from the International Monetary Fund, the World Bank, the US government, and the European Union to gradually remove all non-essential subventions. Military and police officers received raises and new equipment in several countries, both to buy their loyalty and assure their ability to control newly activated crowds. The newly empowered Arab citizens await redress for the many ills that they see around them, such as unemployment, an underfunded poor-quality education system marked by inordinately large classes and increasing deficiencies in the training of teachers, and rampant corruption.

To reiterate, it would be foolish to expect smooth transitions after a mass uprising of Arab citizens. It will take several years, perhaps decades, before we see new political orders emerge. In the meantime we will see unexpected events and new forces attempting to influence the initial post revolt period.

Likewise, we should expect to find weakened states in places where dictators ruled. This is inevitable, since the institutions and main individuals that ran the dictatorships have been broken, old rulers have been exiled or imprisoned, and new forces have not consolidated enough power or established effective new states. In the non–oil-producing states, with most economies in shambles because of a fall in tourism and the drying up of local and foreign investment, job creation, a major popular demand, has had to be put on hold, thereby making an expectant population ever more frustrated and angry. Many of the countries in the MENA region have become mass societies, ready to be mobilized.[19] They are waiting for leaders to emerge who can rally electoral majorities and rule effectively. Tensions will mount to provide for these expectant populations, including those living away from the coasts, whom the old dictators largely ignored. The revolts are not over yet, for we are witnessing only the first stages of a longer process of transformation we can expect to unfold over the next few decades.

As dictatorships reestablish control over some Middle East states new radical formations, such as ISIS, have garnered support from segments of the population that have been shut out of participation in the political processes. But the excesses of the extremists have already produced a backlash, bringing US air power into the fray and inciting elements of the moderate opposition to regroup and retake the offensive. Despite the reluctance of the Western powers to send in troops to fight the radicals, a consensus was growing by the end of 2014 that something had to be done to stop the radicals from expanding their control over strategic locations. It became clear by mid-2015 that, despite Washington's desire to shift its attention to distant Asia, the growth of Islamic radicalism in the Middle East was drawing the Obama administration into the growing conflicts of the region. With thousands of young Western Muslims volunteering to fight with ISIS in Syria and Iraq, the open question remains: what will happen to these young men and women once they return back to their home countries? Their radicalization makes them time bombs ready to explode. So too, the rise of dictators in some countries following the Arab uprisings has once again radicalized the Middle East, from Egypt to Bahrain, Yemen, Syria, and Palestine. Official attacks against moderate forces demanding equity and jobs can only add to a further radicalization of politics throughout the MENA region.

NOTES

1   Orlando Figes, *A People's Tragedy: The Russian Revolution 1891–1924* (NY: Penguin Books reprint, 1998).

2   Matt Bradley, "Military Regime Draws Support From Egypt's Liberals," *Wall Street Journal*, January 12, 2014.

3   See the excellent chapter on Egyptian developments since the revolt by Paul
     Amar, "Egypt," in his and Vijay Prasshad, eds., *Dispatches from the Arab Spring:
     Understanding the New Middle East*, Minneapolis and London: University of
     Minnesota Press, 2013, pp. 24–62 and a paper given by Stuart Schaar at the 2013
     Middle East Studies Association meeting in New Orleans, "Stages in the Recent
     Tunisian Revolt: Public Space and the Digital Revolution," in the panel organized
     by Odile Moreau, "Public and Private Spaces and the Maghreb Spring."
4   According to the Syrian Observatory for Human Rights on December 3, 2013.
5   These figures were provided by former British Foreign Secretary David
     Millibrand, now the Chief Executive of the International Rescue Committee,
     in an op-ed in the *Washington Post*, January 17, 2014. On January 20, 2014, the
     New York Times reported that Assad's forces had cut off the Damascus suburb of
     East Glouta, denying its 160,000 inhabitants of all supplies. The situation there
     was desperate.
6   *Salt Lake Tribune*, January 19, 2014.
7   For long *durée* analysis of the French, Russian, and Chinese revolutions see
     Georges Rudé, *The French Revolution: Its Causes, Its History, and its Legacy After
     200 Years*, New York: Grove Press, 1994; Orlando Figes, *A People's Tragedy: The
     Russian Revolution, 1891–1924*, New York: Penguin Books, 1998; John Schrecker,
     The Chinese Revolution in Historical Perspective, 2nd ed., Westport, CT: Praeger,
     2004.
8   A cogent discussion of the emerging civil society and the role of the new Arab
     citizen in it can be found in Tirno Behr & Aaretti Sŭtorien, "Building Bridges or
     Digging Trenches?: Civil Society Engagement after the Arab Spring," Helsinki:
     The Finnish Institute of International Affairs, FHA Working Paper 77, January
     2013. I would like to thank a former student in my course on the Arab Spring in
     the Amideast Study Abroad Program in Rabat, Robert Bronstein, for bringing
     this paper to my attention.
9   See James L. Gelvin, "Conclusion: The Arab World at the Intersection of the
     National and Transnational," in Mark L. Haas and David W. Lesch, eds., *The
     Arab Spring: Change and Resistance in the Middle East*, Boulder, CO: Westview
     Press, 2013, pp. 240–241, for a critique of the use of the term "Arab Spring."
     Rami G. Khouri, "Drop the Orientalist Term 'Arab Spring,'" *Daily Star* (Beirut),
     August 17, 2011, was one of the first to criticize its use.
10   See Vijay Prashad, *Arab Spring Libyan Winter*, Delhi: Left Word, 2012; Nonie
     Darwish, *The Devil We Don't Know: The Dark Side of Revolutions in the Middle
     East*, Hoboken, NJ: John Wiley & Sons 2012; John R. Bradley, *After the Arab
     Spring: How Islamists Hijacked the Middle East Revolts*, Houndsmills Basingtoke,
     Hampshire, UK: Palgrave MacMillan, 2012; Raphael Israel, *From Arab Spring
     to Islamic Winte*r, New Brunswick, NJ: Transaction Publishers, 2013; and Pierre
     Pouchot, *La Révolution Confisquée: Enquête sur la transition démocratique en
     Tunisie*, Paris: Sindbad, 2012.
11   For example, see Lisa Anderson, "Demystifying the Arab Spring: Parsing the
     Differences between Tunisia, Egypt, and Libya," *Foreign Affairs* (May-June, 2011)

and Julia Clancy-Smith, "From Sidi Bou Zid to Sidi Bou Said: a *Longue Durée* Approach to the Tunisian Revolutions," in Mark L. Haas and David W. Lesch, eds. *The Arab Spring*, pp. 13–34.

12 See Manuel Castells, *The Information Age*. Vol. I; *The Power of Identity*, Vol. 2, *End of Millenium*, Vol. 3, *Economy, Society, and Culture*, Oxford, UK: Wiley-Blackwell, new ed., 2009–2010.

13 See references cited in note 3 above.

14 The best books on the Arab revolts include James Gelvin, *The Arab Uprisings: What Everyone Needs to Know*, New York: Oxford University Press, 2012; the above-cited Mark L. Haas and David W. Lesch, eds., *The Arab Spring*; David McMurray and Amanda Ufheil-Somers, eds., *The Arab Revolts: Dispatches on Militant Democracy in the Middle East,* Bloomington and Indianapolis: Indiana University Press in association with the Middle East Research and Information Project (MERIP), 2013; Clement Henry and Jang Ji-Hyang, eds., *The Arab Spring: Will it Lead to Democratic Transition?* Houndsmills Basingstroke, UK: Palgrave MacMillan, 2013; *The New Arab Revolt: What Happened, What it Means, and What Comes Next?* New York: Council on Foreign Relations/*Foreign Affairs*, 2011; Bassam Haddad, Rosie Basheer, and Ziad Abu-Rish, *The Dawn of the Arab Uprisings: End of an Old Order*, London: Pluto Press, 2012; Paul Amar and Vijay Prashad, *Dispatches from the Arab Spring: Understanding the New Middle East*, Minneapolis, MN: University of Minnesota Press, 2013.

15 See, for example, Eric Denécé, *La face cachée des révolutions arabes*, Lyon: Ellipses Marketing, 2012 and Maoufed Brahimi El Nili, *Le printemps arabe: une manipulation*, Paris: Editions Max Milo, 2012.

16 See the special issue of *mouvements des idées et des luttes* (2011), *Printemps arabes: Comprendre les révolutions en marche*, La Découverte; Jean-Pierre Filu, *La Révolution arabe: Dix leçons sur le soulèvements démocratiques*, Paris: Editions Fayard, 2011, translated into English as *The Arab Revolution: Ten Lessons from the Democratic Uprising,* New York: Oxford University Press, 2011. *L'année du Maghreb* No. 8, 2012, had a special edition edited by Victor Geiser, *un printemps arabe?*, Paris: CNRS Editions. See also Gilles Keppel, *Passion arabe: Journal 2011-2013*, Paris: Gallimard, 2013.

17 Some excellent Arabic titles include: Muhammad Abu Raman, *Salafists and the Arab Spring: Islam and Democracy in Arab Politics*, Beirut: Center for Studies of Arab Unity, 2013; Ibrahim Allush, ed., *Changes and Popular Revolts in the Arab World: Realities and Future Horizons,* Amman: Middle East Center for Studies, 2011; Hamud Abutalib, *Squares: The People Want*, Beirut: Arab House Sciences Publications, 2011 and Ahmed Manissi, *Movements for Change in the Arab World: An Egyptian Case Study*, Abu Dhabi: Center for Strategic Studies and Research, 2010.

18 Paula Gondalfi, RIVOLTE IN ATTO: *Dai mouvimenti artistici arabi a una pedagogia ivoluzionaria,* Milan: Mimesis Enterotopie, 2012.

19 William Kornhauser, *Politics of Mass Society*, London: Routledge, 2010. Writing this book in the 1950s, Kornhauser argued that mass societies have weak

intermediary structures between the masses and the state, making them vulnerable to authoritarian/totalitarian control, but that this condition also makes these societies available for mobilization for defined ends. Jack A. Goldstone, who has written extensively on comparative revolutions, concludes that in the Arab world "Large unemployed and underemployed youth populations are vulnerable to radicalization and recruitment to insurgent movements." "The New Population Bomb: Large Cohorts of Educated, Unemployed Youth," *Key Reporter* (Phi Beta Kappa Magazine), Spring 2011.

PART I
COUNTRY AND
REGIONAL STUDIES

|||||||||||||||||||||||||||||||||||||||||||||||||||||||||||||||||||||||||||||||||||||||||||||

The Islamic State (ISIS) movement needs to be understood as a political project whose primary objective is to establish a viable entity in areas it can control rather than engage in permanent insurgency against more powerful adversaries. The conditions for its emergence were created by the US occupation of Iraq, the dissolution of the Iraqi state and its replacement with a sectarian political system and conflict, and the collapse of central government authority in regions of Syria. The available evidence indicates that ISIS is at best uninterested in achieving the conventional forms of legitimacy and integration pursued by other Islamist movements; engagement is therefore unlikely to prove a viable option.

There are no quick or simple solutions to the challenges posed by ISIS. Those being considered, particularly Western military intervention, are almost guaranteed to make a catastrophic situation worse, while a strategy that relies on disaffected Sunni tribes and sectarian Shia militias is unlikely to succeed. A comprehensive approach is needed, one involving a reevaluation of policy toward the Syrian crisis, engagement with regional parties on a much broader spectrum of relevant issues, and a focus on establishing legitimate institutions that are able to address deep-seated grievances and resolve the conflicts that allow movements like ISIS to thrive.

|||||||||||||||||||||||||||||||||||||||||||||||||||||||||||||||||||||||||||||||||||||||||||||

CHAPTER 1*
THE UN-ISLAMIC STATE
MOUIN RABBANI

INTRODUCTION

Since the Islamic State (ISIS) movement seized control of Iraq's second city of Mosul in early June 2014, it has achieved unprecedented levels of success in Iraq and Syria, seized territory in Lebanon, and expanded to the border regions of most surrounding states. As a result, the international community, which had virtually forgotten about Iraq and was growing increasingly uninterested in Syria, put these conflicts back at the top of its agenda virtually overnight. The US is once again engaged in hostilities in Iraq and considering direct, less covert means of involvement in Syria, as are a number of its partners. Governments in the region, which had previously seen ISIS as either a distant threat or a useful proxy, seem to be overcoming their differences to confront what is perceived to be a common and growing challenge.

|||||||||||||||||||||||||||||||||||||||||||||||||||||||||||||||||||||||||||||||||||||||||||||||||||

* This chapter, now updated, was originally published on September 8, 2014 by the Norwegian Peacebuilding Resource Centre (NOREF): www.peacebuilding.no. Used by permission of the author and NOREF.

Much has been written about the genesis, ideology, objectives, and practices of ISIS. Most of these writings have characterized the movement as puritanical in nature—as either an extremist incarnation or a radical distortion of Islamic orthodoxy. The more pertinent observation, that ISIS represents a thoroughly modern project and that explanations for its existence are primarily to be found in the political landscape in which it operates rather than Islamic theology, is less frequently made.

ORIGINS AND DEVELOPMENT OF THE ISIS MOVEMENT

The roots of ISIS are located in the 2003 US occupation of Iraq and the still-ongoing Syrian Civil War that first erupted in 2011. The US administration in Iraq systematically dismantled the Iraqi state and its institutions and replaced them with a sectarian political system that saw conflict reproduce itself throughout government institutions. Unsurprisingly, Iraqi politics gradually came to be dominated by fundamentally incompatible identity-based political forces rather than national ones competing on the basis of different political platforms. While the ascendancy of Islamist parties among the disenfranchised Sunni community was not a foregone conclusion, it was helped along by the increasingly religious milieu of the Arab world in recent decades and the intensified Islamist character of opposition politics in the region—both of which are to some extent a legacy of the Cold War—as well as the prominence of Islamist militias in the struggle against both the occupation and the new regime in Baghdad.

Similar dynamics were at work in the ranks of the armed Syrian opposition in the period 2011–13, where—as in Iraq—those with the most effective military forces also obtained the greater share of foreign funding, weapons, and skilled cadres. Locally, a steady supply of recruits was ensured by endemic socioeconomic decay, particularly rampant unemployment among the youth and its debilitating impact on individual lives; a deep-seated sense of perpetual injustice; and the opportunity to redress these realities while simultaneously affirming a sense of self-worth and improved opportunities—all with a bit of adventure thrown in.

What made Iraq and Syria, rather than more conservative societies like Jordan and Saudi Arabia or polarized polities like Lebanon and Palestine conducive to the emergence of such movements, was the withdrawal and, in some regions, collapse of the state. A similar process can be observed today in Libya and, to a lesser extent, Yemen. Indeed, the breakdown of central authority and the absence of national institutions with sufficient legitimacy to address grievances and mediate political conflict have not only empowered subnational phenomena like sectarianism and tribalism as social defense mechanisms, but have also provided militias adopting such agendas with the space to develop and the opportunity to expand.

Nevertheless, this does not explain why ISIS in particular succeeded where other movements failed—or, rather, was able to seize the initiative and dominate or eliminate so many of its competitors. Here, ideology and the particular variant of Islam promulgated by ISIS are largely negligible factors. Rather, this phenomenon can be attributed primarily to the movement's thoroughly contemporary rather than atavistic modus operandi. First of all—unlike so many of its competitors, whose raison d'être is confrontation with the state, or what might be called a conventional guerrilla insurgency—from the outset ISIS (as its name suggests) has pursued a strategy of establishing and consolidating a political entity in regions where the former state no longer functions or can be expelled. ISIS is in this respect a fundamentally political rather than religious project—even though it insists the two are inseparable.

Secondly—and closely related to the first—the ISIS strategy has focused on obtaining the resources and means required to function as a state. For this to happen, it has sought to implement core functions including control of territory; the provision of governance, administration, and services; and the regulation of society and the economy. Territorial expansion is not prioritized and pursued for its own sake, as with many of its competitors, but rather pursued only when there is a reasonable prospect that such territory can be integrated, defended, and governed. While ISIS's proclamation of a caliphate in late June 2014 was motivated by a host of factors—including a determination to settle accounts with al-Qaeda, to subordinate other participants in the Iraqi Sunni rebellion and Syrian armed opposition to its will, and, of course, to capitalize on its spectacular successes of the previous months—its willingness to take a step eschewed by similar movements reflects the reality that statehood is germane to the ISIS project.

THE ISIS MOVEMENT: STRATEGY AND OBJECTIVES

Much has been written about the background to ISIS's sudden expansion and the interplay in this respect between the Syrian and Iraqi arenas, and there has been an equal amount of speculation about where ISIS might seek to expand next. Its response to the latter question in late 2014 and as of this writing—i.e. Erbil, the capital of the Kurdish region of Iraq—seems somewhat out of character in light of the consequences. Then again, perhaps speculation is correct that ISIS deliberately sought to provoke Western intervention in order to profit from direct conflict in the knowledge that the US and its allies lack the will to repeat the invasion of Iraq and the means to defeat ISIS in Syria. As for the question "Baghdad or Damascus?" the response is almost certainly "neither."

The former is too heavily defended, the latter too distant, and both are the seats of central authority.

A no less interesting question is whether the recent vast expansion of ISIS territory, and therefore of assets at potential risk, might motivate the movement to deal more pragmatically with the world around it and perhaps even to seek informal or other understandings with adversaries to enable it to consolidate its position and govern more effectively. In this respect some have looked to Lebanon's Hezbollah and more recently the Palestinian organization Hamas as examples of radical, armed Islamist movements that have either achieved or seek conventional forms of legitimacy after attaining significant political power and the responsibilities of governance. An initial informal nonaggression pact between ISIS and Iraq's Kurdish Regional Government (KRG), which allowed the latter to maintain control of Kirkuk and expand its territory by some 40% while ISIS consolidated its hold on Iraq's Arab Sunni heartland, seemed to suggest this could be a possibility.

Yet ISIS is fundamentally different in character and agenda from these other movements, and to extrapolate ISIS policies on the basis of the trajectory of other militant Islamists would be akin to inferring Khmer Rouge conduct from the record of the Bolsheviks after they established the Soviet Union. The tacit alliance with Iraq's Kurds was thus exceptionally short-lived and no more stable than ISIS's periods of coexistence with other elements of the Syrian armed opposition. To return to the Soviet analogy, the brief dalliance with the KRG might be compared to the 1939 Molotov-Ribbentrop pact (which · allied the Soviet Union briefly with Nazi Germany), although ISIS's strategic calculations in this instance more closely reflect those ascribed to Hitler (who ultimately intended to attack and conquer the Soviet Union), with the KRG fulfilling the role of Stalin (who some say allied with Hitler to gain time to prepare for defense against Germany's future invasion of the USSR).

Perhaps the greatest irony of the ISIS phenomenon is that the movement's vision of an Islamic state that correctly applies the pristine and unadulterated practices its leaders ascribe to the religion's inaugural practitioners would almost certainly be disavowed by the latter as a monumental parody. Indeed, from what is known about the statecraft of the Prophet Muhammad and the first caliphs, they would in all likelihood have rather quickly run afoul of ISIS's caliphate. No less importantly, fulfillment of the ISIS platform requires the systematic dismantling (and in too many cases the physical demolition) of fourteen centuries of Islamic civilization and tradition.

Few of the ideas ISIS promulgates are without theological foundation, nor are its practices entirely without precedent. Nevertheless, the movement can hardly claim to be rooted in well-established Muslim tradition or jurisprudence, and should therefore be primarily understood as a thoroughly modern interpretation and application of a faith whose imagined past is a projection backward of contemporary agendas rather than a revival of early Islamic rule. ISIS's reclamation of Islam's essence is thus on a par with the (Cambodian) Khmer Rouge's insistence that it represented the pure soul of communism even as its extremism distorted communist rule.

Similar to the Khmer Rouge, and returning once again to the comparison with other Islamist movements, ISIS branding is in large part based on a categorical rejection of either compromise or concession to an imperfect world, or a gradualist approach to achieving its objectives. The pragmatism and interaction with existing states and institutions exhibited by other Islamist movements is therefore something ISIS has condemned not only when in opposition, but more importantly after achieving power. Although the movement derives its theological roots from eighteenth-century Wahhabi doctrines that serve as the state ideology of Saudi Arabia and have for several decades been energetically disseminated throughout the Muslim world, ISIS rejects the Saudi state as a distortion of Wahhabi tenets.

As attested by the rapidity and ferocity with which ISIS has eliminated the presence of minorities in areas under its rule, suppressed erstwhile Sunni allies in Iraq and Syria, and criminalized tradition and local custom, initial post combat statements reassuring populations under its control that their rights would be respected pursuant to traditional Islamic practice have proven to be nothing more than a tactic to encourage a false sense of security and thus prevent the premature emergence of significant resistance to its designs.

CONCLUSION: FUTURE PROSPECTS

Under the circumstances, the assumption that history is on the verge of repeating itself and that ISIS will be removed much as its Iraqi precursor led by al-Qaeda's Abu Musab al-Zarqawi was defeated by foreign-sponsored local forces seems far-fetched. The ISIS movement is no longer a clandestine insurgent group that can be evicted by stronger militias and prevented from resurrection by internal security forces, but—not unlike the KRG—an increasingly conventional military force that can only be dislodged by taking physical control of its fiefdom. The coalition that occupied Iraq in 2003 appears to have little appetite for a rematch, and should its position change it is inconceivable that a renewed foreign occupation of Iraq would not make an already catastrophic situation more so.

Additionally, ISIS appears to have rather methodically put to sleep most of the leaders of the previous Awakening movement and potential kingpins of a new one. This notwithstanding, mechanisms to empower a cowed population to assert itself without exposing its members to mass slaughter need to be examined. On a related note, the risk that any operation to suppress ISIS will degenerate into a sectarian campaign to blunt Sunni aspirations has already been realized and needs to be addressed. In the current, highly polarized environment, the subcontracting of Iraqi national security functions to sectarian Shia militias is a particularly dangerous approach liable to have a lasting, disastrous impact.

Secondly, as many analysts have pointed out, there is a fundamental contradiction in Western policy toward Iraq and Syria. Seeking to strengthen the government opposed to ISIS in Iraq while acting to weaken its counterpart in Syria may serve any variety of policy objectives, but defeating ISIS is not one of them. Similarly, given the near-apocalyptic perceptions of ISIS that have gripped Western capitals in recent months, the approach of continued demurral and deflection concerning the extent to which the policies of regional allies have empowered and assisted ISIS needs to be revised. One might also note that complacency toward the propagation of *takfiri* thought—the Islamic counterpart of George W. Bush's belief that one is "either with us or with the terrorists"—is particularly hazardous, given the heterogeneous societies of the Levant and Iraq.

In the short term there are no easy responses to the challenges posed by ISIS. Military containment may succeed, but to do so it needs to be led by local and regional forces rather than those who have already brought Iraq to the brink of dissolution. Even limited US military intervention is likely to bolster ISIS at least as much as it weakens it. Secondly, policy on the Syrian crisis requires a comprehensive review. One need not endorse the Assad regime's brutal policies or assist with its implementation to recognize that the regime is a reality in the Middle East that will continue to exist at least until a political transition commences in Syria. Those who accord relative respect and recognition to such leaders as Omar al-Bashir (president of Sudan), Nouri al-Maliki (former Shiite prime minister of Iraq), Benjamin Netanyahu (Prime Minister of Israel) and Abdel Fattah el-Sisi (President of Egypt and ex-army general) lack persuasive grounds for rejecting engagement with Bashar al-Assad on matters of common concern.

Thirdly, neighboring states need to be dealt with as participants in a potential solution rather than part of an existing problem. This applies equally to Iran, Turkey, and Saudi Arabia, whose leaders, along with those of other

||||||||||||||||||||||||||||||||||||||||||||||||||||||||||||||||||||||||||||||||||||||||||||||||||||||||||

takfiri (Arabic: takfīrī) denotes a Muslim who accuses another Muslim (or an adherent of another Abrahamic faith) of apostasy. The accusation itself is called takfir, derived from the word kafir (infidel).

countries, should be encouraged—and if necessary pressured—to revise policies that enable and empower ISIS by design or default.

Finally—and crucially—political transition must be actively pursued not only in Syria, where it has been reduced to a slogan for regime change, if not regime suicide, but equally in Iraq. Only the emergence of institutions enjoying sufficient popular—and not necessarily electoral—legitimacy can address deep-seated grievances and peacefully resolve the conflicts that allow movements such as ISIS to thrive, and thereby reassert governance and authority on a national scale that ultimately forms the only durable solution to this challenge.

Based on his personal experience in Tunisia for more than half a century, Stuart Schaar describes how President Zine al-Abdine Ben Ali's dictatorship affected his own life and friendships there. On a hopeful note, he sees the development of a vibrant civil society as one of the revolt's major achievements. As newly liberated Tunisian citizens claim the right to participate in the country's decision-making processes, women, under attack by conservative forces, have taken the lead in creating new organizations as part and parcel of this bustling civil sphere. Taking everyone by surprise, the revolt, which began with the immolation of the fruit peddler Mohamed Bouazizi in the town of Sidi Bouzid in December 2010, spread first through Tunisia, then to the rest of the Arab world, and then around the globe.

CHAPTER 2
TUNISIAN REALITIES
STUART SCHAAR

I have been visiting Tunisia on and off since 1960 and have lived there for extended periods over the decades. When I retired from teaching at City University's Brooklyn College in New York in 2007, I moved to Tunis, intending to use that city as my base in North Africa and as my permanent home. The fact that the Ben Ali regime had previously devalued the Tunisian currency by one-third meant that it cost little to live there for anyone, like myself, receiving a pension in US dollars.

I had many friends in Tunis from all social classes and spent a great deal of time with families and friends in poor and working class districts, such as Cité Zehour, Sijoumi, Mellasine, and Mourouj, as well the swank suburbs of Carthage, Sidi Bou Said, El Menza VI, El Manar I and II, and La Marsa. I made it my business to cross class lines and not stay only with the rich and powerful. I felt that I had to check out what the elite told me against the realities of life lived at the edge by people who were barely eking out livings. Many of my wealthy Tunisian friends thought I was mad for spending so much time in the slums and working class neighborhoods, something they themselves would not dream of doing.

By 2008 I'd had it with Tunisia. Ben Ali's dictatorship affected all aspects of life. When I went to dinner parties no one said anything meaningful, for fear either that the conversations were being recorded or that people present would report what was said to the police. Ben Ali, a former police officer and ex-minister of interior, had exaggerated the number of police officers in the country. The figure we heard mentioned was that some 150,000 policemen and policewomen watched over a population that then numbered some nine million Tunisians and is today 10.5 million. The former president, Habib Bourguiba, was said to have had some 25,000 police officers working for his regime. After the revolt, in 2012, we learned from Muhammad Lazar Akremi, a high official in the Ministry of Interior, that, in reality, Ben Ali's Tunisia had only 49,000 internal security operatives (whether police officers, National Guard, or civil defense forces). After Ben Ali's ouster, the transitional government recruited 12,000 more police officers, and probably fired some of the force's worst offenders [1] An exaggerated figure of 150,000 had earlier been diffused most likely to make people feel paranoid that the police were everywhere listening in on conversations and tracking people's lives.

The oppressiveness was palpable. I often took walks with politically committed friends on the beach in order to escape security officers' eavesdropping and wiretaps. I must have walked hundreds of miles along the Tunisian seashore in order to discuss politics with friends who feared otherwise being overheard and reported.

No one ever threatened me personally, but some of my close friends were summoned to police stations where detectives asked them about my comings and goings and what I was up to in Tunisia. Sometimes these interrogations lasted for days. These friends later told me that they felt as if they had been subjected to mental torture and some of them announced that it was consequently best not to see each other anymore. And so I lost several of my closest friends. Without in any way exaggerating my importance, I came to realize that I was becoming dangerous for Tunisians around me.

By 2008, unable to take it any longer, I gave up my rented apartment, gave away my furniture, and moved to Rabat, Morocco, where I also had many friends. From then on, when I returned to Tunisia I stayed in short-term rental apartments, and I wrote a series of articles on what transpired.[2] I visited the country during the revolt and returned for the October 2011 elections and again in the summer of 2012, alternating my accommodations between the rich suburbs and poor neighborhoods where garbage piled up outside and street lights were shut off at night. I traveled around Tunis mostly by streetcar and, since the revolt, I have made many new friends anxious to speak their minds after so many years of repression.

Right after Ben Ali's overthrow in January 2011, I returned to Tunisia and interviewed young male and female cyberactivists who helped initiate the upheaval (See Chapter 14).[3] They expressed surprise that their online appeals to demonstrate had so much resonance and they understood early on that things had changed and that fear had evaporated quite rapidly. New solidarities formed on the Net, supplemented by mosque-goers who used Friday prayer to organize new recruits for the demonstrations. Many women, especially, used social media sites to provoke men into joining them in demonstrations—"to protect them," they mockingly said, shaming the men into participating along-side them. (See Chapter 11.) In the first stage of the Tunisian revolt, anarchists held sway, using the Web to sow confusion among officials, calling strikes in the name of the country's main trade union, and succeeding in convincing unionists that their officials had in fact called them out on strike.[4] (See Chapter 14.) The more success they had, the more these young anarchists upped the ante and joined forces with cartoonists who lampooned the regime, confiscating public spaces for their artwork[5] (see Chapter 16); and allied with rap artists who sang the regime into the ground (see Chapter 17) and with graphic artists who appropriated public space once controlled by the state.

The Islamist movement in Tunisia had been forced underground under Ben Ali's rule. Before December 2010 any man wearing a beard who walked on urban streets could be arrested. Any woman wearing a *hijab* could not enter a public building such as a post office, police station, or municipal government headquarters, and any who did so were also under threat of arrest.[6] Sections of Tunis, such as the popular quarter of Ibn Khaldūn, a sprawling district, harbored many Islamists who secretly built communities of resistance to the state.[7] When activists served prison terms, the Islamists provided stipends to their families, sometimes for years on end. As corruption—both that of the state in general and of Ben Ali's family in particular—increased to the point of obscenity (see Chapter 12)[8], fewer and fewer jobs were created, and people searched in the informal economy for alternate livelihoods. The Islamists distributed cheap Chinese goods to young men on credit or charged nominal prices, allowing such vendors to sell them on the streets despite bans on doing so and the threat of police confiscating wares when sellers were caught.

In a country where the marginalized populations rarely ate meat, the Islamists occasionally sold beef and lamb at half price, allowing the poor the luxury of indulging themselves more than once a month. During Ramadan, the Islamists distributed food at low prices, allowing the indigent to eat well at evening meals. Over the years, out of sight of the police, the Islamists had built a vast underground network of support for the day when they could emerge. And emerge they did after Ben Ali and his family fled the country.

In a January 2013 study of the growth of civil society in the Arab world over the past few years, the Finnish Institute of International Affairs put the charity and largesse of the Islamist party, the Ennahda Movement, in a longer and larger context:

In the Arab world, religious charities, guilds and educational institutions represent an age-old form of organization that date back many centuries. The principle of charitable giving is a cornerstone of Islam and has enabled the growth of an Islamic charity and relief sector that is based on the traditions of *zakat* (obligatory charity), *sadaqah* (voluntary charity) and *waqf* (public endowment). According to some estimates between $200 billion and $1 trillion are distributed annually by Islamic organizations … through alms and voluntary charity across the world.[9]

Since religious parties throughout the Muslim world have engaged in massive charitable activities, they have built solid popular followings, contributing to their post revolt electoral victories. The fact that such activities endured during the years in which these parties were forced underground adds to their aura of sanctity and, therefore, their initial popularity.

THE TUNISIAN UPRISING

If Mohamed Bouazazi had survived his immolation, he would have been the most surprised of Tunisians that his act sparked a revolt and had significant repercussions on other Arab states. Similar to many Tunisian men, he could not marry, since he didn't have the funds to rent an apartment and buy furniture to set up a household. He was a bachelor with some education who could not find work. Instead, he sold fruit off of a pushcart in the middle of his small god-forsaken town of Sidi Bouzid located in the interior of Tunisia, far from the glamor of Tunis or the preferred tourist destinations, such as Sousse or Hammamet on the coast. As had happened many times before, a female police officer confiscated his produce and a borrowed scale since he had no permit to sell anything. This time, however, he cracked. Running to the police station, he demanded his property back but received only rebuffs. At that point, he poured kerosene over himself and lit a match. His cousin Ali filmed the entire scene on his cell phone and immediately sent it to YouTube, where it went viral. A few weeks later Bouazizi died from his burns, setting in motion what we now call the Arab Spring, a revolt that forced four Arab presidents from office and convulsed the MENA area from one end to the other.[10]

Luckily for those who joined the revolt, the Tunisian army had become jealous of the police who had dominated Ben Ali's state. The armed forces sided with the demonstrators, giving them the ability to organize and grow the movement exponentially. Within a few short weeks Ben Ali and his family fled to exile in Saudi Arabia. Delirium erupted throughout the country. The emperor proved to have no clothes.

THEN THE HARD PART BEGAN

The state literally melted away. Streetcar conductors lost the ability to collect fares. Few riders would pay. Packs of young men armed with sticks and bats descended on neighborhoods, breaking into houses, stores, and apartments and carting away whatever they could carry. Rumor spread that the old single party that had run Ben Ali's electoral campaigns had organized brigades to steal and spread terror so as to facilitate the reestablishment of a new dictatorship. Immediately local vigilante committees, made up of men from each few city blocks, formed to protect people and property and establish roadblocks, searching for arms in the trunks of cars. These vigilantes reestablished a semblance of order and provided needed security.

In the countryside, landowners hired peasants as security guards, but fifteen or so men protecting farms were no match for groups of armed bandits, often roughly 100 men, who roamed through rural areas, stealing farm machinery and livestock to sell to the highest bidders. After the interim government formed, the newly established state distributed compensation to many victimized landlords—up to 40 percent of the worth of the stolen property. But repeated thefts meant that landowners after continuous robberies often received no further compensation. Backlashes began against the new order and many people—especially the owners of large properties—expressed nostalgia for the law and order provided by the old dictatorship. [11]

Demonstrations continued daily in Tunis at the *Kasbah*, outside the prime minister's offices, and downtown on Habib Bourguiba Avenue in the city center. Families of martyrs set up a tent city on a major thoroughfare near downtown, and shopping streets were inundated by hundreds of rural youth whose families gave them the equivalent of a couple of hundred dollars to buy cheap goods, both locally made and imported from China, to sell on the capital's busiest thoroughfares. Previously the police would have confiscated such goods and chased the vendors back to their villages. Now, following the revolt, the forces of order were powerless to stop this mass migration. Asef Bayat, the author of the terrific 2010 book *Life as Politics* [12], would have called this a "nonmovement movement," one in which rural youth expropriated public space formerly controlled by the state. They remained in place for more than a year, until the country's newly elected authorities removed them from the streets they had occupied and set them up in a flea market far from the maddening crowd.

The new leaders appointed a scion of a great Tunisian ulema family—Ayadh Ben Achour, the former head of a law school—to head a commission of some 150 people, including youth from the uprisings, to put in place an interim government until a permanent one could be elected by universal suffrage. This group also set up a framework for organizing a new constitutional assembly. The transitional government was headed by octogenarian Béji Caïd Es Sebsi, who was born in Sidi Bou Said in a family close to the ruling bey. He studied law in Paris, passing the Tunisian bar in 1952. After Tunisian independence, he headed the national police force and then became Minister of Interior from 1965 to 1969, then Defense Minister, and Ambassador to Paris, becoming Foreign Minister in 1986, and then Speaker of the Chamber of Deputies under Ben Ali. Chosen for his governmental experience and his openness to a new democracy, as interim head of the transitional government he steered the country through a troubled period where a modicum of law and order had to be provided. [13]

Finally, free elections in October 2011 brought to power the Ennahda Movement, dominated by Islamists, as the major force in a new government, but not possessing a majority. Its leaders had lived in exile, prison, or underground for decades. Whoever demonized this party lost votes, though the two secular parties, which had allied with Ennahda, won sufficient seats in the new assembly to share power.

A new force emerged that had never existed legally or surfaced before in Tunisia—namely, the Salafists. Mostly tolerated by the Ennahda Movement, these extreme Muslims acted as moral arbiters, raiding bars and brothels, and attempting to place Salafist leaders as imams in many mosques throughout the country. They succeeded in implanting 400 imams, but the newly mobilized population rebelled against them, and only seventy-five remained in place once the dust settled. Customers in bars and brothels beat up many of the Salafist moral crusaders and chased them out of their establishments.

The Salafists had more luck with their cultural crusades, and shut down cinemas and private television channels that showed films that displeased them and art galleries that displayed paintings and sculptures the crusaders believed insulted Islam.

Ennahda leaders tolerated the Salafists, and initially did little to stop their crusades, since the party needed all the votes it could get; for some of its decisions had begun to alienate parts of the electorate. A critical point was reached when two secular political leaders were assassinated three months apart with the same gun apparently belonging to a Salafist leader whom the police never captured. Popular protests in reaction to these assassinations created a governmental crisis, which led to a "National Dialogue" of all the country's competing political parties meeting with important NGOs: the national trade union, the General Confederation of Labor (CGTT); the Union of Industry, Commerce, and Crafts (UTICA), representing private business interests; the principal human rights organization; and the organization representing lawyers. In the face of mass protests, a slight majority (eleven out of twenty-one) of the political parties chose Mehdi Jomaa, a former minister of industry, to head a cabinet of independents, which had six months from January 14, when the new government took power, to adopt a new constitution (which Parliament voted on at the beginning of January 2014), establish a new electoral law, and hold parliamentary elections. For the first time in the MENA region an Islamist party had relinquished power peacefully. The transition process was brokered in a meeting between Ennahda head Rachid Gannouchi and the head of the previous caretaker government, Caïd Es-Sebsi. Es-Sebsi's party, Nida Tunis, defeated Ennahda in parliamentary elections in October 2014. He won the presidential elections later that year, leading his party to form a new government.

THE JIHADIST THREAT

In spring 2013, the most radical of the Salafist groups, Ansar al-sharia, tried to stage its third national convention in the town of Kayrawan. The minister of interior banned the meeting, so the group changed its venue to a poor neighborhood in Tunis. When its members gathered in Hay al-Tadamen, police came out in force to block the entrance to the group's meeting place. Clashes with the police followed. One person was killed and eighteen wounded, including fifteen officers. Ansar, through its principle leader, is tied to al-Qaeda and was responsible for earlier attacks on the US Embassy in the suburbs of Tunis on September 14, 2012. Pressures mounted on Ennahda since that attack to reign in the movement, especially since the appearance of al-Qaeda-linked jihadists close to the Algerian border and the discovery of arms flowing into Tunisia from neighboring Libya and Algeria. The conflict in Mali involving the Tuareg, al-Qaeda in the Maghreb, and French intervention forces has further highlighted the danger of radical Islamists spreading throughout the region.

Tunisians make up a disproportionately large number of international jihadists fighting in Syria. Al-Qaeda set up training camps for its fighters in the mountainous area on the Algerian border in December 2012. After French troops dislodged their fighters from Mali in Janaury 2013, many of them returned to the border area of Tunisia and joined other jihadists dislodged from the Algerian Sahara by that country's military. Violence has mounted between the Tunisian army and these irregulars since then. Western pressures on the Tunisian regime most likely contributed to Ennahda's decision to crack down on Ansar al-sharia. Ennahda had to balance its Islamist ideology against the real security concerns of the Tunisian state, which it could not ignore. Compromise became mandatory. Such trends, if they continue, bode well for a smooth transition in the small North African country.[14]

JOBS

Tunisia, lacking large quantities of oil and gas and having much smaller quantities of phosphates than does Morocco, embarked on a strategy of economic growth under Bourguiba and Ben Ali, based on developing a mass tourism industry—as contrasted with Morocco, which caters mainly to wealthy Europeans—wherein profits per tourist are very low. It also invested heavily in the textile industry and clothing manufacturing, but since the domestic market was long protected, the lack of competition yielded shoddy production. Simultaneously, Tunisia hosted world famous fashion designers in its textile sector, yielding enhanced quality controls. Such offshore industries flourished and continue to do well, but the local textile and ready-made clothing industry has, in effect, collapsed as liberal treaties, which the country signed more than a dozen years ago, gradually took effect and allowed countries such as China to export to Tunisia large quantities of cheap garments at very low prices, in effect wiping out large segments of this labor-intensive Tunisian industry. Salafist contestation has frightened away many foreign investors, who are increasingly looking to Morocco as a substitute site for investments.

The uncertainties produced by the uprising have reduced the number of foreign tourists, forcing hotels to discount their rooms up to 50 percent, close entire wings, and in some cases, entire hotels. The tourist industry suffered major blows from attacks by radical Islamists against the Bardo museum on March 18, 2015 where 21 tourists were killed and a further 37 tourists lost their lives on June 26, 2015 in another radical Islamist attack at a beach resort near the town of Sousse. Artisans and traders who depend on tourists as customers have suffered, yielding widened unemployment in a country that already unofficially faced upward of 18 percent unemployment and much higher percentages of jobless youth.

The demand for jobs led Caïd Essebsi's transitional government to set up a job-creating institute headed by a competent economist, who began laying plans to create 42,000 jobs quickly. This contrasted with promises made by candidates in the October 2011 elections to create between 100,000 and 400,000 jobs in short order without saying how that was to be done. As soon as the Ennahda–dominated government was installed, however, the job-creating institute was dissolved and the new government had to start from scratch—a disheartening prospect for the country's armies of unemployed.

The problem is critical, since the International Monetary Fund, the World Bank, and their US backers have for some time demanded privatization of employment and refuse to sanction the creation of any more government jobs, which burden debt-laden state budgets. The international private sector, despite some exceptions, such as call centers and high-end clothing production, is reluctant to invest in North Africa, since 1930s legislation from the colonial period still on the books guarantees those workers with employment contracts decent wages with good benefits. In consequence, private foreign and local businesses refuse to give all but the most educated, well-connected, and gifted graduates coveted employment contracts, but rather hire them on a short-term basis so they can avoid providing such perks as benefits and bonuses. Only the brightest and most qualified workers and executives can expect to get long-term employment contracts from most corporations.

The small towns in Tunisia's interior especially need jobs. Their populations see themselves as responsible for having ignited the revolt and expect immediate compensation in the form of heavy investment and new jobs. For decades they have been ignored by the elites along the coast, so now they feel that their turn has come.

Besides creating more jobs, any Tunisian government must decentralize investment and locate industries on or near farms to process agricultural produce. Unlike Morocco, where 40 percent of national income comes from agriculture, Tunisia has reduced dependency on the agricultural sector to about 18 percent of its GDP. (See Chapter 13.) Industrialization of agricultural production seems like the next logical step to decentralize the economy and provide jobs for the army of the unemployed throughout the country.

A NEW, VIBRANT CIVIL SOCIETY

Perhaps the most exciting by-product of the revolt has been the development of a vibrant civil society across the country. People now speak their minds. They have organized new associations everywhere to challenge and watch over government activities. Few matters escape their attention, and for the first time in recent Tunisian history, they have questioned the actions of the highest officials of the land, asking them hard questions and even threatening to bring matters to the courts. The most important of these associations are[15]:

- Reform (reforming the police force)
- Equality Parity (gender equality)
- *Touensa* (creating space for civil society, developing and acting as political watchdogs)
- *al-Bawsala* (promotion of open government)
- *Sawty* (training young people to participate in civil society)
- Citizen Bus Collective (enhancing public awareness of proposed constitutional reforms)
- National Anticorruption Network (publicizing cases of corruption and bad administrative practices)

- *Amal* (defending women and unwed mothers)
- Tunisian Association for the Defense of Infants' Rights (protecting infants and establishing their constitutional rights)

Secular Tunisian women, feeling especially threatened by the coming to power of Islamists, and fearful that their rights would be taken away, have led the way in forming and activating these associations, working side by side with men.

Other groups have formed around other issues. Some are staging literacy events downtown, on Avenue Habib Bourguiba—distributing books and pamphlets to passersby and sitting on the sidewalks with them while holding collective read-ins in order to acclimatize people to the very process of handling books and helping them to understand what they have read. [16]

Culture has blossomed: art and music have developed critical political edges (see Chapters 16 and 17) despite new restrictions imposed by the new regimes (see Chapter 15). Theater groups, building on a long Tunisian tradition going back to the 1920s and earlier, [16] and street theater of the 1970s, have proliferated, putting on new plays with political and social themes. Older students have formed groups to work with elementary and high school students to sensitize them to new possibilities in post revolt Tunisia.

The revolt has, indeed, produced new citizens, and onlookers feel the vibrancy of their participation everywhere.

CONCLUSIONS

Whatever happens, needed transformations will not occur overnight. It took Turkey's Justice and Development Party ten years to diversify its country's economy and establish industries in rural areas outside of Istanbul, Ankara, and Izmir. As a result, Turkey grew by a respectable 8–10 percent yearly until recently. The same can happen in Tunisia, since the country has an abundance of skilled talent and educated leaders to accomplish such a transformation if the will and capacity exists to do so.

There is a basic pragmatism at work in Tunisia that does not exist to the same degree elsewhere in North Africa. For example, Ennahda Movement's rank and file tried to push through constitutional changes that would have defined women as "compliments" of men rather than their equals. An uproar developed against the proposed changes to the point that the leadership of Ennahda withdrew these plans from consideration. That pragmatism must prevail over dogmatism in many other areas of policy-making and public life as well. It remains to be seen how successful the pragmatists will be in convincing their fellow citizens that it lies in the country's best interests to follow a Bourguibist utilitarianism so as to create a new consensus for change, one that might allow this small country to flourish once again. Whatever happens, such changes will take decades or even generations to achieve, and the road ahead will be filled with contention as an expectant population demands immediate redress and takes collective action to achieve rapid change.

NOTES

1   Querine Hanlan, "Security Sector Reform in Tunisia a Year After the Jasmine Revolt," Special Report 304 (March 2012), p. 6, United States Institute of Peace, www.usip.org/files/resources/SP304pdf Accessed April 21, 2013.

2   I have published the following: "Arab Dictatorships Under Fire in the New Information Age," and "Epilogue," in Marvin Gettleman and Stuart Schaar, eds., *The Middle East and Islamic World Reader*, New York: Grove Press, 3rd ed., 2012, pp. 353-357 and 378–381; "Revolutionary Challenges in Tunisia and Egypt: Generations in Conflict," *New Politics*, Vol. XIII-3, Whole # 51 (Summer 2011); "Democracy Triumphs in Tunisia's First Free Elections," *Maghreb Center Blog* (Washington, D.C.), November 2011; "The Arab Citizen's Revolt and its Impact on Tunisia, *The Maghreb Review* (London), Vol. 37, Nos. 3–4 (2012): 334–341; "Wither the Tunisian Citizen's Revolt?" *ZNET* (January 18, 2013).

3   For the most complete assessment of cyber activism in Tunisia starting in 2000 see Romain Lecomte, "*Les usages 'citoyens' d'Internet dans le contexte autoritaire tunisien: analyse de l'émergence d'un nouvel espace public de la critique,*" in Sihem Najar, ed., *Le cyber activisme au Maghreb et dans le monde arabe*, Paris: Karthala IRCM, 2013, pp. 55–75.

4   Conversation with the late Tunisian sociologist Abdelkader Zghal, La Marsa, October, 2012, who characterized the youthful cyberactivists who helped ignite the Tunisian revolt as "anarchists."

5   See the terrific photographs by Tunisian journalist Muhammad-Salah Bettaïeb in *Dégage: La Révolution Tunisienne Livre-Témoignages 17 décembre 2010–14 janvier 2011*, Tunis: Editions de Patrimoine, 2011; Asnières-sur-Seine, France: Editions du Layeur, 2011.

6   On several occasions in the 1980s and '90s I was walking with bearded friends (five o'clock shadows being stylish in the Middle East, and especially among male popular singers there) when plainclothes police officers stopped us and took my friends to a local police station for interrogation. Wearing a beard, in the minds of security officers, was tantamount to being an Islamist. My landlady in the Tunis suburb of Mornag in the early 1990s, an Islamist, complained to me often that she was harassed continuously whenever she tried to enter a post office, police station, or municipality. She wore a *hijab* and swore that she would never take it off in public for any regime.

7   In the 1990s I had an automobile in Tunis and was often called on by my working-class friends to help them transport women relatives to and from wedding ceremonies. In this way I entered the home of a bride of a close friend of mine in Ibn Khaldun—a home inhabited by an Islamist family where I stayed

with the women for a few hours and saw the community of resistance they and their family were building against the Ben Ali regime.

8 See "Corruption in Tunisia: What's Yours is Mine," from Wikileaks, in Marvin E. Gettleman and Stuart Schaar, eds, *The Middle East and Islamic World Reader*, pp. 346–348.

9 Timo Behr & Aaretti Siitonen, "Building Bridges or Digging Trenches? Civil Society Engagement After the Arab Spring," The Finish Institute of International Affairs (Helsinki), Working Paper 77, January 2013, p. 11.

10 Besides spreading through the Arab world, the revolts had repercussions on such other places as Israel (see Chapter 20), Bangladesh, and the United States in the form of the Occupy movement (see Chapter 21). For Bangladesh see Ansar Ahmad Ullah, "The Youth of Shahbagh: A Bengali Spring?" *Open Democracy* (February 15, 2013). www.opendemocracy.net, accessed February 16, 2013.

11 In conversations with landowners in the Menzil al-Bab area of Tunisia over a period of six months in 2012, either in personal interviews or follow-up phone calls, I gained insight into rural banditry and the government's initial distribution of compensation for thefts, plus the landowners' disillusionment with the revolt. In calls to contacts in that region on May 7, 2013, I was told that things have calmed down and bandits no longer prey on landowners. They expected a bumper wheat crop by the end of May 2013.

12 Asef Bayat, *Life as Politics: How Ordinary People Change in the Middle East*, Stanford, CA: Stanford University Press, 2010, esp. pp. 1–39.

13 See Marwane Ben Yahmed, "Béji Caïd Essebsi [interview]", *Jeune Afrique* (Paris), No. 2621, April 2–9, 2011: 58–63.

14 See Daniel Wagner and Georgio Cafiero, "Can Democrats and Jihadists Coexist in Tunisia?" *Before It's News*, January 1, 2014, http://beforeitsnews.com//middle-east/2014/01/can-democrats-and jihad (accessed January 6, 2014).

15 Taken from Frida Dahmani, "Tunisie: On ne se tiara plus," *Jeune Afrique*, No. 2729–2730, April 28–May 11, 2013: 59.

16 Ibid.

17 See Stuart Schaar, "Creation of Mass Political Culture in Tunisia [After World War I]," *The Maghreb Review*, 18, 1–2 (1993): 2–17.

REFERENCES

A number of books and book chapters have been written about the Tunisian revolt: The most important include:

Jalal Ayyed, *Tunisie: La Route des Jasmins*, Paris: Editions de la Differences, 2013.

Amor Cherni, *La Révolution Tunisienne s'emparer de l'histoire*, Paris: Dar Albouraq, 2011.

David McMurray and Amanda Ufheil-Somers, eds., *The Arab Revolts: Dispatches on Militant Democracy in the Middle East*, Bloomington and Indianapolis, IN: Indiana University Press, in Association with Middle East Research and

Information Project (MERIP), 2013, pp. 13–56 on Tunisia.

Olivier Piot, *La Révolution Tunisienne: Dix Jours qui bralérent leMonde Arabe*, Paris: Les petits matin, 2011.

Pierre Puchot, *La Révolution Confisquée : Enquēte sur la transition dēmocatique en Tunisie*, Paris :Sindbad Actes Sd, 2012.

Boujemaa Remili, *Quand le Peuple Reussit la ou toute la société a échoué*, Tunis: Editions Nirvana, 2011.

IMPORTANT ARTICLES AND PAPERS INCLUDE:

Michele Penner Angrist, "Morning in Tunisia: The Frustrations of the Arab World Boil Over," in *The New Arab Revolt*, New York: Council on Foreign Relations/ Foreign Affairs, 2011, e-book, 1274–1352 out of 6984.

Freedom House, "COUNTRIES AT THE CROSSROADS: Tunisia," www.freedom-house.org/report/countries-crossroads/2012/tunisia. Accessed 9/24/2012

Francis Ghilès, "TUNISIA: Secular Social Movements Confront Radical Temptations," in *notes internationals CIDOB*,Barcelona, 64 (December 2012).

Julia Clancy-Smith, "From Sidi Bou Zid to Sidi Bou Said : A *Longue Durée* Approach to the Tunisian Revolution," in Mark L. Haas andDavid W. Lesch, eds., *The Arab Spring: Change and Resistance in the Middle East,* Boulder, CO: Westview Press, 2013, pp. 13–34.

Anne Wolf and Raphaël Lefevre, "Commentary: Revolution under threat: the challenges of the 'Tunisian Model,'" *The Journal of North African Studies*, Vol. 17, No. 3 (June 2012): 559–563.

Nouri Gana, "Tunisia," in Paul Amar and Vijay Prashad, eds., *Dispatches From the Arab Spring: Understanding the New Middle East*, London and Minneapolis: University of Minnesota Press, 2013, pp. 1–23.

Egypt being the most populous Arab country, with over eighty-five million citizens, whatever happens along the Nile Delta has immediate repercussions on the entire MENA region. Through its news outlets, movie industry, television soaps, print media, writers, educators, and religious sheiks in the mosque university of Al-Azhar, the country acts as a trend setter for the other Arab countries. Arab nationalism under Gamal Abdel Nasser flourished there and spread through the Arab world. The Muslim Brotherhood, founded in the 1920s, prospered there and later founded branches elsewhere. It initially ruled over the Egyptian government following free and fair elections until the military staged a coup and reestablished a new army-led regime in the summer of 2013, which greatly restricted liberties. Omar Foda, who witnessed a good part of the initial revolt, gives us a view into what transpired and what we might expect in the future.

CHAPTER 3

THE BALLOT BOX AND THE PUBLIC SQUARES: A HISTORY OF THE JANUARY 25 MOVEMENT IN EGYPT
OMAR FODA

The notion of revolution going "viral" across the Middle East is an appealing narrative that fits well with the conception of the ever-increasing connectivity of our lives across social media. However, as I will show, the significant political upheaval that occurred in Egypt after January 25, 2011, was more the result of a critical mass of destabilizing factors for the ruling regime than of a contagion of revolution spreading to Egypt. In a mere eighteen days, a group of nonviolent protestors were able to overthrow an entrenched dictator who had ruled for thirty years. This turnaround was truly historic and immediately vaulted the January 25 Movement into the company of other epic events in the country's past, including the 'Urabi Revolt of 1881, the Uprising of 1919, and the Free Officers Movement of 1952.

This chapter uses a tripartite analysis to delve deeper into the January 25 Movement. The first section, by looking at the events and conditions that led up to it, shows that when Egyptians were faced by a stunningly corrupt political system, a wildly inequitable and stagnating economy, and a brutal security apparatus, they took to the streets. The second section looks at what happened once they were in the streets and how a series of specific actions by the protestors and the government transformed protests into an insurrection. The final section examines how the path from revolutionary rhetoric to substantive change is unpredictable and how after February 11, 2011 (when President Hosni Mubarak resigned) Egypt quickly fell back into established political structures.

A CLIMATE RIPE FOR CHANGE

On the most basic level, the Hosni Mubarak–led Egyptian government made very little effort to represent its people. Mubarak sat atop a political system rigged in his favor and that of his ruling party, the National Democratic Party (NDP).[1] This control included not only parliamentary and presidential elections but extended to all elections in the country.[2] Nevertheless, the lack of democracy itself was not cause for insurrection; Egypt had not witnessed free and open elections since the 1950s.[3] Rather, the revolt was triggered by the new level of glaring government corruption that the Mubarak regime reached in 2010. Under the leadership of Ahmed 'Izz, the *bête noire* of the Tahrir protestors and the NDP's Secretary of Organizational Affairs, the NDP won 97 percent of the seats and declared for itself a "crushing victory" in the 2010 parliamentary elections.[4] Ballot-box stuffing was all the more galling when paired with the fact that the previous presidential and parliamentary elections had seen some loosening of the strictures on the opposition.[5] Thus, many Egyptians believed these parliamentary elections would provide some indication of Mubarak's policies for the future of Egypt.

The main issue for most Egyptians was that of succession (*warātha*). Unlike Nasser or Sadat, Mubarak had not appointed a vice-president or anointed a designated successor. The lack of a clear successor not only encouraged debate, but also held out the possibility of a significant change in leadership. However, in the 2000s, with the rise of the political and economic fortunes of the president's son, Gamal Mubarak, the specter of hereditary succession became a real possibility.[6] Thus, Egyptians were looking to the parliamentary elections as a bellwether on the possibility of succession. The blatant disregard for the electoral process confirmed what many feared—that the presidency of Egypt would become a hereditary position.

The beyond-the-pale electoral corruption, while astounding, was not the sole motivating force for the January 25 Movement. In fact, most Egyptians under thirty-five, as evidenced by low voting turnout, had lost faith in the electoral process long before the movement emerged. Only 28 percent participated in the 2005 parliamentary elections and only 23 percent did so in the 2005 presidential elections.[7] The increased manipulation of the ballot box was matched by an increase in the corruption of government officials who surrounded Mubarak. While charges of corruption had been leveled at the Egyptian government since the constitutional period, it was under the regime of Anwar Sadat that corruption really took root.[8] As Tarek Osman notes, it was with the *al-Infitah* (opening up), an economic program started in 1973 by Sadat that aimed to push Egypt away from statism to liberal capitalism, that the line between power and wealth began to blur.[9] In a trend that began under Sadat and accelerated under Mubarak, those best able to reap the benefits of the opening up of Egypt were those closest to the regime.

Ahmed 'Izz is an ideal example of this synchrony. Using his close friend-ship with Gamal Mubarak, who used his own personal connections to position himself as the leader of Egypt's technocratic businessmen, 'Izz rose from a modest start to establish a steel business that owned more than sixty-five per-cent of the market.[10] His friendship with the younger Mubarak also gifted him a political career that saw him become a power broker in the NDP, and he used his position both to protect his economic interests and, as shown previously, stack the political deck.[11]

Corruption was not limited to the governmental elite but was an institu-tionalized phenomenon that pervaded "almost every aspect of the country's socioeconomic life."[12] For example in 2008, Transparency International rated Egypt 115th out of 180 countries on a scale where a lower score (1-10) indicates higher levels of perceived corruption. Egypt scored 2.8. [13] The average Egyptian faced not only wide-scale corruption, but also a growing chasm between rich and poor. While a select few made a tremendous amount of money off the government's neoliberal economic policies—the World Bank designated Egypt one of the top ten most improved economic reformers three years in a row—there was little trickle down.[14] The great majority of the population faced rising inflation (double digits for much of the 1980s and 1990s), high rates of unemployment (effective rate of 18–21 percent among those aged 18–54), and a general economic malaise (real wages lower in 2006 than in 1988).[15]

While the presence of an unresponsive and unrepresentative political system may have caused great consternation among the population, eco-nomic realities such as the rising cost of food and the inability to find jobs, proper housing, or healthcare drove Egyptians to the brink. As Heather Sharkey shows in her monograph *Living With Colonialism*, even the most ardent Sudanese nationalists, despite their strong antiregime rhetoric, were generally concerned with carving out a living under British colonial rule. They became activists only when the deprivations caused by the regime af-fected their daily lives.[16]

Likewise, in Egypt, a broken political system was tolerable to many citizens under previous regimes because it provided tangible successes. The massive economic and social changes the Nasser government brought to Egypt (e.g., land reform, nationalization, construction of the Aswan Dam, expansion of the public sector, and the five-year plan) made its authoritarianism more tolerable. Similarly, Sadat's *al-Infitah* brought the promise of new goods and wealth to Egypt, which, coupled with his success in the Sinai war of 1973, helped soften his Pharaonism. However, Mubarak, despite a promising beginning, headed an economic system that was racked with corruption and was characterized by a yawning chasm between the wealthy and everyone else. In addition, his extraordinarily long rule produced a whole generation of people (forty-five million under the age of thirty-five) who knew nothing but the troubled economy of his regime.[17]

In light of the morally bankrupt political system and uneven economic growth that Egypt experienced, the longevity of Mubarak's reign was truly remarkable. Part of his staying power can be attributed to his pragmatism in both foreign and local affairs, where he aimed more for continued stability than assertions of Egypt's leadership in the Middle East.[18] A larger part can be tied to the regime's total suppression of opposition voices.

Although Egypt after Nasser was no stranger to suppression of dissent— e.g. Nasser's treatment of Sayyid Qutb, whom he had killed, and the Muslim Brotherhood that Qutb headed—the Mubarak system was at another level of magnitude.[19]

As both the executive power and key economic broker, the government could use the promise of economic or political gain to quiet dissent.[20] While the use of patronage was no doubt effective, what truly set the Mubarak regime apart was the brute suppression of opponents, mainly through the police. As Salwa Ismail shows, for the average Egyptian, the police were a powerful and extremely visible presence. Their reach extended into most daily activities including "markets, transport, roads, food supply, public utilities, public morality, and taxation, in addition to public security and national security."[21] The relationship between the police and the public was an asymmetrical one that included not only petty extortion and intimidation, but also the significant use of violence.[22]

However, for those undeterred by the diffuse and daily power presented by the police, there was a force dedicated to eliminating those elements that proved openly hostile to the regime, the State Security Agency (SSA). This institution, which had roots in the Nasser era, became a major player in Egyptian internal politics with the declaration of a state of emergency after the assassination of Anwar Sadat in 1981. This declaration granted it nearly unlimited power to pursue those actors actively working against the government. The tactics used by the group were extralegal, extremely brutal, and highly effective.[23] One needs only to look at the two oldest political parties, the Muslim Brotherhood and the *Wafd*, and their absence from the political discourse to understand the extent of the SSA's power. In particular, the Muslim Brotherhood, whose suppression was used as evidence of Egypt's stance in the war on terror, was forced to operate almost exclusively underground to survive in this climate.[24]

However, as the regime embarked on its third decade and Egypt entered the new millennium, the SSA was called on more and more as the population skewed ever younger and grew increasingly tired of the repressive regime. As Joel Beinin shows, there was increasing worker mobilization demanding better wages and other benefits.[25] In fact, the April 6 Youth Movement, which many scholars point to as a predecessor to the Tahrir Movement, was an attempt to organize a nationwide labor strike. In addition, middle class Egyptians with fixed incomes, such as lawyers and teachers, took to the streets to protest the deprivations that the neoliberal economy was causing.[26]

Similar disturbances were taking place in the political realm. Perhaps the most significant was the *Kefaya* Movement in 2004. This movement, as communicated by its name *Kefaya* (enough), organized intellectuals and community activists around their total dissatisfaction with the regime.[27] Their protests targeted corruption, the perpetual state of emergency, and the possibility of dynastic succession.[28] Of course, no accounting of the increasing dissent of the 2000s would be complete without taking note of the rising fortunes of the Muslim Brotherhood. Filling the void left by neoliberal policies of the regime and bearing the banner of political Islam, which had become a more viable alternative in light of the failed policies of Mubarak and the mass immigration of Egyptians to the Gulf in the 1970s, the Brotherhood gained massive amounts of political capital in the 2000s.[29] This was especially true in the countryside and poor areas, where for many it provided the infrastructure, support, and powerful message that government failed to give.[30] Nevertheless, no movement was able to effect serious change, because the regime kept each of them local, divided, and well contained. For example, the government used both repression and token concessions to diffuse workers' strikes at Mahalla al-Kubra.[31] It also ultimately doomed the candidacy of the liberal Ayman Nour (Nūr) and his *al-Ghad* party. Ayman Nour came to national prominence when he finished a distant second to Mubarak in the first multicandidate race for president in 2005. However, he was unable to transform this success into anything tangible because his time on the political stage was short. Almost immediately after the announcement of the results, the regime accused, convicted, and jailed Nour on the charges of falsifying signatures for his election campaign.[32]

The heavy-handed tactics of the police force had reached a breaking point prior to January 25. And it was here where Web 2.0 (e.g. Facebook, YouTube, and Twitter) played a significant role. Through this media, Egyptians were able to publicize the brutal tactics of the police and to transform personal tragedy into a countrywide black mark. The most famous example is the "We Are All Khalid Said" Facebook page, which publicized the capricious beating given to Khalid Said that led to his death.[33] Thus when Egyptians took to the streets on January 25, 2011, it was one of their only options in dealing with a corrupt political system, a stagnating economy, and a brutally oppressive police state.

VECTORS OF SUCCESS

The events that took place in Tahrir Square are a poststructuralist's dream. There is no hegemonic narrative that can claim to definitively portray the events as they "really happened," rather the discourse around these events is multivocal with numerous sources claiming accuracy simultaneously. This multivocality can be linked to the potent mix of new and old media present in Egypt at the time.

While the teleology of progress would assert that new would replace the old, the reality is that often new and old sit uncomfortably side by side. [34] For example, Nancy Reynolds has shown in her study of twentieth-century Egyptian consumption patterns that as opposed to the traditional narrative that posits the "total annihilation of traditional crafts from the influx of cheap and seductive foreign goods," both foreign and Egyptian goods sat next to each other in Egyptian newspapers and markets, and Egyptians consumed them in tandem.[35] In the case of the media in Egypt, this meant that Egyptian newspapers, flyers, pamphlets, and public television coexisted with Web 2.0, satellite television, and international newspapers.

Most importantly, whether it was the *al-Ahram* newspaper, with its roots in the nineteenth century, or the Tahrir protestor with his frequently updated Twitter feed, every claimant to the narrative was linked up to the Internet in some way and thus each was recording his own version of history. Although some have argued that this revolt was unique because it was documented tweet-by-tweet, its true uniqueness lies in the multitude of narratives that it produced.[36]

While the absence of a hegemonic discourse is an interesting source of study to the scholar and extremely freeing to nontraditional media, for the consumer the panoply of voices is frequently a source of confusion and consternation because it undermines the notion that any source can comprehensively say what "really happened." A good example is the continued confusion over the events surrounding a vital moment in the Tahrir Struggle, the "Battle of the Camel". On February 2, 2011, men astride camels and horses attacked protestors in Tahrir Square. While the matter of the attacks on protestors is undeniable, as there is visual evidence in both video and photos, a debate still rages in both the courts and the media over who ordered the attack and why.[37] As such, it is not my intention to present a definitive narrative of the events that transpired in Tahrir, which would require a book-length work. My intention is only to look at some of the factors that made this event more powerful and more successful than any of the other civil movements that took place in Egypt under Mubarak.

Although the idea of revolution going viral is problematic, it would be equally facile to imagine that the events in Tahrir occurred inside a bubble. As evidenced by both the Egyptian and foreign newspapers, it did not take much to imagine the events in Tunisia carrying over to Egypt. For example, the January 16, 2011, edition of *Al-Shuruq*, an independent and left-leaning journal founded in 2009, featured a front-page spread with the headline, "Tunisia … A Gust of Change," with several pages dedicated to the events in that country. This was followed by articles on how those events related to Egypt: "The Leadership of the NDP Denies Comparisons of Egypt to Tunisia and Rules out the Possibility of A Repeat Uprising (*al-intifāḍa*)"; "The Tunisian Revolt in the Eyes of the Official Opposition"; "Analysts: A Repeat of the Tunisian Uprising … is Coming to the Arab Domains"; and "The Brotherhood: The Tunisian Revolution is a Warning to All."[38]

Perhaps the most concrete example of the effect of the Tunisian movement was the wave of attempted self-immolations (see Chapter 18) that occurred in Egypt after the Tunisian uprising forced out President Ben Ali on January 14th. The most famous was that of Abduh Abd al-Hamid, who lit himself on fire in front of the People's Assembly (*Majlis al-Shaab*) building after demanding his share of state-subsidized bread on January 16th. These actions were clearly inspired by the self-immolation of Mohamed Bouazizi, a produce vendor, whose own self-immolation served as one of the spurs for the Tunisian movement.[39] The successful uprising in Tunisia also put the international community on watch for the next domino to fall. For example, the *Washington Post* ran an article that adumbrated the need for Mubarak and his regime to strive for change or face a revolution.[40] Likewise, an article in Al Jazeera on January 13 spoke of the possible effect of the events in Tunisia on Egypt.[41] Thus, when things started to transpire after January 25 the international community was watching and ready to report. Such external attention, in addition to the presence of social media and satellite television channels, assured that no matter how hard the regime tried (e.g., shutting off the Internet) this movement would not be bottled up or silenced.[42]

However attuned the international media may have been to Egypt, it would have made little difference if there was nothing to report. Thus, if we are to understand why the Tahrir Movement succeeded we must look at Egypt itself. One of the most important factors for its success was the message it was built upon. As opposed to other movements, the protests that started on January 25, National Police Day, had no concrete goal other than to display popular dissatisfaction with the police and the regime they supported. The buzzwords as the movement started were not "revolution" or "minimum wage," but rather nebulous concepts such as "anger" (*ghadab*) and "change" (*taghyiīr*).[43]

When the movement grew from ten thousand to hundreds of thousands and millions, and when the message then changed, it remained inclusive with the people demanding "bread, freedom, and social justice" (*Aish, Ḥurriyya, Karāma Isāniyya*).[44] Even the openly aggressive slogans such as "the people want the regime to fall" (*al-shaab yurīd yasquṭ al-niẓām*) could be supported by the wide political spectrum that wanted change.[45] The broad and antiregime, rather than partisan, slogans were vitally important to a movement that was built on the backs of a wide range of contradictory ideologies. It was only with this very wide net that this movement could incorporate liberal secularists, Salafists, and communists without fracturing.

Another aspect of the movement that made it more successful than any that preceded it was its speed. While the rapidity of the removal of Hosni Mubarak, a mere eighteen days after the beginning of the protests, would seem to imply that the government was caught off-guard, it appears that it had ample warning. The Egyptian media reported about the "Day of Anger"/National Police Day protests extensively for several days before they took place.[46] Thus, the protests themselves were not unexpected, but rather it was the exponential growth of the numbers that was. In the course of one day's news cycle, the movement grew from a significant protest into an insurrection.[47]

If there is any place where the presence of Web 2.0 was absolutely vital it was in this initial moment. Where typically the government met previous disturbances with significant police suppression and media silence, in this case social media enabled the movement's message to move faster than other traditional media and faster than the government security apparatus. In addition, Web 2.0 was important because it was a key mobilizer of the youth. As Tarek Osman noted, one of the main reasons Egypt was on the brink was the existence of a massive youth population that had absorbed the greatest burden of Egypt's financial difficulties.[48] When the initial foray on January 25 proved more successful than anyone could have imagined and the results were placed on Twitter, Facebook, and YouTube, it was those disenfranchised youth who were the first to hear the call. And, fortunately for the movement, they proved to be an intractable force willing to suffer death and injury for the cause.[49]

Nevertheless, it is important not to overemphasize the role that new social media played in this movement. As the new media sat adjacent with "old" media, the social organizations on Facebook and driven by Twitter coexisted and were in dialogue with more traditional forms of social organization such as mosques, churches, unions, political parties, and soccer fan clubs. It is hardly a coincidence that the numbers grew tremendously on the first Friday after the January 25 Movement formed, as mosques served as an ideal vector through which to mobilize and direct the population.[50] The nexus between faith and politics would only grow stronger as the movement progressed, and Tahrir Square became a staging ground of mass prayers.[51] Proof of the power of these traditional forms of organization can also be seen in the activism of the Ultras of the two most powerful football teams, *al-Ahly* and *al-Zamalek*, during and after the revolt.[52]

Thus, by Friday the 28th, the movement had grown from protests of thousands of "angry" Egyptians to hundreds of thousands, and had extended beyond Cairo and Alexandria into the cities of the provinces.[53] That Friday, the "Friday of Anger" (*JumaAt al-Ghadab*), also revealed another reason this movement succeeded—the delegitimizing response of the regime. There is no doubt that by January 26th everyone in Egypt realized the momentousness of the events occurring, evidenced by the coverage the protests received on the front page of all the local newspapers, including the government-owned *al-Ahram*.[54]

What truly emboldened the movement was the failure of the government, which had proved itself for so long to be capable of quashing any dissent, to respond adequately to the movement. Once the traditional tactics of tear gas, rubber bullets, hoses, and cordons proved ineffective, the government tried a gambit to prove its essential role by pulling the police force out completely on that Friday.[55] However, this step was a critical misreading of the movement. By vacating the scene at this critical juncture, the government turned previously passive bystanders against them as the country descended into chaos and the people became solely responsible for their own protection.[56] For everyone else, this withdrawal represented a forfeit of any legitimate claim to rule. This loss of control was epitomized by the declaration of the army, one of Mubarak's last pillars, that it was unwilling to fire on the people.[57] *Al-Shuruq* intimated as much when it titled one of its articles on the withdrawal of the police as "The Night the Government Fell."[58]

The state soon realized its folly, and for the first time made concessions to the movement by dissolving the government and appointing Umar Suleiman as vice-president and Ahmad Shafiq as prime minister.[59] This response validated the movement and changed the debate from one over change to one over the end of Mubarak's rule. While the feasibility of Mubarak retaining power after the events of the first four days of the movement was questionable, the events of February 2 nearly assured that the days of his regime were numbered.

Although the identities of the Battle of the Camel's perpetrators are still being debated in court, there is no denying the violence of the day. As *al-Misry al-Yawm* describes it, on that day Tahrir Square transformed into a war zone as a battle broke out between the anti- and pro-Mubarak supporters with the pro-Mubarak supporters astride horses and camels and carrying canes.[60] This violent and bloody day, which was documented with stunning images in both the old and new media, marked a significant turning point. If the removal of the police validated the power of the movement, the Battle of the Camel made patent the need for the immediate removal of the Mubarak regime. It also marked a significant turning point in the army's calculus of the situation. From that point forward the army actively made an effort to appear neutral.[61] Only nine days after the Battle of the Camel, Umar Suleiman would announce the removal of Mubarak and the handing over of power to the Supreme Council of the Armed Forces (SCAF), thus ending the first stage of the January 25 Movement.

A FRACTURED MOVEMENT

As I have shown, the rapidity with which Mubarak went from entrenched dictator to deposed despot was truly stunning and a testament to the power of the January 25 Movement. Nevertheless, the two years that followed this triumph were characterized by the almost immediate fracture of any political consensus and the reversion of Egypt to reliable and entrenched political forms. The number of political organizations that appeared during and after the Tahrir Movement was astounding, but surely not unexpected considering the years of political oppression. By November 2011, thirty-one new parties had formed, covering the entire spectrum of political thought.[62] The common denominator of all of these parties was that each had a unique vision of what Egypt should look like in the future.[63]

In the immediate aftermath of the SCAF takeover of power, these political parties and organizations directed their energies into two different vectors to effect change in the country, protests, and electoral politics. The protests that initially followed the ouster of Mubarak were built upon much of the same constituency that preceded it and had continuity in goals. In particular, the protestors aimed to protect and expand the gains of the revolt by rooting out the remnants (*fulūl*) of the ruling regime and assuring that those individuals who had committed crimes against the people were punished.[64] The protestors were quite successful in the aftermath of Mubarak's exit in ensuring that he, his family, and men such as Ahmed 'Izz were tried in court. They also were able to remove pro-Mubarak forces from the interim governments that the SCAF put in place. In general, the protestors were able to use their established mobilizing networks and the new public sphere of the square, with Tahrir being preeminent, as a check on many of the SCAF's absolutist tendencies.[65]

Nevertheless, as time progressed and the rebuilding of the country became as pressing a need as the extirpation of the old guard, constitutional and electoral politics began to share the spotlight with the demonstrations in the public squares. Contingent to the beginning of the politics of rebuilding Egypt was the gradual exclusion of more and more voices. The first signpost in this narrowing was the constitutional referendum on March 19, 2011. It aimed to determine if the people wanted to proceed with parliamentary elections while using a revised constitution (a "yes" vote) or if they wanted to delay them until a new constitution was written (a "no" vote). Although many of the secularist parties that had formed during the movement argued for a "no" vote in hopes of providing themselves time to build a constituency, 77 percent of the vote went to "yes."[66]

This resounding defeat inaugurated a period where the protestors would slowly be marginalized as representatives of Egypt, a role that they had acquired on the Day of Anger, and come to represent a single part of the movement, Egypt's New Left.[67] This disassociation was accompanied by the rise of the religious right in the political sphere. From the parliamentary elections, in which both the Muslim Brotherhood and the Salafists did extraordinarily well, to the Presidential elections where the Muslim Brotherhood candidate, Mohamed Morsi (*Mursi*) won, the religious right showed itself capable of transforming its broad-based message of "Islam is the solution" into electoral victories.

The most overt signs of the bifurcation of the left into the squares and the religious right into office were the two candidates who advanced to the presidential runoff.[68] While Morsi no doubt carried the support of many of the religious groups involved in the January 25 protests, the presence of Shafiq, who bore the black mark of the *fulūl*, represented a significant silencing of the Tahrir Movement. As Egypt transitioned to rule under its first democratically elected regime, it continued to be plagued by these fissures. In particular, President Morsi's aggressive maneuver to push through a new constitution tailored to his and the Brotherhood's liking was met with a victory in a referendum and massive demonstrations.[69]

Due to the centrality of the Tahrir protests and flood of information that surrounded the January 25 Movement, it was easy to project the images of the movement to the whole of Egypt. While, surely, this act of transference was defensible in attributing the feelings of disenfranchisement and dissatisfaction to the Egyptian population that lived outside urban centers, which comprised 42 percent of the population, it was less defensible to superimpose the image of the young middle class activist driving the change onto that of the Egyptian *fellah* (peasant, pl. *fellahîn*).[70]

There is a tradition as old as electoral politics in Egypt of urban intellectuals using the fellaheen as the medium on which to map out their visions for the country's future.[71] When the protestors in Tahrir imagined that their largely urban movement spoke for all of Egypt, they were unconsciously participating in that tradition. However, when the *fellah* was given an opportunity to speak through the ballot box, he or she did not speak of Tahrir and revolution, but of Islam and the establishment. This message was most clear in the first round of the presidential election. Hamdeen Sabbahi, the candidate most appealing to the revolutionaries due to his distance from the previous regime and his Nasserite credentials, won handily in Cairo, Alexandria, and Kafr al-Shaykh, but was shut out in rural Egypt where Morsi and Shafiq split the vote evenly.[72]

His exclusion was so great that Shafiq was able to ride his rural victories to second place in the presidential runoff elections. Why did Morsi and Shafiq succeed in the rural areas and thus claim the top two spots in the presidential runoff? It was due largely to the old style political constituencies they had built in these rural areas. As Anthony Shadid displays so cogently in his examination of the village of Bagour, the NDP over the course of thirty years had built a network through a system of personal patronage that, even after the removal of Mubarak, could be used to mobilize support.[73] Likewise, since the 1990s the Muslim Brotherhood had built a political network under control of its unified directorate that could be mobilized effectively.[74] This strong and obedient voting base, the fact that the Islamic movement as the main counterpoint to the Mubarak regime had become "everything to everyone," and the strong participation of the Muslim Brotherhood in the Tahrir Movement can account for its track record of electoral success.[75] And it is here in electoral politics that the idea of January 25 as a social media–driven movement falls apart. While the people who seized political power in Egypt two years after the movement's birth no doubt dabbled in new social media, they relied heavily on tactics as old as politics itself. These tactics were essential because more than 60 percent of the population had no access to the Internet, let alone social media.[76]

Not only did the series of electoral results in the two years following the ouster of Mubarak represent the fracture of the Tahrir Movement, but also the marginalization of a group that comprised a significant portion of the movement itself, women. There are numerous examples of the prominent role women played in the January 25 Movement. One of the best is Asma Mahfuz, who was a founding member of the April 6 Youth Movement and whose impassioned cry on YouTube for participation in the January 25 protests was a seminal moment.[77] Since women had been an active and visible part of the revolt and are a significant part of the population, it would have appeared their right to be part of the shaping of Egypt's future. However, this was not to be the case. They were excluded by a process that has deep historical roots, the use of the woman's body as a national battleground.[78]

In this case, violence against women in the streets during and after the removal of Mubarak, including sexual assault, was used to silence that half of the population which had been denied its say for so long.[79] One of the most iconic images of the post-February 11th protests was the exposed blue bra of a women protestor after she had been beaten by the police and soldiers on December 16, 2011.[80] While the violence on the streets did not transfer to electoral and constitutional politics, the degradation of the position of women did. Not only did women's presence in the government decline after the removal of Mubarak, but with the confirmation of Morsi's rushed constitution, many of the hard fought gains for women that were made under Mubarak came under question.[81] This questioning was due in large part to the fact that the constitution contained no provisions to protect the individual rights of groups that had traditionally been the most vulnerable.

These groups included not only women but also religious minorities, which in the case of Egypt are primarily the Coptic Christians. The place of Coptic Christians in the Egyptian national community was a hotly debated issue prior to the Tahrir Movement and was shaped by two discourses that both originated from the Coptic community. The first of these, referred to in Egypt as the "national unity discourse," had its origins in the elite Coptic community in the nineteenth century, and proffered the idea that Coptic Christians were an inseparable part of the Egyptian nation and had worked alongside their Muslim brothers in building it. As for the "persecution discourse," which grew out of Pope Shenouda III's consolidation of the Coptic Orthodox Church in the 1980s and found a receptive audience among middle class Copts, it posited that Christians were a persecuted minority that needed to stand together to protect themselves from the encroaching threat of Islam.[82]

This debate continued after January 25 with the choice of discourse drastically affecting interpretations of the events that followed. The most prominent example was the tragic Maspero Demonstrations on October 9–10, 2011. On these two days, thousand of Egyptians, many of whom were Christians, marched in a peaceful protest on the Maspero television building from Cairo's Shubra district to decry the government's refusal to rebuild a destroyed church in Aswan.[83] However, the peaceful protest soon devolved into a battle between the protestors and the police forces. More than twenty people were killed and over three hundred were injured. When viewed through the national unity prism this incident was an example of Christians and Muslims standing side by side to protest, fight, and die for a human rights issue. However, when viewed through the persecution discourse this event was another example of the mortal danger that all Copts faced in Egypt and the fact that neither the Muslim government nor the Muslim security forces were there to protect them.

While there can be debate on whether certain events in the aftermath of January 25 represented overt attacks on the Coptic Community, it is beyond doubt that their situation did not markedly improve after the deposal of Hosni Mubarak. Violence was directed at the Coptic community, and the issue of sectarianism was one openly debated by Muslim and Christians.[84] In addition, the ballot box was exceedingly unkind to the Christian community as the victories of the Muslim Brotherhood and Salafists came at the expense of candidates the Copts had supported.[85] While those who ascribe to national unity discourse would be assuaged by the Muslim Brotherhood's affirmation of their support for the essentiality of the Coptic Christian community to Egypt, it is undeniable that Copts and women have been left without true representation in the political processes that for a short time determined the country's future.

CONCLUSION

The movement that began in Egypt on January 25, 2011, while no doubt influenced by the volatility in the rest of the region, was an outgrowth of very specific conditions in Egypt. The eighteen days between January 25 and February 11 saw a vanguard of millions of dissatisfied citizens fill the streets and use the power of nonviolent protest to overthrow a regime that had become blatant in its repression and corruption. Through its long reign, the Mubarak presidency had raised a generation of Egyptians denied of so much that to fight and to die for the cause of "change" became the only viable option. The rapidity with which this change came was truly astounding and rightfully belongs in Egyptian history with the movements of 1881, 1919, and 1952.

While Web 2.0 did not cause this movement, it was present to document it, and as such our picture of the events is much more complex and multivocal than any of the major movements that preceded it. Nevertheless, we must not let the multiplicity of these voices delude us into thinking this Movement brought a sharp break with the past. This Movement no doubt brought positive changes to the country. In particular, it reinvigorated the streets and the public squares as viable vectors through which antiestablishment views could be expressed. However, the two years that followed those eighteen days in January and February also showed that the transition from a rhetoric of revolt to actual systematic change is a long and difficult process, and that the imagined Egyptian citizen remains male and Muslim. Nevertheless, for the moment, the destiny of the country lies with the army, which reassumed power during the summer of 2013 following a popular (perhaps orchestrated) mass movement against the Morsi government. The crackdown against all forms of dissent and new laws restricting protests are all too reminiscent of Mubarek's regime, only that this time a majority of the weary Egyptian population, fed up with inaction and economic paralysis, have legitimized the new order. Not only have Muslim Brotherhood militants been given long prison sentences, so have the leaders responsible for initiating the revolt. Once the military leaves its barracks and assumes power, it becomes very difficult to dislodge it and return to civilian rule.

With that said, using these two years as predictive of the future is hazardous territory for the historian. For it was nearly two years after the Free Officers Movement that Gamal Abdal Nasser took the reins of Egypt and led Egypt on a path that few, including deposed President Mohamed Naguib, would or could have imagined.

NOTES

1   Ann M. Lesch, "Egypt's Spring: Causes of the Revolution," *Middle East Policy* 18 (2011): 36.

2   Joel Beinin, "Egyptian Workers and January 25th: A Social Movement in Historical Context," *Social Research* 79 (2012): 329–30.

3   Israel Gershoni and James Jankowski, *Redefining the Egyptian Nation, 1930–45* Cambridge: Cambridge University Press, 1995, pp. 3–4.

4   Lesch, "Egypt's Spring": 40.

5   Ibid., 39.

6   Ibid., 38.

7   Tarek Osman, *Egypt on the Brink: From Nasser to Mubarak*, New Haven, CT: Yale University Press, 2010, p. 207.

8   Malak Badrawi, "Financial Cerberus: The Egyptian Parliament, 1924–52," in *Re-Envisioning Egypt*, Arthur Goldschmidt, Amy Johnson, and Barak Salmoni, eds., Cairo: American University in Cairo Press, 2005, pp. 110–118.

9   Osman, *Egypt on the Brink*, ch.4.

10 Hazem Fahmy, "An Initial Perspective on the 'Winter of Discontent': The Root Causes of the Egyptian Revolution," *Social Research* 79 (2012): 365

11 Lesch, "Egypt's Spring": 42.

12 Osman, *Egypt on the Brink*, p. 141.

13 Ibid., p. 141.

14 Ibid., p. 130.

15 Beinin, "Egyptian Workers and January 25th": 326.

16 Heather Sharkey, *Living with Colonialism: Nationalism and Culture in the Anglo-Egyptian Sudan*, Berkeley: University of California Press, 2003, pp. 95–119.

17   Osman "Young Egyptians," *Social Research* 79 (2012): 299.

18   Osman, *Egypt on the Brink*, p. 166.

19   P. J. Vatikiotis, *The History of Egypt*, 3rd ed. (Baltimore, MD: Johns Hopkins University Press, 1985), pp. 418–419.

20   Anthony Shadid, "In a Town Built upon Patronage, A Test of Egypt's New Order," *New York Times*, February 20, 2011, www.nytimes.com/2011/02/20/world/middleeast/20nile.html?pagewanted=all&_r=0

21   Salwa Ismail, "The Egyptian Revolution against the Police," *Social Research* 79 (2012): 436.

22   Ibid., 437. (Eds.: For more on the heavy-handed tactics of the police against the Egyptian citizenry, see Paul Amar, "Why Mubarak Is Out," in Marvin E. Gettleman and Stuart Schaar, eds., *The Middle East and Islamic World Reader*, New York: Grove Press, 3rd ed., 2012, pp. 357–362.)

23   Hazem Fahmy, "An Initial Perspective […]": 357–360.

24   Ibid., 355–356.

25   Beinin, "Egyptian Workers and January 25th": 327.

26   Osman, *Egypt on the Brink*, p. 142.

27   Juan Cole, "Egypt's New Left versus the Military Junta," *Social Research* 79 (2012):488.

28   Lesch, "Egypt's Spring": 43.

29   Osman, *Egypt on the Brink*, pp. 100–1.

30   Nathan Brown, "Contention in Religion and State in Post Revolutionary Egypt," *Social Research* 79 (2012): 545.

31   Beinin, "Egyptian Workers and January 25th": 335.

32   "Egypt's Nour released from jail," February 18, 2009, BBC News, news.bbc.co.uk/2/hi/middle_east/7897703.stm.

33   Hazem Fahmy, "An Initial Perspective […]": 373.

34   Talal Assad, *Formation of the Secular: Christianity, Islam, Modernity*, Stanford, CA: Stanford University Press, 2003, p. 222.

35   Nancy Reynolds, *A City Consumed: Urban Commerce, the Cairo Fire and the Politics of Decolonization in Egypt*, Stanford: Stanford University Press, 2011, p. 143.

36   D. Parvaz, "The Arab Spring, chronicled Tweet by Tweet," Al Jazeera Online November 6, 2011, www.aljazeera.com/indepth/features/2011/11/2011113123416203161.html. cited in Wiebke Lamer, "Twitter and Tyrants: New Media and its Effects on Sovereignty in the Middle East," *Arab Media and Society*,16 (2012). www.arabmediasociety.com/?article=798.

37   Samar Marzban, "*Bakār alā Twitter: Lam Adil bi-tasriḥāt ḥawl masʾūliyya al-Akhwān An Mawqiat al-Gamal*," *Yawm al-Sabi*, February 19, 2012, www1.youm7.com/News.asp?NewsID=951717&SecID=65°; "'Battle' of the Camels' acquittals shock Egypt," BBC News, October 11, 2012. www.bbc.co.uk/news/world-middle-east-19910446.

38   *Al-Shurūq*, Jan 16, 2011.

39 Muhammad Abd al-Radi, et al. "*Ḥummi al-Iḥtijāj al-Intiḥārī Tuṣīb Misriyīn*," *Al-Shurūq*, Jan 19, 2011.

40 Editorial, *Washington Post*, January 15, 2011, www.washingtonpost.com/wpdyn/content/article/2011/01/15/AR2011011503141.html.

41 *"Tunis Abra lil-Arab,"* AlJazeera.Net, January 13, 2011, www.aljazeera.net/news/pages/4ded9ec2-a5d8-489f-bd06-fba02b41ad56.

42 Matt Richtel, "Egypt Cuts off Most Internet and Cell Service," *New York Times*, January 28, 2011, www.nytimes.com/2011/01/29/technology/internet/29cutoff.html?_r=0 cited in Wiebke Lamer, "Twitter and Tyrants: New Media and its Effects on Sovereignty in the Middle East," *Arab Media and Society*, 16 (2012), www.arabmediasociety.com/?article=798, accessed March 7, 2013.

43 *"Al-Mutazahirūn w-al-Amn fi al-Yawm al-Thanī: La Taraju'...wala 'Istislām"* al-Misrī al-Yawm," January 27, 2011.

44 *"Al-Shaab Yurīd al-Taghyiīr"*, *Al-Shurūq*, January 29, 2011.

45 Hazem Fahmy, "An Initial Perspective [...]": 350.

46 *"Al-Muzahirāt al-Muhtajjīn īdiyya lil-Shurta fi īdihā,"* *Al-Shurūq*, Jan 24,2011; Khaled Abd al-Rasul, *"Sitīn Alf Nāshit 'Iftirādī yushārikūn fi Mudhāhirat īd al-Shurta,"* *al-Shurūq* January 21, 2011.

47 Muhammad Shoman, et al., *"Tazāhurāt Hashida bil-Qahira wa al-Muhāfizāt Istishād Mujannad Amn wa Shābīn bil-Suīs."* *Al-Ahram*, January 26, 2011. www.ahram.org.eg/archive/Al-Ahram-Files/News/60419.aspx

48 Tarek Osman, "Young Egyptians": 314–316.

49 Muhammad Fuad, Esam Amir, and Abd al-Rahman Yusuf, *"Qanābil al-Shurta tafshil fi mana al Muzāhirāt fi Wust al Balad"*, *Al-Shurūq*, January 29, 2011.

50 Carrie Rosefsky Wickham, "The Muslim Brotherhood and Democratic Transition in Egypt," *Middle East Law and Governance* 3 (2011): 212.

51 Talal Assad, "Fear and the Ruptured State: Reflections of Egypt after Mubarak," *Social Research* 79 (2012): 276.

52 Ismail "The Revolution Against the Police": 454–457.

53 *"Al-Shaab Yurīd al-Taghyiīr"*, *Al-Shurūq*, January 29, 2011.

54 *Al-Shurūq*, January 25, 2011; *al-Ahram*, January 25, 2011, www.ahram.org.eg/Archive/news/2011/1/25/index.aspx; al- Misry al Yawm January 26th 2011, today.almasryalyoum.com/default.aspx?IssueID=2027.

55 Safa Esam al-Din, Rania Rabi, and Daha al-Gindi, *"Baad al-Insihāb al-Shurta... Shibāb Yunazzamun al-Murūr fi al-Shawāri,"Al-Shurūq*, January 30, 2011.

56 Esam al-Din et al.,*"Baad al-Insihāb al-Shurta [...]"*

57 Haytham Radwan, *"al-Qawat al-Musalaha li-l-Shaab: Nahnu hena l-tamīnukum wa tahqīq mutālibukum,"* *al-Shurūq*, January 30, 2011.

58 Muhammad Abu Zayd et al., *"Laylat Suqut al-Hukūma,"* *Al-Shurūq*, January 30, 2011.

59 Muhammad Said et al., *"Al-Shaab Yataqadum wa Mubārak Yabda Al-Taraju"* *Al-Shurūq*, January 30, 2011.

60 *"Tahrir Yathawwal ilā Sāhit ā Harb wa al-Watan Yutālib bit-tahdīa"'* *Al-Misry al-Yawm*, Feb 3 2011, today.almasryalyoum.com/article2.aspx?ArticleID=286468.

61 Atef Said, "The Paradox of Transition to "Democracy under Military Rule," *Social Research* 79 (2012): 410.

62   Talal Assad, "Fear and the Ruptured State": 281.

63   For an accounting of some of the ideas and plans put forward see Tahrir Documents, www.tahrirdocuments.org.

64   Juan Cole, "Egypt's New Left versus the Military Junta": 506–507.

65   Juan Cole, "Egypt's New Left versus the Military Junta": 505.

66   Talal Assad, "Fear and the Ruptured State," For a survey of the arguments for "Yes" see Tahrir Documents, www.tahrirdocuments.org, under the header "Constitution"

67   Juan Cole, "Egypt's New Left versus the Military Junta": 488–489.

68   "Relive Vote Count in 1st Round of Egypt presidential race: How Morsi and Shafiq moved on," *Ahram* Online, englienglish.ahram.org.eg/NewsContent/4/0/57314/Opinion/Egyptdivided-a-reading-into-a-crisscrossed-map.aspx.

71   Michael Ezekiel Gasper, *The Power of Representation: Publics, Peasants and Islam in Egypt,* Stanford, CA: Stanford University Press, 2009.

72   Hani Shukrallah, "Egypt Divided."

73   Anthony Shadid, " In a Town Built upon Patronage, A Test of Egypt's New Order," *New York Times*, February 20, 2011, www.nytimes.com/2011/02/20/world/middleeast/20nile.html?pagewanted=all&_r=0

74   Osman, *Egypt on the Brink*, 100.

75   Ibid., 101.

76   "Internet Users, Population, Facebook Stats for Africa 2012 Q2," *Internet World Stats*, www.internetworldstats.com/stats1.htm, accessed March 5, 2013.

77   Talal Assad, "Fear and the Ruptured State": 292.

78   Beth Baron, *Egypt as a Woman: Nationalism, Gender, and Politics*, Cairo: American University in Cairo Press, 2005, pp. 45–56.

79   Margot Badran, "A Proper Revolution," *Ahram* Online, January 27, 2013, english.ahram.org.eg/NewsContent/4/0/63412/Opinion/A-Proper-Revolution.aspx

80   Juan Cole, "Egypt's New Left versus the Military Junta": 495.

81   Dina Samir " Egyptian women still struggling for rights 2 years after revolution" *Ahram* Online, February 12, 2013, english.ahram.org.eg/NewsContent/1/150/63114/Egypt/-January-Revolution/Egyptian-women-still-struggling-for-rights--years-.aspx.

82   Paul Sedra "Class Cleavages and Ethnic Conflict: Coptic Christian Communities in Modern Egyptian Politics." *Islam and Christian-Muslim Relations* 10 (2): 227 cited in Talal Assad, "Fear and the Ruptured State," p. 284.

83   Yusri el-Badri, et al. "*Masbīrū" Taḥawwūl ilā Sāḥat Ḥarb wa 19 Qatīlan wa 183 Muṣaban fī Ṣufūf al-Mutaḍḥāhirīn wa al-Amn*," *Al-Misry Al-Yawm*, October 10, 2011; Talal Assad, "Fear and the Ruptured State": 288.

84   Talal Assad, "Fear and the Ruptured State": 283.

85   Mike Elkin "Egypt's Christians Prepare for New Political Climate," *New York Times,* November 30, 2011. www.nytimes.com/2011/12/01/world/middleeast/egyptianchristians-get-political.html.

II

Jordan and Morocco, two monarchies still standing after the Arab revolts, have more resiliency, according to Jack A. Goldstone, well-known theoretician of revolutions, than what he calls "sultanistic regimes," such as those of Libya's Muammar Gaddafi, Tunisia's Zine al-Abadine Ben Ali, and Egypt's Hosni Mubarak. The staying power of kings, he argues in Foreign Affairs *(May/June 2011), lies in the pluralism of their regimes. If crises hit, the kings can always dismiss their prime ministers or dissolve parliament, thereby defusing those crises before they explode. This thesis, however, came under attack in Jordan in November 2012, when demonstrators for the first time called for the fall of the Jordanian monarchy. An aberration, or a trend? In addition, the Syrian war next door will, according to United Nations estimates, create some million Syrian refugees in Jordan by the end of 2015, putting new strains on the monarchy. Curtis R. Ryan in this chapter discusses the vulnerabilities and strengths of King Abdullah ibn Hussein, the country's ruler.*

IIIIIIIIIIIIIIIIIIIIIIIIIIIIIIIIIIIIIIIIIIIIIIIIIIIIIIIIIIIIIIIIIIIIIIIIIIIIIIII

CHAPTER 4
THE ARAB CITIZENS' REVOLT AND THE HASHEMITE KINGDOM OF JORDAN
CURTIS R. RYAN

Jordan, like the rest of the Middle East, was deeply affected by the regional wave of revolts. Unlike Tunisia, Egypt, Yemen, Libya, and Syria, however, the Hashemite Kingdom had not been seized by revolutionary fervor, regime change, or civil war. Yet Jordan had seen waves of protests emerge as early as those that toppled the Ben Ali regime in Tunisia. In both Tunisia and Jordan, large-scale antigovernment protests emerged in December 2010. The difference, however, was that Jordanian protests mostly called for reform rather than removal of the ruler. While Tunisians called for the overthrow of the Ben Ali regime, Jordanians called for the king to sack and replace the prime minister and his cabinet. Still, a different kind of political instability can be seen in Jordanian governance itself, as the kingdom had five different prime ministers, and hence five different governments, during the first two years after December 2010.

This essay examines the Arab uprisings in the Jordanian context, including precursors to the current protest movement, an analysis of the protests and protestors in the Jordanian version of contestation, and finally, the regime's attempts to reform its way out of a regional crises. As usually happens in such cases, the Hashemite regime has attempted to steer a moderate and middle course through otherwise turbulent events. In this case, it has attempted to shore up its external alliances as it responds to spillover from regional change (especially in the form of the Syrian Civil War) and also to create reform within domestic politics that carries Jordan through internal and regional crises. In short, the Hashemite monarchy is trying to create its own unique path and one that relies on evolution rather than revolution. For the regime's critics and for prodemocracy activists, the key questions are always the same two: is Jordan moving far too slow on the road to political reform? Or, is it moving forward at all?

JORDAN TOO: PROTEST MOVEMENTS

While Jordan had not experienced a revolution, it had no shortage of protests during the period of the regional revolts. Indeed, protests and demonstrations occurred almost every Friday throughout 2011 and 2012, and continued in 2013. Protesters denounced corruption in government and in economic transactions associated with the state's neoliberal program of privatization. That program involved selling many state assets to private investors, and triggered rampant charges of nepotism and corruption as the economic transition continued. In addition, demonstrations called for a return of the kingdom's declining social safety net (in terms of extensive government spending on social services and employment opportunities in state institutions and state-run industries). And, like their colleagues across the region, Jordanian protestors called for openness, transparency in governance, reform, and democratization.

The protests drew on both old and new forms of political opposition in the kingdom. The older opposition consisted mainly of leftist and pan-Arab nationalist parties and—in much larger numbers—the Islamist movement. Jordan's large Islamist movement includes the Muslim Brotherhood as well as its political party wing, the Islamic Action Front. Islamism in Jordan also includes a separate Salafist movement as well, although Salafists were rarely part of the pro reform protests across the kingdom, and have only recently taken more public roles in terms of political activism.

Newer forms of opposition and protest in Jordan drew more heavily on independent nonpartisan activists and on populist social movements that emerged in almost every town and city in the country. These grassroots movements, known as the *Herak*, were often youth-organized and emerged especially in areas that had previously been regarded as centers of East Jordanian, tribal, and loyalist regime support. They emerged first, in fact, in southern cities such as Tafila, Kerak, and Maan, and they therefore took many pro regime elites by surprise. Protests led by Palestinian Jordanians in the country's many refugee camps or demonstrations by the Islamist movement would not have startled anyone in the regime. What was most troubling to many, however, was the fact that, aside from cities such as Amman, Zarqa, and Irbid, most other protests were taking place in areas that had previously been seen as solidly royalist, while most Palestinian camps were largely devoid of contestation.

Yet as important as these new social movements such as the *Herak* are, especially in terms of extensive youth activism in Jordanian politics, it is also important to remember that protest movements did not emerge in a vacuum in 2010 or 2011. In Jordan, as indeed throughout the region, there is a long history of public activism, demonstrations, and protests. The difference today is how extensive these have become, and how successful some movements have been throughout the region in toppling entire regimes. In the Jordanian context, the protest wave of 2010–2013 was a reminder especially of the protests and resultant reform efforts that rocked the country in an earlier round of national demonstrations, in April 1989.

EARLIER PROTESTS AND REFORM IN 1989

The situation in 1989 was similar in several ways to the situation Jordan finds itself in today.[1] The economy was in recession, unemployment and the cost of living had increased dramatically, and negotiations with the International Monetary Fund (IMF) had led to difficult and painful economic austerity measures. In 1989, King Hussein's regime implemented the IMF austerity program, removing many basic subsidies (including on staple foods). The resultant surge in prices was the last straw, triggering demonstrations and even riots, starting in the south of the country and spreading steadily north. The regime was clearly caught off guard by the vehemence of the protests, and it responded by sacking the prime minister and his government, and promising elections and a revival of parliamentary life in the kingdom.[2]

As the riots subsided, King Hussein launched a fairly ambitious program for political liberalization. Parliamentary elections were held in 1989 and these resulted in significant victories for both leftist and Islamist activists. Together, the secular left and religious right members of parliament (MPs) amounted to a parliamentary majority, and even elected a member of the Muslim Brotherhood, Dr. Abd al-Latif Arabiyat, speaker of parliament. The kingdom shortly thereafter legalized political parties, loosened many restrictions on the media, and created a National Charter calling for greater pluralism and liberalization, in return for loyalty to the Hashemite monarchy. Since then, Jordan has held several more rounds of elections for the lower house of parliament (the upper house, or senate, is royally appointed)—in 1993, 1997, 2003,

2007, 2010, and 2013. Yet many in the reformist opposition still pine for the 1989–1993 era, seen as a golden era of reform, and one that produced a very diverse parliament.[3]

From 1993 onward, however, Jordan shifted to the Single Non-transferable Vote (SNTV) system, known in the kingdom as the "one person, one vote" system. Voters had a single vote in multiple-member districts, and more problematically, districts were unequal—over representing predominantly East Jordanian rural areas and under representing more heavily Palestinian urban areas. The former, mainly tribal areas, have historically been seen as bastions of loyalty to the regime, while the latter have historically proven to be more fertile ground for the Islamist movement. As noted above, however, in recent years, opposition to the regime, and especially to its economic privatization policies, has increased markedly in tribal communities and other, nominally royalist areas. Thus while identity politics and loyalties are far more variable than is often assumed, nonetheless the inequality of electoral districts remains, and hence the resulting parliaments are not as representative of the Jordanian public as they could or should be.

REFORM AND ELECTIONS

On January 23, 2013, Jordanians returned to the polls to elect the first new Jordanian parliament in the era of the Arab revolts. Among the main questions surrounding the election, of course, was this: do the elections actually matter? Earlier rounds of elections, especially those in 2007 and 2010, had been marred by extensive charges of rigging, and each produced a lackluster parliament that was disbanded long before its term was up. Opposition parties and activists argued that the electoral law was unrepresentative, the election process was rigged, and that parliament itself was too weak to be in any way significant, especially relative to the power of the monarchy itself. Opposition groups demanded greater (and faster) changes. In particular, they called for extensive changes in the electoral law and, after the elections, for a shift in governance toward empowered elected parliaments and a more constitutional monarchy.[4]

Yet the Jordanian regime was emphatic that the 2013 elections were different. The king argued that Jordan itself was different, and that it was a case of a regime and a country reforming itself. The Arab uprising, he insisted, was an opportunity, not a constraint.[5] In an effort to engage public debate and encourage voter participation, the king even published a series of brief political treatises. A third of these explicitly addressed the transition to a more parliamentary government. "After the upcoming elections, we will start piloting a parliamentary government system, including how our prime ministers and cabinets are selected," the king wrote. "International experience suggests this will require several parliamentary cycles to develop and mature. The key driver of the timeline for this transition is our success in developing national political parties." [6]

After the elections, the revolving door of prime ministers and governments was to stop, with a new PM and government ideally to remain in office throughout the four-year term of parliament. The king argued that the elections, the new parliament, and the new government were the next steps in a broader reform agenda launched by the regime during (and in response to) the regional revolts. These included amendments to the constitution, a new constitutional court, an independent electoral commission (IEC), and new laws on political parties and elections.

But many in the opposition remained unconvinced. The Muslim Brotherhood, several leftist parties, and most of the regional popular movements (*Herak*) boycotted the polls. Other opposition forces, including a national list that combined several leftist and pan-Arab nationalist parties, chose to participate. The IEC attempted to clean up and modernize the entire electoral process, reregistering more than two million voters, and taking multiple steps to ensure that the polls were clean, free, and fair. The IEC invited hundreds of foreign election observers and more than 4,000 domestic observers (from Jordanian civil society organizations) to observe every step of the process, including voting and vote tabulation.

Despite the objections of many in the Jordanian opposition, the kingdom called for parliamentary elections on January 23, 2013. In addition to their other objections, many in the opposition questioned the mid-winter timing, suggesting that given the lack of consensus on the electoral law—and, indeed, given widespread opposition to it—the elections should perhaps be postponed at least until the spring. Yet King Abdullah had asserted repeatedly that elections would be held by the end of 2012, and felt that moving into January 2013 was already a delay. In some respects, the timing was influenced by regional events, especially by the steadily worsening situation in Syria and fears regarding what this might mean for Jordan.

The opposition remained divided. While many leftist parties, *Herak* activists, and the Islamic Action Front (the political party affiliated with the Muslim Brotherhood) boycotted the elections, others participated, including a national list of leftist and pan-Arab nationalist candidates and a moderate "Islamic Centrist" list. The former list failed to gain any seats, but the latter garnered three—the largest of any list in the country, while adding thirteen more seats via district representation. Fifteen women were elected via the women's quota, but three others also gained seats. Television journalist Rula Hroub became one of three women to win a seat without the women's quota, by leading the Stronger Jordan list. The other two women were Marian Lozi (Amman) and Wafaa Bani Mustafa (Jerash), who each won their district seats outright. So of the 150 parliamentarians, eighteen are women—not an enormous number, but a record high for Jordan. Overall, the elections were not without problems, but compared to the previous several rounds, they were a marked improvement. The process, in other words, was greatly improved, even if the electoral system remained highly problematic.[7]

Still, given the nature of the electoral law, and despite the IEC improvements, the new parliament was predestined to resemble the previous several. Most members of parliament (MPs) were East Jordanian men with deep tribal roots, who ran as independents (rather than as part of any political party) and who espoused generally conservative political views. Thus the electoral system and the system of governance remain key points of contestation in Jordanian politics, despite the very real improvements in the electoral process. For all the fury of the regional uprisings, and for all the deep frustration felt by most Jordanians regarding both the economy and the political system, most still supported the monarchy. Yet most Jordanians also rejected cosmetic reform and strongly supported greater pluralism and democratization in the kingdom.[8]

CONCLUSIONS

Like most states in the Middle East and North Africa, the "Arab Spring" has impacted Jordan too—but not yet in a revolutionary way. Yet the country has seen a striking increase in citizen activism, not only in demonstrations and protests but also in extensive political debates across social media, from Facebook groups, to blogs, to Twitter. Jordan's well educated youth have become increasingly politically aware and active, but have been often uncertain about precisely where and how to exercise their political energies.

As the Jordanian economy struggled through severe crises, including IMF austerity measures and rising energy costs, these economic constraints remained even more volatile and combustible within Jordanian politics than questions of political reform, elections, or governance. Yet the kingdom had few real options to ameliorate its severe economic difficulties, even as these carried the increasing risk of social unrest and political instability. Added to these internal constraints were those of the region itself, especially from tensions between Israel and the Palestinians to the west, an unstable Iraq to the east, and most alarming, fears of a spillover of violence from the Syrian Civil War to the north. For many in the regime's intelligence and security services, these various concerns amounted to yet another reason to slow or even halt the kingdom's limited reform efforts. Yet the volatility of the domestic and regional situation actually made domestic political reform that much more urgent—vital, in fact, for Jordan to navigate its way through, and even prosper in, a region in revolt.

NOTES

1   For details on the transition from King Hussein to King Abdullah, and changes in Jordanian politics in both eras, see Curtis R. Ryan, *Jordan in Transition: From Hussein to Abdullah,* Boulder, CO: Lynne Rienner, 2002.

2   Rex Brynen, "Economic Crisis and Post-Rentier Democratization in the Arab World: The Case of Jordan," *Canadian Journal of Political Science,* 25/1 (1992): 69-97, Malik Mufti, "Elite Bargains and the Onset of Political Liberalization in Jordan," *Comparative Political Studies,* 32/1 (1999): 100–129, and Glenn E. Robinson, "Defensive Democratization in Jordan," *International Journal of Middle East Studies,* 30/3 (1998): 387–410.

3   On Jordan's decades of struggles with reform efforts, see Marwan Muasher, *A Decade of Struggling Reform Efforts in Jordan: The Resilience of the Rentier System,* Washington, D.C.: Carnegie Endowment for International Peace, 2011, and also International Crisis Group, "Popular Protest in North Africa and the Middle East (IX): Dallying with Reform in a Divided Jordan," *Middle East Report* no. 118, March 12, 2012. www.crisisgroup.org/en/regions/middle-east-north-africa/iraq-iran-gulf/jordan.aspx

4   Curtis R. Ryan, "What to Expect from Jordan's Elections," Middle East Channel, *Foreign Policy,* January 18, 2013. mideast.foreignpolicy.com/posts/2013/01/18/ what_to_expect_from_jordan_s_elections 5 Author interview with H. M. King Abdullah II. Basman Palace, Amman, Jordan, May 21, 2012.

6   Abdullah II ibn Al-Husayn, kingabdullah.jo/index.php/en_US/pages/view/ id/249.html "Discussion Paper: Each Playing Our Part in New Democracy," March 2, 2013.

7   For a detailed analysis, see Curtis R. Ryan, "Jordan's Unfinished Journey: Parliamentary Elections and the State of Reform," POMED Project on Middle East Democracy, Policy Brief, March 2013.

8   Curtis R. Ryan, "Elections, Parliament, and a 'New' Prime Minister in Jordan," Middle East Channel, *Foreign Policy,* March 11, 2013. www.mideast.foreignpolicy.com/posts/2013/03/11/ elections_parliament_and_a_new_prime_minister_in_jordan.

Much speculation surrounds the Assad regime in Syria. Will it survive an extensive internal revolt, which has torn the country apart and caused more than 320,000 deaths by June 2015, with 1.5 million people wounded since March 2011, according to the Syrian Observatory for Human Rights. More are being killed daily. Cities have been bombarded and four million refugees have fled to bordering states. The region surrounding Syria faces instability and has to deal daily with the ravages of nearby war. Yet, the Assad regime has withstood inordinate internal and external pressures to resign and make room for a new order. With the backing of Russia, Iran, and China externally and the support of most Alawites, the minority group ruling over Syria, the regime has—as of this writing—outlasted most doomsayers' predictions of its imminent demise. Joshua Landis tells us why in this chapter.

The infiltration of foreign jihadists into northern Syria, the Anbar Province of Iraq close to the Syrian border, and Hezbollah-controlled territories of Lebanon, where they have been fighting under the initially al-Qaeda–affiliated umbrella Islamic State (ISIS) from the end of 2013, adds new uncertainty in a volatile war-torn zone and threatens to enlarge the Syrian war into a regional conflict. The evacuation of most US troops from Iraq (with about 3,500 still there by the summer of 2015) and the Obama administration's fear of aiding Syrian opposition movements because of the presence among them of al-Qaeda elements has created a dangerous vacuum, which extremists have filled. The attempt at the beginning of January 2014 to quell the power of ISIS fighters in both Iraq and Syria by Iraqi government forces (in alliance with some Sunni tribal elements) and a coalition of Syrian non-ISIS rebel leaders signifies that both the Iraqi government and the Syrian opposition take the presence of outside jihadists in their countries as a major threat to stability and an impediment to peace. The Geneva 2 conference on Syria in late January 2014 had Syrian opposition forces regrouping to purge the most extreme elements from their midst. Meanwhile the Assad military's loyalists, in an attempt to reconquer territory lost to the opposition, intensified their fighting and dropped barrel-filled cluster bombs from airplanes, wantonly killing large numbers of both civilians and opposition fighters. The world stood by as the Syrian quagmire intensified and spread into neighboring states.

After attacks on Syrian civilians with chemical weapons in 2013, for which no one claimed responsibility, the Assad regime, under pressure of an imminent air attack from the United States and bending to the urgings of its main ally and benefactor, Russia, agreed to surrender all its stockpiles of chemical weapons for destruction. Syria had created these weapons as an antidote to Israel's nuclear warheads. But preventive steps in Israel combined with new weapons technology (both locally manufactured and imported from the US) and missile shields have made Israel less vulnerable to chemical attacks. The Syrian stockpiles therefore had become obsolete *and more symbolic than real weapons of mass destruction. Giving them up bought the Syrian government time and halted the Obama administration's threats to bombard Syria. The peace conference planned and organized by the United Nations in late January 2014 left intact the Assad regime's hold on power. Assad's forces went on the offensive and recaptured previously lost territory, while much of the armed opposition to the Syrian state has refused to give up its arms and has rejected compromises with a regime that it mistrusts, making projected negotiations flawed even before they began. Some groups have even announced plans to boycott the talks. It seems as if Assad's Baathist regime, which is willing to destroy large parts of the country to stay in power, will be around for some time to come. The UN Security Council is paralyzed because of Russian and Chinese opposition to armed foreign intervention, while Western electorates, tired of fighting long wars in distant Iraq and Afghanistan, have despaired of more military intervention in what many view as quagmires and fighting without end, producing frightful results. In addition, millions have come to realize that extremism flourishes as wars expand.*

||||||||||||||||||||||||||||||||||||||||||||||||||||||||||||||||||||||||||||||||||

CHAPTER 5*
THE SYRIAN UPRISING: THE STAYING POWER OF BASHAR AL-ASSAD'S REGIME
JOSHUA LANDIS

Will President Bashar al-Assad continue to hold power? Chances are he will. Despite his regime's rapid loss of legitimacy, its growing isolation, and Syria's tanking economy, no countervailing force has yet emerged that can take it down.

Many opposition and foreign leaders predicted that the regime would fall. Syrian Muslim Brotherhood leader Mohammed Riad al-Shaqfa stated that Bashar would fall "in the next few months."[1] The US State Department called President Assad a "dead man walking." Israel's defense minister insisted that Assad would fall in a matter of weeks. Certainly, the revolutionary process that began to sweep the Middle East in 2011 is powerful; most Syrians want change, and many are willing to fight for freedom and dignity. One cannot envision the

|||||||||||||||||||||||||||||||||||||||||||||||||||||||||||||||||||||||||||||||||||||||||

*Adapted from Joshua Landis, "The Syrian Uprising of 2011: Why the Assad Regime Is Likely to Survive to 2013," *Middle East Policy*, Spring 2013. Used by permission of the Middle East Policy Council.

Assad family retaining power in the long run; all the same, predictions of its rapid demise may be wishful thinking.

Four elements are important in assessing the regime's chances of survival: its own strengths, the opposition's weaknesses, the chances of foreign intervention, and the impact of sanctions and economic decline.

I. ASSAD REMAINS STRONG MILITARILY

First, let's place the regime in regional perspective. The Assads stand atop the last minoritarian regime in the Levant and thus seem destined to fall in this age of popular revolt. If they do, the postcolonial era will draw to a final close. Following World War II, minorities took control in every Levant state, thanks to colonial divide-and-rule tactics and the fragmented national community that bedeviled the states of the region. It is estimated that, due to their over-recruitment by the French Mandate authorities, Alawites already by the mid-1950s constituted some 65 percent of all noncommissioned officers in the Syrian military.[2] Within a decade, they took control of the military leadership and, with it, Syria itself.[3]

Unique among the Levant states was Palestine, where the Jewish minority was able to transform itself into the majority at the expense of Palestine's Muslims. Neither the Christians of Lebanon nor the Sunnis of Iraq were so lucky or ambitious. Nevertheless, both clung to power at the price of dragging their countries into lengthy civil wars. The Lebanese war lasted fifteen years; the Iraqi struggle between Shiites and Sunnis, while shorter, has yet to be entirely resolved. The Alawites of Syria seem determined to repeat this violent plunge to the bottom. It is hard to determine whether this is due to the rapaciousness of a corrupt elite, the bleak prospects that the Alawite community faces in a post-Assad Syria, or the weak faith that many in the region place in democracy and power-sharing formulas. Whatever the reason, Syria's transition away from minority rule is likely to be lengthy and violent. Even though the Alawites make up a mere 12 percent of the total population, the regime continues to count on support from other minorities who fear Islamists coming to power and from important segments of the Sunni population who fear that the civil war will arrive on their doorsteps, too.

The Assads have been planning for the day of popular insurrection all their lives. Bashar's father, Hafez al-Assad, did not make the mistake of former Egyptian President Hosni Mubarak, allowing his sons to go into private business, while leaving the military in the hands of others who ultimately turned against him. (See Chapter 3.) The Assads were less trusting, and for good reason. Syria's urban Sunnis looked at the Alawites as interloping aliens when they first took power—*muwafidiin*, as they were called. It was not long before the Muslim Brotherhood took up arms against them, labeling them as non-Muslim and non-Arab (*shuubiyun*)—only to be crushed brutally after the notorious Hama uprising in 1982. The use of excessive force was then a clear sign of the regime's determination and sectarian nature; the forces sent to retake Hama were largely Alawite.

The Assads tutored their children in the arts of war so they could take command of the military and police their population. They marshaled in-laws, cousins, and coreligionists into the upper ranks of the security forces. Despite the rhetoric of Arab nationalism, the Assads were keenly aware that only the traditional loyalties of family, clan, and sect could cement their rule. In essence, they upheld the notion that it takes a village to rule Syria, a formula that successfully brought an end to political instability. For over two decades following independence, Syria had been known as the banana republic of the Middle East because of its frequent coups and changes of government. Under the Assads, loyalty quickly became the ultimate qualification for advancement into the upper ranks of the security forces. They packed sensitive posts with loyal Alawites and members of the ruling Baathist party. Some analysts have estimated that as much as 80 percent of Syria's officer corps is Alawi. This is undoubtedly an exaggeration, but it underscores the sectarian safety measures the regime has taken.[4] The main strike forces, such as the Republican Guard led by Bashar's brother, are overwhelmingly Alawi. Many of the divisions made up of enlisted Sunnis have not been deployed to quell the uprising. Instead, the regime has built up special forces and irregulars, often called *shabiha*, which include mostly Alawites or Sunnis of known loyalty. Policing loyalty in order to coup-proof the regime has been a paramount concern. Alawites were placed in strategic ministries other than defense. The foreign ministry is a case in point. Recently a Syrian ambassador who has sought refuge in Turkey told the newspaper *Hurriyet*, "There are 360 diplomats within the Syrian Foreign Ministry. Of these, 60 percent are *Nusayri* [Alawi]." He added, "The number of Sunni diplomats does not exceed 10 percent."[5] Even if these numbers are an exaggeration, there is little doubt that the regime has been careful to staff the upper ranks of important ministries with loyalists and coreligionists. This attention to staffing is a key reason that major defections have not occurred in the top ranks of government and why we have yet to see a repeat of the Libya example, where whole sections of the country fell out of central control and turned to the rebel cause within weeks of the uprising's debut. Ironically, the minoritarian character of the regime makes it more durable than its counterparts in North Africa.

The sectarian nature of the regime may protect it from major desertions when economic difficulties make paying for the far-flung patronage networks impossible. Patronage serves as essential glue, binding the interests of disparate social groups to the regime. Just as important, patronage frustrates the emergence of corporate groups that might compete with the government. The regime has skillfully doled out jobs and benefits to fragment the opposition and buy off opponents.[6]

For this reason, opposition leaders hope that sanctions will promote the collapse of the regime. They reason that, once government money runs out, widespread defections will take place, a coup by top-ranking Alawi officers may occur, or a Tahrir Square moment will overwhelm security forces in the major cities. Such hopes have not been fulfilled in years of growing violence and protest. There is little reason to think they will be anytime soon. Despite increasing defections among the military's rank and file, the elite units, special forces, and intelligence agencies may have little choice but to rally around the Assad regime, given their bleak prospects in a post-Assad Syria. Heavily Alawite elite units with sizable numbers of loyal Sunnis will likely see no alternative.

The broader Alawi community is also likely to remain loyal to the regime, even as the economy deteriorates.[7] Almost all Alawi families have a least one member in the security forces as well as additional members working in civilian ministries, such as education or agriculture. Most fear collective punishment for the sins of the Baathist era. Not only do they assume that they will suffer from wide-scale purges once the opposition wins; many also suspect that they will face prison or worse. Opposition leaders have tried to calm Alawite anxieties provoked by hotheaded sheiks. The most notorious is Adnan Arur, who threatened, "We shall mince [the Alawites] in meat grinders and feed them to the dogs."[8] The head of the Muslim Brotherhood has assured ordinary Alawites that they will be protected. Those guilty of crimes will face proper courts and be tried according to the law.[9] Such assurances only go so far in calming Alawi anxieties. Many Alawites do not expect an orderly transition of power, just as many remain convinced that a spirit of revenge may guide the opposition, which has been so badly abused. In short, because the Syrian military remains able and willing to stand by the president, whether out of loyalty, self-interest, or fear, the regime is likely to endure for some time.

2. THE OPPOSITION IS WEAK

The strength of Assad's rule is relative and can only be measured in relation to that of the opposition. Many analysts point out that his regime is brittle, narrow, and ideologically bankrupt. All the same, the opposition is weaker. The regime has been able to count on the factionalism and bickering of its opponents to survive. Syria's feeble sense of political community has been the regime's greatest asset.

The Free Syrian Army (FSA) assembled in Turkey under the leadership of Colonel Riad al-Asaad (no relation to Bashar al-Assad)—who remained in this position until being replaced in December 2012—has proved to be no match for the Syrian army. Although armed opposition to the regime was an important development early on, such groups represented a minimal existential threat given their size, structural limitations, and predominantly Sunni character. They had limited command and control, no dependable communications, and offensive capabilities that are restricted by their lack of heavy weapons. In the initial stages of the country's civil war, at least, they did not present a real danger or alternative to the Syrian military. In fact, Western authorities had pleaded with the Syrian opposition not to militarize, for fear that the insurgency would actually weaken the opposition rather than strengthen it.[10]

The main political representative of the Syrian opposition, the Syrian National Council (SNC), claims to have gained control over the FSA, which in turn claims to have control over some 15,000 defectors and armed elements in Syria. This alleged hierarchy is, by most accounts, fictional.[11] Whether peaceful or armed, the opposition cells in Syria work independently. *The New York Times* concluded in December 2011, "Factionalism has been hindering the drive to topple Assad."[12] Most observers doubt that the FSA had the number of followers it claimed or was responsible for many of the attacks against the Syrian army. Resistance groups in Syria were organized locally, depended on civilian volunteers as well as defectors from the military, and did not take orders from Colonel Asaad or other leaders, although many called themselves part of the FSA. The term "FSA" nonetheless became prevalent among disparate resistance groups whose common goal was to bring down the regime and protect Syrian protesters from the military.[13] The SNC did not invite the leaders of the FSA to its December 2011 meeting in Tunis, a snub to the organization, although it subsequently sought to repair the relationship.

The political leadership of the Syrian opposition remains divided. The SNC claims to speak for the entire opposition but has been struggling to contain divisions within its own ranks as well as to unite with competing opposition parties. The United States and much of Europe recognize the SNC as the rightful leader of the opposition and have sought to build up its legitimacy and authority, but they continue to wring their hands over its internal weaknesses. It is composed of three main factions: The Muslim Brotherhood, the National Bloc—primarily secular, whose members tend to come from elite Syrian families—and members of the National Coordinating Committees, who are resident inside Syria and cannot reveal their names. There are also many independents, a handful of representatives of the Kurdish Bloc, and a few representatives of other minorities, although Alawites seem to be absent.

Secular supporters of the SNC often complain that the Muslim Brotherhood is the real power behind the organization, although there is little concrete evidence for this.

The SNC's first leader, Burhan Ghalioun, who served from August 2011 through May 2012, was a professed secular Sunni who teaches at the Sorbonne in Paris. Although capable and savvy, Ghalioun was anything but assured in his role. When the SNC was first announced, the various factions could not agree on the organization's leadership. Three different executive lists were announced in a two-month period. Ultimately, the more Islamist members confirmed Ghalioun as the leader, perhaps because he was an effective spokesperson in the West, but limited his tenure as executive to three months. He told the *Wall Street Journal* in December 2011, only weeks before his term was due to end, that he did not know whether he would be given a second term.[14] Ultimately, Ghalioun's presidency was extended, but it was to end in less than six months.[15]

The SNC failed to unite other opposition groups that challenged its leadership. In December 2011 unity talks between the SNC and the National Coordination Body (NCB) for Democratic Change, a coalition of leftist parties led by Haytham Manaa, caused a storm of recrimination. Ghalioun led these discussions with Manaa. He initially stated that the two groups would combine forces on December 31, but his hasty announcement caused heated protest from the more conservative and Islamist SNC membership. Even some of Ghalioun's closest allies joined in the criticism. Members of the Muslim Brotherhood attacked him for being a "dictator" because he didn't send the agreement to the appropriate SNC committees before announcing it.[16] Ghalioun quickly backed away from the agreement, calling it a draft, and the SNC leadership promptly voted against union with the NCB. The SNC leadership criticized the NCB for being willing to negotiate with the regime, for refusing to recognize the Free Syrian Army, and for standing against any foreign intervention. A number of SNC members accused Manaa and his NCB associates of working for Assad's *mukhabarat* (secret police).[17]

For its part, the NCB officials accused the Syrian National Council of betraying Syrians by supporting military action that would result in widespread bloodshed. Imposing a no-fly zone—which in late 2011 had still been an option openly considered by political and military leaders in America and Western Europe—would have required neutralizing the regime's air defenses, which would have led to heavy civilian casualties, NCB officials said. Even worse, they have long argued, foreign intervention would result in an "occupation" of Syria similar to the prolonged US military presence in Iraq after the ouster of Saddam Hussein's regime in 2003. "The SNC wants the devil to come and protect them against this regime," said Khaldoon Alaswad, a member of the NCB's executive committee.[18]

The incident weakened Ghalioun and caused many secular and left-leaning opposition members to worry that they may become increasingly marginalized by the revolution as Islamists assert themselves, as happened in Egypt.

More and more opposition parties and groups announced themselves each week. For example, Murhaf Jouejati, a Washington-based academic and member of the SNC, announced the formation of a new political party, the National Consensus Movement. A new Islamic Front announced itself in Cairo in December 2012. The Kurdish parties sat on the sidelines. They did not trust Turkey, which has been sponsoring the SNC, nor did they trust Arabs, who surmised that Kurdish demands for "national" recognition and autonomy were but a prelude to an eventual call for independence.[19] The religious minorities remained fearful of Islamic parties elsewhere in the region. Many saw—and continue to see—the "Arab Spring" to be a thinly disguised "revenge of the Sunnis."

Perhaps the most important divide among the opposition is not that between the Islamist and secular Syrians, which gets much attention, but rather the divide between those living abroad and those on the inside, who are waging the daily battles on the streets.

Neighborhood committees and armed groups formed in ever-greater numbers. Most used the word "coordinating" in their title, but few relinquished local authority. They preferred to keep decision making local. Some of this is for practical purposes, since spies are everywhere. In Aleppo the local coordinating committees discovered that their efforts to put together surprise demonstrations were being foiled by informants. One opposition statement admitted that their ranks had been riddled with double agents.[20]

Opposition disunity was to be expected. The Assad regime thoroughly destroyed rival parties and suppressed most forms of civil debate and organization over four decades preceding the country's latest conflict. Little wonder that Syrians have found it hard to unite. All the same, disunity has been a luxury the Syrian opposition can ill afford. Tunisians and Egyptians could be leaderless and disorganized because their militaries turned against their presidents. In Syria, the military has stood by the president, shooting at protestors in the early stages of the revolt and later waging an all-out civil war.

As the uprising dragged on in a stalemate, opposition leaders saw the limits of their capabilities and became increasingly eager to get foreign powers involved. On finishing its meeting in Tunis on December 21, 2011, the NSC issued a statement to the international community demanding "international protection, the establishment of safe zones ... and prompt intervention."[21]

3. THE INTERNATIONAL COMMUNITY IS UNLIKELY TO INTERVENE

In the United States, Europe, and the Arab world, there is only limited support for intervention in Syria. However, the same could also have been said in the lead-up to operations in Libya. Only weeks after Washington's intervention there, then Secretary of Defense Robert Gates confessed that, if anyone had told him two months previously that the US military would be involved in Libya, he would have asked them what they were smoking.

Although former Secretary of State Hillary Clinton did an admirable job of isolating Syria and mobilizing the Western world and Arab League against it, she discouraged the notion that the United States would intervene—implicitly acknowledging that Syria would be a much harder nut to crack than Libya. In some respects, Syria—which is to say, a relatively stable government that at least controls the country's armed forces and much of its vital infrastructure—remains in the realm of "too big to fail." One US military intelligence officer who spent four years in Iraq recently explained to me that, if Iraq slips back into civil war at the same time as Syria fails, the region would face a "hell of a mess." Europe was sidetracked by its financial crisis, and President Obama was touting his success in withdrawing US troops from the Middle East as part of his reelection campaign. He did not want to step on his own message of withdrawal by launching another US military intervention in the region.

Saudi Arabia and Qatar are constrained from leading an intervention for fear of their Iranian neighbor. Turkey has little to gain from intervention, despite Turkish Prime Minister Recep Tayyip Erdogan's tough talk about democracy and Bashar's tyranny. Turkey's Kurdish "problem" is again on the upswing, and Iraq has become less stable. Ankara does not need a war with Syria.

Most important, foreign powers are unlikely to intervene if Syrians cannot unite and build a military force capable of providing, at the very least, a credible promise of stabilizing Syria on its own. Many ordinary Syrians who are sitting on their hands even as they decry government brutality will not support the opposition until they are assured it can provide a real alternative to the regime and impose order on the country. None want to follow the path of Iraq. Many worry that President Shukri al-Quwatli, the first president of postindependence Syria, was right when he lamented to Egypt's Gamal Abdel Nasser on the eve of the creation of the United Arab Republic—the political union between Egypt and Syria that lasted only from 1958 to 1961—"You have acquired a nation of politicians: 50 percent believe themselves to be national leaders, 25 percent to be prophets, and at least 10 percent to be gods."

Granted, there were circumstances in which the United States might have supported Arab League and Turkish efforts to lead an intervention in Syria.

Washington might have been convinced to "lead from behind," if key Middle Eastern states had committed themselves to intervention. But the withdrawal of American troops from Iraq left many questions about the future role and influence of the United States, especially in the context of strategic competition with Iran. Instability in Syria presented Washington with the opportunity to undermine Iran's regional posture; to weaken or change the leadership of one of its key allies, Syria; and potentially to downgrade the Islamic Republic's role in the Arab-Israeli conflict through the Lebanese Shiite movement, Hezbollah. Directing the orientation of Syria away from the Shiite Crescent toward the Sunni leadership of friendly Saudi Arabia and Turkey was enticing, especially as it might have counterbalanced Iraq, which has moved into Iran's orbit.

All the same, the Syrian opposition has to date been largely disappointed in the international community. Both NATO and the United States have stated in no uncertain terms that they would not intervene in Syria. What is more, Russia and China have vetoed efforts in the UN Security Council to condemn Syria. For these three reasons, Syria's opposition has asked for intervention in vain, and this seems likely to continue. Like Syria's opposition leaders, foreign powers remain in disarray over the issue of how to topple Assad.

4. THE ECONOMY IS PROBLEMATIC

Syria is a classic case of the failure of the Arab authoritarian bargain. Many specialists have focused on the economic drivers behind the Arab revolts, and their analysis encompasses Syria.

During the 1950s and 1960s, Arab regimes, whether republics or monarchies, turned to similar socioeconomic measures to buttress their rule. In return for political quiescence, governments redistributed wealth, subsidized food, and provided minimal shelter, education, and health care. The result was a distinctive "authoritarian bargain." State-owned enterprises and bloated government ministries absorbed tens of thousands of workers and guaranteed stable employment and a minimum wage.[22] These measures solidified autocracy but at a tremendous price. They paralyzed Arab states and saddled them with unproductive economies and unsustainable expenses. Runaway population growth acted as a time bomb, guaranteeing that expenses ballooned in an environment of low growth. This bargain was unsustainable.

Syria met the challenge to liberalize later and more hesitantly than most Middle Eastern states. Bashar al-Assad's efforts to open up the Syrian economy and copy the "China model" were bolder than his father's during the 1990s, but remained hobbled by half measures and caution. All the same, he introduced private banking, insurance companies, and liberalized real-estate laws. He dropped tariff barriers with neighboring countries, licensed private schools, and permitted use of the Internet in an effort to encourage private and foreign investment.

But, even as Assad sought to boost private initiative, he was wary of its results. To avoid the emergence of a capitalist class that would be largely Sunni and not beholden to the regime, Assad turned to his cousin Rami Makhlouf, who became "Mr. Ten Percent" of the Syrian economy. He assumed a majority stake in many major enterprises and holding companies and ensured that the Assad family maintained control over the economy. Office holders at every rank of the state bureaucracy replicated this model of crony capitalism, exemplified by the presidential family. A new class of businessmen drawn from the progeny of major regime figures—called the "sons of power" (*abna al-sulta*)—became notorious for its wealth and economic assertiveness. The result was an explosion of corruption and public resentment at the growing inequality and injustice of Syrian life.

A new form of crony capitalism, which failed to provide jobs or economic security to the broad masses, replaced socialism. Growth was skewed in favor of the wealthy. The poor, particularly the rural poor, were abandoned. This was the social sector that provided the original base of support for the Baath party, but it is now up in arms. The wealthy have remained quiet.

GROWING POVERTY AND INCOME GAP

Poverty in Syria rose in the years leading up to its civil war—from 30.1 percent in 2004 to 33 percent in 2007—even as the upper class prospered with globalization. According to the 2004 UN poverty report, "While between 1996–1997 and 2003–2004 poverty declined, the wealth gap widened." Since then, both the wealth gap and poverty have been on the rise.[23]

Growing poverty has underscored the failure of the Baathist regime and was a leading factor in the Syrian uprising. It also helps explain why the most persistent centers of the Syrian revolt have been centered in poor agricultural regions such as Deraa, Homs, and Idlib.

Syria's growing income gap is mainly due to three causes. The first is the severe drought of the last five years, which devastated Syrian farming and drove an estimated one million people off the land and into urban slums. As a result, some 40 percent of Syria's housing stock is estimated to have been built without permits and in areas with no state-provided water or electricity. The drought is estimated to have plunged 800,000 Syrians in the eastern part of the country into extreme poverty, according to a 2010 United Nations report.[24]

The second factor is the rising price of food. Global commodity prices have been soaring. The average basket of Syrian foodstuffs increased in price by close to 20 percent in 2010, led by wheat, which increased by 30 percent.[25] Syria's poor, which spent over half its per capita income on food, have been particularly hard hit by inflation, which soared 15 percent in 2008. Inflation has been compounded by government reductions in price supports for basic commodities. In the case of fuel oil *(mazūt)*, subsidies were slashed in 2008, causing its price of fuel oil to rise 42 percent between December 2008 and September 2010.[26] Since the beginning of the Syrian uprising in 2011, inflation has exploded. Five circumstances account for this rise: foreign sanctions; the 30 percent tariff on all goods coming from Turkey; the failing ability of the government to pay for remaining subsidies; hoarding; and the limited funds now available to Syria's main allies, Iran and Russia, which face sanctions and therefore have little extra to loan to Damascus to make up for Syrian shortfalls.

The third factor is increasing unemployment. The Syrian economy has been unable to provide jobs for the rapidly growing population. The story of the Arab youth bulge is well known, and Syria has been particularly affected, with an enormous demographic shift since around 2000. Around half the population of the Arab world is under the age thirty. Syria is worse off than most: More than half its population is under the age of twenty-five, with 23 percent bunched in the ten-year segment aged fifteen to twenty-four.[27]

By the mid-2000s, about one in four young Arab men was unemployed, with the situation in places like Jordan (28 percent), Tunisia (31 percent), and Algeria (43 percent) being even worse.[28] Syria's unemployment figures have been notoriously unreliable. Until recently, official Syrian figures placed unemployment at a fanciful 9 percent. In December 2011, the new Minister of Labor and Social Affairs, Radwan Habib, confessed that unemployment in the country stood between 22 and 30 percent.[29] The effects of the revolt since March 2011 have sent figures skyrocketing.

ECONOMIC EFFECTS OF THE REVOLT

The Syrian Civil War has sent the economy spiraling downward, but how quickly real economic crisis can lead to regime change is unknown. By the eleventh month of the revolution, many signs of severe economic stress began to appear. Adib Mayalah, governor of the Central Bank of Syria, described the situation as "very serious" in November 2011. He ran through the problems the economy is facing.

Unemployment was rising, imports were falling, and government income had diminished. In areas where there were protests, there was no economic activity—so people weren't paying taxes. Because they weren't working, they were not repaying their loans—so the banks were in difficulty. And all this is weakening the economy.[30]

Syria's gross domestic product shrunk by almost 50 percent in dollar terms in a single year starting in early 2011—from $55 billion to $25 billion—as the Syrian pound collapsed from 47 to 72 to a dollar. Merchants interviewed on the streets of Damascus reported a 40 to 50 percent fall in business as consumers hoarded cash and ceased spending on all but the most essential items. Tourism skidded to a halt, representing a loss of $8.4 billion.[31] A ban on oil imports, applied by America in August 2011 and the EU a month later cost Syria $400 million a month.[32] Sanctions have also taken their toll on the Syrian economy in unexpected ways. Trade with Iraq has been reduced by 10 percent because of banking restrictions.[33]

A ballooning deficit closed at 17 percent of the GDP in 2012.This elevated it well above the danger mark for default, usually estimated to be 10 percent of GDP. Elias Najma, an economist at the University of Damascus, estimated that tax revenues in 2012 would be less than half those of 2011 and would pay for only 60 percent of projected government expenditures. He thought that the budget deficit would be 529 billion Syrian pounds out of a total budget of 1.326 trillion pounds[34]—equal to nearly $9 billion, or 17 percent of GDP, assuming a GDP of $55 billion.

The government has had no access to credit markets in order to make up for its deficit spending. Not only has it failed to develop a local bond market, but it no longer has access to international credit markets. This has forced the government to turn either to foreign friends such as Iran or Iraq or to Syria's large businesses. Some local economists recommended that the government impose special levies on big business and businessmen. President al-Quwatli imposed such extraordinary taxes in 1948 to pay for the war in Palestine.

By 2012, the government had ordered all ministries to slash expenditures by 25 percent. Fuel subsidies, which had been estimated to cost the government close to $8 billion annually, were unofficially cut. The government simply stopped providing most sources of energy to the public. Heating oil and cooking gas became scarce, and electricity in most cities was shut off for hours on end during peak usage. Rateb Shallah, a prominent Damascus businessman, said, "The whole system has been shrinking—and very fast."[35]

According to one Syrian banker, no one in Syria pays his debts. Large companies refuse to make payments to banks on their loans, bill discounting, or letters of credit. Bankers expect businessmen to default. Many have left the country. What is even more telling, explained this banker, is that some state banks have refused to make payments to private banks; instead they make excuses.[36] Banks began treating defaults as "delayed payments," but the day of reckoning cannot be postponed indefinitely. When it comes, how will the Syrian Central Bank respond? Where can it get money?

The fiscal pressures on the government are rapidly becoming unsustainable. Before the outbreak of the revolt, the government was already borrowing heavily in order to pay both the salaries of its countless employees and energy subsidies. With no ability to borrow, the government will have to reduce expenses by cutting what subsidies remain and by halting salary payments. To raise revenues, it will impose draconian taxes on the remaining Syrians of means. It will also print money, which will lead to inflation and the possible collapse of the Syrian pound. As one Syrian banker explained, "The banking system will soon be hit with a wave of defaults at both the corporate and retail levels, as deferred payments can no longer be ignored."

HOW LONG?

The economy is not going to collapse overnight. Even as it unravels, the Assad regime may survive for some time, if no alternative forces organize to destroy and replace it. It may be able to live off the fat of the land for a while. It is worth keeping in mind that Saddam Hussein's regime did not fall due to the deep economic crisis brought on by war and sanctions in the 1990s, despite the deaths of some 300,000 Iraqis, according to UN estimates. But, of course, Syria is not Iraq. It does not have the energy resources of Iraq, and its people have long been in full rebellion.

All the same, Syria continues to have friends. Most of its neighbors are unwilling to ban trade. Iraq, its second-largest trade partner after the EU, has been supportive; so has Lebanon. Even Jordan has refused to join sanctions. Some of Lebanon's banks are likely to act as a haven for Syrian money. The Assad regime said it would look to other countries, such as China and Russia, for trade and support. Iran will undoubtedly pitch in, so long as its own economy can stand up to Western sanctions. But the open question remains: for how long?

Collapsing institutions and the state's inability to provide basic services should play into the hands of the opposition. The regime gave the business elites and middle class a piece of the pie and stability. Today, it can offer neither incentive. All the same, the Baathist regime will be a tough nut to crack. Alawites and religious minorities view the failure of the regime with great apprehension. So do Sunni Baathists and those who fear chaos.

Perhaps the biggest question mark is the opposition. Its lack of leadership was an asset during the first months of the civil war, but today it is a liability. Without effective leadership, the opposition will continue to have difficulties inspiring more Syrians to take the sorts of risks and exhibit the courage of those who have already stood up to the government.

So far, no force has emerged with the might, unity, or leadership to bring down the regime, at least none that is yet discernible. One must conclude that the Assad regime will remain in power until such a force emerges.

NOTES

1 Interview with Mohammed Riad Al-Shaqfa by Mohammed Al Shafey, "Bashar al-Assad Is Mentally Unbalanced – Syrian Muslim Brotherhood Chief," *Asharq Al-Awsat,* May 12, 2011, www.asharq-e.com/ news.asp?section=1&id=27573.

2 Hanna Batatu, "Some Observations on the Social Roots of Syria's Ruling, Military Group and the Causes for its Dominance," *The Middle East Journal* 35, Summer 1981: 341.

3 Nikolaos Van Dam, *The Struggle for Power in Syria: Politics and Society under Assad and the Ba'th Party,* London: I. B. Tauris, 2011.

4 Bruce Bueno de Mesquita and Alastair Smith, "Assessing Assad: The Syrian Leader Isn't Crazy. He's Just Doing Whatever It Takes to Survive," *Foreign Policy online,* December 20, 2011, www.ForeignPolicy.com/articles/2011/12/20/ is_Assad_crazy_or_just_ruthless?page=full. Alasdair Drysdale and Raymond A. Hinnebusch wrote in 1991 (*Syria and the Middle East Peace Process,* New York: Council on Foreign Relations): "Since the Baathi regime ultimately owes its position to the loyalty of the armed forces, Alawis are disproportionately represented in the armed forces. By one estimate Sunni officers only commanded between 25 and 30 percent of armed units between 1965 and 1971." Nevertheless, the contention that the Syrian military is an exclusive preserve of the Alawites is false and simplistic.

5 *Hurriyet,* November 17, 2011. Under the Sunni Arab who served as Syria's president in 1953–54, Adib Shishakli, minorities, in particular the Druze, were discriminated against in key government positions. The US ambassador wrote in 1953: "Recognizing the clannishness of the Druze community, its secret religion, and social differentiation from the rest of Syria, General Shishakli has appeared to follow a policy of limiting the number of Druzes holding key positions." In the ranks of Syria's foreign service at the time, for example, the only Druze to hold an important post was the ambassador to Washington, Farid Zayn al-Din, and he was a Lebanese Druze who had officially converted to Sunni Islam. Druze members of the Syrian diplomatic corps complained bitterly that they had abandoned all hope of career advancement because the "authorities would not permit two Druzes to serve at the same Foreign Service post," presumably because of their traditional unreliability. See Joshua Landis, "Shishakli and the Druzes: Integration and Intransigence," in T. Philipp & B. Schäbler, *The Syrian Land: Processes of Integration and Fragmentation,* Stuttgart: Franz Steiner Verlag, 1998, pp. 369–373.

6 Yahya Sadowski, "Patronage and the Ba'th: Corruption and Control in Contemporary Syria," *Arab Studies Quarterly* 9, no. 4, 1987: 442–461; and Volker Perthes, *Political Economy of Syria under Assad,* London: I. B. Tauris, 1995, p. 181.

7 "What Do Sunnis Intend for Alawis following Regime Change?", *Syria Comment,* August 30, 2006, www.joshualandis.com/blog/?p=14. The anonymous author

of this article is an Alawi whose father served as a government minister under Bashar al-Assad.

8   "Syrian Sunni Cleric Threatens: 'We Shall Mince [the Alawis] in Meat Grinders,'" Memri videos, accessed December 1, 2011, www.youtube.com/watch?v=Bwz8i3o sHww&feature=related.

9   Interview with Mohammed Riad Al-Shaqfa, "Assad is mentally unbalanced."

10   "Assessing the Risks of Military Intervention," January 5, 2012, posted on the Syrian National Council website, accessed January 5, 2012. www.syriancouncil. org/en/special-reports/item/488-instability-insyria-assessing-the-risks-of-military-intervention.html.

11   Ghaith Abdul-Ahad, "Inside Syria: The Rebel Call for Arms and Ammunition," *Guardian*, December, 11, 2011.

12   Dan Bilefsky, "Factional Splits Hinder Drive to Topple Syria Leader," *New York Times*, December 8, 2011.

13   *Al Jazeera* interviews Nir Rosen, uploaded by *Al Jazeera* English on January 10, 2012, accessed January 11, 2012, www.youtube.com/ watch?feature=player_embedded&v=yu8jxX5JhgM.

14   "Syria Opposition Leader Interview Transcript, 'Stop the Killing Machine,'" *Wall Street Journal*, December 2, 2011, online.wsj.com/article/SB100014240529702038 33104577071960384240668.html.

15   Email communication with Ausama Munajed, December 2011.

16   "A Member of the Syrian National Council: 'Bashar Uses Ghalioun, and the NCB Are Mukhabarat,'" *Syria Politics*, accessed January 8, 2012, syriapolitic.com/ar/ Default.aspx?subject=297#.Twn15yMVm_u.

17   "Lies in the Announcement of Burhan," NCB website, accessed January 3, 2012, bit.ly/skP4TV. See the criticism of the union on Al Jazeera English by Ashraf al-Muqdad of the Damascus Declaration. He claimed that most opposition members want foreign military intervention. Interview on Al Jazeera, Dec 31, 2011, www.youtube.com/watch?feature=player_embedded&v=ooiv3tWXFIY.

18   Ashish Kumar Sen, "Syrian Opposition Row over Foreign Military Action Nixes Unity Effort," *Washington Times*, January 6, 2012.

19   The best report on the Kurdish parties and their attitude toward the uprising is "Who Is the Syrian-Kurdish Opposition?: The Development of Kurdish Parties, 1956–2011," Kurdwatch, European Center for Kurdish Studies, December 31, 2011, accessed December 31, 2012, www.kurdwatch.org/newsletter/index. php?cid=186&z=en.

20   See the "Syrian Revolution News Round-up: Day 278: Saturday, 17 Dec 2011," Strategic Research and Communications Centre (SRCC), bit.ly/yajKfb.

21   Syrian National Council Announcement, accessed December 21, 2011, bit.ly/ wjfBr1.

22   Ariel I. Ahram, "State-Breaking and the Crisis of Arab Authoritarianism," unpublished, 2011; Tarik Yousef, "Development, Growth, and Policy Reform in the Middle East and North Africa since 1950," *Journal of Economic Perspectives* 19, no.3, 2004; Steve Heydemann, "Social Pacts and the Persistence of

Authoritarianism in the Middle East," in Oliver Schlumberger, ed., *Debating Authoritarianism: Dynamics and Durability in Non-Democratic Regimes,* Stanford: Stanford University Press, 2007. For an excellent history of the region's political-economic transition, see Alan Richards and John Waterbury, *A Political Economy of the Middle East,* Boulder: CO: Westview, 2007 [3rd edition]; Stephen King, *The New Authoritarianism in the Middle East and North Africa,* Bloomington and Indianapolis: Indiana University Press, 2009.

23 Dalia Haidar, "Drawing the Poverty Line," *Syria Today,* May 2010, accessed December 29, 2011, www.syria-today.com/index.php/ focus/7730-drawing-the-poverty-line.

24 "Drought Had Significant Impact on Syria's Northeast, UN Official Says," *Syria Report,* September 13, 2010, accessed December, 12, 2011. Abigail Fielding-Smith, "Uprising Exposes Syria's Economic Weaknesses," *Financial Times,* April 26, 2011.

25 David Biello, "Are High Food Prices Fueling Revolution in Egypt?" *Scientific American,* February 1, 2011, accessed January 4, 2012, blogs.scientificamerican. com/observations/2011/02/01/are-high-food-pricesfueling-revolution-in-egypt/.

26 Armand Hurault, "Syria: It's the Economy, Stupid!" Transnational Crisis Project, posted on 11/11/2011, accessed January 4, 2012, crisisproject.org/ syria-its-the-economy-stupid/.

27 Nader Kabbani, "Arab Youth Unemployment: Roots, Risks and Responses," Director of Research, Syria Trust for Development. Presented at the Conference on Arab Youth Unemployment: Roots, Risks and Responses, Carnegie Middle East Center, Beirut, Lebanon, February 10, 2011. Accessed January 3, 2012, carnegieendowment.org/files/Nader_Kabbani.pdf.

28 Ragui Assad and Farzaney Roudi-Fahimi, "Youth in the Middle East and North Africa: Demographic Opportunity or Challenge?" Population Reference Bureau, 2007, accessed December 29, 2011, prb.org/pdf07/YouthinMENA.pdf.

29 He said the new findings were the result of a field survey conducted by his administration. Jihad Yazigi, "Syrian Unemployment at Twice Previously Estimated Level," *Syria Report,* December 19, 2011, accessed Jan 2, 2012, www.syria-report. com/news/economy/syrian-unemployment-twice-previously-estimated-level.

30 Liz Sly, "Syria's Economy Is Key to Assad's Future," *Washington Post,* November 14, 2011, accessed November 14, 2011, www.washingtonpost.com/world/middle_ east/syrias-economy-is-key-to-Assads-future/2011/11/14/gIQAZvfMMN_print. html.

31 Ibid.; Phil Sands, "Syria Sees Tourist Numbers Leap 40%," *The National,* January 25, 2011, accessed January 5, 2012, www.thenational.ae/business/travel-tourism/ syria-sees-tourist-numbers-leap-40.

32 "Sanctions against Syria As Effective As Bullets, Maybe," *Economist,* December 3, 2011.

33 Sly, "Syria's Economy […]"

34 Dr. Elias Najma as quoted in "To Cover a Budget Deficit of syr. 500, a Financial Expert Advises the Government to Require Rich Businessmen to Pay

Extraordinary Levies," *Syria Steps*, December 28, 2011, accessed December 28, 2011, www.syriasteps.com/?d=126&id=294&in_main_page=1.

35 Sly, "Syria's Economy […]"

36 Interviewee asked not to be named, January 2, 2011.

This chapter examines the symbolic interactions between Palestinian social and political movements and Arab protest movements. It also seeks to show the influence of the Arab revolts on the reconfiguration of social movements in the West Bank, the Gaza Strip, and their transnational connections. Likewise it examines political and social issues, different modes of mobilization, and symbolic practices by Palestinian activists. While some might argue that these youth groups' views are the result of old parties and ideologies of political organizations, their actions, this study demonstrates, are independent of any direct political affiliations with specific parties, while they maintain a presence within the resistance movement. The chapter deals primarily with the Palestinian youth movements, whether Islamist or leftist, providing a new political map in the form of new political movements and their associations, especially as a result of the mobilizations of 2011 and 2012. It begins with a brief historical analysis of the role these movements played in Palestinian society, examining first the conditions of their emergence and then their sociological context. It then explores the dominant groups of actors within these organizations, and how they behaved. In doing so, it shows the novel modes of communication used, especially in the new virtual media, to influence public opinion. Finally, the author explores the literature produced by these movements, including leaflets and flyers, which elucidates their political aims, visions, and demands. The information presented here is based on direct observation or testimonies of participants in the new movements. The author relies on interviews with activists, as well as on direct observations.[1] [Eds: Meanwhile, as war raged in Gaza in summer 2014, US Secretary of State John Kerry embarked on a mission to get the Israelis and Hamas to reach at least a truce—a far more modest goal than those he had at the end of 2013 and the beginning of 2014 as he sought then to entice the Palestinians and Israelis to enter into negotiations for a peace settlement, a process that had failed many times before. While the Israelis announced that they succeeded at destroying tunnels from Gaza into Israel, they responded with overwhelming force to Hamas's firing of rockets into Israel amid Hamas's insistence that Israel lift its blockade of Gaza. As for the broader peace process—which Kerry had focused on starting more than six months earlier, shuttling between Israel and the Palestinian territories trying to narrow the differences between the protagonists—the main sticking points continued to be Israel's building additions to its settlements in Palestinian territory and continued pressures from Palestinians not to give up the Right of Return of Refugees to their homeland. With such intractable issues on the table, Kerry's efforts at that point failed to bear fruit, and Hamas's enhanced prominence ensuing from the Gaza war seemed likely to further complicate any such negotiations in the near future.]

CHAPTER 6

PROTESTERS OF THE PALESTINIAN YOUTH SOCIAL MOVEMENT
ABAHER EL-SAKKA

INTRODUCTION

In Palestine, the phenomenal expansion of the number of advocacy groups is a response to the political situation we are living under. This expansion has resulted in a simultaneous double transformation, transnational and internal. Palestinian militant social mobilization against colonialism has a very old history, beginning even before the creation of Israel. In the struggle that ensued after the British conquered Palestine, Palestinians organized a six-month strike in 1936. Today, many of my interviewees are facing either directly or indirectly the danger of Israeli settlements impinging on their existence.

The youth involvement in Palestine is based on a culture of significant interest in the political. Youth groups form and are influenced by politics, impacting on their identity formation, which is an important part of their socialization process. This process influences them politically as well as culturally. The political socialization of young Palestinians leads some to claim that these youth activists are ideological and nationalistically influenced. They are already in conflicts and identify with social groups. One youth movement from the past, *al-shabāb*—"youth"—were the main players in the First Intifada (1987–1993). (These al-shabāb should not be confused with the Somalia-based al-shabāb, or Al-Shabaab.—Eds.) Many of my interviewees[2] knew about it and see it as a model to follow. Abir[3,] one of the interviewees, said that "the model for our current actions is the First Intifada." Indeed, during the First Intifada, the central aim of the Palestinian uprising was to organize civil disobedience, in the form of a fight for Palestinian nationalism. Furthermore, the formation of committees for organizing volunteers led to new and different events, such as sweeping the streets, helping farmers harvest olives, and teaching kids reading and writing when schools were closed. "Citizen initiatives" of this nature, mainly social and political, often relied on charitable, educational, and religious networks found in clinics and schools. Their actions included organizing general strikes or demonstrations.

Another example of these initiatives was the establishment of committees of "Youth for Social Action," which organized self-help activities and cultural events ranging from teaching farmers how to make jam to taking care of the needy. Cultural events were celebrated on important dates, such as the passing of the Balfour Declaration on November 2, 1917. Young people justified their actions by referring to notions such as "civic consciousness" and the ideology of *sumud* (resilience), as well as "passive resistance" characterized by various survival strategies, all of which have now been emulated by the new youth groups. We found that young people have within their collective imagination mythical notions about how they represent this prior period.

THE CRISIS OF THE NATIONAL MOVEMENT

The Palestinian national movement is now at a crucial moment in its history. The failure of the Oslo Accords (signed on September 13, 1993), the upheavals in the region, and the realities of Palestine being divided into smaller enclaves are factors that have culminated in the current crisis. Deficiencies include a failure of socioeconomic policies of the Palestinian Authority (henceforth PA), clientelism and corruption, its inability to meet the needs of the Palestinian population, as well as an increase in the numbers of Israeli settlements in the territories. This is all paralleled by the view that the PA has achieved nothing. One can argue that nothing in the realities of occupation has changed to show a positive light to Palestinians during a period of twenty years of negotiations with Israel. The signing of the Oslo Accords and the establishment of a Palestinian autonomous authority, in a small part of Palestine, was perceived at the time as the creation of a "new state," the "State of Palestine." Even if it was not independent, this "imagined" state might have been sufficient to satisfy the desire of the Palestinians to live with at least a semblance of "normality." But the Oslo Accords ended in an open conflict. Moreover, the current Palestine no longer corresponds to the one described by the Oslo Accords, whose achievements many Palestinians thus see as illusory: symbolic independence, the right to use national symbols, and a symbolic right of return. This sense of crisis, and everything surrounding it, led many of my interviewees to criticize what they see as the reduction of the "Palestinian state" to a new form of symbol, so that we are now the owners of a "state symbol that is the state itself." All these factors explain the profound crisis of the national project, which in turn manifests itself in weak public participation, lack of vision, a general sense of paralysis, rising consumerism, life in a bubble where one imagines a lack of direct occupation, internal divisions, passivity, lack of confidence in politicians and in the resistance alike, and witnessing the PA's growing authoritarianism toward its opponents. Also, many ex-activists harbor intense bitterness stemming from painful experiences including severe punishment (such as imprisonment, torture, injury, loss of family members, and destruction of houses by the Israelis)—suffering that was, in the end, used by politicians to mobilize for party gains or political purposes. The consequently negative image of political power has given rise to these new activists who are either independent or to opposition voices within the political parties to which they belong. Most of the interviewees are members of political parties or identify themselves as supporters of one party or another even though not members. As Aghsan[3] explained:

> We do not rely on political parties. Our aim is to form an independent political group. It is our new way of practicing politics, and in leading the fight. We stand as an opposition to the methods of the Palestinian authorities that we see as based on trading for 20 years. So we blame the political leaders of all parties for their inability to lead the fight. We are members of political parties, ex-prisoners. ... Our common goal is to fight in two directions. On the one hand, fight against the social and economic policy of the Palestinian Authority, and on the other hand, lead the fight against [Israeli] colonialism. We're here to fill a void in the struggle and lay the foundations for a new national project. We provide unity for small groups formed by individual initiatives and so we started to think about how we can take action.

This statement shows the growing social discontent operating in the background of an oppressive colonization, and it also shows a crisis affecting the Palestinian political parties' mobilization of the youth. Likewise, it points at the effect of that discontent within the Palestinian project itself.

THE NEW PALESTINIAN PROTEST MOVEMENT

This study concerns itself with all forms of protest movements. While the Palestinian population can be said to be generally overpoliticized, whether we are speaking of Palestinians in the Palestinian territories or those in the diaspora, their national targets are clear.

The fall of the Tunisian regime energized the new Palestinian protest movement, with young Palestinians forming an "independent youth movement" and focusing on the cause of national reunification. Indeed, Palestinian society has for seven years been divided into those people living in the Gaza Strip and those on the West Bank. Two political forces—the Palestinian Authority under Fatah in the West Bank and Hamas in Gaza—have divided the control of our territories.

The new youthful protesters form a constellation of varied initiatives and heterogeneous structures. The party divisions are due to diverse factors relating to general discontent as well as opposition to local policies. The leaders of this new movement I have studied are mostly from the middle class and therefore have formed a somewhat cosmopolitan environment that has even led to their being viewed as "Westernized." Skilled in communications, they produce slogans in Arabic and English. The activists of these social movements are new actors on the political scene. Many of them are young and well-educated, which serves them in their leadership roles. They are politi-cized and refer to nationalist and social frameworks to defend their actions. Leaders of these movements interact with each other within networks, and have excellent organizational skills. Their leadership talents and achievements have secured them the trust that they enjoy among the members of the move-ment. They have gained the moral authority and legitimacy to lead. These traits are reinforced through social relationships that have developed between the participants in the struggle. They are strengthened through the shared experience of collective actions, even by their failed experiences. The events of May 15, 2012, which I will discuss below, contributed to their aura of success. These youth have, through their leadership of new organizations, increased their social and symbolic status. Their socialization within these movements produces systems of rules—what the French sociologist Pierre Bourdieu calls a deeply differentiated *habitus,* or mindset that generates certain practices and dispositions.[4] They have gained recognition and legitimacy through their leadership of strikes, the boycott of Israeli goods, and civil or other actions of disobedience. However, there may be a downside to such activity, for engaging in a movement, especially for those younger activists with little experience and coming from a poor political culture, gives them a kind of political affiliation that can be manipulated to serve the pursuit of personal interests.

THE INFLUENCE OF OTHER MODELS OF ARAB PROTESTERS

All began with the spark triggered from the Arab street in 2011. A small group of young people decided to stage a solidarity march on March 15, 2011. As Fadi said:

> Once the "Arab Spring" began, these revolutions gave us life (a breath and a pulse) to start our job. Finally our Arab roots were awakened! We began to be interested in establishing contacts with our Arab brothers. Our goal was to popularize the resistance; to call for the boycott [of Israeli goods and institu-tions], to open again the door for the election of the Palestinian National Council, and to restore strength to the Palestinian cause, all to be done by a call for a return to the Arab cause.[5]

Névine agreed with this and almost said the same:

> I've never been an activist, but when the events in Tunisia began, they in-spired me. I was hooked on following the events and I followed the info hour by hour and we made t-shirts signed with slogans like "we are all Tunisians, we are all Egyptians." Other friends made t-shirts on which they wrote "thank you Tunisia, Egypt thank you." There is a slogan dear to my heart, "Finally, we are proud to be Arabs."[6]

Sabih's words echo the same emotions: "The revolution in the Arab world was the spark of my involvement in the youth movement. Suddenly, I resembled my Arab colleagues. I experienced that because I was born in Tunisia, so I have personal affinities with them. I then took to the streets with a lot of pride."[7] As another interviewee told me, "I started to get involved as the Arab Spring began; I participated to support the Tunisian and Egyptian people."[8] Huria said, "Before the Arab revolutions, I had no sense of Arab nationalism, but when the events started, I read more and more about Egypt and Tunisia. As for demonstrating, this was the first time in my life that I find myself face to face with the Palestinian police who were forbidding me from confronting the soldiers of the colonizing state."[9]

From this perspective, the spark was Tunisia. As the Tunisian revolt got underway, Palestinian students took to the streets waving slogans such as "Thank you Tunis." This movement was concentrated mainly in two cities, Ramallah and Gaza, where many Palestinians spontaneously expressed their support for the Tunisian revolt, quickly causing violent or physical confrontations with the police.

Indeed, the Palestinian leadership forged close links with the Tunisian government and with the Tunisian state bureaucracy during the fifteen years that top PLO figures spent living in Tunis and its suburbs. Fadi told me, "In the early demonstrations, Palestinian security services confiscated the Tunisian flag." Several other witnesses confirmed his testimony in describing the repressive methods of the security apparatus and paramilitary forces, which, they said, outnumbered the participants in the events. Moreover, the Palestinian police banned demonstrations in Ramallah; to enforce a guideline that was so often used by Yasir Arafat: "We should not intervene in Arab affairs."

As Housam explained, "I was ordered by the Palestinian security services to close my blog and my website. They threatened me with jail if I participated in the protest outside the Egyptian embassy in Ramallah. We went down the street and there were people who were demonstrating in support of Mubarak (most likely members of the civil security service and other people whom they had rallied as participants)."[10]

On March 15, the two ruling parties (Hamas and Fatah), aiming to quell the momentum of support for the movement, sent members of their security organs and other officials to attend the event—not to infiltrate, but instead to divide the group through physical, but nonviolent, means. They worked their way through the crowd, pushing the core of those representing the movement toward the outside. They also led demonstrators to shout a single slogan: "It's the end of the internal Palestinian division." At the same time, they pushed away the militants who carried other banners, which called for the return of the PLO as a political representative of all Palestinians and demanded the election of a new Palestinian National Council that was supposed to meet the expectations of all the Palestinian people and not just those living in the West Bank and the Gaza Strip.

Palestinians are especially prone to mobilize around May 15, which marks the creation of Israel in 1948 (the Nakba)[11], and June 10, the date marking the Arab defeat in the Six Day War in 1967. Both dates played a fundamental role in the establishment of modern Palestinian identity and both thus have importance in the construction of collective memory, especially for the Palestinians living in the diaspora. They have consequently become reference points in the history of modern Palestine. One can also argue that it was 1948 that shaped modern Palestinian national consciousness. Today, the Palestinian collective memory is composed of all the elements that enable the past to be recreated in the present.[12] The function of collective memory can be seen in two factors: it allows the cohesion and integration of past and present, and ensures the continuity of the past into the present. These can be formed by processes such as manipulation, invention, selective forgetting, and memory repression, as well as the shaping of images, symbols, and even practices in the interests of a group.[13] All this fits the past of a group to its present needs, as it ensures social cohesion and contributes to the process of national identity formation. This memory is based on the diffusion of collective images of the past and their transformation into collective memory and incorporated into our culture[14.] There are sequences of behavior that take on ceremonial or ritual significance that also play a role in shaping and strengthening identity formation. These include ceremonies in the form of political liturgies, which occur during national holidays or official commemorations. Such celebrations and commemorations stand as important moments in social life. They seem essential to the promotion of group cohesion and the dissemination of its values and the core elements of its ideology. These festive commemorations, both in the past as in the present, have already marked their social space. Some dates, like that of May 15, are well known and are used to pass on the national image of identity, as well as emphasize all the political and cultural questions that are important to the Palestinian people.

With all of this in mind, the question of fixing a date for a mobilization becomes extremely significant, so for these activists, the choice of a "date" is a way to respond to the policies of the PA. By marking their difference with the PA, we see here emerging what Arno Mayer called the "duty of memory" as a form of "ownership of the past." He writes, "And we were able to circumvent this vision of the Palestinian Authority and we decided to commemorate the Nakba. This is our way of speaking back to the PA; we speak in actions and not in words, and we do so by confronting the soldiers of the occupation. Thus, we do all what we are not supposed to do, we are not silent."[15]

Ultimately, only by *not* interfering in the new Palestinian movement in support of the Arab revolts could the PA avoid provoking the same revolts among Palestinians. It did this while displaying an officially neutral position with regard to the Arab uprisings. This can be seen in Hamas's mixed stance in Gaza. While favoring the Tunisian revolt, Hamas awaited the outcome of events in Egypt. Hamas officials remained silent until the fall of Mubarak. The PA, knowing that this was an important movement in Palestinian society, decided to reattach the youth movement to its side to regain public support. By sending some members of its security forces into the streets dressed as civilians, it hoped to be a mobilizing force for its own agenda. These newly minted civilians had ready-made slogans, demanding an end to Palestinian division—a play on a popular sentiment. Its task was, on the one hand, to reinforce this division, and counter other demonstrations by being present and by trying to derail the movement by other means. The dealings of such a PA-made group is explained in the words of another one of our interviewees: "During the youth movement march in support of the Arab revolts, the youth belonging to the security service harassed girls or beat up Palestinian activists and arrested others." He also commented, "In Gaza, youth were assaulted in a repressive manner by Hamas's security services." Through its security apparatus, the state's tentacles are now being felt in almost all sectors.

REOCCUPATION OF PUBLIC SPACE

In Palestinian society, the anticolonial struggle has laid the foundation for a culture of social mobilization that was organized to appropriate public space. There is also a tradition of signing petitions. However, unlike neighboring Arab peoples, Palestinians have long voiced their views in public. But now, for the first time, they were directly challenging the Palestinian authorities. In what seems like one voice and might thus be quoted as such, my interviewees said, "In the past, we were as angry and as full of disagreements as we are now. And even if we wanted to react, the circumstances were not suitable to act. Now it is time to speak." Another interviewee, Mūhib, told me that young people started shouting, "Get out of your homes and demand your rights. Speak up; do not let freedom pass you by."[16] They were motivated by the Arab unifying slogan, "The people want the fall of the regime"—modified by the Palestinian movements to "the people want the end of divisions." This slogan was immediately taken to the streets and met with approval, but demonstrators added others, such as, "When the people decide to live, then the chains of slavery are broken." Mūhib noted, "This is what we sang in our school time and time again." In this way,

Palestinian streets became "contaminated" with the spirit of revolt flowing through the Arab world.

Indeed, activists accused the Palestinian Authority of holding a double public discourse that has always worked in two directions or was addressed to two audiences. The first audience is the international community—the ostensible aim being to establish a "peace" process, apply "international law," and, hopefully, create an internationally recognized independent state. The second audience is the Palestinian people—voters, exiles, refugees, combatants, and, by now, citizens of the PA who do not always agree with the diplomatic policy the PA pursues. Indeed, such groups have asserted their independence from the Authority's wishes by managing to organize raids on the Kalandia military roadblocks (near Ramallah) and against the Israeli settlements of Betil. In doing so they have sent a message to the PA that they are in no mood to commemorate the Nakba without mobilizing against the occupation forces, without confronting the Israeli army.

On May 15, Palestinian activists called on their colleagues in the diaspora to come down to the Arab-Israeli borders of Jordan, Lebanon, Syria, and Egypt. Only two fronts responded. They did so by meeting at the borders of Lebanon and, to a lesser extent, Syria. In Egypt, the authorities have not allowed local activists to support the Palestinian movement's calls, and in Jordan the government suppressed thousands of people seeking to gather at the border to meet the Palestinian activists. However, at the Lebanese border many Lebanese and Palestinians crossed the borders into Israel, causing several casualties among them but strengthening the Palestinian resistance movement. By walking on foot past a border Israel has for more than sixty-five years maintained as impossible to cross, they not only demonstrated their defiance but also undermined Israeli supremacy. The activists in this group regarded this crossing as their first victory, especially since they were able to represent the different components of the Palestinian people as one community, whether in the diaspora or not. In this action some Palestinians were killed in northern Israel by Israeli forces, while a large number of Palestinian refugees—who had been mobilized to reestablish and maintain continuity with their lost, previously inaccessible territory—managed to reach Jaffa and Haifa, where they visited the homes of their fathers and their grandfathers. Many of my interviewees insist that these actions nullified the security logic of Israeli colonization, because for sixty years these border areas were considered impenetrable military zones, protected by mines. In this episode of nonviolent civil disobedience, the Israeli military could not prevent Palestinian youths from realizing their symbolic return to their land. These actions gave all Palestinian youth movements a huge boost in struggling for their cause.

In contrast with this achievement, the Palestinian Authority wanted Palestinian young people to commemorate the Nakba in the scope of a well-organized gathering on Al-Manara Square in Ramallah. Such a legalistic approach has contributed to what the youth see as the PA's gradual abandonment of the principle of the right of return. Many, then, took to the streets to remind the PA and others that the generational transmission of memory is still manifested at such festivals—that that they will not abandon the right of refugees to return.

It is partly through such "nonviolent" mobilizations that Palestinian youth have expressed their disagreement with the PA's position not only on the issue of the right of return but also many other issues. The right of return for Palestinian refugees is based on UN Resolution 194, and the aspiration to "return" is a fundamental issue within Palestinian society. By focusing on the future of the land and its people, Palestinian officials and negotiators effectively marginalize the status of those in the diaspora. This becomes a major identity question for more than four million people, the majority of whom still have refugee status. For a significant number of my interlocutors the right of return is seen to be guaranteed by international law, and for them this is not a negotiable issue. As I have already mentioned, the negative image of the political leadership is one of the main factors behind the commitment of these "new" militants, who ironically view the PA as just another Arab regime.

Following the success of these events, the Palestinian protest movement has consistently mobilized youth to speak in all areas. Much popular solidarity has formed around these young people, who began their new actions as a protest against the official dismissal of a campaign to boycott Israeli products, and their rejection of the PA's attempts to normalize relations with Israel. When the PA acts to normalize relations with the colonialists, they are bringing to the public space a rhetorical discourse that legitimizes their actions—all of which these youth are trying to counter in action and in words.

This youth movement has expanded to form small groups, anticolonial opposition groups, and groups focused on opposing the policies of the PA. In response, the PA has created a dependent movement called *Yalla Ninhi al-ihtilal*, a group calling for "an end to the Israeli occupation." The PA was concerned about these actions by the Palestinian youth as well as the public's discontent with the rise in claims by Israel that it has the exclusive right to use certain roads.

Palestinian youth activists have borrowed forms of collective action from social movements elsewhere. As Fadi said, "With groups of Palestinian and international activists, we boarded buses used only by settlers in the West

Bank. We carried banners reading, 'End the Colonial State' and 'End Racism.' Our model derived from the US civil rights struggle of Black Americans against racial politics, but we also borrowed examples from the legacy of South Africans' fight against racism."

It should be noted that at present these movements are not major political actors or movers on the political scene, because of the low number of people coming to their events. Small turnouts are due to an atmosphere of mistrust among fellow Palestinians and the general sense of crisis. However, these movements continue to organize events such as a demonstration on March 21, 2013, against the visit of Barack Obama, accusing him of neglecting Palestinian rights and against his pro-Israeli policies, but also against US policies around the world as well.

The protesters in these youth movements in 2011 had different demands and views from those who mobilized the protests of 2012. The following section seeks to better demonstrate the differences between the two years.

PROTESTERS' MOBILITY 2012

Thousands of people took to the streets to protest against the socioeconomic policy of Salam Fayad, the former Palestinian prime minister, who was looked upon favorably by the international community because of his liberal economic policies. Those demonstrators leading the protests consisted of drivers of public service taxis; they were dubbed "Fordists" after the Fords they typically drove. They were joined by a significant number of other Palestinians, many of whom were at the forefront of other protests—against the sudden increase in the cost of living (higher gas, water, and electricity prices), for example. Rising fuel costs had an immediate negative impact on household incomes. The protesters's key slogan was "Block the Movement" (of traffic). This was indeed a radical slogan that led to the physical blocking of roads and by the refusal of taxi drivers to carry passengers. These movements are, of course, part of the growing discontent against the policies of the PA, but are also linked to the conflict between the former Palestinian prime minister and certain segments of Fatah. Overwhelmed by the "spontaneous" demonstrations and other independent actions, such as those organized by different labor unions and politicians, Fatah finally bowed to public pressure, and the PA decided to make some changes in its economic policies. Unlike the movements of 2011, those of 2012 were organized by political parties, some related to the fragmentation of Fatah, but also to the various centers of power within the PA. There is, therefore, a potential for the future formation of new associations for public action.

NEW MODES OF COLLECTIVE ACTION, THE NEW VILLAGES: THE CASES OF BAB AL-SHAMS, AL-KARAMA, AND AHFAD YŪNIS

Before engaging in these movements, several activists already belonged to popular committees. They were involved in nongovernmental organizations of Palestinian and international "peace advocacy organizations" all working to promote the fight for freedom in Palestine and the end of the Israeli occupation. These groups and organizations advocate methods of nonviolent resistance and direct action to confront and challenge the Israeli occupation forces and policies. One of the founders, Abu Rahma[17], spoke to me about their ambitions: "[We have to] broaden participation in popular resistance to the Israeli settlers, expand the boycott against the colonial state, etc." He fought for his own village: "Our village is the smallest of the Ramallah region. The army has confiscated 58% of its land. We are in contact with all the activists, most of whom are in jail, and we have lost martyrs." Activists have long been involved in resistance, as Abu Rahma explains: "I was already active during the first Intifada in response to the decision of the Israeli government to construct structures in the center of our village." Indeed, these villages to the west of Ramallah—Bilin, Nailin, and Nabi Saleh—have become both "direct resistance locations" for Palestinians and international symbols of unarmed resistance to the Israeli occupation. Festivals, conferences, and other events are held regularly with the plight of these places in focus—not least, demonstrations organized every Friday by activists. As Abu Rahma explained:

> At the beginning we started to demonstrate every day, and then we decided to do so only every Friday. Creative and new ways of action have attracted the attention of activists around the world, first of all because the participants use innovative nonviolent methods. We worked hard to find imaginative ways of resistance that are in accord with our peaceful views. Following this success, we decided to conduct several creative actions.
>
> The Israeli army marked some trees in the village to cut down in the next few days. So we gathered fifty-five people in the morning and we contacted the international press. We then found chains and padlocks, tied fifty-five people firmly to each tree for cutting. This meant that the Israeli operation could not be realized. This act of resistance has been very successful. On a global scale, we were named the "Palestinian Gandhis." On a different occasion we decided to go together, stood narrowly in an iron container, while extending our heads and our hands, which were attached by chains. We were dressed as Navii, the movie character in *Avatar*. On another occasion, we built a large prison, and we put it on the juncture of a road, blocking Israeli bulldozers. The prisoners—that is to say, "we"—carried crosses on our backs just like Christ. We had animals and plants with us in this mock prison. Symbolically, we aimed to represent the entire life of the Palestinians enclosed between four walls of a

jail cell. At a previous demonstration, a great pianist named Jacob Elfer came to play for us while soldiers posed nearby for action. Another time, a Swedish religious choir came to sing in front of Israeli settlers.

These activists along, with other Palestinian militant groups, have sought to develop new forms of action that highlight the threat to villages that comes with Israel's moves to confiscate Palestinian land. The first in the E1 area, they called Bab al-shams (The Gate of the Sun). These activists have experience struggling against land confiscation in various villages. Following the success of this movement, they replicated their actions and coordinated all activities. A small group met frequently to decide on modes of action

> We decided on midnight with a lot of discretion: It is a secret plan, so nobody was to know about it before the act took place. To keep it secret and mobilize people we announced an activity in Jericho that we named "summer camp." We gathered the signatures of a hundred people (all dedicated activists). We decided on the day of departure that is on the day a snowstorm was supposed to arrive, to go there. Each group of activists led a bus. They then informed the participants about their intentions to create a new Palestinian village called Bab al-shams. ... Once we arrived, we set up tents. There were 150 people at the site along with media groups and the international press.[18]

At the same time, during the establishment of the camp, Palestinian lawyers filed requests to freeze the "the military order to confiscate village land" in Israel's high court. Activity at this village lasted three days, all during a snowstorm. The Israeli army blocked all roads leading there to deprive the militants of their livelihoods and reinforcements. This event marks a turning point in the popular Palestinian movement because all politicians supported their efforts. Other steps followed, as Maher explained:

> We built a new village, and called it Burqin. In it we celebrated a marriage of two activists. We had the marriage performed by an Imam. The village did not survive for more than four hours, because the Israeli army landed its helicopters on it. As for the marriage ceremony, it lasted only two hours. The following week, we built a new village, which we called al-Hfad Yūnis, which means the grandchildren of Yūnis (which in turn is named after the hero of the novel *Bab al shams*).[19]

Support groups from around the world also aided the movement, with many forming on the Internet. A large media campaign got underway, all to show global solidarity with this popular approach; consuls at foreign missions took part, as did representatives of European countries. Meanwhile Israeli Prime Minister Netanyahu ordered the army to evacuate these villages by force, and that did occur, with Israeli soldiers arresting all of the protesters and injured and beat up a large number of them. This action was one means by which to decolonize villages and demonstrate the identity of these places as part of historic Palestine. The struggle around the reaffirmation of the old names of Palestinian villages unveils the reality that colonialism seeks to hide by destroying real places and their memory. Such actions reaffirm the existence of prior communities, which have been made to disappear and which the colonizers are attempting to erase from the map and remembrance. The activists' attempt at naming and establishing new village realities is a way to preserve, in the event of a peace agreement with Israel, the principle of law, but also to nullify, even if symbolically, the impact of exile and to affirm the Palestinian people's will to resist.

THE VIOLENCE OF NONVIOLENT DISCOURSE

While these nonviolent activities attracted criticism, they also received popular support and were celebrated by many Palestinians. These actions bridged the gap between Fatah and Hamas, since these parties have come to appear to many Palestinians as two quasi monopolies that exclude other political forces. Secondly, these actions of the youth highlight the PA's nonconfrontational policies and its lack of a resistance strategy. Third, the recovery movement actually may have strengthened those who sought to take advantage of the youth movement, trying to use this mobilization for its own political purposes and enhance its own popular legitimacy. We have therefore seen politicians station themselves in front of cameras during these events to increase their visibility and untarnish their images. Fourth, they tried to channel and create their own institutions around the actions of these militant groups. Indeed, former Palestinian Prime Minister Fayad Salaam formed a committee to manage these villages, as the authority did in the past when the PA established a Ministry of the Wall in response to Israel erecting a concrete, electric-gated wall separating itself from the Palestinians.

Such political responses have sought to tame the activists by offering them new political careers. By doing this, the PA has attempted to integrate the activists into the dominant party (Fatah) giving them a "career in activism" in the sense argued for by Olivier Fillieule.[20] Palestine is an example of one of the last bastions of colonialism conforming to patterns explained in binary fashion by Albert Memmi and Frantz Fanon in the 1950s.[21]

Apart from some NGOs funded by western governments and organizations, most of these citizens' initiatives do not have access to international funding or to foundation grants. However, European and other international institutions have contributed to the development of Palestinian social movements by encouraging what they regard as legitimate, nonviolent resistance and the sharing of their experience within global networks. "Pacifist" approaches that have consequently become more popular among some Palestinian activists are based on models developed not only by Mahatma Gandhi in India but also in the "dominant world" by such leaders as Martin Luther King, Jr. Many activists have assumed a universal discourse that speaks of such values as freedom, equality, social justice, change, democracy, and civic consciousness.

Many Palestinians, however, harbor a deep sense of distrust as regards perceived outside influence and "lessons to follow" in their resistance to the colonial power, Israel. The economic resources of the foreign institutions, together with their ability to manage information within global communication systems has, however, allowed them to establish considerable authority over some aspects of Palestinian social movements. In addition, the nonviolent actions that have resulted have forced the Israelis to respond to the resistance in ways ostensibly less violent but still decidedly oppressive. Israeli military forces have, indeed, adopted new repressive measures at every Friday demonstration—such as spraying Palestinian activists and the villages they are in with waste water, water contaminated with petrochemicals or other pollutants, or dyed water. The mobilization of this technology of "power," which Michel Foucault termed "biopolitics,"[22] targets the Palestinians' very right to life and their integrity, which is the primary object of colonial biopolitics.

Although "nonviolent" resistance does seem to be gaining acceptance in Palestine, old forms of armed struggle still remain strong. The use of violence is still considered by many to be a legitimate source of resistance in the colonial context, since violence is a major component of the colonizer-colonized relationship. Colonizers dominate the colonized with violence and are fought back with the same methods, as Frantz Fanon explained in an Algerian revolutionary context against French colonialism. Moreover, Palestinian activists often avoid using the term "peaceful" and prefer to it the term "popular" instead, as shown in Abu Rahma's response:

> It is not because we participate in the popular resistance that we are fighting against the army, but I chose my own method of struggle and others can make their own choices. In fact, for me, some people try to use excuses that lack any sense of logic to avoid participating in any of the initiatives taken to mobilize in favor of the current struggle.

The same is expressed by Abir when she says: "I'm not against all forms of resistance, including armed resistance, but armed struggle is fomented by small groups, while the popular struggle is a form of struggle that is extended to all social groups and allows all to participate. On the personal level, I think the popular struggle is complementary to the armed struggle."

A VIRTUAL WORLD AS A TRANSNATIONAL SOCIAL BODY

In the words of another interviewee, Nidal[23]:

> We are mobilizing activists from around the world—including jurists, lawyers, artists, writers, and politicians. These friends of ours represent various political orientations—left, green, socialist, and communist—and lobbies, from human rights to environmentalism. They conduct regular activities on the ground in the Palestinian territories. Their nonviolent direct action campaigns have slogans such as "Do not respect curfews" and "Do not follow Israeli orders decreeing civilian areas." These campaigns involve providing humanitarian assistance and seeking to maintain a presence during Israeli raids and assaults. International peace activists are a boon for the Palestinians by their presence as witnesses to both our daily humiliation and the injustice of the Israeli occupation. They also provide practical, logistical, and legal information and aid.

Young Palestinian activists have meanwhile increasingly used social networks, employing the Internet, text messaging, Twitter, and more to mobilize and to influence public opinion. Various websites have become debate forums. More generally, new technologies have facilitated mass mobilization that censorship has otherwise circumvented. But such efforts do not always succeed, as Fadi explained:

> At the beginning of the protests, the Palestinian security services confiscated the Tunisian flag. The "virtual control" arm of the PA's Preventive Security Service interrogated me for four hours. An officer told me at that time that the Arab uprising was an Iranian plot against the Arab world. At the end of the discussion, he asked me to delete a Facebook page calling on support for the Arab people's revolt.

The majority of interviewees deemed alternative information networks to be the most valuable of all—including local activists' newspapers, flyers, electronic petitions, collaborative websites, and blogs, many of them with transnational reach. These networks have also conducted their own actions and cyberattacks; on April 7, 2013, for example, they supported international hackers depicted in black masks and Palestinian *keffiyeh* who acted to "defend the Palestinian cause"—namely, by attacking Israeli government and individual websites to paralyze them or to bombard them with information and pictures of Palestinian political prisoners, images of torture committed by the Israeli army, or messages accusing Israel of war crimes. Other social networks have served as a collective database for the visual memory of the resistance. Activists have recorded all events of significance to their cause, thus providing photographs and videos aplenty to news outlets. In doing so they aim to counter the effects on international public opinion of information they perceive as disseminated by Israel and international news agencies and dominated by the pro-Israel US lobby. Via Twitter and blogs in particular, activists have recorded the arrests and expulsions of Palestinians. However, some of my interviewees believe that online engagement is less efficient than traditional methods, such as being on "the Palestinian street."

CONCLUSIONS

The Palestinian youth movements have been forming and expanding for some time now, but the years 2011 and 2012 in particular saw them achieve unprecedented publicity by resisting not only the occupation but also the PA—the latter realm of action including anticorruption campaigns and protests against the PA's economic policies and negotiation strategies. Although these movements have begun to draw a large sector of the youth—and in turn seen the creation of a wide range of social networks—they have been unable to rally large numbers of Palestinians. Perceived by many as elitist, they lack the authority to lead the masses.

NOTES

1   This chapter is based on field research done in the West Bank and the Gaza Strip in 2012–2013, in the course of which few but long interviews were conducted with several activists. The interviewees, who are quoted in the text, were either unaffiliated social activists or members of Palestinian revolutionary groups, popular resistance movements, or independent youth movements. Their selection took into account variables such as gender, age, religion, socioprofessional category, sociogeographic origin, political/ideological orientation, and involvement in various organizations. Some of the interviewees did not want to be named while others gave permission to use their names in this chapter. The former group will be referred to with pseudonyms.

2   Activist from Nazareth, possessing a master's degree in political journalism

3   Aghsan, a thirty-year-old activist who graduated from Birzeit University and is a founder of this movement

4.   Pierre Bourdieu, *Raisons pratiques: sur la théorie de l'action*, Paris: Seuil, 1994, p. 114.

5   Twenty-three-year-old student from al-Bireh, working toward a masters degree in human rights

6   Student in journalism at al-Quds University

7   Activist in the movement, twenty-six years old, from Nablus

8   Activist with a master's degree in journalism, from Jerusalem

9   Student of sociology, Birzeit University

10   One of the founders of the youth movement in Bethlehem

11   On May 15, 1948, 800,000 Palestinians were expelled from their land and

property and became refugees. Palestinians annually commemorate the anniversary, which they call the Nakba (from the Arabic word for "catastrophe"). A total of 550 cities and towns were lost, of which 417 were totally or partially destroyed by Israel.

12 Maurice Halbwachs, *The Collective Memory*, New York: Harper & Row, 1980.

13 Pierre Nora, *Les lieux de mémoire*, Paris: Gallimard, 1992, p. 19.

14 Abaher El Sakka, "The Palestinian Collective Memory Formation of a Plural Identity Based on the Memory of Founding Events" in C. Suaud, P. Guibert, and G. Moreau (eds.), *Time*, Nantes: MSH Guépin /Cens, 2001, pp. 45–57.

15 Arno Mayer, "Les pièges du souvenir," *Esprit*, juillet 1993: 45–59.

16 A founding member of the youth movement in Ramallah; also a former Fatah member and an ex-prisoner of Israel

17 Abu Rahma, who has been honored for his human rights work and who holds a master's degree in Arabic studies from Birzeit University, is from Belin.

18 Many Palestinians have read *Bab al-shams* (The Gate of the Sun), a novel published in 1998 by the well-known Lebanese writer Elias Khoury, which tells the epic story of the Palestinians who have lived as refugees in Lebanon since the *Nakba* in 1948. Subtly evoking the ideas of memory, truth, and testimony, the book has been made into a film by Egyptian director Yūsry Nasrallah.

19 One of the founders of the youth movement, this twenty-three-year-old lives in the Kalandia refugee camp in the West Bank.

20 Olivier Fillieule, "Propositions pour une analyse processuelle de l'engagement individuel," *Revue française de science politique*, 2001, 1–2, vol. 51: 201.

21 Albert Memmi *The Colonizer and the Colonized*. Boston: Beacon Press, 1991 (published originally in French in 1957) and Frantz Fanon, *Les damnés de la terre*, Paris, Gallimard, 1961 (published in English in 1963 as *The Wretched of the Earth*).

22 Michel Foucault, *Society Must Be Defended: Lectures at the Collège de France, 1975–1976*. New York: St. Martin's Press, 1997, pp. 242–244.

23 A twenty-seven-year-old teacher and a leftist, this interviewee lives in the al Almari refugee camp in Ramallah.

REFERENCES

George Balandier, "The Colonial Situation: a Theoretical Approach," *International Journal of Sociology*, Volume 11: 44–74, 1951.

Asef Bayat, *Life as Politics: How Ordinary People Change the Middle East*, Stanford CA: Stanford University Press, 2010.

Pierre Bourdieu, *Practical Reasons, on the Theory of Action* (In French). Paris: Ed. Threshold, 1994.

Claude Dubar, *Socialization Building Social and Professional Identities* (in French), Paris: A. Colin, 1996.

Abaher El Sakka, "The Palestinian Collective Memory Formation of a Plural Identity Based on the Memory of Founding Events" in C. Suaud, P. Guibert, and G. Moreau (eds.), *Time*, Nantes: MSH Guépin / Cens, 2001, pp. 45–57.

Frantz Fanon, *Les damnés de la terre*, Paris: Gallimard, 1961.

Olivier Fillieule, "Propositions pour une analyse processuelle de l'engagement individuel," *Revue française de science politique*, 2001, 1–2, vol. 51: 201.

Michel Foucault, *Surveiller et punir*, Paris, Gallimard, 1973. English translation:
Discipline and Punish: The Birth of the Prison, New York: Vintage Books, 1979.

Maurice Halbwachs, *The Collective Memory*, New York: Harper & Row, 1980.

Arno Mayer, "Les pièges du souvenir," *Esprit,* juillet 1993: 45–59.

Albert Memmi *The Colonizer and the Colonized*. Boston: Beacon Press, 1991.

James Scott, *Domination and the Arts of Resistance* (In French), Paris: Editions
Amsterdam, 1992 & 2008.

Alain Touraine, *Social Movements Today* (In French), Paris: Les Editions Travailleurs,
1982.

Michel Wieviorka, "Sociology: Post Classic Decline of Sociology?" *International
Journal of Sociology*, 108, January-June, 2000: 5–35.

SITES AND BLOGS

www.facebook.com/groups/103054189780933/
Alhirak Alshababi, youth mobilization
www.facebook.com/Herak.Shababi?fref=ts
(Herak Shababi Mustakel) the independent youth mobilization
www.facebook.com/groups/yalaninhii7tilal/?fref=ts>
Yalla Ninihi Alihtilal (We'll End the Occupation)

This chapter describes the counterrevolutionary steps taken by the monarchies that rule the Arab states of the Persian Gulf to control the impact of the wider revolts that shook the Arab world starting in December 2010. Christopher Davidson demonstrates how the Internet served the opposition. Its use expanded despite the attempts of the Gulf Arab states to censor and limit access to sites. Likewise, he demonstrates the potential importance of Jordanian and Moroccan militaries, which may be deployed in the event of full-scale revolt in the Gulf States. The first install-ment of aid by the energy-exporting Gulf states to those distant monarchies in the amount of $5 billion is predicated, he concludes, on using their well-trained troops and pilots as mercenaries if the need arises. In May 2015, a Moroccan pilot flying one of six Maghribin F-16 jets stationed in the United Arab Emirates and working in tandem with the Saudis in Yemen was shot down by the Shiite Houthi rebels in the northern Yemeni province of Saada.

CHAPTER 7
THE GULF MONARCHIES AND THE ARAB REVOLTS
CHRISTOPHER M. DAVIDSON

The Arab states of the Persian Gulf have faced down different opposition movements over the years, but these have represented only narrow sections of the indigenous populations. Moreover, the Gulf monarchies have gener-ally been strong and confident enough to placate or sideline any opposition before it has gained too much traction. They have also been effective in demonizing opponents, either branding them as foreign-backed fifth col-umnists, as religious fundamentalists, or even as terrorists. In turn this has allowed rulers and their governments to portray themselves to the majority of citizens and most international observers as being safe, reliable upholders of the status quo, and thus far preferable to any dangerous and unpredictable alternatives. When reformist forces have affected their populations—often improving communications between citizens or their access to education, the Gulf monarchies have been effective at co-option, often bringing such forces under the umbrella of the state or members of ruling families, and thus continuing to apply the mosaic model of traditional loyalties alongside modernization even in the first few years of the twenty-first century.

More recently, however, powerful opposition movements have emerged that have proved less easy to contain, not least because they are making the most of potent new modernizing forces that have been less easy for governments to co-opt. As a result an increasing number of regular Gulf nationals have become emboldened enough to protest against and, often for the first time, openly question their rulers.

In 2011, spurred on by developments elsewhere in the region, these opponents and critics presented the most serious challenges yet to the ruling families. In something of a perfect storm for the incumbent regimes, the uprisings in Tunisia, Egypt, Libya, Yemen, and Syria not only gave hope for those Gulf nationals and Gulf-based movements committed to serious political reform and to unseating the current autocracies, but they also made it harder for the Gulf monarchies to depict their new enemies as anything other than prodemocracy activists or disillusioned citizens who recognized the inevitable collapse of the political and economic structures underpinning their rulers.

Furthermore, the 2011 revolts—or at least the first few waves of protest in Tunisia and Egypt—also helped expose the Gulf monarchies' strong preference for supporting other authoritarian states in the region and their fear of having democratic, representative governments take shape in neighboring states. The initial responses of most of the Gulf monarchies were markedly antirevolt, even if they later tried to change tack. This had a massive delegitimizing effect on the ruling families and governments involved, since in the eyes of many of their citizens they positioned themselves as part of a distinct and anachronistic counterrevolutionary bloc.

Unsurprisingly, the post-2011 opposition in the Gulf monarchies has manifested itself in different ways depending on the circumstances and pressures in each state. This has ranged from full-blown street riots complete with killings and martyrs in the poorer Gulf monarchies to more subtle intellectual and even Internet-led "cyber opposition" in the wealthier Gulf monarchies. But in all cases the regimes have responded with more repression than ever before, thus further exposing the ruling families to opposition. In some instances brutal police crackdowns have taken place and foreign mercenaries have been deployed, while in others political prisoners have been held, judicial systems manipulated, and civil society further stymied. Thus far only Qatar has avoided such heavy-handedness, mostly due to its more favorable circumstances and its rather different stance on the Arab uprisings. Nevertheless, even its ruling family is not without critics, and there are already indications that opposition is building and greater repression may follow.[1]

EVOLVING OPPOSITION

Much of the early opposition in the Gulf monarchies focused on economic grievances and the frustration of merchant or worker communities in the postpearling industry era, and—especially in the 1960s and early 1970s—the ruling families' perceived connections to non-Arab, non-Muslim powers and the need to bring these states closer into line with the region's Arab nationalist republics. Particular hotbeds were in Dubai, Bahrain, and Kuwait, although there were also some protests in Qatar from indigenous oil workers concerned with the excesses of their ruling family.

Several national fronts were established, but only one of these—the Dhofar Liberation Front, later the Popular Front for the Liberation of the Occupied Arabian Gulf—ever led to an armed insurrection. In many ways the Gulf monarchies were well-placed to counter these threats, as Israel's victories over the main Arab military powers in 1967 and 1973 had taken much of the gloss off Arab nationalism. Moreover, with increasing oil exports and expanding state treasuries this was also the period when many of the region's wealth distribution practices were inaugurated. Not only were most Gulf nationals enjoying better lifestyles than hitherto, but many were kept busy with the new activities and opportunities resulting from the first major oil booms. In Dubai's case, many of the families that had been involved in national front activity and opposition to the ruling family in the 1960s became massively enriched in the 1970s, mostly due to being granted exclusive import licenses for the various products demanded by the emirate's fast-growing economy. And today their descendants, now regarded as key allies of the ruling family, are at the helm of some of the region's biggest trade and retail empires.[2]

Subsequent opposition movements have been more difficult to contain, as most have focused on the illegitimacy of the Gulf monarchies and in particular their manipulation of Islam. Given that they have often been based on religious platforms, or led by disillusioned population groups subject to discrimination, these movements have not been entirely placated with material benefits. In Saudi Arabia, for example, the most serious opposition to the ruling family in the 1990s came from a diffuse movement of young religious dissidents and conservative university students. Critical of the official religious establishment's seemingly hypocritical support for American bases on Saudi territory following the 1990 invasion of Kuwait, this *Sahwa* or awakening movement was dealt with only by granting more control over social institutions and the education sector to religious conservatives. Confirming a long-held view in the ruling family that their main opposition would eventually come from religious circles rather than liberal reformers, this was deemed a necessary if unpleasant maneuver in order to head off further criticism.[3] Similarly in the UAE and

Kuwait, where Muslim Brotherhood organizations or "reform associations" have existed for many years, there was a tacit understanding in place that these groups would be tolerated and given some influence over the religious and educational establishments. In the UAE this led to the Brotherhood's de facto control over the Ministries for Education and Social Affairs, with its members presiding over curriculum committees and—for many years—dominating the UAE's principal university.[4] Up until 2003 senior members of the Abu Dhabi ruling family were even holding meetings with Brotherhood representatives, trying to establish a set of compromises.[5]

Following 9/11, the subsequent US-led War on Terror, the CIA's capture of a major Al Qaeda figure in the UAE in 2002[6], and a violent campaign launched against the Saudi oil industry and Western expatriates in 2003 by al Qaeda on the Arabian Peninsula, the Gulf monarchies have made a *volte-face* on such Islamist opposition movements. Partly this has been out of fear, with unpublished polls in Saudi Arabia after 2001 indicating that most young Saudi men sympathized with Osama bin Laden and opposed any form of Saudi cooperation with the US over the Iraq War.[7] But it has also been due to the increasing ease the monarchies have experienced in simply branding opponents as "terrorists" or alleging their connections to ill-defined al-Qaeda plots. Indeed, in recent years the Gulf monarchies' security services have usually been able to arrest activists and repress any Islamist organizations in their territories without fearing any international scrutiny. In many cases these crackdowns have in fact won praise from Western powers, being described as part of the monarchies' "commitment to battling terrorism."[8]

In the UAE, for example, the previous concessions granted to the Muslim Brotherhood were reversed in 2006, with hundreds of teachers, academics, and ministry employees fired from their jobs on the grounds of Islamist affiliations. Some have since been accused of "dual loyalties" or threatening "violent acts in the occupied Arab emirates,"[9], and in 2008 a large number of activists were imprisoned and accused of being part of an "underground movement in the UAE trying to promote their own strict view of Islam."[10] Meanwhile, in Saudi Arabia new antiterror legislation has been repeatedly used to imprison men who have been described by international human rights organizations as being political activists. In late 2010 Canada's *Global Post* reported on sixteen Saudi nationals—including businessmen, university professors, and a judge—who were charged in a secret court with "supporting terrorism and plotting to overthrow the government." Having been held in custody for more than four years, they were believed to be "widely known for peacefully demanding political reforms." Their case was not reported in the Saudi press, although some Saudi nationals commented on the matter, claiming that the accused were only "seeking reform and to open people's minds" and that they were "extremely anti–al Qaeda." Moreover, fellow activists complained that such terrorism charges are now widespread in the kingdom as they are "one of the most convenient charges [because] no one will defend you and you will become hopeless."[11] There are now countless other such examples in Saudi Arabia and elsewhere in the region, with a Saudi surgeon having been held in custody and accused of "backing and funding terrorism" since appearing on Al Jazeera television and criticizing the government.[12] Similarly, in Bahrain a trial was held in late 2010 for a group of twenty-five dissidents who were accused of "financing terrorism" and "inciting hatred of the ruling family." Reportedly beaten, tortured, and with the Bahraini media barred from covering their case, the men included prominent bloggers, journalists, and even a member of a human rights group.[13]

Overall, the branding of such opposition movements as extremism- or terrorism-friendly and the positioning of the Gulf monarchies as a better, safer alternative to Islamist-dominated governments or other such scenarios has been highly effective. Indeed, as described in a book, written originally in French, on the Arab revolts, these "rulers became well versed in their routine of no alternative argumentation: towards the West, they posed as the only ones able to deter an Islamist takeover."[14] Moreover, it was argued that there is now a "sad irony that the powers in place have ended up believing their own fantasies about the Islamist threat; they not only displayed that card for external consumption, but they also fed their own masses with gory stories about the inevitability of … ruin."[15] And that the Gulf monarchies—and their now fallen Arab autocrat neighbors—have been responsible for "rushing to enroll in the global War on Terror, provided that their domestic opposition would fall under the extensive category of al-Qaeda supporters." The antiterrorism legislation and emergency laws that have been used to neutralize opponents have since been heavily criticized for being an "oxymoron to describe the suspension of the rule of law and the absolute vulnerability of the citizen."[16]

In much the same way as the Islamist groups, some opposition movements in the region, especially in Bahrain and Saudi Arabia—where there are substantial Shiite populations—are now being branded both as terrorists and as part of some greater plot to further Iran's interests in the Gulf monarchies. Linked to growing hawkishness toward Iran, this has been another relatively straightforward and convenient mechanism in these states with which to portray opponents—no matter how peaceful—as being dangerous fifth-column movements serving a foreign power or entity. Again this has allowed the monarchies to discredit opponents in the eyes of other citizens, while also allowing them to demonstrate their willingness to support Western policies on Iran. Frequently in Bahrain, for example, the government has claimed that the opposition is either being funded by Iran or is receiving from that country weapons or other logistical support. In May 2011 military officials alleged that the opposition was made up of "traitors and saboteurs" who were drawing "guidance lines from Iran that drew the acts of sabotage and barbarism in the kingdom."[17] And even following the publication of an independent report into Bahrain's crackdown in November 2011—as discussed below—concluding that the "Iranians are [merely] propagandists and that they can't be expected not to take advantage of the situation" and that "to say they were funding, agitating … we found no evidence of this," Bahraini government officials still claimed that there was a link, stating that they had "evidence you cannot touch or see physically, but we know it is there."[18]

MODERNIZING FORCES

Since the beginning of the oil era and the rapid socioeconomic transformation of the Gulf monarchies, many of the modernizing forces impacting on the region were, as described, expected to lead to significant political openings or, at least, more conscious and demanding national populations. In many ways what happened instead was the careful control or, in some cases, even harnessing of these forces by the regimes. Despite massively improved access and a large number of schools and universities being established, educational curricula have usually been tightly monitored or even shaped to support directly the state or the ruling family in question. This has usually led to skewed or inaccurate history being taught in the region, the absence of some fields of political science and law from university departments, and a reliance on self-censoring, often expatriate, staff in these institutions. Similarly, with regard to communications, the Gulf monarchies have invested considerable resources and efforts to finding ways to censor interactions between their citizens and between their citizens and other parties. As such, each new communications technology and print media that has become available in the region has either been sponsored by the state (for example, state-backed newspapers, radio stations, and television stations), or—if that proved difficult—has been blocked (such as unpalatable foreign newspapers, unwanted foreign radio and television signals, satellite broadcasts, local blogs, and foreign books).

A case can even be made that the Internet itself—predicted by many to lead to sweeping changes in such tightly controlled societies—was also successfully co-opted by the Gulf monarchies, at least in the early days. Offensive websites, including blogs critical of the regimes, have been blocked, while many other basic Internet communications methods, such as email or messenger software, can either be blocked—or more usefully—monitored by the state so as to provide information and details on the opposition.[19] Moreover, some Gulf monarchies have actively exploited Internet communications and arguably done so much better than most governments in developed states, with an array of "e-government" website services having been launched—most of which allow citizens to feel more closely connected to government departments and thus help echo the earlier era of direct, personal relations between the rulers and the ruled.[20] Meanwhile, as demonstrated, the rulers themselves have often established presences on the Internet, and their self-glorifying websites usually also feature discussion to facilitate interaction between themselves—or, rather, their employees—and the general public. Many other lesser ruling family members, ministers, police chiefs, and other establishment figures in the region have set up interactive Twitter feeds and Facebook fan sites for the same purposes, and some of these are now followed by thousands of citizens and other well-wishers. The Twitter feed of the ruler of Dubai, for example, exceeded one million subscribers in July 2012. Tweeting on this success, he emphasized the participatory nature of the software: "Together we came up with many social, humanitarian, and cultural initiatives and I have personally benefited from your constructive thoughts. Thank you all, and I hope that we take our communication and interaction to the next level soon, for the good of our communities."[21]

More recently, a wave of new Internet technologies—often loosely bundled under the banner of "Web 2.0" applications—seems to be finally having the kind of impact on the region's access to education and communications that would have been predicted or desired by the earlier modernization theorists. Popularly defined as "facilitating participatory information sharing, interoperability, and user-centered design," these applications allow users to connect to each other using social media that is based on content created by themselves in cooperation with other users, rather than simply retrieving information from the Internet in the format presented to them. Among the best examples of such applications are the more recent incarnations of Facebook, which is now no longer just focused on personal pages and fan sites but has become home to thousands of active discussion groups; the more recent versions of Twitter, which is now host to thousands of third-party applications that aid users in finding and following the most appropriate content and personalities based on their interests; and YouTube, which allows regular users to upload, share, and comment on videos from their mobile phones, or even create their own television channels. While these and other Web 2.0 applications can still be blocked in their entirety by cautious regimes, this is now unlikely to happen in the Gulf monarchies, as the inevitable outcry from the large numbers of users would be difficult or perhaps impossible to appease.

Inevitably these applications are being increasingly used to host discussions, videos, pictures, cartoons, and newsfeeds that criticize ruling families, highlight corruption in governments, and emphasize the need for significant political reform or even revolution in the Persian Gulf. Leading opposition figures are now attracting as many followers on these applications (often anonymous Gulf nationals) as members of ruling families. While there have been some attempts by regimes to counterattack against this cyber opposition, often by deploying fake social media profiles so as to threaten genuine users, or by establishing "honey pot" websites to lure in activists and help reveal their identities, for the most part the applications are effectively bypassing censorship controls and the mechanisms used to control earlier modernizing forces. As such they are facilitating an unprecedented set of horizontal connections forming between Gulf nationals and between Gulf nationals and outside parties—connections that are crucially now beyond the jurisdiction or interference of the ruling families and their security services.

The exact role played by Web 2.0 applications, social media, and other such modernizing forces in the 2011 Arab revolts is still not clear, as at present it is unknown what proportion of the populations of North Africa, Yemen, and Syria actually had access to the Internet or were using it for revolutionary purposes. Indeed, some have argued that Web 2.0 applications did not lead to "Revolutions 2.0," as not everybody was Internet-savvy in these countries and that the *abtal al-keyboard* or "keyboard heroes" of the Arab world may have posted many angry messages online but did not necessarily take part in street protests.[22] Nevertheless, many observers do hold the view that the very recent Internet-led expansion of the Arab youth's public sphere has been of enormous consequence and was certainly an "important instrument added to the protest toolbox."[23] In January 2011, for example, the newly installed Tunisian minister for Youth and Sports (himself a well known blogger—Eds.), claimed that "in reality we have been ready, we people of the Internet, for a revolution to start anywhere in the Arab World." Stressing the interconnectedness made possible by the Web 2.0 applications, he stated that "we've been supporting each other and trying hard since a long time, and you know how important the Internet was for the revolution."[24] Indeed, in both Tunisia and Egypt human rights defenders and activists were believed to be using social media and proxy websites, often hosted in other countries, to keep track of the repression taking place and to keep countering inaccuracies reported by the state-backed media. (For more on this, see Chapter 14.)

Claims of a direct link between opposition activity and Web 2.0 applications in the Gulf monarchies appear much stronger in many respects than in North Africa, as the considerably higher Internet and smart phone penetration and usage rates in these relatively more developed states indicate that most Gulf nationals—and the overwhelming majority of the younger generation—not only have the necessary access to such technologies but are also well acquainted with their capabilities. With regards to Internet-enabled phones, for example, four of the Gulf monarchies now have the highest per capita penetration rates in the world, with 1,030 for every 1,000 persons in Bahrain, 1,000 per 1,000 in the UAE, 939 per 1,000 in Kuwait, and 882 per 1,000 in Qatar. This compares with an OECD average of only 785 per 1000.[25] In 2011 it was also reported that high-speed broadband Internet subscriptions had risen massively in the region, with 50,000 new subscribers over the first half of the year in the UAE alone, taking the country's total number of Internet-enabled households to about 1.3 million. Over the next few years the penetration rate will continue to increase, as will the quality of access, with many of the Gulf monarchies having invested heavily in fiber-optic networks. Interviewed in summer 2011, the chairman[26] of the UAE's largest state-backed telecommunications provider[27] even claimed that the UAE was going to be "one of the top five connected countries in the world" following government investments of more than $15 billion in such networks.[28]

Web 2.0 and social media usage in the region is a little harder to measure, but most indications are that it is increasing rapidly. An April 2011 report published by the Governance and Innovation Program at the Dubai School of Government claimed that the total number of Arab Facebook users had increased by 30 percent in the first quarter of that year, bringing the total to over 27 million.[29] Only a year later, in May 2012, Facebook's operating company announced that it had reached 45 million users in the region, with a penetration rate of about 67 percent, and had decided to open a regional office in Dubai.[30] Significantly, the 2011 report claimed that over 70 percent of Arab users were in the 15–29 age bracket. It also estimated that there were over one million active Twitter users in the Arab world, who had collectively posted over 22 million tweets during the first quarter of 2011. Significantly, the report claimed that the UAE, Qatar, Bahrain, and Kuwait, together with Lebanon, were the five leading countries in the region in terms of the proportion of their population using social media, with over 400,000 Twitter users in Saudi Arabia and 200,000 in the UAE. It was also estimated that there were about four million Facebook users in Saudi Arabia, and that over 50 percent of the UAE's population was using Facebook, while 36 percent and 30 percent of Qatar's and Bahrains' populations, respectively, were using Facebook. Claims were also made in the 2011 that there had been a "substantial shift in the use of social media from social purposes toward civic and political action" in the region, with social media usage being perceived by many of the report's interviewees as being "mainly for

organizing people, disseminating information, and raising awareness about …
social movements." Interestingly, the majority of Tunisian and Egyptian interviewees also argued that their ousted regimes' attempts to block social media
access "actually provided a boost to the [opposition] movements, spurring
protesters to more decisive and creative action."[31]

COUNTERING THE ARAB REVOLTS: THE WRONG SIDE OF HISTORY?

During the first Arab revolts in Tunisia and Egypt most of the Gulf monarchies
quickly and instinctively positioned themselves on the side of the region's remaining autocracies. Perhaps assuming that the revolutions would fail, or that
American and other Western interests in the area would ultimately deny the
opposition movements sufficient international support, a number of the Gulf
monarchies' governments and advisors seemingly misunderstood or underestimated the scale of these uprisings. Consequently they chose to portray their
states as being bastions of authoritarianism and—collectively—as something
of a counterrevolutionary bloc. Although the full impact of this stance is not
yet clear, it is likely that the new post revolt electorates and governments in the
Arab world will not view the Gulf monarchies favorably, even if they remain
open to Gulf investments and development assistance. Moreover, and arguably
more significant, it is likely that many of the younger and more idealistic Gulf
nationals will also view their governments and ruling families with distrust
or as being "on the wrong side of history," especially as more and more of
these nationals study the Arab revolts and correspond and interact with fellow
Arabs from post revolt states. In early February 2011, for example, at the height
of the Egyptian uprising, a new region wide group of Gulf nationals including academics, journalists, and human rights activists gathered to "urge the
conservative monarchies which have ruled the region for centuries to embrace
democracy and freedom of expression." Referring to itself as the Gulf Civil
Society Forum, the group issued a statement calling for "the ruling families in
the Gulf to realize the importance of democratic transformation to which our
people aspire," and warned the Gulf monarchies not to crack down on activists
planning to stage peaceful protests. Significantly, the statement also called for
the ruling families to "understand that it is time to free all political detainees
and prisoners of conscience and issue constitutions that meet modern day
demands" and claimed that "the Gulf peoples look forward to their countries
to be among nations supporting freedom, the rule of law, and civil and democratic rule which have become a part of peoples' basic rights."[32]

At the same time as these statements were being issued, however, Saudi
Arabia's leading religious authority and Grand Mufti, the aforementioned

Abdul-Aziz bin Abdullah Al-Shaykh—a septuagenarian cleric who had earlier claimed that "reconciliation between religions was impossible"[33]—was publicly criticizing the Tunisian and Egyptian revolutions. After claiming that "these chaotic acts have come from the enemies of Islam and those who serve them," he went on to say that "inciting unrest between people and their leaders in these protests is aimed at hitting the nation [the Muslim world] at its core and tearing it apart." Having already provided the ousted Tunisian president with asylum in a Jeddah palace, and with the Saudi King having earlier telephoned the embattled Egyptian president, Hosni Mubarak, to offer his support and to "slam those tampering with Egypt's security and stability,"[34] it was abundantly clear that the Saudi ruling family both feared and opposed the Arab uprisings. Moreover, soon after Mubarak's ouster, members of Egypt's Supreme Council of the Armed Forces went on record to claim that they had "received information that certain Gulf countries had offered to provide assistance to Egypt in exchange for not bringing Mubarak to justice."[35] (Eighty-seven-year-old ex-President Mubarak was set to be tried for a third time in November 2015 on charges that he was responsible for killing Egyptian demonstrators in 2011.—Eds.) Thought to refer to Saudi Arabia, this again seemed to indicate the kingdom's position on the revolts and perhaps how its government hoped to use development aid to limit or influence the actions of any new Egyptian government. On a foreign policy level Saudi Arabia also made it quite clear that the new Egyptian and other post revolt Arab governments posed a risk to regional security, not least undermining the Gulf monarchies' aforementioned stance on Iran. After the post-Mubarak administration granted permission for Iran to sail two warships through the Suez Canal in February 2011[36] and then announced it would restore diplomatic relations with Tehran, Gulf-based analysts quickly remarked that "Gulf policymakers are concerned about Iran making inroads into Egypt," that "there's no doubt the Saudis are very concerned about Egypt's new foreign policy orientation," and that "Saudi Arabia is seeking to regain its heavyweight position in the region and doing so in a very assertive manner. It does not want to see Egypt erase any Saudi gains."[37]

The UAE's official position on the Arab uprisings, at least in the early days, appeared in line with Saudi Arabia's. An attempted rally to "silently and peacefully protest against Mubarak" by Egyptian activists outside their country's consulate in Dubai was swiftly broken up by the police.[38] And a UAE national[39] who had apparently tried to express support for Tunisian and Egyptian demonstrators in a mosque was later seized from his home in Sharjah on the grounds that he was "disturbing public security." For several days his location was unknown, with Amnesty International filing a request with UAE authorities to confirm his legal status and whereabouts.[40] Two weeks after protests began in Egypt, the UAE's minister for foreign affairs[41] became the first—and only Arab—international diplomat to meet with Mubarak during the revolt. Described by another Arab diplomat as "showing extraordinary political support for Egypt," the UAE visit was treated with great suspicion by many Egyptian protestors, not least because the crown prince of Abu Dhabi[42] had stated earlier in the week that "the UAE rejects all foreign attempts to interfere in the internal affairs of Egypt."[43] Moreover, soon after Mubarak's fall one of the crown prince's aides was reported by Reuters to have "vented his frustration over the downfall of a major ally who Gulf Arab rulers once thought was as entrenched in power as they are," and to have questioned "how could someone do this to him [Mubarak]?" before explaining that "he was the spiritual father of the Middle East. He was a wise man who always led the region. ... We didn't want to see him out this way."[44] Meanwhile, in Dubai's most read state-backed newspaper, *Gulf News*, a leading member of the emirate's merchant community argued that "there is a very real danger that mob rule is destroying Egypt's reputation, stability and economy while Mubarak was the symbol of stability, economic prosperity and peace."[45]

As with Saudi Arabia and some of the other Gulf monarchies, the UAE was also reportedly alarmed that Mubarak would have to face the indignity of a trial. As claimed by Egypt's *Al-Masry Al-Yawm* newspaper, "certain princes offered to pay the hospital bill of deposed President Hosni Mubarak, when they heard that the Egyptian government would not meet the costs of his [private] medical treatment."[46] More recently, even after the success of the Muslim Brotherhood's Mohamed Morsi in Egypt's May 2012 elections, senior UAE officials have gone on record with inflammatory statements. Dubai's veteran chief of police[47], for example, claimed in July 2012 that members of the Brotherhood had "been meeting people from the Gulf and discussing toppling Gulf regimes" and warned the Egypt-based group that they would lose a lot if they challenged the Gulf states.[48] Beyond Egypt, the UAE's diplomatic stance has been much the same on other Arab revolts, at least when they began. In April 2011, nearly two months after the beginning of the Bahrain revolt and a month after the deployment of UAE and Saudi troops in the kingdom—as discussed below—the crown prince of Abu Dhabi received a delegation from the Bahraini government that had come to "express its gratitude ... for the supportive stance that had contributed to establishing security and stability in the kingdom." Despite the crown prince having no formal foreign policy role in the UAE's federal government, he reportedly welcomed the delegates by "stressing the deep fraternal bond between the UAE and Bahrain as well as all other Gulf countries" and stated that "these relations are based on strong historical ties, shared interests, and mutual destiny." Despite the brutal crackdown that was taking place in Bahrain that very week, the crown prince also expressed his "support for Bahrain and its people as well as the measures adopted by Bahrain's wise leadership for establishing peace and security." He further "hailed the efforts of the king and the crown prince [of Bahrain] for reforms and development as well as for protecting the values of national unity, tolerance, and peaceful coexistence among sects."[49]

On a broader level, there are indications that the Gulf monarchies are now working harder than ever to portray themselves collectively as being inherently different from the Arab authoritarian republics. A concerted effort has been made to convince both their own populations and the international community that there are somehow enough structural differences between their style of authoritarianism and that of their neighbors such as to exempt them from the revolts. Most notably, there have been recent attempts to broaden the Gulf Co-operation Council to include the fellow Arab monarchies of Jordan and Morocco. Despite these states being geographically separated from the Gulf monarchies and having few economic or social commonalities with them, it has nonetheless been reasoned that their survival now matters to the Gulf monarchies. Jordan and Morocco have faced serious protests since early 2011, but the regimes remain in place for the time being, and thus provide some temporary evidence for the "monarchy is different" theory. In May 2011, delegates at a GCC consultative summit decided to offer both Jordan and Morocco GCC membership. Though the talks took place behind closed doors, the summit's main topic of discussion was presumably the Arab revolts and how the Gulf monarchies could best find ways of delivering financial aid to the region's two other monarchies. Moreover, given that the usefulness of foreign mercenaries has become increasingly apparent since the beginning of the Arab uprisings, it is likely that Jordan and Morocco—both of which are manpower rich—were viewed as possible suppliers in the event that the Gulf monarchies have to rapidly expand their security services.

Shortly after the summit, the Moroccan minister for foreign affairs[50] visited Abu Dhabi to convey the "gratitude of King Mohammed VI to the UAE under the leadership of Sheik Khalifa for the sincere and fraternal call stated in the final statement of the recent GCC consultative summit for the accession of Morocco to the GCC." Adding that "such a move would further strengthen bilateral ties," the minister also referred to the "fraternal coordination and cooperation that bind us with these countries since a long time at all levels," despite Morocco having never had any previous formal engagements with the GCC.[51] Unsurprisingly, within a few months of this and similar meetings between Jordanian officials and GCC representatives, the GCC announced in September 2011 that it would fund a five-year development program in

Jordan and Morocco. Finalized in December 2011 with $2.5 billion allocated to each state, the deal was viewed by some analysts as being a "consolidation of monarchies that are solidly Sunni" and with the "attraction [for the Gulf monarchies] being assistance … from [Jordan's] well-trained military."[52] Similarly, Reuters reported that the deal reflected the Gulf monarchies' need for "closer ties with Arab kingdoms outside the Gulf as part of efforts to contain the pro-democracy unrest that is buffeting autocratic ruling elites throughout the Arab world."[53]

NOTES

1   Allen J. Fromherz, *Qatar: A Modern History*, London: IB Tauris, 2012, p. 7.
2   For a full discussion of the Dubai opposition see Christopher M. Davidson, "Arab Nationalism and British Opposition in Dubai, 1920–1966," *Middle Eastern Studies*, Vol. 43, No. 6, (2007).
3   Leigh Nolan, "Managing Reform? Saudi Arabia and the King's Dilemma," Brookings Doha Center Policy Briefing (May 2011).
4   University of the United Arab Emirates, in Al-Ayn.
5   According to a study of the Muslim Brotherhood in the UAE published by *Dar Al-Hayat* newspaper in Saudi Arabia. *Dar Al-Hayat* (September 12, 2010).
6   Abd Al-Rahim Al-Nashiri was captured in the UAE in November 2002.
7   Nolan, "Managing Reform?"
8   *Wall Street Journal*, August 30, 2010, with reference to the crackdowns in Saudi Arabia.
9   *Dar Al-Hayat*, September 12, 2010.
10 *The National*, April 6, 2010.
11 *Global Post*, December 22, 2010.
12 Agence France Presse, December 30, 2010.
13 *Los Angeles Times*, December 23, 2010.
14 Jean-Pierre Filiu, *The Arab Revolution: Ten Lesson from the Democratic Uprising*, London: Hurst, 2011, p. 76.
15 Filiu, *The Arab Revolution*, p. 74.
16 Filiu, *The Arab Revolution*, p. 75.
17 Bahrain News Agency press release, May 2, 2011.
18 *Washington Times*, November 23, 2011.
19 Regimes have also used "deep packet inspection" to censor private emails. See Filiu, *The Arab Revolution*, p.46.
20 For example, the case of Abu Dhabi's burgeoning e-government. See Christopher M. Davidson, *Abu Dhabi: Oil and Beyond*, London: Hurst, 2009, Chapter 6.
21 *Gulf News*, July 30, 2012.
22 *Foreign Policy*, September 21, 2010.
23 Filiu, *The Arab Revolution*, p. 46.
24 Filiu, *The Arab Revolution*, p. xiii.
25 Filiu, *The Arab Revolution*, p. 44.

26 Muhammad Omran.

27 Referring to *Etisalat.*

28 *Arabian Business*, July 2, 2011.

29 *Kipp Report*, June 8, 2011. Citing the second Arab Social Media Report published by the Governance and Innovation Program at the Dubai School of Government.

30 *Gulf News*, May 31, 2012

31 *Kipp Report*, June 8, 2011; *Time* Magazine, 12 July 2012.

32 Agence France Press, February 9, 2011.

33 This was Al-Shaykh's initial reaction to Pope Benedict XVI's Regensburg lecture on September 12, 2006.

34 *Asharq Al-Awsat*, February 5, 2011.

35 *Al-MasryAl-Yawm*, April 10, 2011.

36 BBC News, February 22, 2011.

37 Reuters, April 27, 2011. Quoting Shadi Hamid, an analyst at the Brookings Center in Qatar and Theodore Karasik, a defense analyst based in Dubai.

38 *Gulf News*, January 28, 2011.

39 Hassan Muhammad Hassan Al-Hammadi

40 Amnesty International press release, February 9, 2011.

41 Abdullah bin Zayed Al-Nahyan.

42 Muhammad bin Zayed Al-Nahyan.

43 *The National*, February 9, 2011.

44 Reuters, April 27, 2011.

45 *Al-Ahram*, April 30, 2011. Quoting Khalaf Al-Habtoor.

46 *Al-Masry Al-Yawm*, May 23, 2011.

47 Dahi Khalfan Al-Tamim

48 BBC News, July 31, 2012.

49 WAM, April 11, 2011.

50 Al-Tayeb Al-Fassi Fihri.

51 WAM, May 16, 2011.

52 *The National*, September 13, 2011; Reuters, December 20, 2011.

53 Reuters, December 20, 2011.

||||||||||||||||||||||||||||||||||||||||||||||||||||||||||||||||||||||||||||||||||

The intervention of NATO forces in Libya, ostensibly to protect civilians from pro-Gaddafi troops and mercenaries, provided sufficient air cover and military support to topple the dictatorship. Russia and China did not veto the action, but neither did they sanction the overthrowing of the regime or the bloody killing of Muammar Gaddafi. NATOs escalation in Libya so infuriated the Russians and Chinese that they later refused to back any UN sanctioned intervention in the civil war in Syria. This chapter is written by an Indian doctor living in Tripoli, Libya for several years before, during, and after the Libyan revolt against Muammar Qaddafi's regime. Prashant Bhatt presents an eyewitness account of what transpired. In interviews with survivors, he gives us precious insight into the revolt that toppled the long-lasting dictator. By mid-2015 the country stood on the brink of anarchy as multiple militias fought for influence and territory. The government was powerless to stop the breakdown of law and order and had been relegated to a new makeshift capital in Tobruck.

||||||||||||||||||||||||||||||||||||||||||||||||||||||||||||||||||||||||||||||||||

CHAPTER 8*
TRIPOLI IS "FREE"?
PRASHANT BHATT

"Tripoli is free," read a slogan widely seen among the graffiti decorating the walls of the former Libyan capital—a slogan that summed up the outcome of the February 17, 2011 revolt that led to the end of Colonel Muammar Gaddafi's forty-two-year-old reign. The brutal reaction of the regime to the democratic aspirations of the people led to militarization of the opposition, and more than half a million expatriate workers fled the conflict. Since then I have come across several people who stayed behind, braving all odds—ordinary people who do not figure in the big power narratives to do with billions of dollars transferred abroad, of assets frozen, or of high-minded UN Security Council resolutions.

"Tripoli is free," sounds like a contradiction in many ways. The forces of the February 17 revolt gained freedom from a despotic regime with overwhelming support provided by the North Atlantic Treaty Organization (NATO), which interpreted United Nations Security Council Resolution 1973 in favor of protecting civilians in Libya and establishing a no-fly zone in a very broad manner. This support amounted to covertly arming and training the rebels and

||||||||||||||||||||||||||||||||||||||||||||||||||||||||||||||||||||||||||||||||||

*This chapter, now updated, originally appeared in Prashant Bhatt, *Shafshoofa Maleshi: Life Narratives of the Libyan Revolution* (February 17, 2011), e-book, Smashwords Ed., 2013, Chapter 3. Used by permission of the author, who owns the copyright.

backing their advance with heavy aerial bombing. Though the logic of protecting civilians was applied in March 2011 when Benghazi, the country's second largest city, was threatened by Gaddafi's army, the same logic did not hold for "loyalist" cities where there was support for the deposed dictator. Also, there is no accounting for the large number of weapons that were looted from the arms depots of the regime during the insurrection and after it. Surely having porous borders through which these weapons can find their way to anywhere in the world cannot be a good thing. For that matter, almost everybody in Tripoli now possesses a firearm, and while the National Transitional Council (NTC) has no real authority, armed militias rule the roost.

Against this backdrop, which shows the pitfalls in the path of nationalism in today's world, the accounts presented here, based on interviews, involve a Libyan Arab, a Berber, a Nigerian migrant, and an Indian doctor. They point to the multilayered and complex realities that characterize this region, something anyone attempting to consolidate a central authority in the country will have to contend with.

THE DISSIDENT GENERATION

Salem, who left Libya for the UK in 1981, is forty-two. Studying and later working there as an engineer, he married a Briton in 1988. He visited Libya in 2002 and resettled in Tripoli six years later. Having played an active role on the ground during the revolt, he now does liaison work and also earns money by giving English lessons. He represents a generation of Libyans who worked and waited in exile for decades, hoping to see the day Gaddafi and his army would get what in his assessment they deserved.

Salem holds British and Libyan passports, but did not leave Libya when there was an evacuation of British citizens at the beginning of the conflict. "I belong to this land. Whatever happens to its people, will happen to me," he answered when asked about the wisdom of his decision.

His marriage came apart after his 2002 visit, when he expressed a desire to raise his children in Libya. As he spoke of his marriage, traces of emotion flitted across Salem's face. Yet the precepts of his faith offer him comfort.

"My marriage broke down when I began insisting that my children live in Libya. I have four children—two sons, two daughters. As a Muslim it was very important for me to give everything I could to my wife and children. I am happy I could give my savings and the house built in England to them. It secures their future." He added he had no regrets, but rather was satisfied that he had given it all up for the sake of his children.

"This is it! There are a lot of casualties and now there is no going back," Salem told me over the phone on August 21, the second day of the Tripoli uprising. "The first Tripoli uprising, in February, was brutally suppressed by the regime," he went on to say. "So we prepared for a long time. Benghazi broke free in four days on February 20. What we had read in books about revolutionary situations, where things change within hours, came true there. However, in Tripoli, there was a brutal counterrevolution, and we decided to step back and prepare."

Many district-level organizers in Tripoli worked through their associations to procure weapons and form local self-defense committees. When the rebel advance from the western Nafusa Mountains overran Zawiya (about 50 km, or 30.07 miles, west of Tripoli) and moved rapidly toward the capital on the evening of August 20, mosques in the city exhorted people to go out and secure their streets. The districts of Tripoli then rose up in defense of their localities in a plan that had been organized for several months.

Gaddafi's forces tried to terrorize the population the way they had done in February, but this time the people were well prepared. Local committees secured their districts and no one from outside was allowed to enter. If anyone tried to break through the barricades set up in all street corners by the residents, they were stopped by force. Despite this, there were house-to-house searches and killings in some areas—Ras-Hasan, Fashloom, and Suq Juma—by armed mercenaries from sub-Saharan African countries. This led to reprisals and there were hundreds of casualties, but ultimately, those opposed to the regime prevailed.

The citizens' committees thus successfully fought off the regime loyalists, who once again tried to intimidate people. Unlike in February, there was also a successful advance from outside Tripoli and there were NATO bombings. But it was the heroism of common people who bravely stood up for their rights that, to a large extent, prevented the state security forces from going "*zenga zenga*" (or *zanqat zanqat*; i.e., alley by alley) into the many neighborhoods of the capital. Hundreds paid the ultimate price for this, and many thousands were injured and had to go without proper medical treatment as the healthcare system had been severely compromised.

When unrest against his government gained strength in February, Gaddafi made a televised speech in Arabic vowing to hunt down the "rats" (as he called the insurgents) "inch by inch, room by room, home by home, *zenga zenga.*" This imported a catchy phrase into the lexicon of the revolution, and a "*Zenga Zenga*" song parodying the speech went viral on the Internet. August showed the *zenga zenga* strategy gaining new significance in Tripoli, but in exactly the opposite way from what Gaddafi had intended.

Salem telephoned me about a week after the August 27 liberation of Tripoli, and his call made it clear that the hospitals in the capital were still struggling to cope. "My mother had a fall," he said. "We went to the oldest and largest teaching hospital in Tripoli. It was chaotic, but people were trying their best to help. I met a neurosurgeon there who works in the private sector but had volunteered to work in the public hospital."

A LIBYAN BERBER

Khawla, a staff nurse in her twenties, told of her uncle who died in June 1996 when state security massacred some 1,200 political prisoners at Abu Salim prison south of Tripoli. He had been arrested and detained without trial. Her family still bears the scars, like those of many Libyans who "disappeared" in the decades of tyranny. Abu Salim became a powerful symbol of state repression, one that drove thousands of the country's rebels to action.

Talking to Khawla brought to light a significant but often suppressed detail about the country. "Yes," she said, "we are Muslims, but we are not Arabs. We are the original inhabitants of this land—the Berbers."

The Berbers, or the *Amazigh* community, are the original inhabitants of North Africa, forced to leave the more prosperous regions following the Arab advance from the east, beginning in the seventh century AD. In Libya, many of them live among the plateaus and hills of the Nafusa Mountains, as well as in the Oasis of Fezzan in the southwest. In several African countries, the Berbers have been assimilated into the Arab population.

Gaddafi called Berbers a "product of colonialism" who were created by the West to divide Libya. Seeing them as a threat to his view of Libya as a homogeneous Arab society, the Amazigh language, Tamazight, and script, which is distinct from Arabic, was officially banned and could not be taught in schools. Giving children Amazigh names was forbidden. Those attempting to promote Amazigh culture, heritage, and rights were persecuted, imprisoned, or even killed. The suppression of the Amazigh community has been highlighted by Amnesty International, which has asked the National Transitional Council to end all discrimination against it. More specifically, Amnesty has said that a Libyan law from 1949 that prohibits the use of languages other than Arabic in publications, official documents, public spaces, and private enterprises, as well as the use of "non-Arab, non-Muslim" names, should be amended in line with international law and standards.

Not surprisingly, the first successful attack on Tripoli from outside came from the western Nafusa Mountains, which is home to Berber communities. And the ranks of these inexperienced fighters included doctors, professors, students and even taxi drivers. Libya is known as an Arab state and is part of both the Arab League and African Union, but its Berbers, who make up more than 5 percent of the country's population of six million, do not usually figure in its modern narratives and mental maps.

"I was raised in Tripoli, but my grandparents live in the Nafusa Mountains," Khawla said. "I cannot follow their dialect easily."

This ancient divide, which was aggravated by Gaddafi, has to be properly addressed if there is to be any true democracy in Libya. The coming election could provide the Amazigh community with a sense of self-determination a step, they hope, that will lead to its rights being guaranteed by a new Libyan constitution and to full national and regional recognition.

A NIGERIAN IMMIGRANT

Carlos, a twenty-seven-year-old Nigerian, used to play in the Libyan football league and worked in the San Francisco church of Dahra. His father died when he was young. This probably shaped his character, as he was always willing to help the disadvantaged as a part of his faith and as a service to the community. He now helps train footballers in the Egyptian league. "The church is why I stayed and survived in Libya though my aim was to play in the leagues of Europe," said Carlos. "In my spare time, I help to prepare papers for my community members who have fallen into drugs, prostitution, prisons. It is not easy for them, and I like to do God's work. The bishop has asked me to find out about the cemetery in Misrata, as the cemetery in Tripoli is full and the community needs to preserve the dignity of its dead."

Community work has helped Carlos find meaning and stability in life, but many other black African migrants in Tripoli have not been so fortunate. Expatriate communities in the Tripoli region are free to follow their religions, though their priests are not allowed to convert people. There are functioning Greek Orthodox, Anglican, and Catholic churches in the capital and, through volunteers like Carlos, they render various services to the community. While it is true that Gaddafi employed mercenaries, not all of the nearly one million black Africans in Libya were soldiers of fortune. Sub-Saharan residents in Libya—mainly from Chad, Niger, Somalia, Eritrea, and Nigeria—were targeted by rebel forces from the moment they took control of Tripoli. There were reports of mass roundups and abuse of the migrants as well as looting of their homes and rapes. Rebel fighters barged into residences, shouting *murtazaka* (mercenary)—a word every black African in Libya knows too well.

There are no reliable figures on how many foreign mercenaries Gaddafi employed. Yet, it was almost certainly far fewer than the rebel fighters suspected. Most black Africans in Libya have been in the country for years doing casual manual labor. But just as it was easier to suspect foreigners of doing Gaddafi's bidding and carrying out some of the worst excesses of the conflict, so it is now easier to persecute those who can be easily distinguished by the color of their skin.

Being black and African in Tripoli after the revolt was not very safe. Public transport was regularly stopped, and armed men detained those who were dark-skinned. "Filipino *mafish mushkila*" (Filipino, no problem), they said to the nonblack migrants, some of whom were Filipinos.

THE INDIAN CAMP

Around 18,000 citizens of India were evacuated by the Indian embassy in Tripoli, which showed marked efficiency during the crisis. Those working for companies in Libya did not have much choice but to leave, and the Indians fleeing the conflict from the Misrata region in the initial days of conflict in February and March had not slept, eaten, or washed properly for days. Those who chose to stay behind did so for their own reasons and at their own risk. Indian medical workers, for instance, had a base among the population they served and were not dependent on companies.

Bachchoo Singh, an Indian doctor who has been in Libya since 1988, politely but firmly told one of his "friends" who insisted that he flee the fighting, "How I reached here is a long story, which you have neither the time nor inclination to hear. Please do not impose your opinions on me. Leave me to my resources and judgment."

Recounting some of his experiences in Libya, the doctor said, "My father-in-law used to work for the hydrology department here. He introduced me to this country." Bachchoo Singh speaks Arabic fluently and is on familiar terms with Libyans of all classes as well as expatriates from India.

Long before all the present troubles, a *bhajan* group—for chanting devotional songs—was organized for the Indian community in Tripoli by the Khemlanis, a Sindhi trader family settled in Libya since 1933. The prayer group served as a focal point for Indians.

In addition, big, Sikh-owned construction companies like SSB and DS used to organize *jagratas* (all-night devotional festivals) and celebrate Guru Nanak Jayanti, the holiday celebrating the birthday of the first Sikh *Guru*, Nanuk, one of the most sacred festivals in Sikhism. Rich, long-term expatriates working in the oil sector and Sindhi trader families were at the forefront of the activities of these prayer groups.

"Now the community will take at least three years to restart life here," said Bachchoo Singh. "One year for the workers to return, another year for the families, and a third for some proper teachers to organize education."

During the turmoil of the revolt, some Indian construction company sites were looted. Indian workers who stayed on in a camp outside the capital related their encounters, first with the loyalists and then with the revolutionary forces.

"They never harmed us physically, but very systematically took away our computers and televisions. When the rebels reached the camp, there was no serious fighting. The loyalist soldiers who had been camping here made good their escape by discarding their uniforms and boots. They always seemed to have civilian clothes under their uniforms but had to run barefoot because their boots would have given them away. We hid in a container for a few hours. Some people ransacked the whole camp but they did not drive away with our vehicles, as we had removed the batteries. They did not search to kill anyone."

REVOLUTIONARY JUSTICE

Libyans have a tradition of marking dates and of building monuments around them. While the world knows about the February 17 revolt, April 7 marks the day in 1983 when public killings took place at the University of Tripoli. Those who carried out these killings continue to be marked men and are in hiding, many of them outside Libya.

During the revolution and its aftermath, leading doctors who were close to the Gaddafi regime either fled the country or were detained. There was costly diagnostic equipment, drugs, and supplies in Tripoli's hospitals. But the director of the largest teaching hospital, the Markis Tubbi, or Tripoli Medical Center, was detained for questioning and his passport had been confiscated so that he could not flee the country. With a new judicial process yet to be established and no functioning courts, justice was what the *thuwaar* (revolutionaries) dispensed.

In the Zawiya and Zuaara areas of western Libya, on the road to Tunis, there were incidents of intertribal fighting, which had more to do with settling scores than being pro- or anti-Gaddafi. Also, there were reports of killings in the town of Tawerga in the Misrata region. When the city of Misrata was being besieged, Gaddafi's forces waged many indiscriminate attacks against it from Tawerga, and fighters from Misrata later sought to pay it back.

While this had been happening on the ground, Amnesty International demanded that all those arbitrarily detained, including in the context of the conflict, be released and capricious arrests and detentions cease immediately. But this was—and is—a tall order. With the dissolution of known mechanisms of the state even months after the liberation of Tripoli, Libya remained devoid of established procedures or legal institutions, and as time has shown, the situation is not much better today.

CONCLUDING THOUGHTS

When Libyans who supported the overthrow of the regime were asked about the attitude of the victors toward Gaddafi supporters who sought after the revolt to express their views peacefully, and about the detentions of black Africans, some became thoughtful while others were dismissive of the questions. Yet others said this was a transitional phase, and that a mature culture of intellectual enquiry and tolerance would take time and effort to emerge.

That may well be true. Libya's new leaders have excelled in many ways, not least in how they guaranteed the freedom, dignity, and justice that so many died for. But if it is to mean anything, it must apply to all, and as events have borne out, the path ahead for Libya will continue to be a challenging one.

Born in the context of the "Arab Spring," Morocco's February 20 Movement (henceforth F20) helped revitalize a stagnant Moroccan political life. This movement is a "bizarre" form of protest action. In addition to the country's most radical Islamist organization (which later broke away), its basic political components were elements from the secular far-left parties. Communications (especially its protest slogans) emanating from the movement were peaceful in a naïve style imbued with a touch of youthful and playful Moroccan creativity. However innovative it may be, F20 carried the seeds of its own weaknesses. The state designed a strategy to delegitimize the movement before Moroccan public opinion. This included holding a referendum on new constitutional amendments and presenting a reform package. It also created a new alignment between society's political components and its intellectual elite. The politicized population divided either in support of, or in opposition to, the popular protests. Yet, one of the challenges the movement had to face concerned breaking the divide between political, social, and religious issues. The authors of this chapter deal with these weaknesses.

CHAPTER 9
MOROCCO'S FEBRUARY 20 MOVEMENT: HAS THIS PROTEST MOVEMENT PETERED OUT?

MOHSINE EL AHMADI AND AZIZ RADI

We begin this chapter with a few questions: Are we really living in a historical moment in which old Arab authoritarian regimes are crumbling in favor of new democratic systems? If so, are we witnessing the birth of an Arab citizen who possesses a new political culture? Can the new, transformative processes now at work lead not only to democracy, but also to changes in the old social system and the traditional cultural worldview—by allowing a new society based on the rule of law and the values of dignity, solidarity, and rationality to emerge? An examination of the evolution of social movements in Morocco might help us find responses to these questions.

THE HISTORY OF SOCIAL MOVEMENTS IN MOROCCO
For decades during the 1970s and 80s, Morocco underwent large-scale social struggles. As part of that process, until the early 1990s, the kingdom experienced conflict between the authoritarian state, leftist political parties and, initially, labor unions, as well as radical Islamist organizations.

Moroccan social movements were not born in 2011. For years, protests took various forms, such as sit-ins by unemployed graduates; labor movement strikes; student demonstrations; protests against high prices; women mobilizing for access to wider rights, including through the reform of the *Mudawana* (the family code); and protests against poor social services. The recent Arab revolts broadened the spread of such claims and strengthened their legitimacy. The spillover effect helped, above all, to publicize criticism hitherto only whispered or restricted to a very limited segment of the population.

The "years of lead," as they have come to be known, comprised a dark era in the contemporary political history of Morocco. Over the course of this period (the 1970s to the mid-1990s), Moroccans organized protests several times in big cities such as Casablanca, Fez, and Marrakech, demanding democracy, freedom, and social justice.

If the political claims were the result of previous struggles, the merit of F20[1] was to bring those claims back on the Moroccan political stage. Since the very beginning of the recent uprisings in North Africa, political activists, union militants, intellectuals, and engaged artists have become more and more involved in social movements and have come to occupy a central role in national debates and actions.

Both the previous and the present movements are anchored in Moroccan contemporary protest history. While the demands and goals of both the old and new movements seem to be quasi identical, those in every generation seeks to exploit the means and technical tools available to them to realize their goals. This includes mobilizing through music, theater, cinema, dance, and multimedia, not just the traditional forms of political and NGO organizing.

The activists who initiated F20 at the beginning of 2011 aspired to create a revolt similar to those elsewhere in North Africa and the Middle East (the MENA region.). All the Arab dictatorships had little tolerance for protest, which was considered an act of disobedience and defiance to the state. But with the fall of the Ben Ali regime in Tunisia, mass social mobilization in Morocco, which for decades had been considered unlikely, began to gather pace.

Faithful to its own history and political heritage, the Moroccan state—both the *Makhzen,* as the central authority, and local powers—has, to some extent, faced contention as happened in other Arab countries. But unlike elsewhere in the region, protesters in Morocco involved in F20 did not call for the fall of the nation's leadership but, simply, for the end of "authoritarianism," "cronyism," and "corruption."

After this brief description of the national, regional, and global environments in which F20 emerged, we will introduce the movement, analyze its strengths and weaknesses, and explore its role as a catalyst for change. We will try to assess the collective actions and social struggles that have been under-taken by F20 so far, but also emphasize the future challenges lying ahead for the movement; and we will conclude by pointing out the reasons why it has so far failed to create an autonomous social movement.

To profile F20 activists, we can broadly define them as young people aged 18-40 and unknown figures of political life in Morocco. They have been politicized in the aftermath of ongoing demographic transitions. Mostly they were born in the late 1980s and the 1990s, and are among the 60 percent of the Moroccan population under forty. They are the products of the social consequences of the Structural Adjustment Program imposed on Morocco by the World Bank and the International Monetary Fund from 1983 up to 1992, under which severe budget cuts were made in vital public sectors such as education and health.

THE "BIZARRE" NATURE OF F20

Emulating Emile Durkheim's French word *bizarrerie* in *The Elementary Forms of Religious Life*[2], F20 is a "bizarre" sociopolitical form of protest action in the sense that it is neither a pure religious movement nor a firm secular one. It is, rather, a hybrid combining both components, as we will demonstrate below. The religious components of this movement, notably the Islamists and very few Salafists, defend their point of view that, when making propos-als for the reform of Moroccan society and the state, F20 should be inspired by the experience of the Prophet Muhammad in the town of Medina during the seventh century. While Moroccan Islamists think that modern Moroccan society should be re-Islamized step by step from the top (the state) down to society, Moroccan Salafists think sharia law should be applied by a bottom-up strategy and by all methods, including, if necessary, violence. The Salafists are not numerous but extremely active.

On the contrary, secularist components, namely leftists and some of the Berbers, advocated that F20 should be oriented to the creation of a new social order free of any religious and sectarian influences. Also, despite appearances, F20 is not a reformist movement but rather a radical one, which dares not express loudly that its ultimate goal is to jettison the existing political system.

F20's mode of action and form of protest—such as its Sunday demonstra-tions, the boycott of the constitutional referendum, or peaceful sit-ins—were not new, but rather old forms of social mobilization. What was new and original was that Moroccan young people dared to organize and mobilize themselves without the backing of the traditional political parties and trade unions.

F20 did not work with the logic of a labor movement, because the latter represents the interests of a specific social category, unionized workers with professional demands. Indeed, it deliberately eluded transformation into a social movement by adopting a very loose structure, allowing all who wished to enter to do so as long as they desired to reform the traditional Makhzen as an old form of political and cultural domination and replace it with a sound modern system giving much more room for Moroccan citizens to expand civil society. They also hoped to reform a system characterized by "corruption and clientelism." To reach this end, they launched a series of collective actions in response to the harshness of the state, or any other sort of institutionalized violence, by setting up a series of ephemeral, unorganized actions, without defined leadership, or concise social demands. Theirs is the opposite of a social movement—a labor movement, for instance, which is devoted to the defense of workers' interests—whereas a mass or popular movement is one whose core issues are much more related to the broader demands of a wider sector of society. In many cases, the actors involved in F20 are the underprivileged young people excluded or marginalized from the system of production of material and cultural values.

Social movements come and go, and may generate either the biggest revolutions or relatively "quiet" ones as during the 2011 global waves of prodemocracy movements.[3] The "diffusion of collective action" across the MENA region bears witness to the fact that there are waves within waves. The general wave of mobilization (Tunisian, Egyptian, and Libyan) actually transcended nation-specific waves.[4]

F20 did not operate with the logic of a political party, it should be noted. The core support for a party derives from members sympathic to the party's political line and cognizant of its constraints. The goal of a party is to win elections, access political power, and implement a reform program. Eventually, the focus of a party's struggle is a process that sees the party itself become but a tool used to serve the broader interests of the elites who control its functioning. However, the partisan logic of each party inevitably compels it toward the use of this struggle's framework for the purposes of narrow partisanship and discipline.[5]

As a unique, huge mass movement in postcolonial Morocco, F20 gave voice to the voiceless. Thousands of Moroccan young people and some of their elders, male and female, urban and peasant, broke their silence and took to the streets to demand universal principles such as freedom, dignity, and democracy.

THE STRENGTHS AND LIMITATIONS OF POLITICAL ACTORS

Moroccan leftist parties and associations characterized by a disparate mix of revolutionary and nondemocratic orientations grouped together to form F20. These included the United Socialist Party (USP), the Federal Congress Party (FCP), the Democratic Way (DW), the Moroccan Association for Human Rights (MAFHR), the *Amazigh* (Berber) Democracy Movement (ADM), and the Vanguard Party *(Hizb al-Taliaa)*, as well as the most important Islamist association—known as Justice and Charity or, in Arabic, *Al-Adl wa al-Ihsan*[6]—and other small groups.

Youth organizations affiliated with some mainstream political parties and with two Islamist parties—the Justice and Development Party (PJD) and *Al-Adl wa al-Ihsan*—helped substantially to give birth to F20, providing both militants and other resources [7]. But the PJD leadership later pressured its party youth to withdraw; for the involvement of the party's youth was seen as weakening the party's allegiance to the monarchy and hence as an obstacle to access to power by means of behind-the-scene negotiations with the state following general elections. Alongside *Al-Adl wa al-Ihsan*—the most radical Islamist association—secular radical left parties were the basic political components of F20, for young people on both ends of the spectrum wanted significant social and political change.

THE INFORMATION AGE AND F20

Without necessarily following evolutionary stages, as was the case in the West, Arab societies have been thrown very rapidly into the Information Age and modern communications. In this respect, Morocco's F20 represents an opportunity to learn a great deal about how the media affects programming, which media diffuses information about protests, and how the information thus circulating affects the F20 itself. Interestingly, some differences may arise as the information flows reach some actors but not others. Furthermore, as the information travels through cyberspace and/or the mass media, it is inevitably subject to filtering and distortion. The result can further enhance or denigrate responses.

On top of the list are mobile phones permitting SMS (Short Message Service) and MMS (Multimedia Messaging Service) as well as Facebook, YouTube, Twitter, and blogs. New technologies of information and communication dominate Moroccan youth as is the case with young people worldwide. This helps raise the question why society is technologically lagging behind its youth and why society fears technological innovations even when the latter can serve it well.

Breaking away from the wall of silence and collective fears, young people found space in social networks, free from most intrusive state controls, for public deliberation, and a freed virtual dialogue, since "people have become skeptical in the ability of traditional political parties to make any difference in their daily lives. In fact, Moroccan political parties are conservative in the face of a society yearning for change, and have lost much of their power to mobilize and articulate societal interests."[8]

The new debate was initially distorted by self-censorship and political waffling, given that the fear of politics was ingrained in the minds of Moroccans, terrified as they were of being persecuted and prosecuted for speaking their minds. But then it suddenly gave way to freedom and individual effusion that eventually generated a vibrant public space. Group dynamics created by collective migration onto virtual platforms has become a force ready to come forward whenever the opportunity arises.

F20'S MODES OF COMMUNICATION

Peaceful and professional communication imbued with a touch of creativity is certainly one of the most defining features of this movement, even if this image was sometimes tarnished by violent and reprehensible outbursts in Casablanca, Marrakesh, Fez, and Tangier, to name a few. Initially, news and slogans were issued only in standard Arabic. But the need for clear communication then compelled the movement's participants to use both colloquial Arabic and French as well. Often, the banners were written in the two languages, implying that the messages were also meant for external consumption. The Amazigh alphabet, known as Tifinagh, was also used. Remarkably, a new idiom emerged: "Arench," a mixture of Arabic and French frequently used by private radio stations and on the Moroccan street, served to bring together a new community of "bilingual illiterates." Engendering in its speakers a newfound pride in its constituent languages, the same linguistic register has been used in folk art (tags) and music, much like Moroccan rap, which has a growing popularity and appeal among the younger generations. (See Chapter 17.)

THE MESSAGE AND POLITICAL LEXICOLOGY OF THE F20 MOVEMENT

The content of protest slogans itself is the subject of tough negotiations between competing ideological trends and the F20 leadership. The wording of protest slogans is not an opportunity for the emergence of new leaders, as much as it confirms and reinforces political pluralism inside F20. Some of these slogans include:

"Oh Makhzen, oh coward, Moroccans are not to be humiliated."
"Oh world, look, look, Morocco is ruled by fear."
"Oh people, revolt, revolt against the dictatorial regime."
"However hard you try to put the fire out, you won't succeed."
"'tis people's fire, a strong fire that would form a flame."
"'tis the will of the people, change is inevitable."
"The people want to end corruption."
"Governments come and go, but our conditions are always the same."
"Regionalism is but a mind game on you and me." (This refers to the state seeking to introduce reforms region by region.)

Gradually F20's coordination committees developed slogan committees that worked to develop, homogenize, and organize effective new slogans during public appearances so the movement might avoid discord and avoid sending confusing messages to the public. That was one of F20's strengths, which may explain the success of this movement in the first weeks after its launch. In fact, F20 has been particularly cautious in preventing spillover effects between oral protest slogans and slogans directly attacking the sacred figure of the king. In this regard, it should be noted that "Down with the regime"—which has proliferated in the other Arab revolts—has been conspicuously absent from the F20's slogans, which instead included "Down with despotism" and "Down with corruption."

F20 protest slogans have mimicked the lyrics of popular Moroccan songs. Striking such a deep cultural-emotional chord has served to arouse and optimize public sympathy while enunciating clearly and deeply the movement's social, economic, and political demands.

Broadly speaking, F20's slogans fall into three categories. Its political slogans have denounced corruption and repression; its socioeconomic slogans have demanded improvement of living conditions; and its communicative slogans have called for a democratic constitution to be drafted by an elected constituent assembly reflecting the genuine will of the people. Its slogans have also called for the dissolution of both the government and parliament and the formation of an interim transitional government subject to the will of the people; for the independence and impartiality of the judiciary; and for bringing to trial individuals suspected of corruption, abuse of power, and looting the country's resources. Other slogans have called for recognition of Tamazight (the Berber language) as an official language alongside Arabic; more attention to the details of Moroccan identity in language, culture, and history instruction as well as the release of all political prisoners and prisoners of conscience; and the prosecution of those responsible for their detention. Yet other slogans have demanded the integration of the unemployed in the civil service through fair and transparent competitive examinations;

enhancing indvidual citizens' more dignified lives by reducing the cost of living and increasing the minimum wage; and enabling all citizens to access social services and improving the cost-effectiveness of such services.

The movement highlighted the big divide between the world of traditional politics—of elections and political parties—and the politics of the street. Often accused of being apolitical, it proved that the young were joining the forces calling for change. Their credo: Moroccan youth are "really politicized," but refuse to "take part in" the current political system.

Weekly street protests were the form the movement gave to that political message—considering it the right of the youth to demand immediate reforms, free of political calculations, that would take Morocco from being a country "aspiring to democracy" to being a staunchly democratic one. The movement promulgated the message that young people had the right to express their aspirations, without any form of political or religious tutelage.

This radical change represents a significant transformation of protest politics: the mobilization of a disempowered and excluded minority against the traditional centers of power. However strong such a contemporary form of protest initiated by F20 may be, with its bottom-up call for political radical action, it carries in it the seeds of its own weaknesses.

WEAKNESSES AND STRENGTHS OF THE MOVEMENT

Even though F20 did become, within months, the leading opposition force in Moroccan political life, it subsequently weakened for a variety of reasons, experiencing an apparent deficit in its capacity to keep the masses mobilized around its major goals. Because it produced no charismatic figures as leaders, no powerful political structure, and no unifying ideology, F20 became easy prey for the more politically experienced traditional political parties as well as the Makhzen. F20 had to confront a lack of ideological harmony between its diverse components, since it suffered from the absence of an integrated political strategy that would gather those various forces into a united front against a multitude of challenges.

F20 faced major difficulties in juggling the interests of diverse and opposing groups. In addition, as Antonio Farro has pointed out, the external political environment—dominated by the Makhzen and by traditional political parties that wanted nothing to do with the movement—limited the effectiveness of F20. The most sensitive of F20's decisions were taken in general meetings where anarchy reigned, with some coordination committees functioning independently, and where blatant disagreements on basic issues surfaced. Besides, the movement was hijacked by the J&B as well as the most radical leftists and Jihadist groups. The J&B Islamists, similar to the Salafists, as mentioned above, hoped

> to reestablish the seventh-century caliphate and aim[ed] to use democracy to achieve their ends. In the long-term, however, a multiparty democracy would not exist in their Islamic caliphate. Their literature speaks of denying the power of the parliament to make laws, replacing it with a judiciary that rules through unchanging sharia law. Meanwhile, the Democratic Way (Maoists) want[ed] an anticapitalist revolution.[9]

Key militants were targeted by state media and spokespeople to discredit them. Official talking heads identified them with the militants of the J&B and other Islamist groups who, they claimed, subversively used F20 to achieve their hidden goal of establishing a theocracy.

The state's credo was that as long as the authorities were not opposing those elements of the youth that were demanding democratic reforms, there was not much to worry about. In reality, the state sought to discredit F20 in the realm of public opinion by suggesting an alliance between its core members and the far left on the one hand and extremist Islamists on the other.

What F20 did see in *Al-Adl wa al-Ihsan* was the promise of financial and organizational support that would serve as an asset and make F20 more popular. Equally important, *Al-Adl wa al-Ihsan* sought political cover in F20, which would make it difficult for state forces to directly target the J&B on the grounds that street protests were conducted under the umbrella of the so-called "Arab Spring" associated with F20.

The official position influenced public opinion sufficiently enough to erode the popular sympathy enjoyed by F20 at its birth. In this sense, the propaganda campaign against F20 and its allies, stressing the radicalization of the movement, did indeed isolate the movement, leaving only a handful of political and labor leaders on the far left to continue to support F20. Did F20 run out of steam? Have Moroccans become suspicious of its appeals for change?

A combination of factors led to the weakening and, perhaps, the apparent demise of F20. As previously mentioned, no charismatic leaders emerged from the movement to channel and direct the young people's zeal. The mixture of far left and radical Islamic parties and associations grouped together under the F20 banner confused many Moroccans and gave the impression that F20 actions could lead either to violence or to a new form of authoritarianism. Furthermore, the state, in combination with the traditional political parties, effectively isolated F20 and shut out of key decisions the youthful activists who conceived and organized the movement. Hence, those activists could play but a minor role in setting the agenda for change in the kingdom. Also, the movement's failure to define realistic and attainable goals further diminished its standing. It is thus important to examine the political issues surrounding the F20's pitfalls and the main factors in its missteps.

THE STATE'S PLAN

From the outset the state perceived F20 as a threat, and hence designed a strategy to weaken it—designing a propaganda campaign, for example, concurrent with its foundation in an attempt to discredit F20 and its goals. Imams—as part of an official religious body in government that oversees mosques, traditional religious brotherhoods, and *zawaya* (plural of *zawīya*, or a mystical religious sanctuary)—as well as religious councils were mobilized to influence the voting population in June 2011 in favor of the yes vote for the referendum on the constitution. Also, government officials succeeded in isolating F20 and depriving it of supporters by opening unprecedented talks with political, civic, and labor union leaders aimed at increasing salaries and granting other concessions. Not too long before, such a move would have been unheard of, due to the prospect of adding to the national debt.

Instead of capitalizing on the social conflict that prompted the talks, the F20 ruled out its participation from the outset by expressing strong skepticism as to the outcome of any dialogue. At the same time, it joined demonstrations of unemployed doctors and post office clerks demanding better jobs and living conditions.

It thus entered into an asymmetrical struggle with the state, which ultimately led to the gradual depletion of its rank-and-file core. Also lacking public support, F20 also lost political legitimacy. The state was able to group around it a front of consensus by opening up an unprecedented democratic dialogue. The movement was able to continue its struggle through peaceful popular demonstrations, but it could not maintain its initial pace of impressive mobilization and expansion.

THE STATE'S EVOLVING APPROACH

If F20 lost much of its momentum, was there some logic in the reaction of the Moroccan state? The response of the latter varied during different stages of the movement's evolution and in response to events in different Moroccan cities. Having tolerated F20's first marches, viewing them during initial moments of doubt and hesitation, the state, after gaining national trust, international support, and mainly after King Mohammed VI's March 9, 2011 speech, intervened more vigorously to disperse sit-ins and occupations of public squares. The authorities wanted to convey the message that it was no longer acceptable to demonstrate after the royal speech. But the movement could not be halted, as tens of thousands of Moroccans took to the streets in more than fifty localities throughout the country. The state was compelled to adjust its approach. It changed its strategy and started working to disparage, in the mass media and on the Internet, leading figures of the F20 movement, painting a picture of a movement at risk of being hijacked by factional infighting. Meanwhile, though, protests continued at a steady pace. Then, the movement decided to shift gear.

It is true that the evolution of a protest movement is always shaped not only by the movement itself but also by the actions of its opponents. From this perspective, in Morocco both the state and F20 used a wide variety of tactics as they sought to recover their respective positions. The state learned to contain and belittle the F20 demonstrations to mitigate the movement's potential to disrupt the established order, while the F20's participants learned to take full advantage of their momentum within the framework of regional uprisings and revolts, while minimizing the risk of bearing severe costs. The regime responded with various concessions or contained violence.

Unlike other Arab states, Morocco adopted a hybrid attitude. It avoided outright repression, urged security officials not to create martyrs, and eschewed mass arrests as happened elsewhere in the Arab world. It responded quickly to the combined "viral" use of social network sites and the mass effect of satellite channels such as Al Jazeera. The king's speech of March 9 significantly reduced support for mass action. Most Moroccans responded favorably to the king's signal for reform. They understood the subtle difference between the use of democracy to create anarchy and its use to build a society based on the values of freedom, responsibility, and tolerance.

Contradictions within F20 have hampered its ability to propose constitutional reforms. In this regard, constitutional and electoral participation can be viewed as the state's bait to highlight the opposing tendencies within the movement and contain F20's expansion. The movement in turn tried to diversify its mobilization strategy by appealing to other social classes and sectors of society—not least, the rich and intellectuals—to join the mobilization. One can see herein a legitimate desire to broaden F20's base of support and stick to its agenda of addressing social issues, but some knowledgeable commentators see the movement's contradictions as a serious stumbling block. However, notwithstanding the movement's serious setbacks, we should also mention its merits.

THE MERITS OF THE F20 MOVEMENT

Born in the context of the so-called "Arab Spring," F20 acquired legitimacy nationally and regionally. It helped revitalize a stagnating Moroccan political life. Within months, the movement's protests yielded results nobody could have predicted. The movement is really an unprecedented gathering of different ideological, intellectual, and political streams. Three significant trends emerged within the movement.

Militants from J&B were religious actors who worked within F20s frameworks, despite their disbelief in the system. A second group—including mostly the youth wings of democratic parties such as the Socialist Union of Popular Forces (USFP), the Independence Party (Hizb al-Istiqlal), the PJD, and others integrated into the kingdom's political life—considered the guidelines set by the royal speech an obstacle to further organizing. Finally, a third entity, comprising members of leftist associations and parties, pressed for the establishment of a true parliamentary political system, although they remained cautious about the possibility of achieving such a goal.

What was amazing about F20 was its ability to surmount ideological and political differences and provide a forum for the exchange of contradictory ideas, which otherwise would have had little audience in the kingdom. It, in effect, hosted an exciting space for exchange.

A POLITICAL PRESSURE FORCE

F20 compelled the state to change its political agenda by introducing changes in the constitution and other reforms. A few days after the first protests, in fact, on March 9, 2011, King Mohammed VI gave the aforementioned historic speech in which he launched the long-awaited project of constitutional reform. In the eyes of constitutional law experts, while the powers of the prime minister and parliament were somewhat enhanced under the constitutional reforms approved by referendum almost four months later, on July 1, 2011, preponderant executive authority remained in the hands of the monarch. For example, the king continues to appoint the prime minister, although he is now required to choose a member of the party with the highest proportion of the vote in the legislative elections. He also appoints and fires government ministers proposed by the prime minister (Art. 47). He likewise retains the ability to dissolve parliament (Art. 51), accredit all ambassadors, and sign and ratify treaties (with certain exceptions that require parliamentary approval) (Art. 55).

In addition, the National Council for Human Rights (CNDH) was installed in Rabat in 2012 in accordance with the Paris Principles the United Nations approved in 1993, stating that human rights councils should be independent from states. Two human rights activists, Driss El Yazami and Mohamed Sebbar, known for their integrity and progressive stances, were appointed to head the CNDH.[9] Unlike the country's former Consultative Council for Human Rights (CCHR), the CNDH has had its purview broadened, especially regarding investigations into possible violations of human rights. Its establishment was accompanied by the release of ninety-six Islamist prisoners, as part of a royal pardon of 196 prisoners, most of whom were Salafists.

In terms of human rights, F20 introduced the principle that universal charters should take precedence over national laws and demanded that Morocco's Reconciliation and Equity Committee (which has investigated alleged transgressions of Hassan II's regime) implement recommendations pertaining to the respect of individual and public rights and the separation of politics (state management) from the spiritual (faith management). As for the country's political framework, F20 protesters demanded the establishment of a parliamentary system in which the government rules, parliament legislates, and justice remains independent. The movement demanded a clear separation of powers and a genuine multiparty system in which parties and civil society could play their role as intermediary institutions. However, the movement's mobilization capacity was dramatically jeopardized by the state's effectively implemented strategies to isolate it.

RECONNECTING SOCIETY WITH ITS ELITES

F20 created a new alignment between the political components of society and its intellectual elites regarding which positions to adopt in support of or in opposition to the popular protests. The movement presented an integrated package of political, social, economic, and human rights demands. One of its most vocal economic demands was the abolition of rent, which, in a capitalist society such as Morocco, demonstrated its profound political immaturity. Contrarily, F20 demanded an economic system based on free entrepreneurship and competition to promote innovation, boost employment, and control inflation. Further, the movement advocated for substantial reform of the country's educational and judicial systems. It also ushered in an unprecedented debate focusing on such political taboos as the Makhzen's influence over the economy and the king's shadow cabinet working parallel to the prime minister's cabinet, as well as governmental responsibility and accountability.

F20 succeeded in taking the debate down from the higher spheres of the state to Main Street, where ordinary people talked about issues once discussed only by the elites. It gave legitimacy to peaceful popular protest, exercised the right to demonstrate on the streets, showing great political maturity by ensuring that this was done peacefully.

THE WEIGHT OF POLITICAL TRADITION

Among the movement's challenges was that of breaking the divide between political and social issues—and conveying to the public that a shift was underway from the old, individualistic concept of a country in need of a charismatic leader to that of a nation that celebrates collective action, and that institutional structures sanctified by tradition were discredited and outdated and thus had to be bypassed.

Even if, at the outset, F20 held the initiative, it would be naïve to believe that the state was oblivious to the movement's disturbing advantage. The state's seemingly lax attitude toward events at the outset was nothing else but an attempt to fully prepare its response. In fact, the royal speech of March 9, in which the head of state promised a revision of the constitution, stripped the movement of its ability to take further initiatives. Since then, the movement seemed to be on the defensive vis-à-vis the palace, unable to find means of mobilizing the masses other than its call for a boycott of the July 1 constitutional referendum.

Some criticized the movement's call for a boycott of the royal commission to reform the constitution without providing any concrete alternative constitutional proposals—accusing F20 of doing so in bad faith. But F20 was in a bind. Had it agreed to participate in the royal initiative, many would have considered the movement an agent in the already obsolete institutional structure. Had it reversed course and cooperated with the king's initiative, it most likely would have lost the support of those who favored the boycott. Had the movement engaged in the business of drafting the constitution, it would have inevitably confronted divisive issues such as freedom of consciousness and religion, as well as individual rights, which the movement had carefully avoided.

THE MOVEMENT'S LOSS OF ITS GRIP ON PROTESTS

F20 made another strategic mistake by organizing its protests within densely populated, lower-class neighborhoods. It did so independent of the trade union movement and without genuine public support. This deprived F20 of its upper middle class supporters, who also desired more access to political decisions. Secular middle class protesters had previously participated in large numbers, balancing the Islamist presence in protests. Furthermore, the migration of F20 protesters to poor neighborhoods angered the authorities.

Finally, routine set in. The F20 movement froze into a repetitive protest mode. Its members gradually abandoned the creative edge that had earlier seen them vary the methods of their demonstrations: they stopped staging sit-ins, campaigns for blood donations, the distribution of flowers to the police, and neighborhood clean-up initiatives. Going out to demonstrate or protest on Sundays no longer excited an average Moroccan, and the movement had no political, labor union, or civic affiliations to fall back on to spread its message. Many people did not know what to think of the state-initiated ongoing reforms or the charges of radicalization levied against the movement. The movement now failed to clearly present its goals and objectives to the general public, which began abandoning Sunday demonstrations in the popular quarters of major cities. As a result, F20 faced major crises.

THE F20 MOVEMENT AND DEMOCRACY

F20 faced a dilemma: it was dominated by political parties and organizations whose democratic credentials were dubious indeed—e.g. J&B and the Democratic Way. Moreover, its constituent organizations competed rather than cooperated with each other. The movement's credo was that the goal of a democratic party was to contribute to the achievement of popular democracy, not to become a party in control of everything in the political arena.

The J&B's leaders have not yet understood that democracy is incompatible with its religious approach. This Islamic movement claims to embrace democracy, while its undeclared objective is to impose a strict ethic and particular religious vision of morality on the whole of Moroccan society. This has scared many Moroccans who fear a new, religion-based political tyranny. It is, after all, evident that some Islamic groups are convinced that the problems facing their country's largely Islamic society derive *not* from the way in which society and its political system are structured, from a lack of social cohesion, or from an unjust distribution of resources, but rather from a lack of religiosity and the nonapplication of sharia law.

DESTINY OF THE MOVEMENT

In the F20's view the July 1 referendum was hurriedly organized in an attempt to take the steam out of the movement. Its leaders dismissed the poll as a stage-managed affair that would not address the underlying causes of Morocco's political malaise. Instead they vowed to continue their protests because, they argued, the constitution was not an end in itself.[10] The movement advocated an overhaul of the state apparatus, as well as the constitution. The latter alone, F20 leaders stated, would not solve the Moroccans' daily problems. Further, they said the king's speech failed to respond to their demands. They wanted a political system that derived its legitimacy from popular sovereignty through a constitutional assembly, not from historical legitimacy.

In terms of the rationalization of powers, the new constitution establishes four distinct powers: the legislative, executive, judicial, and royal. The first two fall within the realm of popular legitimacy and remain subject to the final verdict of the ballot box, but not the last one. Given the preponderance of state power, no electoral process can redefine the fundamental nature of the country's political system. The state seems inclined to accommodate the movement only slightly, in a way that does not undermine its core power, so that Moroccans cannot exercise their right of oversight and hold accountable those people with close connections to the political sphere.

There are enormous social challenges ahead for Morocco, and the public debate concerning them will probably continue in the foreseeable future. Street protests show no signs of waning. Yet are these generated by F20 or, rather, by unemployed college graduates and those belonging to other interest groups that existed prior to the creation of F20? Perhaps the protesters will devise more creative ways to make their presence felt in public spaces. Those young people in the movement who previously led quiet lives of relative comfort have given that up to take to the streets. F20 members point out that the state allowed political arrests to continue while exonerating those responsible for human rights violations, political repression, and economic corruption. Indeed, it helped perpetuate the flaws of the Moroccan political system.

Nevertheless, despite the movement's tenacity and perseverance, its future appears dim. In the wake of the reforms proposed by King Mohammed VI, it became clear that the political future of F20 was at stake. Many factors converged to generate this state of affairs. With the ratification of the constitution in July 2011, Morocco demonstrated its willingness to make a significant shift to its democratic structures. Today the core debate seems centered around the question of how to implement the articles of the new constitution in genuinely effective and efficient ways.

Undeniably, the adoption of a new constitution is an important step forward in the process of democratization. Yet, Morocco is still in search of a real democratic system. Simply put, the country needs strong, impersonal institutions, and an actual separation and balance of powers, both genuine bulwarks against arbitrariness.

Technically, the July 2011 ratification solved one basic problem related to state administration and the management of government authorities. How did it do that? What is required? The question remains whether the political parties can keep up with the new constitution. In other words, the state has undertaken reform, but not the parties, which F20 accuses of being too involved in seeking power within the present political system that they are supposed to change.

For F20, a real democratic parliamentary system is about the only formula in the long term that can reconcile the monarchical form of statehood and the principle of democracy. But that begs the question of establishing a constitutional monarchy, which reduces the head of state's powers—a prospect F20 members certainly think of but cannot express publicly, for fear of retaliation. The people have spoken by voting in the referendum on the constitution, and therefore many who support the king's approach think F20 no longer has either the justification to demonstrate or the right to exist. The organizers of the referendum acted on the basis that a "yes" vote was part of a sacred cause that justified all means for its support. The official discourse equated the vote on the constitution with the support of social order, and turned the referendum into a kind of test of allegiance to the monarchy. Yet the existing constitution already guaranteed various core liberties, including the freedom of expression and the freedom to demonstrate.

In short, the king's March 9, 2011, speech concerning constitutional reform, the ensuing overwhelming ratification, the impressive showing of the JDP in legislative elections, and the withdrawal of *Al-Adl wa al-Ihsan* entirely from the F20 movement in March 2012 are factors that seriously jeopardized F20s, continued existence. Since the referendum, the movement has been unable to function as a cohesive entity capable of mobilizing significant actions. No longer does it have the support of either *Al-Adl wa al-Ihsan*'s vast membership or its disciplined leadership.

CONCLUSIONS

It seems clear that the founders of F20 and their militant supporters sought to reproduce the huge demonstrations that took place in Tunisia and Egypt, but they failed because social and political conditions in Morocco were so different. First, more than a decade earlier Morocco had implemented a wide range of reforms, both political and social, under King Hassan II, who opened the political system to his opponents in 1998, a year before his death. Also, his son and successor, King Mohammed VI, inaugurated his reign by reforming his father's political system and some of Morocco's legal system (for example, changes in the law regulating marriage and family issues) and launched an ambitious "National Initiative for Human Development" to combat poverty. Second, F20 could not reproduce the mass-scale demonstrations in Morocco that the Egyptians or Tunisians did in their countries, because the king is genuinely more popular than were either Hosni Mubarak or Zine al-Abdine Ben Ali. And he has inherited a kind of political savoir faire in governance that gives him the ability and thus far a real legitimacy to rule.

Comparing Morocco with Jordan is more tenable, because both countries introduced reforms for fear of succumbing to revolts. For the moment, these efforts are working in both, although demonstrators did call for King Abdullah's removal in Jordan in 2013. Jack A. Goldstone argues in *Foreign Affairs* that monarchies are stronger than "sultanic presidencies" (Algeria, Egypt, Libya, Tunisia, Syria, and Yemen) because power is more diffused under kings.[12] A sovereign can lay the blame on the parliament and dismiss it, or on the prime minister and his cabinet and dismiss them. He can diffuse tensions and conflicts. By contrast, the centralization of all power in a president means that if he goes, the regime collapses. All other institutions depend wholly on the presidency, and they too fall once the head is cut off. F20 could not and did not attack the king directly in part because doing so is considered an act of defiance to his person. Also, Morocco's monarchy has historical legitimacy and religious authority. Taken together, that makes kingship in Morocco more sustainable than the "sultanic presidencies" to be found in some other countries.

The F20 seems to have failed because unlike other movements in the Arab world, which had a clear objective from the start—i.e. the fall of the regimes that governed their respective countries—F20 could not make such demands. Demonstrators in Tunisia and Egypt and elsewhere were relatively free to chant "*Ashaab yourid isqaat annidhaam!*"—"The people want to topple the regime!" Even if the F20 movement did sympathize with such a goal, it could not declare its sentiments as clearly as in other Arab countries. Instead, it tried to maneuver more subtly in the hope of creating a political environment conducive to triggering a final meltdown of state order.

That is not to mention that the experiences of Tunisia and Egypt in 2011 show that the fall of a dictator does not necessarily lead to fundamental changes in such a system and does not usher in a political system to everyone's liking. (See Chapters 3 and 15, for example.) As long as militant movements within a specific society are politically immature, organizationally weak, and lack the ability to initiate, adapt, or create, those movements are unlikely to succeed in achieving their goals of ushering in wide-scale political change.

By and large, F20 has three survival options. It can, on the one hand, continue protesting and so confirm its identity as a movement accommodating all expressions of civic protest, including those voiced by citizens from marginal neighborhoods. But the greatest challenge to this option is F20's ability to assemble components of social unrest in the absence of the support of labor union or human rights organizations.

F20 could also switch to clearer political expression—that is, clarifying its positions and establishing fixed goals through a process of consensus. Without *Al-Adl wa al-Ihsan* in its ranks, F20 is relatively homogeneous ideologically, making the task much easier now than was previously the case. The challenge it now faces is to forge consensus among competing and differing ideological tendencies of leftist parties and associations.

Finally, the movement may call for a radical change in the structure of the Moroccan political system and try to reproduce the experience of the popular revolts in Tunisia and Egypt. This option has very little chance of succeeding, because of the lack of internal cohesion among the remaining leftist factions.

The decision *Al-Adl wa al-Ihsan* took to withdraw its support of F20, and the current political context that is characterized by the installation of a new

PJD government led by moderate Islamists loyal to the monarchy, definitely affected F20's political future; Islamist movements are highly suspicious about the secular agendas of the leftists within the movement.

Unlike *Al-Adl wa al-Ihsan*, the PJD vigorously defended the Commander of the Faithful status for the king, ensuring a "state fundamentalism" that coincides with PJD's religious values. Clearly, the current government does not have the magic wand to address the complex political, economic, and social problems Morocco has accumulated over the years. Despite its popularity, the PJD will need more time than determination to convince its own voters and dispel the doubts of the skeptics, who contend that the shift in power in Morocco is really a mirage, for while those in government have changed, their policies remain the same as those who ruled in the past.

Although F20 lasted much longer than other Moroccan protest movements, it has also shown itself to be an ephemeral, sporadic phenomenon. It was the victim of its own boycott strategy. Trapped between two alternatives, either of which seemed equally fatal to its survival, F20 was wary of any exploitation of its endeavors by the state or confiscation of its project by the Islamists. It should be remembered that attractive and convincing models for a different Moroccan society that can gather mass support are in extremely short supply.

NOTES

1   Hereafter, we will refer to the February 20 Movement as F20.

2   Translated from the French by Joseph Ward Swain, republished by Simon & Brown, Hollywood, FL, 2013.

3   Charles Tilly, Louise Tilly, and Richard Tilly, *The Rebellious Century, 1830–1930*, Cambridge, MA: Harvard University Press, 1975.

4   B. Hibou, "Le mouvement du 20 février, le Makhzen et l'antipolitique. L'impensé des réformes au Maroc," CERI, Sciences-Po, May 2011. www.ceri-sciences-po. org.

5   According to Alain Touraine, "The concept of social movement is only useful if it serves to highlight the existence of a particular type of collective action, through which a specific social category challenges a form of social domination, both general and particular, and calls against it to values in the general direction of the society it shares with its opponent in order to deprive the latter of legitimacy." *Le Retour de l'acteur*, Paris: Fayard, 1984, p. 341.

6   See Mohsine El Ahmadi, *The Yasiniste Movement* (in French), Mohammadia, Morocco: *Ittissalat Sabou*, 2006.

7   Al-Adl wa al-Ihsan withdrew from F20 on November 18, 2012, although none of the movement's objectives had yet been achieved. This demonstrated that Al-Adl wa al-Ihsan's participation depended on F20 serving its political agenda.

8   National Democratic Institute, "Youth Perceptions in Morocco: Political Parties in the Wake of Legislative Elections. Findings from Qualitative Research in

Morocco." Conducted in March and April 2012.

9   Ahmed Charai, "The Moroccan Spring," Center for Strategic and International Studies, June 2011. www.fpri.org/enotes/201106.charai.morocco.html. Accessed May 20, 2012.

10   According to Driss El Yazami, "the CNDH's national-level priorities include (1) gender equality (2) the rights of children and young people (3) the rights of 'vulnerable' groups, and (4) the oversight and coordination of a national plan to promote human rights." Cf., Alexis Arieff, Congressional Research Service: Morocco, Current Issues (May 2011). Accessed May 25, 2013.

11   Significantly, the movement's youth employ the expression "*Ma Mfakkin-sh*" (We'll not give up) quite frequently as a slogan, which seems to speak volumes about their actual mindset. (See Mamfakinch.com, "Communiqué *Mamfakinch/ Mamsawtinch*: Appel aux Militant(e)s du 20 Février," June 29, 2011. Accessed July 10, 2012.

12   Jack A. Goldstone, "Understanding the Revolutions of 2011," *Foreign Affairs*, May/June 2011.

REFERENCES

Alexis Arieff, "Morocco: Current Issues," Congressional Research Service, December 20, 2011, pp.1-26.

Ahmed Charai, "The Moroccan Spring," Foreign Policy Research Institute, June 2011. www.fpri.org/enotes/201106.charai.morocco.html. Accessed May 20, 2012.

Alain Touraine, *Le Retour de l'acteur*, Paris: Fayard, 1984, p. 341.

Antimo L. Farr, *Les Mouvements sociaux: diversité, action collective et globalisation*. Montreal: Presses de l'Université de Montréal, 2001.

Azzedine Layachi, "Meanwhile in the Maghreb: Have Algeria and Morocco Avoided North African Unrest?" *Foreign Affairs*, March 31, 2011.

B. Hibou, "Le mouvement du 20 février, le Makhzen et l'antipolitique. L'impensé des réformes au Maroc," CERI, Sciences-Po. (May 2011), www.ceri-sciences-po.org

Charles Tilly, Louise Tilly, and Richard Tilly: *The Rebellious Century, 1830–1930*, Cambridge: Harvard University Press, 1975.

Ismail Hammoudi, "Le mouvement du 20 Février: identité, évolution et perspectives," *Revue Marocaine des Sciences Politiques et Sociales*, Vol. IV *Hors série*, Mars 2012:185–219.

Laila [Layla] Mernissi, "*Le Mouvement du 20 février au Maroc : Vers une seconde indépendance?*"*Revue Averroès*, N° 4–5, 2011, *Spécial Printemps Arabe*. *Mamfakinch*.com, *Appel aux Militant(e)s du 20 Février*," June 29, 2011.

National Democratic Institute, "Youth Perceptions in Morocco: Political Parties in the Wake of Legislative Elections. Findings from Qualitative Research in Morocco." Conducted in March and April 2012.

Youssef Sadik, directeur, *La Révoluion Improbable : Etude des dynamiques protestaire et révolutionnaires dans le Monde arabe*, Rabat : Université Mohammed V, 2015.

Sidney Tarrow, *Power in Movement: Social Movements and Contentious Politics*, Cambridge, UK: Cambridge University Press, 1998.

When the Arab revolts began, small numbers of Algerians poured into the streets to express their solidarity with their Arab neighbors. They were surrounded by police officers. Indeed, the Algerian regime led by President Abdelaziz Bouteflika made it clear that it would not tolerate mass protests. The Algerian population, already traumatized by a long civil war, approached this new series of events with great caution. That conflict had pitted a segment of the Islamist movement, which was on the verge of winning power in free elections, against the military-led state and its supporters, leading to more than 200,000 deaths. The Algerians seemingly did not want to repeat the bloodbath they experienced in the 1990s. Many inequalities exist in Algeria despite large oil and gas revenues. Corruption has siphoned off billions of dollars to army officers, top government officials, and leading bureaucrats, leaving little for social expenditures. Will the threat of revolt change the givens and open state coffers for investment in the social development the country so badly needs? Karim Amellal here tells us why he thinks Algeria avoided a revolt in this last round of regional contestation.

CHAPTER 10
WHY DON'T ALGERIANS START A REVOLUTION?
KARIM AMELLAL

After decades of political sclerosis and inertia, the Maghreb and the Middle East have suddenly become a row of falling dominoes. In this part of the world that had long been considered culturally resistant to any democratic change, values of liberty and democracy have been brandished like banners by young people yearning for a major change in their lives.

Whereas the situation seems paralyzed for the time being, Algeria was not an exception to the rule. In January 2011, it saw several riots take place. Five people were killed and several hundred injured. The unemployed and poor made up the bulk of protesters. All the ingredients were present for a revolution: a spark (the rising price of food), sclerotic politics, an aging leader at the helm for more than a decade, growing inequality despite oil wealth, corruption, and so on. And yet the country remained relatively calm despite the massive upheaval taking place throughout the Arab world. For a nation conceived in revolution, that is quite surprising. So let's try to see why.

First we must remember that Algeria experienced a similar revolution more than twenty years earlier—in October 1988—which has shaped the national imagination and most people's perception of what was now happening abroad. October 1988 was, in a way, a prelude to the 2011 so-called "Arab Spring."

In 1988, the regime was challenged because of a strong economic crisis linked to inept political choices, and huge popular discontent stemming from *hagra*—an Algerian word meaning injustice mixed with resentment. When riots broke out in Algiers and the military (i.e. the National Popular Army, known by the French acronym ANP) reacted with brute force, crowds gathered in the capital, Algiers, to express collective anger. The regime was completely discredited and delegitimized. Corrupt and highly incompetent, President Chadli Benjedid was ousted both by a popular revolt and a cohort of greedy, power-hungry generals who were finally fed up with their own puppet, whom they had manipulated behind the scenes. Thus the road was open for a democratic transition that lasted three short years, ushering in a multiparty system and freedom of the press and association.

However only one party succeeded in matching the Algerians' expectations, providing the only credible alternative to the regime: an Islamist party, the FIS (Islamic Salvation Front), founded in 1989 and immediately legitimized by the state. The FIS, extremely powerful during this period, won the 1990 local elections and was about to win the general elections of 1991, which would have given the Islamists a share in state power. But the military then intervened in a coup d'état to stop the Islamists and regain power. The democratic transition ended abruptly and a civil war began: the GIA (Armed Islamic Groups) emerged and a dramatic struggle against the Algerian government began. The civil war, responsible for approximately 200,000 deaths, finally ended with the election of a new president, Abdelaziz Bouteflika. Most guerilla fighters put down their arms in exchange for amnesty.

In the new, regional context of the Arab Spring, Algerians remembered the unrest and the tragic consequences of their own country's transition process, which started with the fall of President Chadli—in many respects similar to Hosni Mubarak or Zine al-Abdine Ben Ali. Despite the considerable concerns of the public, especially of the youth—half of Algeria's population is under twenty-five—the memory of the civil war is still fresh in people's minds. By weighing the pros and cons of a revolt, most Algerians consider that it is now too early to engage in a process whose outcome is far from certain. The street is not ready for a new revolution that could lead to unpredictable changes—and perhaps bring radical Islamists to power.

The second issue to keep in mind is the important differences that exist between Algeria and its neighbors. Algerians have freedom of expression and a real, if imperfect, multiparty system. These are the components of a centralized regime that is not, however, a dictatorship. In the streets of Algiers, Constantine, or Oran, every Algerian is free to speak and express his or her distrust of the government. The print media are largely free—as opposed to television, which remains under strict state control—and it is very common to read in newspaper columns that a governmental minister is involved in a corruption scandal. Despite all the democratic deficits of the Algerian regime in terms of rights, freedom, and transparency, and the still heavy weight of the military, it would be an exaggeration to describe Algeria as closed, autocratic, or dictatorial, as were Ben Ali's Tunisia and Mubarak's Egypt.

This does not mean, though, that the country's political situation has been fluid. It has, rather, been profoundly entrenched. President Bouteflika began his third five-year term in 2009 and, after changing the constitution to allow him to run again, put an end to general uncertainty (he was suspected to be ill) by running—and winning—again, starting his fourth term in 2014. Moreover, the political landscape was uncertain after Ahmed Ouyahia, former prime minister and leader of the RND (one of the main presidential coalition parties) resigned in January 2013 and Abdelaziz Belkhadem, also a former prime minister, was pushed out of the National Liberation Front (FLN), Algeria's state-dominated party. Therefore, no political heavyweights remain in the game, except President Bouteflika himself.

Thirdly, after the turmoil of the 1990s, Algeria is now a wealthy country with considerable oil and natural gas export revenues, thanks to the economic upturn experienced in recent years and rising oil prices that preceded the downturn of 2014. In 2010, Algeria's foreign exchange reserves reached $150 billion—i.e. more than those of the US ($140 billion), the UK ($118 billion), or Canada ($63 billion). However, with petroleum prices falling to less than $60 per barrel by mid-2015, those reserves were being used up very rapidly. Although these figures mask a tough social reality—with unofficial unemployment rate reaching 25 percent and around 23 percent of the population living below the poverty line—in the past this hydrocarbon prosperity has given the government a certain room to maneuver. It may be losing that cushion faster than ever imagined. In the wake of Ben Ali's fall on January 2011 and Mubarak's the following month, the Algerian regime was also forced to make concessions to ensure that sporadic riots did not degenerate into a mass revolt. The state of emergency was lifted after nineteen years, and during the spring a substantial redistribution plan was adopted, including a massive rise in public spending intended mainly for new housing and job creation. Moreover, in a televised address to the nation, President Bouteflika announced constitutional reform and plans to set up a committee of political leaders and experts to formulate plans to establish a parliamentary democracy. With the president ill and oil prices falling, commentators wondered whether those reforms would be enacted.

Have the promises of more freedom, change, and new social expenditures succeeded in extinguishing the protest movement? Marches regularly organized in Algiers (e.g. in 2012) by the "National Coordination for Democratic Change"—a group of unofficial trade unionists, political opponents of the regime, and human rights activists—had little success and failed to destabilize the government. Perhaps this is why no deep political change has happened in Algeria despite the ongoing feeling of hagra shared by the people: no longer are there strong forces capable of catalyzing protests. The Islamists are still mostly out of the game; even the more moderate among them, who have participated in the governing coalition, have not benefitted from the same level of public support as did the banned FIS at the beginning of the 1990s. Opposition parties—foremost among them, the one with a solid base of popular support, the socialist party (FFS), led by a former opponent Hocine Ait-Ahmed—have been so divided as to be incapable of emerging as a credible alternative to Bouteflika's coalition.

Finally, Algerians have carefully scrutinized the transition process in neighboring Tunisia and nearby Egypt. In Egypt, four years after Mubarak's fall, and two years after the coup d'état that ousted his successor, Mohamed Morsi, Egypt's first democratically elected president, the people are still awaiting the major changes they struggled for. Tunisia, despite a successful democratic transition, still faces major economic problems, due to a drop in tourism and competition from the Chinese in the textile sector.

Algerians now want a democratic evolution, more jobs, and less corruption, not a hazy revolution. But the revolutionary fervor that is firmly rooted in the national spirit could surface again if the legitimate aspirations of the people remain ignored.

PART II
SOCIETY AND CULTURE

||||||||||||||||||||||||||||||||||||||||||||||||||||||||||||||||||||||||||||||||||||||

Any observer of the massive wave of political revolt that has swept the Arab world since the end of 2010 could not help but notice the visible and remarkable role that women have played in it. The author of this chapter, Sahar Khamis, makes it clear that the term "women" refers to all women: young and old, Muslim and Christian, religiously conservative and liberal, veiled and unveiled, rich and poor, reflecting the grassroots, across-the-board movements for political change that they came out to support and for which they rallied. These movements were characterized by egalitarianism and had wide popular appeal. They strove above all for unity, solidarity, and cohesion.

However, this unity and solidarity, whether in countries that witnessed actual political change—such as Tunisia, Egypt, and Libya—or others that are still experiencing tough political struggles—such as Syria, Bahrain, and Yemen—was followed by divisiveness and fragmentation of opinion over which direction societies should move toward in the future. These issues became contentious. Onlookers' assessments of the implications of the Arab citizens' revolt for the future development of the region's political, social, and economic institutions have also differed, as have perceptions of the potential impact on women's movements or the rights of Arab women more generally.

Before discussing the perceived positive and negative implications of the Arab citizens' revolt on Arab women's rights, status, and future, Khamis sheds light on the leadership and activism they manifested amid this wave of political revolts and the iconic images of heroism they created. She also addresses women's dual political and social struggles to secure their own rights and fight for them as women. In both struggles, we read, they relied on cyberactivism.

||||||||||||||||||||||||||||||||||||||||||||||||||||||||||||||||||||||||||||||||||||||

CHAPTER 11
REFLECTIONS ON ARAB WOMEN'S LEADERSHIP AND ACTIVISM IN THE ARAB CITIZENS' REVOLT
SAHAR KHAMIS

THE DUAL STRUGGLE OF ARAB WOMEN

The Arab citizens' revolt produced images of hundreds of thousands of Arab women throughout the region, including in some of the most traditional, conservative countries, such as Libya, Bahrain, and Yemen, taking to the streets alongside men, calling for an end to dictatorship and repression, and demanding dignity, freedom, and democracy.[1] These women did not confine themselves to stereotypical gender roles, such as nurturing or supporting men in their struggle for freedom. Rather, they assumed nonstereotypical roles by taking positions in the front lines of resistance, risking their lives, and exposing themselves to the dangers of arrest or assault. The revolt unveiled "numerous examples of courageous Arab women heroes risking not only their reputations but also their physical safety for the sake of reform."[2]

Beside the political struggles that have been taking place in many parts of the Arab world, there is an equally pressing, ongoing, gender-specific struggle, namely the attempt of women to secure political and social gains for themselves despite many challenges. These include reactionary social forces; the rise of political Islam; the imposition of a top-down cosmetic feminism[3], which only serves those in power; and an unsafe public space, which poses increased risks of rape, humiliation, and harassment. In other words, although Arab women fought alongside men to overcome dictatorship and autocracy, "unlike men, women face two battles: the first for political change and the second to obtain a real change of their societal status to become fully equal to their male counterparts."[4] As Egyptian journalist and activist Yasmine El Sayed Hani remarks, "Our battle is not just fought in Tahrir Square alongside men to oust a corrupt dictator and reform the political system, although we [have] contributed significantly to this struggle. Our battle is also fought in everyday life to demand our rights as women."[5]

This multifaceted sociopolitical struggle has asserted these women's position as members of a "subaltern counterpublic,"[6] as women who form their own resistance communities in political and social domains, both online and offline. By doing so, they are establishing the missing link between private spheres, which have been traditionally (mis)perceived as the feminine domain, and public spheres, which have also been traditionally (mis)perceived as the masculine domain. They can accomplish this transformation by increasing the visibility of women's issues and cultivating support for them in the reordering of their transitional societies. In other words, Arab women's struggle is multifaceted, as it encompasses both political and social dimensions that are closely interlinked and interrelated.[7] As Hani explains, "Our job as women activists is politicizing the social and socializing the political by drawing attention to women's specific needs, demands, and causes and making sure they are taken seriously and incorporated in laws and legislation. For political reform to happen, social reform is also needed."[8]

ARAB WOMEN'S ICONIC IMAGES OF LEADERSHIP IN THE ARAB CITIZENS' REVOLT

Arab women's leadership and activism during the Arab uprisings gave birth to a number of iconic figures who became symbols of resistance and images of heroism. Arab women played an unprecedented leadership role in the uprisings, recognized by the awarding of the 2011 Nobel Peace Prize to Yemeni journalist and human rights activist Tawakkul Karman for her role in inspiring the democratic uprising in her country, which grew from twenty female journalists who gathered to mark the day Tunisia's president Ben Ali fled the country to tens of thousands of women in the weeks and months that followed. She came to be known as the "mother of the revolution" in Yemen and was the first Arab woman ever to win the Nobel Peace Prize. This award was interpreted by many observers as a nod to the Arab revolt and to the great role that Arab women played in it.[9]

Another iconic figure that emerged was twenty-six-year-old Asmaa Mahfouz, who came to be known as "the most brave girl in Egypt," due to her famous online video, or vlog, which was posted on YouTube calling on people to join her on the streets to revolt against Mubarak's dictatorial regime. When Mahfouz heard about the call for Egyptians to take to the streets during the Tunisian uprising, she decided to go to Tahrir Square. Not only did she then participate, she also urged and shamed her male compatriots to do the same. On January 18, 2011, Mahfouz posted on her blog an impassioned plea for solidarity that drew on cultural narratives of males as protectors and defenders of women, challenging them to defend their honor and drawing on the common trope of indignity and rights abuses that had become so prevalent in the few years leading up to the revolt:

> I, a girl, am going down to Tahrir Square, and I will stand alone. And I'll hold up a banner. Perhaps people will show some honor. I even wrote my number so maybe people will come down with me. No one came except ... three guys and three armored cars of riot police ... I'm making this video to give you one simple message: We want to go down to Tahrir Square on January 25. If we still have honor and want to live with dignity in this land, we have to go down on January 25. We'll go down and demand our rights, our fundamental human rights. ... If you think yourself a man, come with me on January 25. Whoever says a woman shouldn't go to protests because she will get beaten, let him have some honor and manhood and come with me on January 25.[10]

Not only did this blog spark mass mobilization and fuel patriotic sentiments, but it also, ironically, challenged gender stereotypes; this, by asserting the right of women to participate publicly in the political arena and encouraging them to do so, while simultaneously drawing on gender stereotypes, which in Egypt traditionally frame men as women's protectors and defenders. Mahfouz conveyed her message brilliantly and achieved the intended outcome of encouraging both men and women to go out onto the streets and protest.

This is representative of Arab women activists' nonstereotypical gender roles more generally during the Arab uprising, when hundreds of thousands of women, young and old, veiled and unveiled, took to the streets across the region, slept in the squares, and climbed atop men's shoulders to rally the public. Pictures of middle-aged women tending to their children in tents, and accounts of older women refusing calls to go inside where they would be safer have become part of the stories told about these revolts.[11]

Asmaa Mahfouz's second moment of fame came with her arrest after Mubarak's overthrow, when she publicly insulted the Supreme Council of the Armed Forces (SCAF), calling it the "council of dogs." She was detained and faced a military trial. But after a huge public outcry, much of it on Twitter and Facebook, the military backed off and released her on bail in August 2011, an act that came to be widely referred to as "released with a hashtag."

In Bahrain, twenty-year-old Ayat al-Gomezi emerged as significant female figure. Al-Gomezi wrote several poems critical of the ruling regime that she recited from the stage on the Pearl Roundabout in Manama, the country's capital, in February and March 2011, when the protests there first began.[12] She became one of the first women revolutionaries to gain international recognition following her arrest for incitement and insulting the royal family. She became an inspiration to many young women in Bahrain, giving them courage and making them proud of their fellow Bahraini citizens.[13]

People shared Gomezi's poems and videos of her performance via Facebook, Twitter, and Blackberry Messenger, and the YouTube video of her recital went viral following her arrest.[14] Although she was the first Bahraini woman to be put on trial following the outbreak of political protests, she was not to be the last.[15] A number of Bahraini women—activists, journalists, or both—followed.[16]

CYBERACTIVISM: A VITAL TOOL FOR ARAB WOMEN ACTIVISTS

Arab women played a pivotal role in inspiring their fellow citizens and other women to take part in the uprisings and build global public support for their cause, often using social media and Internet-based platforms to do so. In nearly each Arab revolt there was a woman who inspired her fellow citizens to join the struggle and stirred the hearts of a global audience that watched on YouTube or joined in on Facebook.[17]

In Libya, for example, as they watched the fall of the regimes in Tunisia and Egypt, young women started talking on Facebook about the need for revolution in their own country. They wrote on each other's walls and started groups to encourage each other and build support for collective action. Others inspired their fellow citizens with their fearlessness in the face of repression and willingness to traverse red lines.[18]

We now know that years before the eruption of the revolts, women activists played a vital role in paving the way for political change and social reform in the Arab world in their different capacities as bloggers, activists, and journalists.

Citizen journalists[19] in the lead-up to the Arab uprisings created awareness among people about their rights and the excesses of the Arab regimes, especially regarding corruption and violations of human rights. One such leading figure was Nawara Negm, the prominent Egyptian activist and blogger, who tackled many of these issues in her popular blog and through her Twitter account, each having tens of thousands of followers.

For many Arab women, posting on Facebook or blogging was the first time they had ever expressed their personal feelings publicly. Cyberactivism, defined as "the act of using the Internet to advance a political cause that is difficult to advance offline,"[20] became a form of empowerment, a way to exert control over personhood and identity while gaining a sense of being able to do something in the face of a patriarchal hierarchy and an authoritarian state. New media provided Arab women with new tools to assert their identities in the public sphere, putting issues of particular concern to them onto the public agenda and making their opinions and voices heard, sometimes for the first time. Cyberactivism provided Arab women the opportunity to play a leading role online and offline by linking virtual dissent with physical protest, by influencing mainstream media, by setting the media and public policy agenda, and by framing the debate about political rights and civil liberties, including the role of women.

One of the main reasons behind Arab women's reliance on cyberactivism is the lingering distrust of mainstream media, cultivated over many years during which dictatorships controlled and manipulated outlets of communication—leading people to rely on personal connections or alternative media to assess the trustworthiness of news. As observed by Yasmine Hani, "Facebook is more trustworthy than mainstream media, because it is based on 'circles of trust.' I connect with people whom I personally know and trust. Therefore we support and propagate each other's causes."[21]

THE FUTURE OF ARAB WOMEN'S LEADERSHIP: PROSPECTS AND OPPORTUNITIES

Looking ahead to the future of Arab women's leadership and activism, we can conclude that there is a general trend of increasing engagement and involvement on the part of Arab women in the political, social, and communication domains. This justifies some optimism concerning women's increasing leadership, continued activism, and rising visibility. It is likely that this leadership and activism will continue to grow, thanks to women's increased reliance on new forms of communication and their mastering of social media tools. This is especially important given that cyberactivism enabled young women in the more conservative countries, such as Libya and Yemen, to participate in the revolts. There are fewer strictures on gender mixing and female comportment online, and anonymity was an option, whereas this was and is not the case in everyday life in most cities and villages, where extended family ties mean that it can be difficult to elude prying eyes and ears.[22]

Yet another reason for optimism regarding the projected future of Arab women's leadership and activism is the increasing prominence of young Arab women among those who shape public opinion in their respective countries—women who have combined online and offline efforts, such as in the cases of Egyptian activists Nawara Negm, Esraa Abdel Fattah, and Asmaa Mahfouz. This has in turn helped boost support for women's issues. For example, Nawara Negm bravely discussed both the issue of women's mass harassment on the streets of Cairo before the Egyptian revolt and the sensitive issue of subjecting female protesters to virginity testing after the uprising; her doing so forced the mainstream media to cover both issues.[23] This spillover in tackling women's issues from the realm of citizen journalism to that of mainstream journalism serves women's interests by drawing attention to their needs, demands, sufferings, and challenges.

By focusing attention on such issues, Yasmine Hani explains, these and other such women used their rising status as prominent public figures and their widely growing popular base of support—due to their large following on social media venues such as Facebook and Twitter—to launch a parallel struggle to support women's rights and to protect them from various forms of assault, violence, harassment, and humiliation. By doing so, Hani told me, "they set good examples and act as positive role models for all citizens, men and women alike."[24]

Those who are optimistic about the future of Arab women's leadership and activism count on their resilience and determination for change and consider them to be the best protection against any possible backlash in women's rights. This camp generally comprises the younger generation of women activists, those who perceive women's rights as only one component of the broader issue of human rights. "Just like there is no giving up on the call for freedom, democracy, and human rights in the Arab world, there is also no giving up when it comes to calling for women's rights, political representation, and equal participation in all walks of life," remarks Nawara Negm, the aforementioned Egyptian political activist and blogger. She adds, however, that "women's rights have to be contextualized within the broader framework of human rights. In other words, Arab women will enjoy their full rights as citizens only when every Arab citizen, regardless of gender, is guaranteed these rights."[25]

Another young Egyptian political activist, Dalia Ziada, who has publicly declared her interest in becoming the "future president of Egypt" when she turns forty—that being the legal age required in the Egyptian constitution to run for the nation's highest office—agrees with this position, indicating that "the change in Arab women's status necessitates a change in the prevailing mindset in Arab societies first."[26]

These young women reflect the pulse of a new generation of Arab women leaders and activists who see no limits to women's progress and achievements in the rapidly changing Arab world, and who are not ready to be hindered by any obstacles or barriers in their political and social struggles.

THE FUTURE OF ARAB WOMEN'S LEADERSHIP: THREATS AND CHALLENGES

Despite the above-mentioned reasons for optimism, there are also a number of limitations and threats that pose challenges to Arab women's continued activism and growing leadership. A host of barriers to full and equal political participation for women remain in place despite regime changes, including unequal economic opportunities, high rates of illiteracy, restrictive personal status laws, and socioreligious systems dominated by men (but supported by many women) that subjugate women to the will of their male family members. The conservative cultures in most Arab countries pose a barrier to women's full participation not only in the real world but also in the virtual world. Therefore it has not always been easy for women to take to the streets or even to become cyberactivists, as they must contend with familial and societal expectations and norms about a woman's ideal role and suitable place in society.[27]

In talking about these barriers to women's political and social participation, however, we need to remember that women have different experiences in each Arab country, and so they cannot be subsumed under one general category. Although the Arab world is generally highly patriarchal, the region varies in terms of women's formal participation in the public sphere. For example, in Egypt, Bahrain, Syria, and Tunisia, women held parliamentary seats prior to the revolt and participated in economic life, while in Yemen and Libya women were largely relegated to the home and not visible in the public sphere.

Another possible threat is the rise of political Islam. Many of the regimes that fell made efforts to staunch the influence of Islamists, who are widely regarded as retrograde on women's rights. Islamists sought political power and influence over the constitutions and laws they drafted to replace those of the previous political systems. For example, the Muslim Brotherhood, long oppressed and banned in Egypt, gained power in fair elections—short-lived though it proved to be, as it and the country's president Mohamed Morsi then fell to a military coup—while the Islamist-influenced Ennahda Movement came to power in Tunisia by the same route. This poses the risk that the space young women need in the public sphere to allow for leadership and activism may continue to be contested, especially for the more liberal and secular among them and those advocating for women's rights.

Additionally, there is the unsafe public space, which poses the risk of rape, humiliation, and harassment, thus threatening Arab women and limiting their political and social participation. For example, when Egyptian women held their first public demonstration on the occasion of International Women's Day on March 8, 2011, "they were vulgarly taunted and bodily assaulted by thugs. … The following day, numbers of women were picked up by the military, beaten, and subjected to virginity tests."[28] Commenting on this incident, which took place one month after Mubarak was ousted from office, Samia Sadek, a journalist with *Rose Al Youssef* magazine in Egypt, remarked, "This march, which was supposed to attract a million women to rally for women's rights, only managed to get five hundred women out to the square. They were shouted at by some men who told them to 'go back to the kitchen.'"[29]

In other countries, especially Libya and Syria, the uprisings were far more deadly and relied on military action rather than peaceful protest—the violence including rape on a massive scale, making women's participation in the streets during the uprisings more risky and otherwise problematic. Women cyberactivists in those countries stayed largely behind the scenes in their homes, taking mobile phone videos, pictures, and reports from the frontlines and uploading them online, as well as spreading information about what was happening elsewhere.[30]

Although Arab women played a central role in the revolts, formalizing their participation in the new political power structures in their transitional societies is proving difficult amid disagreements about electoral quotas, ballot design, constitution drafting, new legislation, and ongoing insecurity. The Arab region is undergoing critical political and social change, but many of the major developmental challenges and deficits in knowledge, freedom, and women's empowerment remain, meaning that women face an uphill battle in their efforts to gain political power or leadership roles. One of the primary points of contention in this regard will be defining the rights of women in constitutional and legal reforms, as well as ensuring their equal representation and participation in elections and decision-making institutions in transforming countries.[31]

Samia Sadek highlights the fact that the number of women who nominated themselves in parliamentary elections in Egypt after the revolt was less than the number of women who were nominated in the last parliamentary election under Mubarak. "This is not an encouraging sign. We need to see more women, not less women, running for elections and nominating themselves for political positions in Egypt," she remarked.[32]

Other like-minded women activists generally fear for the progress and gains women have seen in recent years across so much of the Arab world; which is to say, they are concerned that women may be pushed out of the public sphere of political participation and social visibility and forced back into the private, domestic sphere.

A FINAL WORD

Looking ahead, we can conclude that there is no turning back when it comes to women's pivotal roles in the Arab world. Young women across the region rejected the idea that social relations and the perceptions of women's roles could retrogress to what they were before the Arab uprisings. The translation of online experiences and relationships offline blurs the lines between the real and virtual worlds, public and private lives, and the political and social domains. This provides new and varied opportunities to expand women's circles of influence and to enable them to interact with people they never could have met otherwise.

Arab women's prominent positions of leadership and activism in both the real and virtual worlds provide firm evidence that the Arab uprising has been more than just a political revolt. Rather, it has been a social and communication revolt as well, since Arab women activists have in fact been upending traditional hierarchies, reinterpreting religious dogma, breaking taboos, and bringing new issues into the public sphere.

Yet it is important to bear in mind that Arab women's participation did not start and end with the initial protests in the streets, but rather continues to expand as youth in Egypt, Libya, and Tunisia have fought to consolidate their gains; as Bahrainis and Syrians persist in fighting for political change; and as Yemenis continue to demand their most basic rights. As the uprisings have continued in some places in the region, Internet access has expanded, and the popularity of Twitter and Facebook grown, new groups of women have become inspired to participate both online and offline while redefining the meaning of citizenship, civic engagement, and private versus public spheres.[33]

Almost five years after the eruption of the Arab uprisings, however, Arab women are not as optimistic as they were in the earlier heady days of daily demonstrations and confrontations. According to a recent Arab youth survey[34], young men felt more optimistic about the direction in which their countries were heading (58 percent) than young women (50 percent). This is partly because women must fight to remain visible in the new spaces they have claimed as part of the public sphere and must continue struggling for their most basic rights as citizens.

Yet Arab women have carved out new spaces for debate and discussion in the public sphere, both physically and rhetorically, through activism on the streets, as well as online agenda-setting and mobilization. In doing so, they erased red lines that had previously kept topics such as torture, political succession, and sexual harassment off limits. Therefore they are unlikely to retreat from the public sphere no matter what lies in the future.

However, the impact of such efforts on the political, social, and communication landscapes in their countries, and the speed with which they can bring about actual change in their societies will vary from one country to another depending on a myriad of political, economic, and social factors. In assessing the future roles and leadership prospects of women it is therefore important to remember the uniqueness and individuality of each Arab country.

But in making such projections it would be reasonable to adopt a middle-ground of cautious optimism, one that takes into account the overall picture in this rapidly changing region—with all its political, economic, and social challenges and uncertainties, as well as its unprecedented breakthroughs and victories in support of human rights and political freedom. The mere fact that women in some of the most traditional and conservative Arab societies—such as Libya, Yemen, and Bahrain—broke out of their cocoons and rallied in huge numbers for many months under the most dangerous conditions, exposing themselves to injury, imprisonment, or even death, signals a new era in the history of this region and women's evolving roles in it.

That is not to say that the popular uprisings in these countries or the political transformations they have witnessed will automatically put an end to all forms of discrimination, inequality, or injustice against women. Rather, it means that Arab women today are much more willing to fight bravely and openly for their rights and are much more capable of defending themselves against negative practices. The myriad of political activities that Arab women have been engaging in in recent years in this highly volatile region are serving to write a new chapter in the history of Arab feminism, as well as the history of the entire region. Just as there is no turning back completely in the region's political history—despite the apparent undoing of the revolt and its accompanying democratic ideals in Egypt, the chaos that has taken hold of Libya, and the continuing wars in Iraq and Syria—it may be safe to predict that there is no turning back for Arab feminists, despite the hardships they may suffer or the obstacles they may encounter. They have known the road to freedom and they are determined to reach their goals despite any obstacles or hardships.[35]

NOTES

1   Courtney Radsch. "Bahrain's Young Women Keep the Revolution Aloud," Women's E-News. Last modified July 28, 2011. Accessed November 8, 2012. womensenews.org/story/leadership/110727/bahrains-young-women-keep-the-revolution-aloud; Courtney Radsch. "Unveiling the Revolutionaries: Cyberactivism and the Role of Women in the Arab Uprisings," James A. Baker III Institute for Public Policy, Rice University. Accessed November 10, 2012. bakerinstitute.org/publications/ITP- pub-CyberactivismAndWomen-051712.pdf; Sahar Khamis "The Arab 'Feminist' Spring?" *Feminist Studies*, 37, no. 3, 2011: 692–695.

2   A. al-Malki, D. Kaufer, S. Ishizaki, and K. Dreher, *Arab Women in Arab News: Old Stereotypes and New Media*. Doha: Bloomsbury Qatar Foundation Publishing, 2012. "Arab Youth Survey 2012." ASDAA Burson-Marsteller. Accessed November 12, 2012. www.arabyouthsurvey.com/english/findtop10.php 81

3   The term "cosmetic feminism" refers to an artificial, elite-imposed, top-down, government-sponsored feminism, which doesn't stem from the grassroots and doesn't reflect the pulse or the needs of ordinary women.

4   Wafa Alamm, "Reflections on Women in the Arab Spring: Women's Voices From Around the World." Woodrow Wilson Center. Last modified March 5, 2012. www.wilsoncenter.org/sites/default/files/International %20Women% 27s%20Day %202012_4.pdf, 14

5   Yasmine El Sayed Hani, personal communication with the author. Washington DC, November 15, 2012.

6   Nancy Fraser, "Rethinking the Public Sphere," *Habermas and the Public Sphere*, edited by Craig Calhoun Cambridge, Mass.: MIT Press, 1992, pp. 109–142.

7   Sahar Khamis, "Islamic Feminism in New Arab Media: Platforms for Self-Expression and Sites for Multiple Resistances," *Journal of Arab and Muslim Media Research* 3, no. 3, 2010: 237--255.

8   Hani, personal communication with the author. Washington D.C., November 15, 2012.

9   S. Khamis, "The Arab 'Feminist' Spring?" 2011.

10 C. Radsch, "Unveiling the Revolutionaries," 2012.

11 C. Radsch, "Unveiling the Revolutionaries," 2012.

12 See her blog entry at ayat-algormezi.blogspot.com

13 C. Radsch, "Bahrain's Young Women," 2011.

14   See YouTube video at www.youtube.com/watch?v=K8-qOerX3xI

15   See www.englishpen.org/bahrain-poet-and-writer-arrested-fears-for-their-safety

16   C. Radsch, "Bahrain's Young Women," 2011.

17   S. Khamis, "The Arab 'Feminist' Spring?" 2011; C. Radsch, "Bahrain's Young Women," 2011; C. Radsch, "Unveiling the Revolutionaries," 2012.

18   C. Radsch, "Unveiling the Revolutionaries," 2012.

19   W. Lance Bennett, ed., "Changing Citizenship in the Digital Age," *Civic Life Online: Learning How Digital Media Can Engage Youth*, Cambridge: MIT Press, 2008, pp. 1–24; Stephen Coleman. "Blogs and the New Politics of Listening." *The Political Quarterly*, 76, no. 2 (2005): 272–280.

20   Philip N. Howard, *The Digital Origins of Dictatorship and Democracy: Information Technology and Political Islam*, Oxford: Oxford University Press, 2011, p. 145.

21   Hani, personal communication with the author. Washington D.C., November 15, 2012.

22   C. Radsch "Unveiling the Revolutionaries," 2012.

23   A. al-Malki et al. "Arab Women in Arab News," 2012.

24   Hani, personal communication with the author. Washington DC, November 15, 2012.

25   Nawara Negm, personal communication with the author, Cairo, Egypt, July 30, 2012.

26   Dalia Ziada, commentary by Skype during the event "Revolution and Women's Rights: The Case of Egypt" at the Middle East Program of the Woodrow Wilson International Center for Scholars, Washington, D.C., June 15, 2011.

27   S. Khamis, "The Arab 'Feminist' Spring?" 2011; C. Radsch, "Unveiling the Revolutionaries," 2012.

28   Margot Badran, "Reflections on Women in the Arab Spring: Women's Voices From Around the World." Woodrow Wilson Center. Last modified March 5, 2012. www. wilsoncenter.org/sites/default/files/International%20Women%27s%20 Day%202012_4.pdf, p. 12.

29   Samia Sadek, personal communication with the author. Washington D.C., October 23, 2011.

30   C. Radsch, "Unveiling the Revolutionaries," 2012.

31   S. Khamis, "The Arab 'Feminist' Spring?" 2011; C. Radsch, "Unveiling the Revolutionaries," 2012.

32   Sadek, personal communication with the author, Washington D.C., October 23, 2011.

33   S. Khamis, "The Arab 'Feminist' Spring?" 2011; C. Radsch, "Bahrain's Young Women," 2011; C. Radsch, "Unveiling the Revolutionaries," 2012.

34   Arab Youth Survey, 2012.

35   S. Khamis, "The Arab 'Feminist' Spring?" 2011.

REFERENCES

Alamm, Wafa. "Reflections on Women in the Arab Spring: Women's Voices From Around the World." Woodrow Wilson Center. Last modified March 5, www.wilsoncenter.org/sites/default/files/International %20Women%27s%20 Day%202012_4.pdf.

Al-Malki, A., Kaufer, D., Ishizaki, S., and Dreher, K. *Arab Women in Arab News: Old Stereotypes and New Media*. Doha: Bloomsbury Qatar Foundation Publishing, 2012.

"Arab Youth Survey 2012." ASDAA Burson-Marsteller. Accessed November 12, 2012. www.arabyouthsurvey.com/english/findtop10.php.

Badran, Margot. "Reflections on Women in the Arab Spring: Women's Voices From Around the World." Woodrow Wilson Center. Last modified March 5, 2012. www. wilsoncenter.org/sites/default/files/International%20Women%27s%20Day%20 2012_4.pdf.

Bennett, W. Lance. "Changing Citizenship in the Digital Age," *Civic Life Online: Learning How Digital Media Can Engage Youth*, edited by W. Lance Bennett, Cambridge: MIT Press, 2008.

Coleman, Stephen. "Blogs and the New Politics of Listening." *The Political Quarterly*, 76, no. 2, 2005: 272–280.

Fraser, Nancy. "Rethinking the Public Sphere," *Habermas and the Public Sphere*, edited by Craig Calhoun, 109–142. Cambridge, Mass.: MIT Press, 1992.

Hani, Yasmine El Sayed. Personal communication with the author. Washington D.C., November 15, 2012.

Howard, Philip N. *The Digital Origins of Dictatorship and Democracy: Information Technology and Political Islam*. Oxford: Oxford University Press, 2011.

Khamis, Sahar. "Islamic Feminism in New Arab Media: Platforms for Self-Expression and Sites for Multiple Resistances," *Journal of Arab and Muslim Media Research* 3, no.3 (2010): 237–255.

Khamis, Sahar. "The Arab 'Feminist' Spring?" *Feminist Studies*, 37, no. 3 (2011): 692–695.

Negm, Nawara. Personal communication with the author, Cairo, Egypt, July 30, 2012.

Radsch, Courtney. "Bahrain's Young Women Keep the Revolution Aloud," *Women's E-News*. Last modified July 28, 2011. Accessed November 8, 2012. womensenews org/story/leadership/110727/ bahrains-young-women-keep-the-revolution-aloud.

Radsch, Courtney. "Unveiling the Revolutionaries: Cyberactivism and the Role of Women in the Arab Uprisings," James A. Baker III Institute for Public Policy, Rice University. Accessed November 10, 2012. bakerinstitute.org/publications/ITP- pub-CyberactivismAndWomen-051712.pdf.

Sadek, Samia. Personal communication with the author, Washington, D.C., October 23, 2011.

Ziada, Dalia. Commentary by Skype during the event "Revolution and Women's Rights: The Case of Egypt" at the Middle East Program of the Woodrow Wilson International Center for Scholars, Washington, D.C., June 15, 2011.

II

Tunisia and Syria were among the more preposterous as well as repressive of the region's authoritarian regimes. Preposterous in Syria, as Lisa Wedeen brilliantly illustrated with cartoons and thick descriptions of the cult of Hafez al-Assad, inculcating obedience by requiring performances of fealty in which nobody believed.[1] Ridiculous in Tunisia for having Zine al-Abdine Ben Ali, a mediocre apparatchik from military intelligence services, not only overthrow the supreme warrior, Habib Bourguiba, but also mimic his personality cult with a narrative that was "peculiar in its naïveté" (Chapter 2).[2] Perhaps, as Kai Hafez has argued, the two regimes were also among the region's most repressive because each was defending an unpopular secular ideal.[3] Whatever the possible similarities, however, this chapter underlines major structural differences between Syria and Tunisia that explain the critical variations not only in their recent political awakenings but also why Egypt, not Syria or Libya, could be Tunisia's most faithful echo. The big structural difference concerns their respective private sectors and banking systems. Tunisia, like Egypt, had generated a substantial, if politically subordinate private sector from a restructured socialist economy, whereas Syria, like Libya and Yemen, had consigned theirs, either by design or lack of financial capacity, to the shadows of the informal economy. While the IMF and the World Bank had pressured most of these countries to engage in neoliberal reform, private sector development varied significantly. Tunisian and Egyptian businesses enjoyed considerably more commercial bank financing than the others.

IIIIIIIIIIIIIIIIIIIIIIIIIIIIIIIIIIIIIIIIIIIIIIIIIIIIIIIIIIIIIIIIIIIIIIIIIIIIIIIIIIIIIIII

CHAPTER 12*
POLITICAL ECONOMIES OF TRANSITION
CLEMENT HENRY

INTRODUCTION

This chapter focuses on the specific national differences that explain variations in the mobilization of Arab protest movements and their potential outcomes, possibly "transitions to democracy," rather than on general economic determinants of unrest or "revolution," such as youth bulges and unemployment, rising food prices, growing inequalities in income distribution, the alienation of previously protected public sector labor, and the like that are common to the entire region.[4] Economic grievances were fairly similar throughout the southern Mediterranean,[5] and arguably the countries faced similar pressures,

IIIIIIIIIIIIIIIIIIIIIIIIIIIIIIIIIIIIIIIIIIIIIIIIIIIIIIIIIIIIIIIIIIIIIIIIIIIIIIIIIIIIIIII

*Adapted from Clement Henry and Ji-Hyang Jang, eds., *The Arab Spring: Will It Lead to Democratic Transitions?* Houndsmills Basignstoke, UK: Palgrave MacMillan, 2013. Used by permission.

but my concern is to understand why rising discontent and widespread perceptions of regime illegitimacy took the forms and timing that they did across the region between December 2010 and the following long summer of 2011, with no end of transitions in sight.

Let me also confess at the outset that my argument hinges on a practical convergence of Franco-American with German conceptions of civil society. For the former, as illustrated by Alexis de Tocqueville, the art of association lies at the root of democracy's defense against the tyranny of the majority. For Hegel and Marx, on the other hand, civil society is simply bourgeois political economy—the private sector buttressed by law courts and police forces. These very different intellectual traditions do converge, however, in very concrete ways, whether in Paris, Berlin, Cairo, or Tunis. Associations, whatever their cause, need funding from private enterprises and/or foundations if they are to display any independence in expressing the interests of their constituents. Let me offer two quick illustrations from my portfolio of interviews with Tunisians over the years: Ahmed Mestiri, leader of the liberal opposition within the ruling party in the early 1970s and 1980s, could not sustain many editions of his opposition party's newspaper in 1986 because local businesses did not dare advertise in it for fear of antagonizing the government. More recently, in June 2011, Abdeljelil Bedoui, president of Tunisia's Higher Education Union, announced a new labor party to contest the Islamists. One of his first steps was to contact elements of the business community—presumably in such sectors as tourism, which were concerned with containing the Islamist Ennahda Movement and other, more radical Islamist parties—to raise funds to establish a national network of party offices to campaign in the October elections. Whether in 1986 or 2011, such experiences were inconceivable in Syria or any other of the Arab states with weak to nonexistent private business sectors.[6]

Intermediary bodies or secondary associations, whether they be interest groups or political parties, are weak throughout the Arab region: De Tocqueville's art of association, axiomatic in American political science as expressed in Arthur Bentley's seminal work[7], did not travel well from north to southern Italy, much less points further south.[8] Consequently, "limited pluralism," the defining feature of "authoritarian" regimes, makes less sense in Arab countries than in Franco's Spain, which inspired Juan Linz with the concept.[9] The entire literature concerning transitions to democracy connotes starting and end points, but these points get blurred in the absence of intermediary bodies and at least "limited" pluralism. "Pacted" democracies characteristic of some Latin American and southern European transitions, for instance, entail viable intermediaries representing various constituencies.

This is not to argue that the Arab countries are necessarily stuck in some hybrid halfway house.[10] Rather, terms with emotive meaning like "democracy" and even "transition" are moving targets, bound to specific national contexts. To the extent, however, that "transition to democracy" connotes a move to liberal pluralism (as well as to supposedly free and fair elections), the concept is more applicable to countries that host private business communities and support associations (including labor unions) than to those in whi ch private enterprise remains small, furtive, and informal. Transitions gain more traction in Egypt and Tunisia, countries with more private businesses and stronger associations, than in Libya, Syria, or Yemen.

TYPOLOGIES OF POLITICAL ECONOMIES

Robert Springborg and I presented a typology of Arab political systems before January 2011 that roughly coincided with variations in their respective command and control systems for allocating credit to the economy.[11] On the political front, there was only one true formal democracy, Lebanon, amid a variety of monarchies and undemocratic forms of republican rule. Democracy went hand in hand in Lebanon (as in Turkey) with a relatively competitive, privately owned commercial banking system. Some of the monarchies also harbored banking structures that were privately owned and appeared to be relatively competitive, although ruling families usually wielded decisive influence behind the scenes—as was perhaps still the case in the formal democracy of Lebanon's Rafiq Hariri (1944–2005).

Of special interest for understanding the Arab awakening, however, were the differences among the more authoritarian republics. Egypt and Tunisia, the bully police states depicted in Table 1 (below), had stronger states than the bunkers. They deployed power through relatively autonomous administrative structures and other controlled intermediary bodies interacting with them. In the nineteenth century, Egypt's Muhammad Ali and Tunisia's Ahmad Bey engaged in modern state-building, and these republics, unlike others in the Arab world, enjoyed previous legacies as political entities living off their respective sedentary tax bases.[12]

Both Egypt and Tunisia also substantially altered the commanding heights of their respective economies in the 1970s. To open up their respective economies to foreign investment, they encouraged private ownership in their commercial banking systems, although a heavy influence of state-owned banks remained. As Table 1 also shows, the bankers in these bully state regimes allocated substantially more credit to the private sector than did those in the bunkers, who were not real bankers but usually continued, as in the heady days of state socialism, to be state officials doling out off-budget patronage.

The bunker regimes are legacies of less developed states. There is little civil society: the state, to borrow the expression of French political scientist Jean Leca discussing Algeria, is "folded in" on the society and directly managed by clans, tribes, or personal networks, not developed bureaucracies.[13] None of the bunker regimes allows credible intermediary bodies capable of making "pacted" transitions: there are no principals capable of representing critical constituencies other than primary groups of family, clan, tribe, sect, or clientele. By contrast the bullies maintained appearances of intermediary bodies in supposedly vibrant civil societies, even if the reality was police control, taken to absurd extremes in Tunisia.

Progressive monarchies, notably those of Morocco and to a lesser extent the more recently reinvented dynasties of Bahrain, Jordan, and Kuwait, also nurtured a variety of intermediaries that serve as shock absorbers and might perform "pacted" transitions to democracy. On the smallest scale, Bahrain, which like Kuwait had occasionally experimented with parliamentary representation, might have experienced genuine reform had Saudi Arabia not intervened. The other family-run municipalities and larger members of the Gulf Cooperation Council (GCC) seem more akin to the bunker republics, however, for their prime intermediaries, too, are families, tribes, and patron-client networks, not political parties or other forms of secondary associations. Much wealthier than the other bunkers, however, they have preempted any revolt of their potentially restive populations with substantial social spending programs. Their bunkers, to pursue the metaphor, are more akin to bank vaults than to underground military fortresses.

Table 1 shows that our political typology correlates closely with commercial banking structures, the command and control systems of the political economy. These political and economic structures also bear an interesting correlation with the second column of the table, Contract Intensive Money (CIM). CIM is the percentage of money supply (M2) held by the domestic banks rather than by individuals who prefer to keep their cash away from these public institutions. It indicates the outreach of a country's financial infrastructure and possibly also the security more generally of property rights under the rule of law.[14] As Lewis Snider observes:

> Where institutions are highly informal, i.e. where contract enforcement and security of property rights are inadequate, and the policy environment is uncertain, transactions will generally be self-enforcing and currency will be the only money that is widely used. Where there is a high degree of public confidence in the security of property rights and in contract enforcement, other types of money that are invested in banks and other financial institutions and instruments assume much more importance.[15]

Banking	Structure						
Market	Ownership	As % of GDP	Credit 2007 (constant mm USD 2000)	CIM Ranking (2007)	2007	Regime Type
Competitive	private	75.6%	15,822	Lebanon	97.9%	democracy
Oligopoly	private	69.6%	35,279	Kuwait	96.6 %	monarchy
Oligopoly	private	41.6%	9,222	Qatar	96.2 %	monarchy
Competitive	private	78.4%	6,686	Bahrain	95.4%	monarchy
Competitive	private	64.3%	68,686	UAE	90.4%	monarchy
Oligopoly	private	40.4%	97,777	Saudi Arabia	90.9%	monarchy
Oligopoly	private	32.0%	8,562	Oman	90.8%	monarchy
Competitive	public	50.6%	68,851	Egypt	86.5%	bully
Competitive	private	99.0%	12,731	Jordan	86.2%	monarchy
Competitive	public	64.3%	17,435	Tunisia	85.4%	bully
Oligopoly	private	69.6%	36,512	Morocco	81.4%	monarchy
	public	7.2%	3,265	Libya	82.3%	bunker
Oligopoly	public	13.3%	9,745	Algeria	71.1%	bunker
	public	7.9%	977	Yemen	71.9%	bunker
		12.5%	2,712	Sudan	71.4%	bunker
Oligopoly	public	16.2%	4,315	Syria	68.1%	bunker
		3.9%	799	Iraq	47.9%	bunker

Note: CIM = (M2 minus Money outside Domestic Banking System)/M2
Source: IMF Financial Statistics, lines 14a, 34, and 35, from Henry and Springborg (2010): 81, 95, 104.

Table 1. Regime Types and CIM, Credit, and Commercial Banking Structures

The one Arab democracy and the small wealthy GCC countries enjoy the highest CIM scores, whereas the bunker regimes score lowest, indeed reflecting a general distrust of any public institutions and preferences for informal economy. Libya's Muammar Gaddafi at one point banned money altogether—virtually expropriating the middle classes—but then, floating on oil revenues generating a relatively high per capita income, Libya became the sole bunker to exceed a CIM of 80 percent and surpass Morocco despite its much smaller trickle of credit to the private sector. Table 1 shows the relative amount of credit to the private sector that the various type of regime allocate. It is hardly surprising that the higher the CIM, the greater the amount of credit a banking system may generate. Note that only Iraq, bunkered in its Green Zone, allocates even less credit as a percentage of GDP in the private sector than Libya.

Commercial banking systems tend to be the mirror image of the real economy and to reflect its structure. The banks may be publicly or privately owned, and their market shares may be concentrated into a small number of banks or less concentrated, and therefore potentially more competitive in structure. Table 1 indicates the four possibilities. The bunkers all fall into the category of concentrated public ownership, whereas the bullies, while retaining predominantly public ownership, display more diversified banking systems as well as consistently greater credit allocations to the private sector. The monarchies, by contrast all display predominantly privately owned banks, albeit with varieties of greater competition in Jordan to a relatively concentrated, oligopolistic system of royal control in Morocco.

It seems no coincidence that the bully regimes were the first to experience the Arab awakening. After practicing state socialism in the 1960s, they also developed dense webs of private sector interests, as indicated by outstanding credits to the economy, which could support civil society. Monarchies of course also harbor significant private sectors but usually manipulate them more astutely: Morocco's Makhzen, for instance, used the concentrated banking system to leverage new forms of royal patronage. The bullies were less skilled in not only the political but also financial arts. Their patronage generated substantially larger proportions of nonperforming loans, as regime sycophants as well as public enterprises simply neglected to repay their debts. Politically, too, the presidents who relied on ruling parties appeared less able than monarchs to stay above politics. Bullying their civil societies required ever larger security forces, up to one police person (including plainclothesmen and thugs) for every fifty Egyptians and every seventy Tunisians. (See Chapter 2 for the exaggerated figures given by Ben Ali for his police force.—Eds.)

A cross-sectional view of commercial banking structures taken in the mid-1990s can be interpreted, indeed, as the march of civil society across the broader region of the Middle East and North Africa, including Iran, Israel, and, of special interest to observers of the Arab awakening, Turkey, the bell-wether of praetorian statist regimes that moved furthest toward democracy. In the 1930s and 1940s, before the advent of a multiparty system, that country's banks were largely government-owned and dominated by three or four big banks. By the 1990s, more of them were privately owned and the structure was less concentrated.

Table 2 shows a scatter plot of the region's commercial banking structures, indicating the degree of state ownership along the horizontal (x) axis and the degree of concentration of their respective markets along the vertical (y) axis.[16] Our praetorian bunker states are all lined up in the upper right-hand quadrant of highly concentrated state-owned banking systems. Further down, still largely state-owned, are Egypt and Tunisia, marching in a path toward Turkish and Lebanese democracy, reflected in their diversified, predominantly privately owned commercial banks.

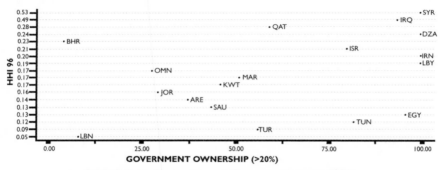

Table 2. Bank Ownership and Concentration, mid 1990s

The monarchies—and Israel for that matter—tend to have more con-centrated banking systems, reflecting the oligopolistic control of their ruling families, who are also heavily steeped in commerce and control the working capital provided by the banks.

This temporal cross-section of the region's commercial banking structures offers further clues about potential political transitions. Among the republics, Tunisia had marched slightly further down the line than Egypt, and both of them are clearly much closer to Turkey than Libya, Algeria, Iraq, and Syria—or Iran for that matter. The two bullies by the mid-1990s had clearly emerged from the bunkers of state socialism. In the heyday of Arab socialism, Egypt, with its four state-owned banks, would have clustered with Algeria, Syria, and Iraq at the extremities of concentration and state ownership, extremes that Tunisia's more prudent leadership had avoided. The two bully regimes had progressed the furthest in structural adjustment by the 1990s and were enjoying steady 5 percent growth rates in much of the following decade. Many social and political strains accompanied the new dynamic.

TUNISIA AND EGYPT

Before 2011 Tunisia's "sweet little" rogue regime, positioned among the "Worst of the Worst," already seemed the ripest candidate in the region for political change.[17] Of the non–oil states its per capita income was second only to Lebanon's. Prudent economic management had generated the highest average per capita wealth growth rate since 1987, the year General Zine al-Abdine Ben Ali succeeded Habib Bourguiba as president. The regime boasted of home ownership for 80 percent of the population as a sign of growing middle and lower middle classes. Its carefully crafted policies of export-led growth had fostered a light manufacturing base with as much value-added as neighboring Algeria's, with triple Tunisia's population. Economic success indeed rendered Ben Ali's crude dictatorship a political anomaly. His police regime tortured dissidents, mugged investigative journalists, imprisoned youth for circumventing Internet filters, and destroyed any semblance of judicial autonomy but could not insulate its largely literate population from constant interaction with their European neighbors, the closest of which was only ninety miles across the Mediterranean. As Jack Goldstone observes:

> For a revolution to succeed, a number of factors have to come together. The government must appear so irremediably unjust or inept that it is widely viewed as a threat to the country's future; elites (especially in the military) must be alienated from the state and no longer willing to defend it; a broad-based section of the population, spanning ethnic and religious groups and socioeconomic classes, must mobilize; and international powers must either refuse to step in to defend the government or constrain it from using maximum force to defend itself.[18]

Such description fitted Tunisia perfectly, if "state" in this context is taken to mean "regime."

By 2010 the government's "irremediable" injustice was as apparent to rural folk as to upscale Tunis's chattering classes. Wikileaks confirmed much of the gossip about Leila Trabelsi, Ben Ali's wife, and other members of her notorious family as well as other Ben Ali in-laws, thanks to judicious reporting by US Ambassador Robert F. Godec.[19] After 2007 the invasion of the Ben Ali and Trabelsi clans into lucrative slices of the Tunisian economy accelerated. Credit to this web of some 114 individuals reached 3 billion dinars by 2011 ($2.2 billion) and even more serious, in the opinion of Dr. Mustapha Nabli, Tunisia's highly respected governor of the Central Bank (from January 2011 until June 2012) brought in to clean up the mess, was how it had doubled in 2009 and again in 2010, revealing how ravenous the appetites of the ruling thieves were becoming.[20] Family members had gained control of two of the country's principal private sector banks. They were highly visible, and information about their predations traveled rapidly across the country via Facebook as well as word of mouth, but mobilizing the population required intermediaries on the ground as well. As the sheer amount of outstanding credit to the private sector noted in Table 1 suggests, civil society had the potential organizational capacity.

Structural variables cannot offer tipping points or explain how one particular case of self-immolation of the many that had happened in Tunisia since the 1990s can set off the sort of chain reaction that got underway on December 17, 2010 and sent Ben Ali packing twenty-eight days later, on January 14, 2011. Nor does the profile of a bully police state explain why one such state started off an Arab chain reaction and not another. Tunisia was perhaps better positioned than Egypt because it was smaller (with an eighth of Egypt's population), wealthier, and had less geopolitical weight. The Americans could be and were, at little cost, on the right side of history.

Tunisia's greater wealth was also correlated with greater associational activity; Internet connectivity; and, proportionate to population, greater Facebook membership, as Table 3 indicates. Perhaps equally important, the country's very success in building up an export-and-services-led economy may have led to the dictator's downfall. The contrast that emerged—a relatively dynamic economy blocked only by visible, top-heavy centralized corruption—became too great for Tunisia's marginalized elites. Yet Tunisia's economic growth could not keep pace with an ever-expanding education system. Over 50 percent of the country's secondary school and university educated were unemployed in 2005, a record in North Africa; and possibly the aftershocks of world recession, coupled with high food prices, affected Tunisia more adversely than it did its neighbors because trade constitutes a substantially larger proportion of Tunisia's GDP.

The other factor conducive to a successful revolution in Jack Goldstone's view was a military "alienated from the state and no longer willing to defend it." There were, and indeed still are, major structural differences between the Egyptian and Tunisian military, but the overriding similarity was that each was prepared to defend the state against a corrupt leadership and dirty police. Egypt and Tunisia, after all, exemplified the strongest, most developed states in the region. The differences were that the Tunisian armed forces were small, professional, and distrusted and marginalized by Ben Ali, whereas the Egyptian armed forces were an integral part of the regime, embedded in its political economy, and headed by a Supreme Council (SCAF) that could trace its ancestry to Nasser's Revolutionary Command Council. These differences, however, did not affect the outbreak of popular protest nor the military's role in each case of defending the protestors against the incumbent leadership's paramilitary security forces and thugs.

The catalyst to Tunisia's revolt of January 14, 2011, mirrored the country's economic predicaments yet also acted out earlier visions of political change. The self-immolated youth, Mohamed Bouazizi, a high school dropout who had aspired to go to university, was a replica of Manfred Halpern's New Middle Class, the putative regional dynamo of the 1960s.[21] But the new catalyst lived in Sidi Bouzid, a rural periphery at Tunisia's geographic center, not the capital city. Village protest in Sidi Bouzid resonated in other peripheral centers, notably Thala and Kasserine, where the Tunisian army prevented further police brutality. As protests spread finally east to Sfax and up the coast to Tunis, the army remained studiously neutral while security forces eventually fractured, accelerating Ben Ali's departure on January 14.[22]

Only eleven days later the "Tunisation"[23] of other Arabs proceeded with Egypt's first Day of Rage. Perhaps some electronic exchanges between Tunisian and Egyptian youth facilitated Egypt's quick awakening. Certainly Egypt's Day of Rage, although planned before Ben Ali's demise, would not have had such a spectacular outcome without the Tunisian precedent. But the two countries also displayed their structural similarities, including a private sector and civil society of sorts. Despite having a poorer, more rural, less literate society, it then took the Egyptians only eighteen days, compared to Tunisia's twenty-eight, to oust their dictator. But just as the structures of political economy underlay these early Arab uprisings, they also conditioned their resultant dilemmas.

In Tunisia the armed forces have few economic interests apart from their own upkeep and have stayed out of politics. The contrast with Egypt could not be sharper. In Egypt, revolt was pretty much confined to major cities, not the rural peripheries that had grounded Tunisian urban protest. And while ostensibly defending the Egyptian insurgents against a counterrevolution managed by security police thugs, the Egyptian military connived to expel the president while preserving its economic interests, hence those of the old regime.

Tunisia and Egypt both experienced political decapitations but with very different consequences. The Tunisian insurgents, liberated from Ben Ali and protected by the military, could purge the old regime, up to a point, whereas their Egyptian counterparts were blocked. Egypt's Supreme Council of the Armed Forces (SCAF), headed by Field Marshal Mohamed Hussein Tantawi, protected the extensive economic interests of the senior and retired officer corps. SCAF was happy to see Mubarak and his sons go because they threatened these interests. But only if popular insurrection precipitated changes within the army command might Egypt clean out the corrupt networks of its political economy.

The business networks of the two bully regimes also displayed significant differences. Corruption in Tunisia was highly centralized and top-heavy. Cut off the head and then the cancer, directly infecting some 113 individuals, is curable with further judicial surgery.[24] Indeed, if Tunisia was to continue its prudent export-oriented economic policies, its new political climate could attract the substantial local as well as foreign investment that the kleptocracy had deterred. In Egypt, by contrast, the cancer was more widespread, and SCAF, committed to protecting its extensive interests, did not wish to probe too deeply. SCAF and the Tunisian transitional authorities might compete with one another in exposing the financial misdemeanors of their former presidential families, but they faced different problems.

Each country enjoyed the advantage—unlike the bunkers—of a state with a functioning bureaucracy detached from social forces. As Shain and Linz have argued, "one of the most important elements for ensuring a democratic outcome by any interim government is for the state to retain sufficient bureaucratic apparatus and minimal respect for the rule of law."[25] In post-Mubarak Egypt, SCAF even enjoyed a certain legitimacy, buttressed by a referendum in March in support of their proposed constitutional amendments. In Tunis, many might also have welcomed provisional military rule, but General Rachid Ammar wisely determined to preserve Bourguiba's legacy of civilian rule. The revolutionary youth and their supporters, however, perceived the incumbent authorities, whether in Egypt or Tunisia, to be illegitimate.

Differences in the respective transitions did not appear immediately. More protests in Tahrir Square led to Egypt's change of prime ministers in early February, preceding a similar change in Tunisia. There, as in Egypt, the insurgents staged sporadic mass protests in iconic locations. Finally on February 27 the protests of "*Kasbah 2*" (referring to the open spaces adjoining and overlooking the prime minister's office where multitudes gathered to demonstrate) induced the long-serving prime minister to resign. He was a technocrat who, however well-meaning, was too tarred by association with Ben Ali to be acceptable. The provisional president's choice of his former patron, eighty-eight-year-old Béji Caïd Essebsi, to be the new prime minister was a stroke of luck, for as a former interior and defense minister under Bourguiba, he had requisite political as well as technical skills. In December 2014 Essebsi was elected the country's president.

Equally important, as a result of *Kasbah* 2, was the expansion of Tunisia's Commission for Constitutional Reform, a technical committee of jurists headed by Yahd Ben Achour, a former law school dean, into the Higher Instance for the Preservation of the Objectives of the Revolution, Political Reform, and Democratic Transition. It became a miniparliament of up to 155 members, representing a variety of self-co-opted political parties, trade unions, professional associations, and human rights groups. At its opening meeting on March 17 it had seventy-one members but then expanded as more of Tunisia's civil society knocked at its doors.[26] Limited to only three seats, however, the Ennahda party officially withdrew in June. Meanwhile the Higher Instance had drafted an electoral law of pure proportional representation, favoring smaller parties, as well as the requirement that women constitute at least half, in fair order, of every party list. It also elected an independent commission to supervise the elections to a Constituent Assembly and managed successfully to negotiate with the prime minister to delay them, originally scheduled for July, to October, to give the smaller parties more time to organize.

In Egypt, by contrast, SCAF retained control of the transition and organized a constitutional referendum on March 19, 2011, to ratify amendments originally promised while Mubarak was still in power. The "no" vote supported by much of the youth in revolt and their senior supporters such as Mohamed ElBaradei obtained only 23 percent of the vote. SCAF then proceeded in the Constitutional Declaration of March 30 to issue its ground rules for the transition process, but meanwhile remained in full control, with a thirty-year Emergency Law still in place. Efforts in Egypt to co-opt civilian advisory councils as in Tunisia failed, and civil society remained disconnected, apart from sporadic rioting, from the transition process. Tacit understandings between SCAF and the Muslim Brotherhood finally led to a series of legislative elections conducted in late 2011 and early 2012. SCAF's guidelines called for the People's Assembly (PA) to designate one hundred members of a Constituent Assembly, but the Supreme Constitutional Court (SCC) invalidated its effort and dissolved the PA in June on the ground that the electoral law had violated the Constitution. Meanwhile SCAF ordered presidential elections in May 2012, while Egypt was still in constitutional limbo. Egypt's Supreme Electoral Commission, headed by the president of the SCC, vetted the candidates, eliminating a number of major contestants. While awaiting the results of the run-off elections in June, SCAF appropriated all legislative powers and designated a new Constituent Assembly. The results announced on June 17 confirmed a narrow victory by Dr. Mohamed Morsi, the Muslim Brotherhood's second stringer, over Mubarak's former prime minister and air force commander Ahmed Shafiq. President Morsi then moved in August to eliminate SCAF's aging leaders and subsequently on November 22, 2012, to appropriate all legislative as well as executive powers and accelerate the drafting and vote by referendum for the new constitution before the judiciary could stop it. The overall results, announced December 25, 2012, were 63.8 percent in favor nationwide, but with a low turnout and only 43.1 percent voting in favor in Cairo. The first stage of Egypt's transition to a new regime concluded in chaos, marked by considerable violence along the way. In March 2013 elections for a new People's Assembly, scheduled for April, were postponed because Cairo's Administrative Court had referred the new electoral law to the SCC. And in July 2013 Morsi was overthrown by the military after little more than a year in office. Less than a year after that, in June 2014, armed forces chief Abdel Fattah el-Sisi, who had led the country since Morsi's downfall, won a landslide presidential election, ushering in a new, if as yet highly uncertain, era of military rule.

Tunisia, by contrast, engaged in a methodical transition process finally leading, in January 2014, to the passage of a new constitution in the elected parliament by a margin well above the required two-thirds majority. Drafts of the constitution had circulated to the public from mid-August 2012 through March 2013, when the United Nations Development Program concluded a two-month outreach program whereby the second draft, released in December, circulated throughout the country with Assembly members and chairs of the six constitutional committees fielding public sessions.[27]

However, amid appearances of orderly progression in Tunisia, and chaos followed by a military coup and eventually new elections in Egypt, the underlying politics are similar. Each country's legislative elections initially gave rise to a strong Islamist party, the Muslim Brotherhood in Egypt and Ennahda in Tunisia, gaining roughly 40 percent of vote. In Tunisia as in Egypt, the newly dominant party then gave rise to a transitional government—though in Egypt that government was to be booted in a popularly supported coup after little more than a year in office. Whether the government was backed by a coalition in the Constituent Assembly (Tunisia) or designated by the president, Egypt's sole elected top official, those in the opposition viewed it as exceeding the boundaries of transitional rule and Islamizing the state administrations. Serious outbreaks of violence marred the transitional process in both countries, leading to widespread dissatisfaction and changes of government in March 2013 in both countries. Neither government could unite their polarized political classes sufficiently to engage in needed economic reform; indeed, the political classes were stymied since they largely opposed political Islam in all its forms yet were less organized on the ground than the new ruling parties.

Consolidating a political transition seemed more likely in Tunisia than Egypt, but even so, the Tunisian fomenters of the revolt faced likely isolation as the remnants of the Destour battled the efforts of Ennahda to achieve hegemony. The Tunisian remnants of the old regime had much deeper historical roots than the discredited cliques of Egypt's National Democratic Party. Béji Caïd Essebsi, who had successfully guided the transition to the October 2011 elections, regrouping the Destourians under a new coalition, the Nidaa Tounes ("Call of Tunisia") that credibly, and successfully, opposed Ennahda. Cleansing it of Ben Ali sycophants, however, was a daunting task in a country where many technically competent people had been obliged, like their counterparts in Baathist Iraq, to join the ruling party and play to the dictator's personality cult.

Egyptian politics were also polarized, but could be viewed as practicing a political culture of contestation embedded in the Constitution of 1923. Under British domination, the king had shared power with a parliament, usually dominated by the nationalist Wafd Party. After the fall of Mubarak, an analogous power triangle pitted the Egyptian judiciary, the Muslim Brotherhood, and the military in a politics reminiscent of the 1940s and contested by the street.

Whatever the outcome of their respective transitions, the two bully regimes had relatively autonomous bureaucracies, grounded in centuries of state development. The other Arab regimes governed more problematic states with weaker administrative and civil infrastructures. Clans within the bunkers of Syria, Yemen, and Libya viciously lashed out at insurgent populations—one family, clan, tribe, or sect against another—without the insulation of either a bureaucracy or a professional military, not to mention associations or political parties with any free life of their own to temper primordial loyalties. In Libya, where Gaddafi had instrumentalized a weak tribal structure, the principal building blocks for a new political order were the scores of militias based on locality and wartime experience. In Syria the repression of spontaneous civil resistance led to hardened sectarian warfare for lack of a strong civil society and state traditions.

THE MONARCHIES

By contrast, monarchies, especially the more progressive ones of Morocco and Jordan, had perfected styles of divide-and-rule of intermediary bodies, coupled with periodic promises of reform that postponed any frontal mass assaults of the type waged in Egypt and Tunisia. Their underlying political economies offer a partial insight into tactics of survival.

The financial command and control structures of the monarchies, clustered, for the most part, in the center of our graph (Table 2), offer a fascinating clue. To the extent that banking concentration reflects royal control of the political economy, as in Morocco, there are ways of controlling businesses and civil society organizations while giving up some formal levers of power.

Morocco effectively deregulated parts of the economy and moved toward a market economy in the early 1990s—but only after the Makhzan had first established effective control of the banking system and some associated conglomerates. In effect King Hassan II reconstructed and expanded his system of royal patronage by commanding many of the spaces of private enterprise. Two decades later, under a new king, the Makhzen's portfolio, concentrated in the holding company SIDER ("of the king," in Latin, spelled backward), has been rationalized. While the centralizing of control and the leveraging of assets may carry some financial risks, they also offer cushions for further political as well as financial engineering.[28]

To contain the awakening of his people, articulated in the February 20 Movement, King Mohammed VI promised on March 9, 2011 to delegate substantial powers to an elected prime minister. Drafted by experts supervised by the palace, the new constitution offers greater powers to an elected prime minister but "reserves for the king three areas as his exclusive domain: religion, security issues, and strategic major policy choices."[29] It was adopted by referendum on July 1 by an overwhelming 98.6 percent majority but contested by the February 20 Movement. It may in reality reenact King Hassan II's political opening in 1997, when he appointed a prime minister from a leading opposition party and allowed him to form a government but reserved key domains for royal appointees. The extensive royal patronage machine serviced by the political economy ensures royal control while offering an appearance of big changes toward constitutional monarchy.

The region's other monarchies rest on less established state foundations than Morocco, which is ruled by a dynasty dating from the seventeenth century and supplemented by a modern administration inherited from the French protectorate that once controlled much of Morocco. There are fewer intermediary bodies, in the sense of either private sector enterprises, or civil society or professional associations, that might transcend primary cleavages. The small wealthy Arab states, with the exception of Bahrain (see Table 3), field few NGOs as most public matters are discussed in ruling family circles, such as *diwaniya*, which serve as receptions for notables. Not even Jordan, much less the GCC members, has Morocco's rich assortment of political parties and civil society associations. Relatively large private sectors point, however, to a potential development of civil society. The GCC countries, with the exception of Oman, are also at the forefront of Islamic finance in the region, raising eventual possibilities of an Islamic bourgeoisie emerging in competition with ruling families. Meanwhile, however, the tragedy of Bahrain reflects a Saudi determination to block any significant reform. As suggested at the outset of this chapter, many of the wealthy oil states still resembled the bunkers.

Bahrain, where oil was first discovered on the Arabian side of the Persian Gulf, was the most educated of the GCC countries, with the most vibrant civil society, but it was also the closest to Saudi Arabia and major oil reserves. Host to offshore banking in the 1970s and to Islamic finance since the 1990s, Bahrain is a miniature Lebanon, the region's financial hub until 1975. Power sharing in Bahrain was as problematic as in Lebanon. The predominately Shiite population enjoyed substantial private wealth, but the monarchy was Sunni, just as wealth had also been spread across various denominations in Lebanon although Christians had retained political hegemony. Bahrain seems also to have suffered Lebanon's earlier fates of sectarian discord and foreign intervention. The treaty founding the GCC in 1981 gave Saudi Arabia license to intervene in any of the peninsula's coastal municipalities, and the causeway completed in 1986 gave the Saudis quick access to Bahrain. Consequently the Saudis could back support for the hardliner Bahraini prime minister with a physical presence and sabotage any efforts of the soft-line crown prince to mediate and contain a predominately but not exclusively Shiite opposition. Bahrain might yet, however, be the catalyst that ignites the rest of the GCC, including its larger neighbor, where young, rapidly growing, educated populations remain underemployed, and the private sector is largely under expatriate management.

The Arab awakening has happened from the ground up[30], and external intervention can only exacerbate it, even if change is temporarily postponed. This chapter has therefore focused on some of the internal drivers for change. Relatively strong states, such as Egypt, Jordan, Morocco, and Tunisia, offered more hospitable environments for mobilization than the bunker states: where necessary, a professional military stepped in to contain the excesses of the police. The monarchies proved their ability to contain protest through adept preemptive maneuvers, whereas bully presidents had to be sacrificed. The commanding heights of the political economy helped to explain why both bullies and monarchies had adequate protection in the form of viable civil societies—heavily policed, to be sure, but available, too, to engage populations in new political experiences, once they gained greater freedom. Each aroused citizenry was grounded in a particular political economy underlying its politics. It is no accident that Tunisians were the first to awaken. Tunisia's blatantly distorted political economy made it the prime candidate for a regime change. Egypt then followed suit, reflecting a material infrastructure that resembled Tunisia's more than those of any other Arab state.[31] Finally, the more politically experienced Moroccan regime could offer modest reforms without endangering its pervasive patronage networks, again amplified by a material infrastructure similar to Tunisia's and Egypt's.

Country	Per capital income $000s (PPP) (2009)	Density of asso-ciations (NGOs per 100,000 pop.) (2001)	Urbaniza-tion (percent pop.) (2009)	Mobile cellular subscrip-tions (per 100 pop.) (2009)	Inter-net usage (per-cent pop.) (2010)	Facebook members (2010)
Qatar	$91,379	95.7	175	51.6	26.5	373,000
UAE	$57,7443	77.9	232	75.9	35.1	1,616,000
Kuwait	$48,631	98.4	107	39.4	16.7	498,000
Bahrain	$35,174	88.6	199	88	27.2	215,000
Israel	$27,656	91.7	121	71.6	38.5	2,901,000
Oman	$25,462	71.7	140	41.7	5.3	152,000
Saudi	$23,480	82.3	177	38.1	8.8	2,901,000
Libya	$16,502	77.7	78	5.5	2.2	144,000
Turkey	$13,668	69.1	84	44.4	31.1	22,552,540
Lebanon	$13,070	87.1	36	24.2	22	931,000
Iran	$11,558	69	72	43.2		
Tunisia	$8,273	66.9	94	34	14.9	1,555,000
Algeria	$8,173	65.9	94	13.6	2.4	845,000
Egypt	$5,673	42.8	67	21.2	4.3	3,360,000
Jordan	$5,597	78.5	101	27.2	14	884,000
Syria	$4,730	54.6	46	17.7	0	0
Morocco	$4,494	56.4	79	33	5.6	1,767,000
Iraq	$3,548	66.5	63	1.1	0.6	189,000
West bank and Gaza		72	30	14.2	4.5	179,000
Djibouti	$2,470	87.7	15	3.5	3.4	29,000
Yemen	$2,320	31.2	16	1.8	0.4	97,000
Italy	$32,430	68	151	35.8	27.6	16,647,260
Valle d'aosta			265			
Trentino-Alto Adige		182				
Puglia		54				

Table 3. Indicators of Potential Social Mobilization

Sources: Salim Nasr, UNDP; Putnam, Italy; World Bank Development Indicators: www.internetworldstats.com/list2.htm; http://www.internetworldstats.com/stats4.htm; www.logicks.com/pdf/2010-05-22-MENA_Facebook_Digest.pdf: www.guardian.co.uk/technology/blog/2010/jul/22/facebook-countries-population-use#data.

NOTES

1   Lisa Wedeen, *Ambiguities of Domination: Politics, Rhetoric, and Symbols in Contemporary Syria*, Chicago: University of Chicago Press, 1999.

2   As observed by Laryssa Chomiak, comparing the cult with that of Assad and various fascists, in *Confronting Authoritarianism: Order, Dissent, and Everyday Politics in Modern Tunisia*. PhD dissertation, College Park, MD: University of Maryland, 2011. Quoted here with her permission.

3   Kai Hafez, *Radicalism and Political Reform in the Islamic and Western* Worlds, Cambridge, UK: Cambridge University Press, 2010, p. 26.

4   For an excellent overview see Omar S. Dahi, "Understanding the Political Economy of the Arab Revolts," Middle East Report, 259, summer 2011:. 2–6.

5   Steven Heydermann, at a conference on November 4, 2011, that I attended, summarized the basic grievances of "a regime-wide structural deficit in job creation that has kept unemployment rates at staggering levels for almost two decades, with especially high unemployment among university-educated Arab youth … the deepening of market-oriented economic reforms that improved macro-level economic performance in some cases, but were accompanied by the erosion of social welfare programs, and by increasing levels of poverty, inequality, and economic insecurity among Arab citizens, and the capture of liberalized sectors of the economy by predatory, privileged economic networks and the exclusion of large segments of Arab societies from such sectors; as well as increasing (and increasingly visible) levels of corruption among political and economic elites." Heydermann stressed the importance of "memories and expectations about the distributive role of the state, its obligation to provide for the economic security of citizens, and its responsibility to ensure economic and social justice in accounting for the escalation of economic grievances that culminated in the Arab uprisings of 2011."

6   See Eva Bellin, "Contingent Democrats: Industrialists, Labor and Democratization in Late-Developing Countries," World Politics, 52, January 2000: 175–205, and Stalled Democracy: Capital, Labor, and the Paradox of State-Sponsored Development, Ithaca, NY: Cornell University Press, 2002. Bellin explains why business and labor were weak and dependent in the countries such as Egypt and Tunisia, whereas I make distinctions between these cases, with their greater potential for autonomy, and less promising ones.

7   Arthur Fisher Bentley, The Process of Government, ed. Peter H. Odegard, Cambridge, MA: Harvard University Press, 1967. The original edition was published in 1908. As Odegard summarizes the axiom, p. xix, "So integral is the relation of individual process and group process that to ask which is the more important is like asking whether the area of a triangle depends more on its base than its altitude."

8   Robert D. Putnam, Making Democracy Work: Civic Traditions in Modern Italy, Princeton, NJ: Princeton University Press, 1994.

9   Recent French comparative political studies also contest the utility of limited pluralism from a somewhat different perspective and tear down distinctions

between modern democracies and authoritarian regimes. See Olivier Dabène, Vincent Geisser, and Gilles Massardier, eds., Autoritarismes démocratique et démocraties autoritaires au XXIe siècle: Convergences Nord-Sud, Mélanges offerts à Michel Camau, Paris: La Découverte, 2008, and Michel Camau and Gilles Massardier, eds., Démocraties et authoritarismes: Fragmentation et hybridation des régimes, Paris: Editions Karthala, 2009.

10   Thomas Carothers, "The End of the Transition Paradigm," Journal of Democracy, 13:1, January 2002: 5–21.

11   Clement Moore Henry and Robert Springborg, Globalization and the Politics of Development in the Middle East, Cambridge, UK: Cambridge University Press, 2010.

12   Karl A. Wittfogel—in his Oriental Despotism: the Comparative Study of Total Power, New Haven, CT: Yale University Press, 1957—presents the classic argument relating taxation to hydraulic engineering, but the extended coastal Sahel of Tunisia was also, like the Nile Valley, a relatively rich tax base. Fernand Braudel offers a somewhat different explanation in his Memory and the Mediterranean, New York: Vintage, 2002: clearing the shores and draining the swamps for agriculture required remarkable social coordination in Neolithic times.

13   Jean Leca, Foreword to Andrea Liverani, Civil Society in Algeria: The Political Functions of Associational Life, Hoboken, NJ: Allen and Francis, 2007, p. xii.

14   Christopher Clague, Philip Keefer, Stephen Knack, and Mancur Olson, "Contract-Intensive Money: Contract Enforcement, Property Rights, and Economic Performance," Working Paper 151, Center for Institutional Reform and the Informal Sector, College Park, MD: The University of Maryland, (revised Oct. 4, 1997): www.springer.com/article/10.1023%2FA%3A1009854405184?LI=true#page-1

15   Lewis W. Snider, Growth, Debt, and Politics: Economic Adjustment and the Political Performance of Developing Countries, Boulder, CO: Westview Press, 1996, p. 9.

16   HHI, the Herfindahl-Hirschman Index of concentration, is simply the sum of the squares of market shares of the commercial banks, ranging from 1, a monopoly, to very small numbers as in Lebanon.

17   Clement M. Henry, "Tunisia's 'Sweet Little' Regime," in Robert Rotberg, ed., Worst of the Worst: Dealing with Repressive and Rogue Nations, Washington, D.C.: Brookings Institution Press, 2007, pp. 300–323. In his "Reverberations in the Central Maghreb of the 'Global War on Terror'"—in Yahia H. Zoubir and Haizam Amira-Fernandes, eds., North Africa: Politics, Region, and the Limits of Transformation, New York: Routledge, 2008, p. 298—the author recommended Tunisia as the best testing ground in the region for promoting democracy.

18   Jack A. Goldstone, "Understanding the Revolutions of 2011," Foreign Affairs, 90: 3, May–June 2011: 8. Note, however, that Goldstone proceeds to conflate our bullies and bunkers into "sultanism" and therefore cannot make necessary distinctions between the various sorts of processes at work in the region.

19   See "Wikileaks," New York Times, November 28, 2011, www.nytimes.
     com/interactive/2010/11/28/ world/20101128-cables-viewer.html#report/
     tunisia-09TUNIS492.

20   Interview with Dr. Mustapha Nabli, June 20, 2011. For a summary of the
     Ben Ali and related family holdings see "Ali Baba gone, but what about
     the 40 thieves?" Economist, January 20, 2011: www.economist.com/
     node/17959620?story_id=17959620

21   Manfred Halpern, The Politics of Social Change in the Middle East and North
     Africa, Princeton, NJ: Princeton University Press, 1963, pp. 51–78.

22   The rumor at the time was that Army Chief of Staff Rachid Ammar had
     elegantly engineered Ben Ali's departure. See Ezza Rurki, "Tout sur la fuite de
     Ben [']Ali," Réalités (Tunis), February 4, 2011. However, many knowledgeable
     Tunisians were still publicly asking about the real conditions under which Ben
     Ali departed. Noureddine Jebnoun points to crucial splits within the security
     establishment, not the army, in "'The People Want the Fall of the Regime': The
     Arab Uprisings and the Future of Arab Politics," a paper presented at the Annual
     Symposium of the Center for Contemporary Arab Studies, March 22–23, 2012.

23   Azmi Bishara, January 21, 2011. Subsequently, however, at a conference on
     Arab revolutions conducted in Doha on April 22, 2011, "Bishara dismissed
     the idea that the experiences of Tunisia and Egypt could be replicated in
     other Arab countries, explaining that other countries do not exhibit the
     same level of social homogeneity and thus no clear institutional separation
     [between state and regime] as in the cases of Tunisia and Egypt." www.
     english.dohainstitute.org/Home/Details?entityID=f4c16d5a-893e-4b10-bce4-
     fda7bb6493c7&resourceId=9e5f7395-fb84-4515-9074-7086ba61b73b.

24   Just seizing the assets of the presidential family turned out to be more
     complex than beheading a snake, however. Ben Ali's three daughters
     by his first marriage, for instance, had parked their assets with their
     mother, who was not under investigation. See Slim Bagga, L'Audace No.
     2, 17-30 March 2011, as reported online: www.paperblog.fr/4302914/
     indiscretions-sur-le-clan-ben-ali-source-le-journal-l-audace.

25   Yossi Shain and Juan J. Linz eds, Between States: Interim Governments and
     Democratic Transitions, Cambridge, UK: Cambridge University Press, 1995, p.
     94

26   Interview with Yahd Ben Achour, June 20, 2011. See also his interview
     in Le Monde, April 23, 2011, and the carefully crafted summary in
     Wikipedia of the High Instance's history online at www.fr.wikipedia.
     org/wiki/Haute_instance_pour_la_r%C3%A9alisation_des_objectifs
     _de_la_r%C3%A9volution,_de_la_r%C3%A9forme_politique_et_de_la_
     transition_d%C3%A9mocratique.

27   Duncan Pickard, "At Last Public Consultation in Constitution making in
     Tunisia," Atlantic Council Viewpoint, February 13, 2013, www.acus.org/
     viewpoint/last-public-participation-constitution-making-tunisia.

28   On Makhzen finances see Henry and Springborg, Globalization, pp.216–224.

Catherine Graciet and Eric Laurent, two investigative French journalists, observe in Le Roi prédateur: main basse sur le Maroc, Paris: Editions du Seuil, 2012, that Mohammed VI is greedier and exercises even tighter economic control than his father did.

29   Marina Ottaway, "The New Moroccan Constitution: Real Change or More of the Same?" Carnegie Endowment, June 20, 2011, www.carnegieendowment.org/publications/index.cfm?fa=view&id=44731&solr_hilite=Morocco. For further analysis see Mohamed Madani, Driss Maghraoui, and Saloua Zerhouni, "The 2011 Moroccan Constitution: A Critical Analysis," International Institute for Democracy and Electoral Assistance, Stockholm, 2012, www.idea.int

30   See Bahgat Korany and Rabab El-Mahdi, "The Protesting Middle East," in Korany and El-Mahdi eds., *Arab Spring in Egypt: Revolution and Beyond,* Cairo: American University of Cairo Press, 2012, pp. 7–15.

The Arab Revolt of 2011 could well be called the North African Revolt. While protests were widespread across the region, citizens in Egypt, Libya, and Tunisia overthrew their existing regimes. Only the Yemen and Bahrain revolts took place on the Arabian Peninsula, and Syria deteriorated into a protracted civil war. The Kingdom of Morocco also experienced major demonstrations and observers watched with fascination to see if another North African country would lose its traditional government. But Morocco's monarch, Mohammed VI, quickly offered constitutional concessions to his citizens and, additionally, prevailed upon the Moroccan police and military (though with some lapses) to avoid bloodshed when managing the country's protests—and thus averted the kind of martyr incidents that can spark a national upheaval.

CHAPTER 13

THE MOROCCAN SPRING AND KING MOHAMMED VI'S ECONOMIC POLICY AGENDA: EVALUATING THE FIRST DOZEN YEARS

EVE SANDBERG AND SETH BINDER

Many in the West were surprised at the vehement demands for change that surfaced in Morocco amid the Arab revolts. Morocco's King Mohammed VI had often been portrayed in the Western press as a modernizing monarch. Further, he was particularly famous for his support for improving the status and rights of Moroccan women. Additionally, the king had permitted an investigation into the human rights abuses of his father, King Hassan II, and paid reparations to thousands wrongfully imprisoned and/or tortured during his father's reign.

No doubt, politics motivated many of those demonstrating in the streets on Morocco's famous February 20, 2011, and afterwards.[1] In fact, at first, the social media protestors had been careful to call for a new parliament and democratic change, something the king himself had said should be goals for a future Morocco. But news accounts of the demonstrations reported that young people wanted jobs and older people were tired of being asked for patience in awaiting the economic gains Morocco continued to seek.

By changing the constitution, calling for new elections, and handing over some of his power to Morocco's political leadership, Morocco's King

Mohammed VI managed, for now, to retain his throne. And though he was forced to turn the parliamentary budget over to the parliamentarians, the king was able to retain those distinct (and secret) budgets that underwrite the country's military and Morocco's royalty.

But Moroccans have had their eyes on the economic affairs of the country as much as they have had them on the country's political institutions. In 1999, at the age of thirty-six, Mohammed VI inherited the throne of a country whose previous monarch had already searched for ways to open politically and to introduce economic reforms.

In this chapter we argue that although under King Mohammed VI key macroeconomic structures and practices have been modified and progress has been made to establish the metainstitutional conditions to support development. But the payoff in the daily lives of Moroccans has yet to be realized, and such lack of economic advancement for Moroccans "in the street" diminishes the legitimacy of the king and his policies. Unless Morocco undertakes economic activities that build its domestic demand structures, prospects for Morocco's economic development will remain linked to the global recovery—of which there is no guarantee, and which may well be slow. This is so largely because it affects tourism, especially from Europe. Agricultural development depends on good rains, a major factor for the economic health of the country and its citizens; and as an energy poor country, it is dependent on oil prices. As is evident, these variables lie beyond the control of Morocco's monarch (and/or its new parliament). In addition, much of the work that has been accomplished to secure economic growth has largely been hidden from public view.

During his first decade in office, Mohammed VI developed the structural foundations of the state, but this hardly translated into better living conditions for the people and income disparities are growing. Yet Morocco's has not been an inactive monarch when it comes to economic development.

BRIEF BACKGROUND TO UNDERSTAND THE CONTEXT THAT KING MOHAMMED VI INHERITED

When in 1999 Mohammed VI inherited the Moroccan throne from his father, he knew the headwinds of history were blowing against him. His grandfather, Mohammed V had reinstated the legitimacy of the monarchy in Morocco. His father, Hassan II, had consolidated his power by careful foreign affairs successes, close attention to his public image, brutally suppressing any who might contemplate opposing the king or any of his policies, and by securing Western allies willing and able to sell him military and police technology for both foreign and domestic uses.

Hassan II also created economic institutions in Morocco that primarily served his immediate circle, and in many cases his sycophants. And although he claimed to want to modernize Morocco's productive sectors, the pace of modernization was uneven, and dismally slow. The ownership of a Moroccan business largely became a privilege

The 1970s saw King Hassan II institute "Moroccanization" measures that brought much of the country's economy under the purview of the king and state control. The king expanded the public sector and required that all companies have at least 51 percent ownership by Moroccans. The king used Moroccanization to create a loyal elite by offering jobs in return for support among the various actors vying for power [2] In large part due to these policies, and due to the military costs of the Western Sahara War, as well as due to the increase in oil prices in the 1970s, incoming international investment slowed and the national debt rose. Hence, in the 1980s Morocco was forced to borrow from the International Monetary Fund (IMF) and, in return, adopt the structural adjustment policies supported by the World Bank and the IMF.

Morocco become reliant on external trade, maintained little diversity economically, and focussed on particular external markets, especially with France, one of the former colonial powers.[3] Morocco fell into this trap as Hassan continued to look to Europe for trade, paid little attention to diversification, and continued to offer loans to those supporting him politically, despite their records of poor management.

In keeping with his structural adjustment policies, King Hassan II devalued Morocco's currency and liberalized the foreign trade sector to spur investment in exports. In addition, he enacted austerity measures that sharply reduced subsidies for education, agriculture, health care, and food staples, while raising interest rates to curb inflation. He also privatized several sectors of the economy. Bread and energy prices rose, causing hardship for many Moroccans, and organized resistance and riots resulted. The king quickly reinstituted bread and energy subsidies.

European policies toward Morocco failed to offer much to Moroccan exporters. Moreover, during the 1980s the Western economic recession saw Western investment in Morocco decline, and Morocco did not receive the European investment it had anticipated. As the European Economic Community (EEC) expanded to include Greece, Spain, and Portugal, farmers in those countries fought alongside their counterparts in core countries of the EEC and, from 1993, the European Union (EU)—who produced many of the same products as those produced by Moroccan exporters—to prevent Moroccan imports to the EU. Thus, when Mohammed VI ascended to the throne in 1999, Morocco had neither a workable plan for economic development nor professionals in state institutions that could support such development.

Mohammed VI completed his graduate work at a university in France, focusing on trade relations between Morocco and the EU. He also drew on the experience he gained by representing his father abroad. He was well aware of alternative economic strategies to those found in Morocco. When he assumed the throne, Morocco's citizens were demanding change both economically and politically, and the new king promised he would oversee an era of reform. To many Moroccans, the thirty-six-year-old Mohammed VI offered the hope of modernization, political democratization, and economic development.

ECONOMIC POLICY STRATEGIES IN KEY ARENAS TO PROMOTE ECONOMIC DEVELOPMENT

Mohammed VI's key economic policies focused on six key areas of strategic concern: economic planning and financial institutions; investment and trade, including agriculture and phosphates; remittances (money sent from abroad into Morocco by workers employed overseas); transport (road, rail, sea, air); tourism; and energy. In 2001 Moroccan government officials underwent training programs to implement key shifts in economic policy—designed to create public sector reforms and to operationalize "results-based budgeting and management" practices.[4] It was especially important for the financial and banking sectors, in which transparency, competent record-keeping, and the security of investments is paramount to attracting investors.

The country's financial and banking systems did indeed achieve high standards of excellent performance from 1999 to 2012. Officials set the goal of broadening the tax base while lowering taxes. In the period from 1999 to 2011, Morocco's banking institutions were strengthened and its business regulatory practices were rendered more attractive, especially to large-scale investors. Additionally, foreign banks were permitted and indeed encouraged to establish operations in Morocco. By 2010, only 27 percent of Morocco's banking sector was owned by the state. [5] The result was credit growth (a major precondition for economic development), and soaring investment in the country's economy from both within the country and abroad.

It followed that Morocco's international monetary ratings saw improvement as well. Standard and Poor's raised Morocco's foreign currency rating to BBB- (its lowest investment grade) and its local currency rating to BBB+ in March 2010 thus attracting new buyers and capital from the international markets. [6] In just one decade, Morocco's banking sector was modernized.

Additionally, Morocco's stock market, though small—only seventy-five companies are listed—is Africa's fourth largest. And, despite the protests that did erupt, the FDI intelligence division of the Financial Times recognized Morocco in 2011–2012 as the "African County of the Future" and as the "best investment destination in Africa."[7]

Morocco's leaders have been careful to modernize in a manner that still offers some shelter to Moroccan citizens from the arbitrary nature of the global economy. In order to combat inflation, instead of adopting strict free-currency, market practices, Morocco pegged its foreign exchange rate to a basket of currencies from its key trading partners. Hence, Morocco's inflation rates over the past decade have been low. Inflation declined from 3.9% in 2008 to 1% in 2009, a level Morocco then maintained during 2010 and 2011.[8] The king and his advisors have not been afraid to run a national deficit since 2007. The king insisted on continuing to subsidize food and energy prices for Moroccan citizens despite the IMF's warning late in 2011 that a good part of its debt would result from such actions.

INVESTMENT AND TRADE UNDER KING MOHAMMED VI

Morocco is sometimes compared to five other aspiring and emerging economies in its greater region: Egypt, Senegal, South Africa, Tunisia, and Turkey. Significantly, Morocco saw more domestic investment between 2000 and 2009 than in any of those countries. Such investment grew at a compounded annual growth rate of 13 percent while Morocco's GDP grew at 10 percent.[9] With regard to foreign direct investment (FDI), initially little investment was captured except when huge spikes occurred that were triggered by Vivendi's acquisition of Maroc Telecom in 2001, and when Altadis acquired 80 percent of the government-owned tobacco monopoly in 2003. But from 2004 through 2008, Morocco accrued a respectable level of FDI. The global crash in 2008 substantially lowered FDI worldwide beginning in 2009, and Morocco was no exception.

As can been seen from Table 1, Morocco's ability to secure foreign direct investment provided important capital for new projects until the effects of the 2008 international economic downturn took hold. [10]

In 2011, when European economies were slumping due to the sovereign debt crisis, Morocco still posted an economic growth rate of 4.5 percent. Mohammed VI and his decision makers had diversified Morocco's economic activities enough to keep Morocco on a program of expansion even as the country's main trading partners suffered economic contraction. This was done through a relentless pursuit of exports and through the heavy funding of domestic transportation infrastructure.

In the domain of trade, Morocco is not the master of its own fate. During the period in which the Arab revolts spread, Morocco was being buffeted by international and climatic challenges that dramatically increased its need for

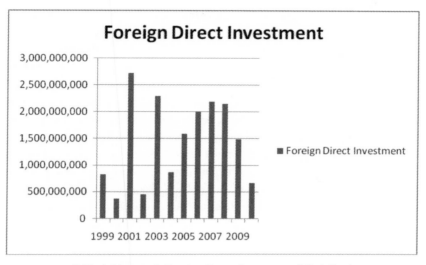

Table 1. Morocco's Foreign Direct Investment (US dollars)
Source: World Bank: http://databank.worldbank.org/data/home.aspx

imports.[11] From January–May 2010 to the same period in 2011, wheat prices rose 66 percent and prices for oil imports rose 31 percent.[12] Morocco purchases much of its oil from Saudi Arabia and imports most of its wheat from France. Due to the international rise in oil prices that prevailed during this period, Morocco purchased 4.7 percent less crude oil than it had the previous year but paid more for it. [13] [moved paragraph up] As a result of international factors and a poor climate, Morocco's trade deficit increased by a whopping 25 percent in the first five months of 2011. Even an increase in the value of its exports could not offset the growing trade imbalance.

Morocco's former colonial powers, France and Spain, remain Morocco's dominant trade partners. They, along with the rest of the EU, accounted for approximately 60 percent of the country's total foreign trade in 2009. But much of this trade is based on Moroccan imports of European goods, not on Moroccan exports to the EU.

Morocco, in fact, has found its exports to the EU curtailed. Greece, Spain, and Portugal produce vegetables, wine, citrus fruits, and olive oil in direct competition with Morocco. The EU's Common Agricultural Policy (CAP) limits these specific Moroccan exports only to certain times of the year, when they cannot be produced in the EU. The EU's subsidization of its agricultural sector makes wheat imported by Morocco less expensive than Moroccan-grown wheat. This impedes the ability of Morocco's rural economy to develop, increases its trade deficit, and creates a reliance on international trade for basic foodstuffs. The agricultural sector employs 40 percent of Morocco's workforce and accounts for 14 percent of the country's output.[14] Poor rural performance in 2012 put pressure on urban areas as rural to urban migration increased.

Trade between the EU and Morocco has been expanding. Between 1995 and 2008, trade volumes grew by over 80 percent amounting to over $30 billion. Trade then contracted by 20 percent due to the global economic downturn.[15] As Table 2 demonstrates, Morocco somewhat diversified its network of trading partners, in part looking more to large alternative consumer blocs and less to European consumers. It saw an increase in imports from its major trading partner, the EU (of which France is the key player). Morocco's exports to the EU also increased. However, despite much fanfare from the United States about signing a free trade agreement with Morocco—this happened in 2004—trade between the two countries improved only slowly.

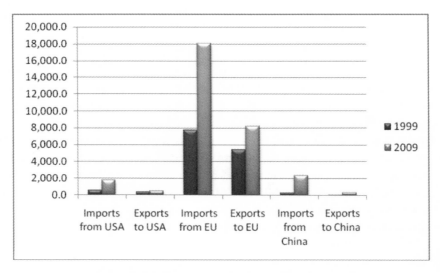

Table 2. Morocco's Imports and Exports with Major Powers
(millions of US dollars) Source: IMF Directions of Trade Statistics

China's much-publicized outreach to Africa has also resulted in some changes in trade with Morocco during the period in focus. As Table 2 shows, imports from China jumped dramatically over the decade. However, Moroccan exports to China (50 million in 1999 to $337 million in 2009) remained low. Many of the obstacles to finding more markets for Moroccan goods can no longer simply be blamed on Morocco's domestic institutions. The king's success in modernizing the country's regulatory structures for doing business with Moroccan nationals has seen Morocco climb to the top 50 percent of countries as regards the ease of doing business.[16]

One major area of exports that continues to benefit Morocco is the phosphate sector, which has benefited from steady production and also price increases. As one of the world's largest producers of phosphates, and with demand growing for the mineral and its by-products (such as fertilizer), transportation problems have all but been eliminated. To address the issue of phosphate supply, Morocco has embarked on a production project that seeks to position the country as a greater global exporter of phosphate, especially as US and Chinese exports are expected to fall. Morocco, with the largest known phosphate reserves, is taking steps to expand production capacity, as is Saudi Arabia. This could mean that the price of phosphates might fall from present highs.

REMITTANCES

While remittances—money sent to Morocco by the country's citizens who are employed overseas—are seen as a positive financial inflow to assist family members back home, some worry that remittances may create a culture of dependency for its recipients or add to inflationary pressures for families that do not receive remittances. Additionally, because many of Morocco's migrants are males and some have high levels of education, remittances have increasingly been seen as a brain drain.[17] Some, however, have argued that more attention needs to be given to the benefits of remittances. And as Mohamed Berrianne and Mohamed Aderghal noted in their 2008 comprehensive study of all aspects of Moroccan migration, "remittances now provide between 8 and 9% of the country's GDP."[18] The money sent back to Morocco often pays for education and health care, and contributes to the nourishment of Moroccan individuals who form the country's work force.

MOROCCO'S STRATEGIC TRANSPORT SECTOR

When King Mohammed VI ascended the throne, almost everyone agreed that the country's transport infrastructure needed a major overhaul—to improve the prospects of tourism, the domestic business sector, and the country's export potential, as well as to attract more foreign investment. Visitors entering Morocco from Europe—whether for tourism or business—should be able to travel to key destinations in Morocco in less time and with more comfort, the king concluded, adding that tourists from other reaches of the globe should be able to fly into Morocco on schedule and with multiple choices of air carriers, and move about from region to region with relative ease.[19]

In 2003, following four years of planning, Morocco announced an ambitious plan to modernize its transport infrastructure. A new Terminal 2 at Casablanca's Mohammed V International Airport was constructed to improve air transportation. Also road, rail, and sea traffic were modernized. The king and his planners set an ambitious goal of hosting ten million foreign tourists annually by 2010. Plans were likewise put into effect to upgrade the country's road transport system. The completion of an expressway connecting Casablanca and Marrakesh in 2007 was a key accomplishment, as was the Tangier to Marrakesh link. When the Marrakesh-Agadir expressway opened in 2010, it completed the goal of linking Casablanca with Agadir as well as Tangier and Agadir (through Marrakesh). Now, instead of driving for fourteen hours from Tangier to Agadir, the trip takes just seven hours.

But it was air and sea freight that the king's transit plans addressed in order to position Morocco as a hub to North and West Africa as well as to Europe. The king and his advisors planned two port terminals in Tangier—the Eurogate terminal and the AP Moller Maersk (APMT) terminal. Hoping to allow Morocco to recruit European manufacturers and industries and ship competitively priced goods back to Europe, Morocco also constructed a free-trade facility and attracted Renault-Nissan to set up manufacturing operations and ship its automobiles to Europe. The Tangier hub also can allow containers to come into port and then be redirected across the region or move on globally. In 2007, when the hub became operational, it was estimated that it could handle about three million containers annually, the goal being to eventually handle eight million containers a year.

TOURISM UNDER MOHAMMED VI

Morocco's leaders adopted some of the most cutting-edge planning techniques used by planners internationally especially the ones to expand the country's tourist industry. As Table 3 demonstrates, in 2001—when the program was first introduced—just over four million foreign tourists visited Morocco. In 2010, 9.3 million tourists visited. The same year saw a global economic downturn sweep through countries that are home to most of Morocco's tourists, suggesting that Morocco has been successful in preparing for, hosting, and advertising its tourist attractions.

Most Moroccan tourists come from the European Union: 75 percent from France, Spain, the United Kingdom, Belgium, and Germany. Overall, between 2001 and 2009, Morocco's tourism industry saw an average increase of 8.4 percent, and if the economic crisis years are removed, growth was at 9.2 percent.[20]

A range of accommodations was to be established for Moroccan and foreign visitors, from the ultra high end to the modest. It was hoped that the availability of modest accommodations would encourage Morocco's domestic tourists to stay not with family and friends but rather in hotels or campgrounds. Additionally, Morocco promoted itself abroad as a second home destination.

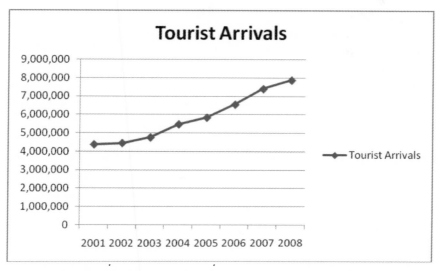

Table 3. Tourist Arrivals Source: Moroccan Ministry of Tourism: www.tourisme.gov.ma/english/5-Tourisme-chiffres/ArriveeTouristes.htm

dependency on oil and other energy imports that gobbles up much-needed capital that could be invested domestically in development projects and the building of human capacity. So Morocco embarked on Project Genesis, a quest for energy self-sufficiency especially through the utilization of renewable energies—mainly solar and wind, but also nuclear and natural gas. Morocco's second major energy goal in recent years was the electrification of the entire country, including rural areas.

It is vital to Morocco that these plans succeed, for the country's appetite for energy is growing and its industrial, tourist, and other sectors are reliant on it. In 2008, Morocco spent $8 billion to import its energy.[21] In 2011, Morocco's electricity consumption grew by 8.4 percent from the previous year, while economic growth for the same year was only about 6 percent.[22] Hence, to reduce its imports, Morocco aims to generate as much as two gigawatts (GW) from wind and 2GW from solar power by 2020, costing $17.2 billion.

In November 2011 the World Bank announced it had agreed to provide $297 million to Morocco to develop one of the world's largest solar power plants.[23] Though the loan only supports the first phase of one part of the country's solar power program, which was expected to cost $9 billion overall, it is an important contribution, as the plant—located near the south-central town of Ouarzazate, built by a Spanish consortium, and was set to become operational by late 2015—is expected to produce 500MW of energy annually.

VITAL STATISTICS

While Moroccan elites and administrators were improving their skills over that decade, Morocco's overall literacy rate was still just 56 percent by 2009. Life expectancy at birth increased from sixty-two to seventy-two between 2000 and 2010. While this was a significant accomplishment, it presented dilemmas for policy makers in meeting the employment needs of a larger workforce.

Adding to the average Moroccan's sense of discontent—of being restrained while the well-connected are unfairly reaping greater rewards from their country's economic achievements—is the perception throughout society that to undertake the most basic economic activities one must pay a bribe or find connections. Thus, in 2010, when Wikileaks released a document from the US embassy in Rabat, according to which "corruption is prevalent at all levels of Moroccan society," many Moroccans simply nodded in agreement.[24] The continuing lack of opportunity for economic advancement is seen by most Moroccans as not just a fact of life but also a choice by those who could redirect the country's resources. This perception is exacerbated by the common perception that the distribution of national assets in the course of privatization has occurred *not* on the basis of merit.[25]

Additionally, Morocco's vibrant shadow economy—and, indeed, the trade in illegal goods, including hashish—has had implications for substate level economic development and possibly political control in the northern part of the country. The state's apparent ambivalence arguably helped shape how those in northern Morocco responded to the protest movement. Hashish is exported from Morocco mostly to Europe, though a significant percent of the harvest is now believed to pass through Mauritania to other parts of Africa as well as to Europe, and some of it remains in Morocco for domestic and tourist consumption.[26]

Many argue that for decades Moroccan officials did little to curb illicit exports. Building on the work of Romero L. Labrousse, in 2002 Michel Peraldi argued that the Rif area produced "about 48,000 tons of plants and 3,000 tons of resin, which feed about 100,000 farmers who benefit from 20 million euros of the 10 billion that the traffic generates."[27]

James Ketterer has chronicled how in 1992 the rival barons of Tangier declared a truce and began building networks, bribing security officials, and corrupting politicians. But with money being centralized in a few hands, the state began "cleansings" that met with stiff resistance from Rif residents. Mohammed VI, Ketterer asserted, assumed the throne on "the horns of a dilemma": he wanted to support the economic livelihood of the Berbers in the Rif areas, but he did not want to cede political power to traffickers. Europe was looking for action against its drug inflow, and the Moroccan government would benefit from taxes on alternative legal activities to those of illicit trafficking.[28]

The 2003 United Nation's Office on Drugs and Crime report shone a light on Morocco's drug problems, and the king then undertook various initiatives: to educate Rif farmers about the dangers of soil erosion derived from the illegal crops; to introduce alternative agricultural practices such as saffron growing and rose petal extraction; and a policy of increased interdiction. By 2008, the United Nations Office on Drugs and Crime would report that although Morocco remained "the world's principle producer and exporter of cannabis resin," with "revenues estimated at over $13 billion annually" ... by 2006 "the percentage of countries citing Morocco as the origin of hashish found in their markets ... dropped from 31 percent to 18 percent."[29]

Then the War on Terror prompted the West to pressure Morocco to crack down on the drug trafficking in its northern territories, because some policy makers abroad linked drugs to Western security concerns and speculated that al-Qaeda in the Islamic Maghreb and affiliated groups might be benefiting financially from the illicit trade despite their denunciations of drug users as Western decadents who lack Islamic piety. A June 2012 report to the US Congress by Alexis Arieff notes that "Moroccan authorities have ... arrested individuals whom they accuse ... of (such) involvement."[30] Also alarming to many is the increasing prevalence of Latin American, especially Columbian, cocaine that now flows through Morocco. Such trafficking has been associated with the destabilization of states.

Yet as Michel Piraldi suggests, Tangier's construction boom has "virtually no relationship with the town's commercial development. ... It's all money-laundering."[31] And with few options that can generate similar profits, illicit trade highlights the lack of alternative economic development paths in northern Morocco, a situation that contributed to the 2011–2012 unrest.

In December 2011, Morocco's unemployment rate stood at 9.1 percent compared to just over 13 percent in 1999 when King Mohammed VI took office. Unemployment among young Moroccan males aged 15–24 was higher than the national average, at 10.1 percent.[32] These figures are merely a conservative estimate of the numbers of Moroccans who seek full gainful employment in acceptable working conditions. Young, unemployed Moroccans have little to lose by expressing their rage.

Approximately 18 percent of workers with an intermediate to advanced education are unemployed and 11 percent of those with a basic education. Nationwide, a whopping 31 percent of young urban males are unemployed and the 3.8 million rural poor below Morocco's poverty line represent 27 percent of the rural population and 19 percent of the entire population.[33]

Does this situation differ for Moroccan women? According to the country's constitution, women are equal under the law. From his first year in office, King Mohammed VI has appointed women to cabinet positions in government, supported their efforts to run for parliament and city councils, and broke with tradition by allowing his wife to be photographed in public. Further, the king encouraged the private sector to employ and promote qualified women to responsible corporate positions. Under King Mohammed VI, Morocco's family code (the Mudawana) was altered in 2004, giving women more legal and economic rights in Moroccan civil courts.

While visible progress has been made to improve the lives of educated Moroccan women, much remains to be done. The Global Gender Gap Report 2011, for example, notes that Morocco's position among the 135 countries surveyed has slipped since 2006, the baseline used for these rankings. In 2006, after much improvement under King Mohammed VI, Morocco ranked 107 among the 135 countries in the relative ranking of its gender gap.[34] In 2011, Morocco slipped to a ranking of 129, just six countries from the bottom of the index.[35] Like its men, Morocco's women are suffering from the international as well as domestic constraints on the country's economic development. But they are also suffering from the choices of men and policy makers as well.

CONCLUSION

Since King Mohammed VI took power in 1999, Morocco's macroeconomic indicators have improved for the most part, though they have suffered from external and global economic downturns. From 2003 to 2010, overall investment doubled. Over this time foreign investors diversified their investments. Under the king's reign, the skills of the states planners and administrators have been professionalized.

As the above discussion of Morocco's core economic sectors demonstrates, huge strides have been made to modernize Morocco, and creative and savvy planning has been accomplished to this end. But while the state has modernized its development practices, Morocco's citizenry remains under supported and under productive. Some contend that the state does not care enough about the living conditions of poor people. Others believe that the king made extraordinary attempts in the space of a decade to improve the lives of ordinary Moroccans—focusing mainly on the foundations of infrastructure and investment that will lead to sustained economic development.

Whatever one's perspective on the policy approaches undertaken by King Mohammed VI, it is clear from Morocco's employment figures, from its ranking on the UN Human Development Index, and from its gender gap data, that millions of its citizens have seen few benefits in their own lives of the economic development that has been underway since King Mohammed VI assumed the throne. The monarchy's activities and the leadership are largely hidden from view and have, to date, had little impact on the struggles of most Moroccans. More must be done in this respect, and more visibility must be given to programs that aim to improve Moroccan lives.

NOTES

1   Morocco's demands for change are often referred to as the February 20 Movement because that day in 2011 marked the first major protests, which were called for through social media outlets.

2   Peter Katzenstein, quoted in Gregory White, *A Comparative Political Economy of Tunisia and Morocco: On the Outside of Europe Looking In*, Albany, NY: State University of New York Press, 2001, pp. 18–19.

3   Gregory White, *A Comparative Political Economy of Tunisia and Morocco....*

4   Such efforts were promoted internationally by the World Bank, which, over time, fine-tuned its recommended budgeting techniques.

5   Marlon Mühlberger and Marco Semelmann, "North Africa–Mediterranean Neighbors on the Rise," Deutsche Bank Research, May 31, 2010, p. 9.

6   US Department of State Bureau of Near Eastern Affairs, Background Note: Morocco. April 20, 2011, www.state.gov/r/pa/ei/bgn/5431.htm (to BBB- from BB+ and to BBB+ from BBB, respectively).

7   Maghreb Arabe Presse (Rabat), "Morocco: Nation Awarded African Country of the Future 2011/12," August 13, 2011, allafrica.com/stories/201108160975.html.

8   US Department of State Bureau of Near Eastern Affairs, Background Note: Morocco. March 12, 2012, www.state.gov/r/pa/ei/bgn/5431.htm#econ.

9   Oliver Wyman, *Overview of Investment in Morocco*, Rabat: Kingdom of Morocco Ministry of Industry, Trade and New Technologies, 2010, p. 3.

10 World Bank: Databank.worldbank.org/ddp/home.do?step=27id=4.

11 Michael Shari, "Country Report: Morocco, March 2012," *Global Finance.*

12 Reuters Africa, June 17, 2011. af.reuters.com/article/investingNews/idAFJOE75G0A020110617.

13 Reuters Africa, June, 17, 2011.

14 Saad Guerraoui, Middle East Online March 28, 2012, www.middle-east-online.com/ english/?id=51460nline.com/english/?id=51460.

15 "Morocco," European Commission: Trade, September 30, 2010, ec.europa.eu/trade/creating-opportunities/bilateral-relations/countries/morocco.

16 World Bank, *Doing Business in a More Transparent World*, Washington, D.C.: World Bank, 2012.

17 Andrea Gallina, "Migration, Financial Flows and Development in the Euro-Mediterranean Area," in *The Journal of North African Studies*, Vol. 11, No. 1, March 2006: 19.

18 Mohamed Berrian and Mohamed Aderghal, The State of Research into International Migration from, to and through Morocco. Country Paper,

Morocco 2008. Prepared for the African Perspective s on Guman Mobility progrfamme, financedx by the John D. and Catherine T MacArthur Foundation.

19 The Oxford Business Group. The Report Emerging Morocco 2007. London: Oxford Business Group, 2007.

20 "The Tourism Sector: Progress Report and Prospective Analysis," Kingdom of Morocco Directorate of Studies and Financial Forecasts, April 2011.

21 Nuqudy English. Moroccan Electricity Consumptiojn Grows.

22 english..nuqudy. com/Morocco_Electricity-599

23 "Morocco," World Bank, Accessed November, 2011, "Morocco,"

24 Ian Black, "Wikileaks Cables Accuse Moroccan Royals of Corruption," *The Guardian* Monthly, December 6, 2010.

25 Samia Errazouki, Economic Reform in Moroccothe Road Not Taken, January 21, 2012. www.fairobserver.com/article/economic-reform-morocco-road-not-taken

26 Pierre-Arnaud Chouvy, "Morocco Said to Produce Nearly Half of the World's Hashish Supply," *Jane's Intelligence Review*, November 2005, Vol. 17, no. 11: 32–35.

27 Michel Peraldi, "Economies criminelles et mondes d'affaire à Tanger" (Criminal economies and the business world in Tangiers), *Cultures and Conflicts La Revue*, No. 68 *Circulation et archipels de l'exception*, pp. 111–125.

28 James Ketterer "Networks of Discontent in Northern Morocco Drugs, Opposition, and Urban Unrest," *Middle East Research and Information Project* (MERIP): 218, www.merip.org/mer/mer218/networks-discontent-northern-morocco. Ketterer notes that in 1996, King Hassan II embarked on several "cleansings," with 18,794 people arrested for drug trafficking in Morocco, of whom 342 were foreign. In June 1996 citizens of the area rioted, particularly young people, with dozens of rioters and police hospitalized and two killed. The Rif riots were conflated by unrelated union strikes and other protests elsewhere in the country.

29 United Nations 2998 World Drug Report. http://www.unode.org/documents/wdr/WDR_2008/WDR_2008_eng_web.pdf

30 Alexis Arieff, "Morocco: Current Issues" *Congressional Research Service*, June 20, 2012.

31 Michel Peraldi, "Economies criminelles et mondes d'affaire à Tanger"....

32 Genesis Morocco genesismorocco blogspot.com/2012/03/milestone-moroccos-novecinitiates-35.html

33 IMF Youth Dialog Summary of the Roundtable Discussions at Al-Akhwayan University, Ifrane, Morocco Roundtable Summary, March 8, 2010.

34 World Economic Forum, The Global Gender Gap Report 2011. Rankings and Scores, http://www3.weforum.org/docs/GGGR11/GGGR11_Rankings_Score.pdf

35 "Labor Statistics, Appendix: Unemployment and Selected Rated," International Labor Organization Department of Statistics, 2010.

Several years before the Arab uprising began in Tunisia in December 2011, young cyberactivists in that country and Egypt were using the Internet to organize actions that questioned the authority of their respective dictatorial regimes. They were in touch and thus learned from each other's experiences. The three Tunisians interviewed by Stuart Schaar were key cyberactivists who were harassed and arrested by the regime of Zine al-Abdine Ben Ali in Tunisia. Their stories follow.

CHAPTER 14

THREE TUNISIAN CYBERACTIVISTS WHO HELPED PREPARE THE WAY FOR REVOLT [1]

STUART SCHAAR

I returned to Tunisia at the beginning of June 2011 hoping to find and interview some of the young activists who helped bring down Zine al-Abdine Ben Ali's twenty-three-year dictatorship. A lunch for the well-known professor and blogger Juan Cole (University of Michigan) and Mark Levine (University of California at Irvine), the author of a book on heavy metal music in Morocco—a lunch organized by Tom DeGeorges, then the director of the American Research Center in Tunis, CEMAT—brought me face to face with two of the three bloggers I later interviewed. They were Sofiene ben Haj Mohamed, alias Hamadi Kaloutchka, twenty-eight years old; and Fatma Riahi, also known by her blogger's name, Fatma Arabicca, thirty-four. Sofiene then put me in touch with a young "cyber pirate," Skander Ben Hamda, alias Bullet Skan, sixteen years old. Very quickly I made three new, incredibly interesting friends who I interviewed separately over lunch.

The three were arrested prior to and during the revolt and therefore became well known in Tunisia. Their cases helped galvanize opposition to the Ben Ali dictatorship although the three of them remain humble about their roles in toppling the old regime and give most credit to the Tunisians who remained on the barricades facing the police, snipers, and armed thugs day after day in late December 2010 and early January 2011—finally forcing Ben Ali and his family to flee the country and take refuge in Saudi Arabia. I therefore concentrated in my interviews with the three bloggers on events they precipitated or participated in prior to Ben Ali's departure, events that saw them enter their country's blogsphere world, in which some 200–300 cyberactivists kept the pressure up on the dictatorial regime, which tried to shut them down. Officials quickly discovered that they could not outwit these young people, who found creative ways to circumvent the censors. Their stories help elucidate how the Information Age has transformed the political landscape in parts of the Arab World.

SOFIENE BEN HAJ MUHAMMAD, ALIAS HAMMADI KALOUCHKA

Sofiene was born in the textile town of Ksar Hillal, not far from Monastir, the home of Tunisia's first president, Habib Bourguiba. His mother was Belgian, his father Tunisian. She was one of two foreigners living in the town, and as a result he grew up, as he sees it, "between two parentheses," suffering in his childhood from being viewed as European, as the son of a foreigner who was a Christian. When his parents divorced, he was nine years old and moved with his mother to the coastal city of Nabeul. She got a job there as an interior decorator for hotels, providing for the family. It all came to a head in his high school in that town, when one of his teachers asked him to recite a section of the Koran, which he was supposed to have memorized. When he stumbled in his recitation and could not remember the lines, the teacher tore into him and insulted him in front of the class for being a "half-breed." Sofiene, in a rage, hit the teacher with his notebook. As he tells it, he was not only thrown out of class but also barred from all Tunisian public schools. He spent two years in the resort town of Hammamet hanging out with "juvenile delinquents," where he learned what street life was all about. He imposed himself on the other kids, beating up a couple of them in order to stand tall among his peers and not suffer as he had in his early years in Ksar Hillal.

Sofiene had thus spent two years in limbo when his older sister, who worked in finance in Tunis and lived in the upscale suburb of La Marsa, enrolled him in a private French high school, the Lycée Gustave Flaubert, near her house. There Sofiene discovered a new world—a democratic educational system where students were encouraged to think for themselves. It was like a breath of fresh air, he told me. His father, an architect, who ran a textile factory in Ksar Hillal, paid his school fees during his first year. Sofiene, in his element, became a student leader and was elected as his class delegate to the administration. The school encouraged the students to participate in governance, and Sofiane took up the challenge. He did such a good job that he was elected the student delegate of the entire school. In the meantime, he met a fellow student, a young woman also of mixed parentage—her father being a German communist, a surgeon who later headed a hospital in Berlin; and her mother being a Tunisian. Sofiene and his new friend later married.

Adversity hit when his father went bankrupt, having spent all of his family's inheritance, and declared that he could no longer pay for his son's private education. Sofiene informed the school administration that he had to leave because he could not pay tuition. The principal, aghast that this star student intended to cease his education, arranged for the school's parent association to pay half of Sofiene's fees while the school would cover the other half with a scholarship. In 2003 Sofiene passed the *bac*, an exam whose successful completion represents the equivalent of a US community college degree. He and his fiancé left for France where, using borrowed money, they travelled for a year, living frugally and doing odd jobs to survive.

Sofiene then enrolled in the Free University of Brussels, working part time and helped by his mother's family in Belgium. Just as he had been discriminated against in Tunisia for his mixed parentage, in his mother's native land he felt similar prejudice, especially as his full name made his foreign origins clear: Sofiene Ben Haj Mohamed. Daily affronts saw him develop a profound awareness of his North African roots and his Tunisian identity. Meanwhile Sofiene discovered the social sciences and excelled in the study of philosophy. He dropped science and math, and opted to major in political science.

I asked Sofiene what had impelled him to study politics. He told me that his family's background, as well the influence of an older friend he'd made in Hammamet, had influenced his decision. He added that his paternal grandfather, a communist who had joined the underground armed struggle against colonialism, had been imprisoned by protectorate officials for attempting to kill a French general. After Tunisia achieved its independence his grandfather often spoke with disgust about Bourguiba's dictatorship that, in his view, had cast a shadow on the postcolonial period. That grandfather had died when Sofeine was twelve. In addition, in Hammamet one of the kids Sofeine hung out with had a father who was a teacher and also a communist. The man had friends in a densely populated district of town and, because of his radicalism, had been under police surveillance. He held secret political meetings in his home, which Sofiene sometimes attended, contributing to his own radicalization. By contrast, Sofiene's father, who had met his mother in Brussels while studying architecture there, disdained all politics. Nevertheless he did, indirectly, help raise his son's political consciousness: His textile factory near Ksar Hillal employed low-wage workers who produced garments in sweatshop conditions. Years later, when Sofiane worked at a Tunisian call center, marketing products in France by phone for French companies, he often had flashbacks to those workers in his father's factory, and felt that he had ended up working under similarly dehumanizing conditions.

Sofiene told me that he began blogging in 2008 on seeing the power of Facebook in helping to elect Barack Obama, the first black US president. Many Arabs like him, he `explained, could not help but notice the manner in which

Obama's campaign had marshaled the support of American young people to raise funds and propel him to the White House. The shift was palpable, and the social media site's potential as a political mobilizing tool became immediately apparent. Tunisian adherents to Facebook grew exponentially within three years. Only 16,000 belonged at the beginning of 2008. By August of that year the number had grown to 28,313, jumping to 304,084 by February 20, 2009, and more than double that by July 26, 2009, to 661,640 adherents. After the revolt—on March 22, 2011—the country had 2,201,780 Facebook users.[2]

But blogging in Tunisia under Ben Ali was a dangerous business. On March 13, 2005, a well-known Tunisian cyberactivist, thirty-seven-year-old Zouhair Yahyaoui, died of a heart attack, presumably as a result of the harsh treatment he had received in prison. Zouhair had established the online satirical website TUNeZINE during the summer of 2001; there, anonymously, under the name of "Ettounsi," he denounced violations of individual liberties and the subservience of the country's judicial system to the executive branch. On June 4, 2002, Zouheir was arrested in an Internet café. Over the next few years, he was tortured in prison before finally being released. His death shocked Tunisia's growing cyber community and impelled several bloggers to create contentious sites in which they clamored for justice and respect for human rights. Sofiene was not among the early bloggers.

Sofiene claims, rightly or wrongly, that Tunisians were more advanced than Egyptians in computer skills, and that a higher percentage of Tunisians thus went online earlier than did Egyptians. The Tunisians taught the Egyptians a great deal, he believes. He also thinks it would have been impossible for any country ruled by tyrants to discover and develop the Internet. It had to come from a democracy, such as the United States, which enjoyed a free exchange of information and ideas. In his words:

> When Facebook entered Tunisia, democracy entered through a cable. Facebook gave us freedom of expression. It gave us the right to speak out and we took advantage of it. In my case, I decided to fight for democracy. In my blog I began attacking popular misconceptions. At first it seemed as if the mentality of Tunisians was not favorable to democracy, and people insulted me for what I wrote. I was accused of provoking censorship.

Between 2008 and 2011 Sofiene initiated a number of actions on the Internet that brought him notoriety. During the late summer of 2008 the Tunisian government tried to block its citizens' access to Facebook and increased censorship. It hired 600 computer engineers who reviewed suspicious online material page by page. When the government then started shutting down sites, Sofiene used the software application Hotspot Shield as a proxy.

Three groups of Tunisian social media users formed to confront state censorship. The first demonstrated in front of a theater in central Tunis. Its action failed. Another circulated petitions to reopen Facebook. That campaign dissipated. As for Sofiene, he formed a group whose members threatened to quit Internet service providers. The servers all belonged to members of Ben Ali's family. According to his testimony, four thousand people joined him. The day before the deadline for withdrawal from Internet service, *Le Temps*, a newspaper then controlled by the state, dared to talk about this movement against censorship. The next day, the Facebook site reopened. That was Sofiene's first major victory against the censors.

When Wikileaks published US diplomatic cables, Sofiene, using Google Translate, posted those dealing with Tunisia into French and Arabic. The site at issue registered 160,000 hits by the end of 2010. Thus Tunisians came to realize that the United States, instead of blindly backing Ben Ali, was in fact critical of the regime and understood the depths of its corruption. In September 2010, when Islam-bashing Florida pastor Terry Jones threatened to burn a copy of the Koran, provoking riots in Afghanistan, Sofiene again decided to act. He wanted to demonstrate the hypocrisy of the reaction to the threat by filming the interior of a mosque on the Manar campus of Tunis University, which had been closed for two years. He filmed a Koran on the floor next to empty beer bottles, used condoms, and piles of shit, since the holy building, while closed, had been used for partying and defecation. Al Jazeera showed the film clip and laid the responsibility for the mess at the mosque on the Tunisian government.

According the Skander Ben Essad (whose interview follows below), at the beginning of the Tunisian revolt—on December 25–26, 2010—Sofiane and another blogger, Aziz, started an online campaign for a large-scale labor strike. They sent out the call over several media outlets and placed it on Facebook on December 25—making it seem as if the government-controlled labor union, UGTT, had called the strike. Few people took to the streets, but the action utterly confused the union's leadership, which, indeed, took responsibility for the call to strike. Sofiene and Aziz soon repeated their action: once again speaking in the name of the UGTT leadership, they called for a demonstration at Mohamed Ali Place in Tunis, which succeeded despite the attempt by police to block public access. They did the same on January 1 and 2, 2011. The police closed businesses in proximity to Bab Jazeera, the proposed site of another demonstration. Meanwhile they tracked down and arrested Aziz. Five days later they arrested Sofiene. After each action, Sofiene had had to lie low, avoiding Internet use for a couple of weeks to let things cool down. His actions had clearly been provocative and had involved great personal risk.

Before his arrest, proxy servers had added to Sofiene's confidence, for he'd found sites to use that were securely encrypted. Those that began with "https" kept the censors at bay. When the revolt began on January 1 and 2, 2011, hackers working for the Tunisian government pirated Facebook in order to get everyone's passwords and cause havoc online. Sofiene received a message from Slim Ben Hassan, a Tunisian student in Paris who headed a revolutionary group, requesting a telephone number so a French cultural TV program could interview a cyber-dissident. Sofeine could not buy a new SIM card, but he sent Slim an old number that he had not used in months. As soon as he did so, the regime's censors traced the number to him, leading to his arrest on January 1. Letting his guard down for an instant had cost him his liberty.

The police found his wife's computer at their apartment. It contained the infamous film of the campus mosque. Hitting him for two hours, the detectives wanted to know the name of his Al Jazeera contact and how much the station had paid him for the film clip. They could not understand that he had filmed at his own expense and had received no payment for his work. They forced Sofiene to sign a six-page "confession" whose contents they refused to divulge. He expected them to call him back six months later and press charges against him after tensions waned. Freed after three days, Sofiene joined the demonstrators in front of the prime minister's office.

After the Ben Ali regime fell on January 14, 2011, Sofiene, as a well-known cyberactivist, was nominated to the initial seventy-member commission headed by the jurist Iyadh Ben Achour that was responsible for safe-guarding the revolution and preparing a roadmap for the transition. He attended many meetings, but since members were not reimbursed for transportation and the building where meetings were held was in an out-of-the-way location accessible only by taxi or car, Sofiene attended sessions only sporadically. He has no regular job, but gets by by freelancing for friends and for companies wanting to stay high up on Google and other sites so that users would easily find them online. He had studied marketing for a few years after dropping political science. Neither field pleased him, and he thought of doing journalism in Paris. He was not sure about his future, but after getting to know him, I'm sure something will turn up that will suit his many talents. Finally I asked him—this was in 2011—what he would do if the Islamist party, the Ennahda Movement, were to sweep the elections for the constituent assembly scheduled for October? He responded, without missing a beat, that he fought for democracy and a risk is always there that groups he disagreed with will win the elections. But that will be a test for them, and if they can not perform according to the people's expectations, they will be thrown out of power. It's a risk worth taking, he added. In closing I would add that while the Ennahda did secure victory in late

2011 that saw it form a government, in January 2014, after a political deadlock, it relinquished power to a government of technocrats.

FATMA RIAHI, ALIAS FATMA ARABICCA

Fatma Riahi, thirty-four, is the oldest of the three activists I interviewed. A teacher of theater arts at a rural school, she began blogging earlier than most Tunisians, making her a pioneer of the cyber world there. Her inspiration for studying theater came from well-known Tunisian dramatist Tewfiq Jebali, who in the 1980s formed a company to perform street theater. Tewfiq and his American wife, the late Janet Stevens, were good friends of mine back then, and I and others admired their audacity at the time in tackling hard subjects under Bourguiba's dictatorship. Fatma became interested in the theater of the oppressed and wanted to found her own theater to teach her students drama from the ground up.

When she finished her preliminary studies, Fatma enrolled in a master's program. After passing a required, highly competitive exam, she was qualified to teach and landed a position in a junior high school. But she first had to work for a year as an unpaid intern—a considerable hardship, since Fatma came from a family of eleven children and she was expected to help support her younger siblings, get married, and raise her own family. Getting through that internship was therefore a major challenge. After the year was over, she was assigned to a school near Monastir, in the village of Moknine, far from her hometown, near Zaghouan. As a single woman it would have been difficult to live alone in Moknine, so she opted to live in Monastir and commute to work. Fatma quickly discovered that she did not fit in in Monastir. Most of the city's residents have light skin, unlike hers, and belong to the middle class. She came from a rural area known for its poverty.

Fatma had no friends, but she compensated for this by blogging. At first she wrote about her family, praising her mother's determination in the face of adversity. She started writing poems in the Tunisian Arabic dialect that were well received. Blogging changed her life and put her into the spotlight, allowing her to make many friends. Starting in 2005 Fatma regularly met with fellow bloggers. That was the year that Zouhair Yahyaoui, the well-known cyberactivist, died soon after his release from prison. That event changed her life, she told me, because she realized that he had given his life to expand freedom of expression in the face of dictatorship. Yet it took Fatma a few more years to analyze political events and fight against the macho society that surrounded her. She did, though, begin writing about social and other issues of public interest such as transportation, municipal elections, the exclusion of certain students from school, and how poor parents sacrifice for their children to succeed. When she began her cyberactivism, the government underestimated the power of local bloggers such as Fatma, so she initially escaped punishment even though she wrote under her own name.

More and more, Fatma's blogging turned political. In May 2008, when the phosphate mining town of Metlaoui exploded in unrest, with the locals mounting protests that lasted months, activists there sent Fatma videos showing police violence against the population, including officers forcing open the doors of stores that had been shut in protest. She published some of these videos on her blog. Al Jazeera broadcast clips of these videos that it found on YouTube, while the French TV news channel France 24 sent journalists to the town to cover the story live. Fatma attacked the corruption in the family of President Ben Ali, beginning with an exposé about a Volkswagon dealership contract signed with a prominent presidential relative. She also wrote two blogs about the lack of press independence. By then, there were 200–300 Tunisian bloggers between the ages of sixteen and sixty feeding information to the media.

On November 2, 2009, the police arrested Fatma and released her the same day. The next day they summoned her and accompanied her to Monastir to get her computer. She had bought it on credit in 2005 and still was paying it off. They never returned it. Luckily, she was able to borrow another computer from a friend.

Fatma was promptly rearrested and kept in jail until November 7—interrogated aggressively, with three groups of police officers taking turns asking her questions. They never hit her, but they kept asking for her computer password. They wanted her to sign a confession without letting her read its contents, at which point, Fatma recalls, she screamed at her interrogators, insulted them, and carried on until they relented, giving her a copy to read. They charged her with libel carried out on the Internet and claimed, falsely, that she was the administrator of the blog DebaTunisie (The Tunisian Debate)—debatunisie.canalblog.com. This site contained slick political cartoons in color that attacked Ben Ali and his family. One showed Leila Trabulsi, Ben Ali's wife, a former hairdresser, cutting Muammar Gaddafi's hair. Others showed Ben Ali as a little Hitler. The administrator and cartoonist was an accomplished architect who had begun the site in 2008, and its high quality had attracted a large following.

Fellow bloggers began a "Free Fatma Arabicca" campaign, and the slogan spread together with the mantra, "We are all Fatma Arabicca." Meanwhile, in prison, she was initially put in a room alone with a young man who had also been arrested—a situation never tolerated in a Muslim society outside of prison. When the prison warden found out what his officers had done, he had her removed and put into a cold room by herself. There she heard the screams of prisoners who were being tortured. Outside her window was a tree from which the police hanged young men and beat them. Finally, they put a drunk woman in the room with her who had been beaten to a pulp. By November 7 Fatma was released.

When she returned to the village of Moknine to resume teaching, Fatma was summoned to the local school administration office, where she was told that she was being docked twenty-five days' salary for missing class without permission. Living from paycheck to paycheck, this was a serious blow. Fatma appealed to the teacher's union, which reimbursed her for her lost pay—but only three months later. In addition, the police arrested her younger brother, taking him from the factory where he worked, accusing him of hitting a woman there. They then initiated a court case against Fatma, accusing her of not paying for clothes that she had purchased in 2002. Her lawyer recommended that she pay up rather then enter the court system, sure to become a victim of "Tunisian justice." Her family, frightened by her notoriety and fearful of further repercussions, verbally attacked her and demanded that she stop blogging.

Three months later—it was now 2010—Fatma was back to blogging, anyway, under the name L'Ami Suspect (Suspicious Friend). The authorities shut down this new blog, and when she then returned to the Internet under her old handle of Fatma Arabicca, they shut down that site, too. She then turned to Facebook, where she opened a debate about people who traded in antique Tunisian currency, attacking them for selling parts of the country's national heritage. Soon she discovered that a Canadian was buying a small island off of the coast of Djerba, and she went on the attack. This time the antiterrorist police intervened. Meanwhile, the government, in an effort to sow confusion among Internet users, created its own Facebook and Gmail pages.

When the revolt broke out, Fatma joined the demonstrators and remained on the barricades until Ben Ali fell. At that point her family celebrated with her, but soon thereafter renewed its pressure on her to marry and raise a family of her own, reminding her that traditions continue to exert a powerful hold on her society. And yet, not having forgotten her first love, drama, Fatma was hoping to mount a project focused on the theater of the oppressed. Given her experience and determination, she should succeed.

SKANDER BEN HAMIDA, ALIAS BULLET SKAN

Skander Ben Hamida was introduced to me by Sofiane, who had spent time in the same prison without ever meeting him. They had recently been introduced at a party and spent the evening talking about their experiences. Sofiene told me that this sixteen-year-old was a cyber pirate, and urged me to call him.

Skander discovered electronics with his first Atari game, which he played on the family TV. His mother, a schoolteacher, bought it for him when he was three years old. In 1997 his mother also bought him his first PC, a Pentium 3 costing $2,000. He immediately took it apart, hoping to put it back together again and learn the machine's anatomy. He and his mother returned the machine to the store, and she protected him from his father, who was displeased at her having bought so young a child a computer—a machine that indeed Skander had proceeded to wreck. She told her husband that they had to encourage their son, for by taking apart the computer he was trying to learn how it really worked. She believed in him, he told me. Before long, he learned how to take the machine apart and put it back together again. Prior to his infatuation with computers Skander played soccer and was a fan of the Club Africain soccer team, in Tunis. But once he had his own computer, he began focusing solely on computers, and no longer shared with his parents what he was doing online.

At first Skander attended a preeminent high school, Lycee Sadiki, which had been founded in 1875 by the Tunisia's reformist prime minister, Khayr al-Din Pasha as a way to introduce secular education into the country. Most of the country's elites had passed through its doors, but in recent years it had allowed into its hallowed halls students from lower class districts. The school administration remained dedicated to student needs, responding whenever called on to mediate between the teaching staff and pupils, and indeed often defended students from tyrannical professors. Skander appreciated the chance he had to attend Sadiki, and, as he tells it, because of his brilliance got into trouble with one of his teachers who thought that he was a wise guy for trying to correct him. The teacher threw Skander out of his class, and Skander immediately went to the principal's office to complain about the teacher's arrogance and unwillingness to be corrected by a student. The principal listened to Skander and returned with him to the classroom where he confronted the teacher and forced him to take Skander back as a student. Skander told me that Sadiki had been student centered, and if someone complained, he or she could expect redress. Disaster hit, however, when Sadiki closed its computer courses, forcing Skander to enroll in the high school in his own neighborhood, where the teachers and the administration tended to be authoritarian.

Skander now began reading about Internet hacking and pirating, and soon decided to learn how to become a cyber pirate and how to phish. "It was sort of a crazy thing to do," he told me. At thirteen years of age he bought a server with excellent security, and then another one. He felt powerful. He hacked a company's computer and then laid low for three months. He had illusions of grandeur and thought that once the company found out who had discovered a major flaw in its system, he would be rewarded. He then visited the company, notifying its representatives that he had hacked it. Instead of lauding him, they had Skander arrested. The police slapped him around. Depression set in and his dreams of grandeur were demolished.

But Skander could not resist hacking and piracy since it gave him a feeling of great power. Still thirteen years old, with outstanding grades (equivalent to staight A's) in computer science at his new school, he pirated all the building's computers, as well as its main e-mail account. The school's administrators waived Skander's obligation to take any more computer courses in exchange for his desisting from piracy against the school. He then spent eighteen hours a day in front of his computer and didn't sleep for weeks, provoking an epileptic fit.

But soon Skander was attracted to a Tunisian anarchist group, Takriz, whose web page had been censored in August 2008 and despite that continued to function. He detested Ben Ali and his regime. The ubiquitous photos of the president posted all around the country disgusted him. Skander too, as was the case with Sofiene and Fatma, was traumatized by Zouhair's death, which impelled him to act. On approaching Takriz asking if he could join, he was told to submit articles to demonstrate his worthiness. Skander wrote a poem about censorship, which the group published. A second poem on dictatorship followed, after which he was permitted to join the organization. He wanted to be able to tell his own children some day that he had fought Ben Ali's dictatorship. He told me that he felt that he had no other choice.

Takriz was the first organization in Tunisia to broach the subject of revolution, beginning in 2010. It put up a Facebook page that was ignored. Skander spoke to one of the group's leaders, who went by the handle Foutus, and was told that he, Foutus, was writing a scenario for a revolution in Tunisia. He gave Skander excerpts to read, including descriptions of Ben Ali's corruption. Skander asked Foutus if they could write together. Foutus had no idea that Skander was merely fifteen, thinking he was in his twenties. By August 2010 Skander had joined Takriz's central committee, responsible for recruitment. He also initiated an action to write a revolutionary slogan on the wall of the telecommunications ministry to protest growing Internet censorship. He went there at 3 AM expecting the area to be deserted. Instead he found the place bustling with people guarding nearby stores. Skander nevertheless succeeded in writing his graffiti on the ministry walls—a crime in prerevolt Tunisia, as it had been under the French colonial regime, punishable by imprisonment.

On December 17, 2010—once news spread about the self-immolation of Mohamed Bouazizi that day, precipitating the Tunisian revolt that was to erupt the next day—Skander attended a meeting of anarchist activists intent on kicking out Ben Ali. They decided to infiltrate demonstrations in order to change the slogans and radicalize the demands, convinced that the protestors would follow suit. Sofiene's and Aziz's above-mentioned action calling for strikes then took place on December 25–26.

Skander also joined Anonymous, the amorphous group made famous by its hacking the websites of those who condemned WikiLeaks. Its Tunisian members initially attacked thier country's main government-operated tourism site, but they quickly realized that they had to up the ante by going after more strategic sites to put them out of business. Skander worked with four people from Anonymous in attacking the site of the prime minister's office—and got rid of it. They left behind the message, "We are Anonymous and we are watching how you are violating your citizen's rights. The police should stop all oppression. If they don't, this will get worse." At the beginning of January, using a proxy, Skander attacked the website of the Ministry of Defense, prompting his arrest. He later realized during his interrogation in prison that he had been under surveillance for a couple of years, that informants had been reporting his activities to the authorities. Skander was in jail January 6–13, 2011, having been forced also to hand over his computer to the Interior Ministry. He was interrogated nonstop and burned with the same cigarettes he himself asked for. He showed me seven burn marks left on his arms. As was the case with Sofiene, he was forced to sign a confession he was not allowed to read. To this day, he doesn't know its contents.

On January 15 Skander gave up his cyber piracy and decided to return to his studies. At the time of this writing he was exploring ways to go overseas on a scholarship to study advanced computer science so as to contribute what he can to a new Tunisia. He concluded our interview by telling me that his body was sixteen, his mind twenty-five, and his experience equivalent to that of a man of forty. In March, after Ben Ali and his family had fled Tunisia, Skander went to the Interior Ministry to retrieve his computer. He found the same people working there and the same structures in place. Little had changed, he told me. [3]

1   The author thanks Dr. Tom DeGeorges, who in 2011 directed CEMAT, the AIMS research center in Tunis, in reading and commenting on this chapter. The author alone is responsible for its contents.

2   www.checkfacebook.com, cited in an unublished paper by Sofiane Ben Haj, "La révolution tunisienne à travers les nouvelles technologies de l'information et de la communication," (March 2011), p. 7.

3   For more on Tunisian cyberactivism see the following chapters in Sihem Najar, ed., Le cyber activisme au Maghreb et dans le monde arabe, Paris: Karthala IRCM, 2013, Romain Lecomte, "Les usages 'citoyens' d'Internet dans le contexte autpritaire tunisien analyse de l'émergence d'un nouvel espace public de la critique,"

pp. 55–75; Hamida el Bour, "Cyberactivisme des journalistes tunisiens avant et après la révolution du 14 janvier 2011," pp. 95–105; Siham Najar, "Les femmes cyberctivistes et les revendications d'un changement démocratique en Tunisie," pp. 148–173; Chirine Ben Abdallah, "L'engagement politique des internautes tunisins au lendemain de la révolution: les pages *facebook* seront-elles une arme à double tranchant?," pp. 125–140; Maryam Ben Salem, "Femmes tunisiennes et usages différenciés de la sphère du *Web* comme outil du participation politique," pp. 141–148; Rym Haloues Ghorbel, "Cyberactivisme tunisien en matière de don d'organes et changements de valeurs," pp. 259–269.

Dr. Viola Shafik, a film critic and documentary filmmaker living in Egypt and Germany, examines in this chapter the burst of cinematic creativity that accompanied the revolts in Tunisia and Egypt. She demonstrates how difficult it is for filmmakers to express themselves freely even now that the Ben Ali and Mubarak dictatorships have fallen. Constraints from bureaucratic regulations, new and old, as well as public attacks undertaken by Islamists and Salafist guardians of morality have further jeopardized freedom of expression. A few directors, both men and women, have found the right formulas to express themselves openly despite new impediments imposed on creative artists since the revolts.

CHAPTER 15
FILM CULTURE IN UPHEAVAL?
EGYPT AND TUNISIA IN TIMES OF REVOLT*
VIOLA SHAFIK

A revolution is somewhat like a tsunami: it sweeps across the land, shaking everything that stands on weak foundations, and finally recedes, leaving behind a completely changed geography. And even if it achieves no real success, as in the case of Egypt, it brings deep uncertainly to everyone who experiences it. Handed-down rules and ideas, long-familiar actors and forms of expression begin to waver and must submit to scrutiny. The entire political and cultural landscape suddenly finds itself confronted by previously unknown challenges, in terms of content, aesthetics, and structure: in short, a society, a culture in upheaval.[1]

I wrote these lines in the spring of 2012, but almost a year later, I find that for Egypt and Tunisia the image of an active volcano seems more appropriate: the so-called Arab Spring as a series of variably intense eruptions, here and there a few new formations, but no fundamental change, rather just enough to raise uncertainties and a whole lot of questions. For neither Egypt nor Tunisia have thus far experienced the outbreak of what the experts call a "great revolution," one that completely abolishes economic and social structures, as well

*Adapted from "Filmkultur im Umbruch? Ägypten und Tunesien zu Zeiten der Rrevolution," in Positionen: issue Arabische Welt, edited by Johannes Ebert, Johannes Odenthal, Sarah Rifky, Stefan Winkler, and Günther Hasenkamp in a joint initiative of Academie de Künste, Berlin and Goethe-Institut, Munich. Göttingen: Steidl Verlag, 2013. Used with permission. Translated from the German by Bernard Heise.

as political institutions, probably because the uprisings in both countries—similar to the case of Eastern Europe after 1989—fail to conform to traditional class struggle but rather began as a peaceful revolt through which a coalition of various social strata and interest groups unsaddled a previously secure regime.

But the alliance between the upper and lower classes, on the one hand, and the military, Islamists, liberals, and the left on the other that precipitated the fall of dictators has thus far been unable to reach a consensus regarding the degree and nature of the necessary changes. Meanwhile, in the areas of the economy, human rights, and personal freedom, some—first and foremost from the Islamist camp—are striving for and effecting measures even more reactionary than the previous government would have dared. After Islamic forces undermined their initial rapprochement with the liberal, democratic, and secular camp as a result of their blatant striving for power, the Tunisian and Egyptian societies today find themselves beset by inner divisions and turmoil. In the case of Egypt, the relationship between the camps has even suddenly changed to open hostility, claiming its first causalities at events around the Egyptian presidential palace in December 2012. In both countries the Islamists have been swept out of power, with a military regime taking over in Egypt and an amalgam of old guard ex-Bourguibists and lower level Ben Ali followers ruling in Tunisia.

During the first year, however, the situation still looked quite different. A revolutionary wind was, in fact, blowing through the society, setting things in motion within the realm of established culture. In the process, during the course of the first eighteen days of the uprising in Egypt, Tahrir Square provided the stage for unparalleled creative commotion: drawings, caricatures, songs, rhymes, chants, self-presentations, and installations. This creative explosion produced the impression of enormous diversity and an initial sense of grassroots democracy and social justice; for, in contrast to ancient democracy, this agora included not only the privileged hand-picked few but also the poor and marginalized, liberals and conservatives, the secular and the religious, women and men. They included a considerable number of more or less famous artists, some of whom—remaining in tents at Tahrir Square after the "Battle of the Camel" on February 2, 2011—later becoming spokespersons for various groups of demonstrators. Other less fortunate individuals lost their lives during the first days of the Egyptian revolt, including the graphic artist Ziad Bakir and the installation artist Ahmed Bassiouny.

In Tunisia, too, first the protests in Avenue Bourguiba and later the sit-in on Kasbah Square produced this creative and inclusive agora. No wonder, then, that many artists felt encouraged—even pressured—to leave their ivory towers (if that was where they were) and take a position vis-à-vis this altered landscape. Inspired by events, questions emerged about what art could offer the people assembled in the squares and how it could respond to the revolt's key slogans: in Egypt, "Bread, Freedom, Dignity, and Social Justice"; and in Tunisia, "Work, Freedom, and Dignity." Thus the first eighteen days of the uprising in Egypt already featured the formation of the Federation of Independent Art (i´tilaf al-thaqafa al-mustaqilla), which also includes the cultural manager Basma al-Husseiny, who with a few other individuals directs the al-Fann Midan (Art is a Square) initiative. As of this writing, on the first Saturday of every month the group was staging a free-admission street festival on the public squares of Cairo and various other Egyptian cities, with exhibitions, handicrafts, and theatrical and musical performances.[2]

In Tunisia in 2011 and during the spring 2012, the Tunisian graphic artist Elektro Jaye, Franco-Algerian's "Zoo project,"[3] the Ahl al-Kahf graffiti group, as well as the gigantic mural "Khaldounia" created jointly by seven different artists brought art into the streets. A film festival launched in 2011 by the Tunisian filmmaker Ridha Tlili in the town of Regueb near Sidi Bouzid, the cradle of the revolt, included the creation of a number of short films about local artistic activities. In addition, Tlili established a documentary film association in the town.[4] (See Chapter 16 for a description of the street art produced during and after the Tunisian revolt.) In Egypt, activists also used graffiti as a direct form of revolutionary communication. In early summer 2011, visual artists decorated the walls of buildings in Cairo's impoverished districts and inner city; artists like Ganzur and Ammar Abu Bakr commented on political events, sprayed mobilizing slogans and caricatures as well as sophisticated murals on walls, and, in 2012, just before the first anniversary of outbreak of the revolt, called for a week of "Mad Graffiti."

Similar developments occurred in the media sector. In a collective exhibition during fall 2011, photographers such as Cairo resident Randa Chaath drew attention to the revolt's unknown and ongoing victims. Media artists from the Egyptian Mosireen initiative, founded by the filmmaker Tamer Sai and the actor Khalid Abdalla (The Kiterunner, 2007), dedicated themselves to "people's journalism" and put together audio-visual recordings of the revolt. Meanwhile, from December 2011 until the military regime was replaced by the new president, political activists of the Kazibun (Liars) movement produced and screened short documentaries in public squares to expose the state media's one-sided reporting on human rights violations. Yet, as of this writing, the immediacy of the revolt's first days was slowly fading away: the Mosireen initiative, for example, created a didactic series on civil rights and no longer only documents current affairs.

The impetus to bring art to the streets and the long-neglected provinces is unmistakably a first-stage revolutionary impulse. During the second year of the revolt and in the wake of the intensified state and military violence, blood-shed, and violent sexual assaults that confronted those who occupied and demonstrated in Tahrir Square, as of this writing the square had degenerated into a stomping ground for hawkers and revolutionary desperados. Likewise, the murals had lost their artistic ease, diversity, and abstraction. Upon the election of Mohamed Morsi from the Muslim Brotherhood, the initial graf-fiti was removed and at the same time the people who revolted went on the defensive; the new wave of graffiti, consisting mostly of realistic portraits of "martyrs," appeared much more sloganistic and dogmatic.

Concurrently with "institutionalization" and "hierarchization," new battlefronts emerged: after the electoral victories by Islamic parties in both countries, artists and intellectuals saw themselves on the defensive. After the Egyptian Muslim Brotherhood's Morsi assumed power in the summer of 2012, legal actions against journalists and politicians—among other things, for alleg-edly defaming the president and attempting coups—multiplied. Anticipating this confrontation, prominent Egyptian artists—first and foremost the film directors Daoud Abd El-Sayed and Khalid Youssef, the producer Midhat al-Adl, the painter Muhammad Abla, the author Baha Tahir, and the poet Gamal Bakhit—founded the so-called Creative Front (*jabhat al-ibda*') as early as January 2012 to defend creativity and freedom of opinion. But the Front provided little protection from encroachments.

In Tunisia, censorship efforts and violent assaults occurred even earlier than in Egypt. A court sentenced Nabil Karoui to pay a fine because his televi-sion station broadcast the Franco-Persian animated film *Persepolis*, classifying one of the film's scenes as blasphemy. Incidents occurred in the visual arts sector as well: Elektro Jaye, for example, accused organizers of the *Printemps des Arts* of taking down one of his paintings for religious reasons. On another occasion, Salafists stormed an exhibition in Tunis, destroying a number of the paintings and installations on display. One of the worst assaults took place in June 2011, when fanatic Islamists forced their way into the AfricArt movie theater and inflicted property damage as part of their campaign against Nadia El-Fani's documentary film *Laicité Inchallah* (2011). The Tunisian filmmaker, whose film confronts religious-moral double standards, among other things, subsequently found herself exposed to media attacks, which she documented in another film, *Même pas mal* (2012).

Under these circumstances, the fact that revolutionary and assimilated or conservative artists have partially closed ranks—which meanwhile can also be observed in the political field—comes as no surprise. The aging Egyptian "King of Comedy" `Adil Imam, for example, whose films since the end of the 1970s constantly resulted in box office hits, had strongly supported Mubarak in a television interview during the uprising. With Mubarak's resignation on February 11, Imam lost so much popularity that a Vodafone advertising campaign launched a short time earlier with him at the helm had to be cancelled. In spring 2012, however, Imam was charged and convicted because he supposedly defamed Islam in a work created decades ago, thus once again assuring for him the solidarity of his fellow actors, artists, and parts of the public.

Consolidation took place elsewhere as well. The state's monopolization of all cultural activities, firmly established in Egypt since the mid-twentieth century, meant that, in practice, the Ministry of Culture even created groups such as the Film Critics Association, which originally launched the International Cairo Film Festival. After a few cosmetic improvements, parts of the old management once again—as of this writing, in the second year of the revolt—took over the festival. The complete restructuring of the Ministry of Culture, as called for by artists, had not occurred. Artists who work in the cinema in Tunisia also urged the creation of a self-governing—that is, independent of the state—national film center to control film ratings and supports films. Despite substantial preparatory work on its statutes, the center was still not really independent. Thus, as late as November 2012, Tunisian producers and filmmakers complained that the appointment of the center's conservative director had been made over their heads.[5]

Thus "traditional" conformative culture has reemerged, whereas "organic" artists need to reorient themselves. Antonio Gramsci defines organic intellectuals as those who express the interests of a certain class, in contrast to traditional intellectuals, who, due to their assimilation, help preserve the existing system's cultural hegemony. Gramsci's classification of traditional and organic intellectuals has naturally been revised and refined by others, including Michel Foucault, for whom intellectuals have the responsibility of exposing the hegemonic "regime of truth."[6] For Julia Kristeva, on the other hand, the intellectual dissident approximates the organic intellectual who dedicates himself to a specific underprivileged group, such as women, homosexuals, or ethnic minorities.[7] Regarding art itself, we must in any event exercise caution when speaking in terms of assimilated and organic art, even if this seems appropriate for ideological polarizations after the revolts. In doing so, we need to consider more than simply the factor of historical change; thus, in his analysis of popular culture, Stuart Hall has indicated that the categories of subculture and elitist art cannot be essentialized, especially since they also constitute a site of struggle between different discourses; that is, what appears nonconformist today can be assimilated tomorrow and deployed to serve a dominant discourse,[8] something that we could actually observe for example in the practices of Egypt's post revolt state media. Even though the Morsi regime was hardly interested in realizing the uprising's goals, its programs and presenters heaped lavish praise on the revolt and its martyrs.

Similarly, recent artistic projects from the region should more appropriately be discussed not in terms of clearly defined categories but as a struggle between discourses. The episodic film *18 Days* (*thamani ashar yaum*), 2011, created on the initiative of Yousry Nasrallah and involving the collaboration of a number of prominent Egyptian directors, celebrated its premier at the 2011 Cannes Film Festival. The work made negative headlines upon the revelation that two of its directors had made campaign ads during the last presidential elections for the now deposed head of state. Entirely fictional in nature, the episodes themselves range from bold accusations of human rights violations under Mubarak to humorous segments, such as one in which a man barricades himself in a store and afterward discovers an altered political landscape. The most jarring contributions, however, come from the project's only two female directors, Mariam Abu Ouf (Awf) and Kamla Abu Zikri, one dealing with the conflicted conscience of a government-hired thug and another with the moral dilemma of a young woman from a humble background who, during the days of the revolt, dyed her hair an unusual color, even though she would be better off concealing her hair beneath a head scarf. But these are hardly examples of formal innovation.

In this sense, we should keep in mind that not everything that purports to be revolutionary is necessarily revolutionary. As in the case of *18 Days*, most of the cinematography created since the turmoil that deals with the uprising itself is more or less descriptive and classical in form. Only a few works try to conquer new cinematic terrain; that is, to revolutionize the medium itself. When watching the first "revolutionary" works of art in the history of film, such as Sergei Eisenstein's *Battleship Potemkin* (1925) or Dziga Vertow's *Man with a Movie Camera* (1929), we notice above all their special form. The two Soviet directors transposed the materialistic concept of the collision of opposites not so much through content—that is, not through any stringent or coherent narrative (Vertow's film lacks such a narrative anyway)—but rather through form. Both films developed—manifest at the level of film montage—a concept contrary to conventional narrative cinema's causally determined unity of space and time, as featured first and foremost in American films. Two other aspects are also apparent: first, the films were created after a decent gestation period, just over a decade after the outbreak of the Russian Revolution; second, with the advent of Stalinism they were superseded by an indoctrinating socialist realism, while Vertov himself was ostracized.

For a better understanding it may be helpful to take into consideration Colin MacCabe's notion of classic realist text, which seems to apply to both socialist and Hollywood realism. MacCabe viewed the latter as reactionary because it organizes discourses hierarchically, primarily through the narrative's uniform perspective by giving the spectator the impression that s/he occupies a position outside of the production of meaning and therefore possesses the whole, absolute truth.[9] Critics challenged MacCabe's conception in part by citing the arguments of Michail Bakhtin, who asserted that the realist text, too, possesses a dialogical and/or contradictory character and therefore could also allow marginalized discourses to be heard.

Nonetheless, even if we cannot assume an absolutely hegemonic realist text, MacCabe's three specific alternatives to the classic realist text—namely the progressive, subversive, and revolutionary text—can still be useful for further film analysis. Hence MacCabe regards a formally classic realist text whose content contradicts the dominant ideology—for example, a film that recounts an economic struggle from the perspective of trade unions—as a progressive text, while a subversive text opposes any kind of dominance, including narrative dominance as well. The latter would therefore be a narration that offers various versions of one and the same story. In turn, the revolutionary text would be a more self-reflexive or even a deconstructive text that includes and problematizes itself in the process of the production of meaning.[10] Naturally, the difference between all three categories is rather fluid, especially since the classic realist text can include dialogue just as can the self-reflexive text.

Considering the circumstances of the Egyptian film industry, dominated by a star system and monopolized by just a few interregional distribution companies, the two latter text categories hardly stand a chance of being realized or distributed. To be accessible to a larger public, a film can appear at most to be progressive, like *Winter of Discontent (al-shita illi-fat)* (2012) by Ibrahim El-Batout (al-Batut) and Ahmad Abdalla's *Mattress and Covers (farsh wa ghata)* (yet to be released as of this writing), both relatively stringently narrated films that take a critical stance toward the old regime. Yet the very first works by these two directors, created prior to the revolt, feature a very vigorous polyphony. They were rightly evaluated as forerunners of alternative filmmaking, especially since they also sought to move into new terrain with production methods that were relatively independent from the industry.

Abdalla's *Microphone* (2010), for example, is a kaleidoscopic music film that deals with the exclusion of the Alexandria alternative art scene—including rappers, filmmakers, and graffiti artists—from the state's Art Center in favor of more assimilated artists, and at the same time examines the individuals' private lives. It owes its charm and spontaneity to the fact that the musicians and artists comprising its protagonists developed their stories and characters themselves; thus the result should be viewed as a collective effort. This conglomeration is what lends the film its polyphony. As a heavy lifter for the box office, the famous actor Khalid Abu El-Nagga (Khalid Abu al-Nagga) joined the team in a secondary role. He also stood at the frontlines during the revolt. In a certain way, with its focus on alternative, nonconformist young artists and its collective orientation, *Microphone* seems to anticipate the image of the creative Egypt in revolt. Its cinema debut, however, foundered amid the excitement of Mubarak's departure, which had just taken place.

Ain Shams (2009), by El-Batout, on the other hand, is a film about a young girl from Cairo's impoverished neighborhood of Ayn Shams who suffers from cancer. For her entire life she has wanted to see Cairo's inner city, but she needs to wait a long time for this to happen because her father, a humble taxi driver, has his hands full. Apart from his own taxi, he also needs to chauffeur a rich industrialist and, in addition, grapple with the latter's familial problems. The film is distinguished by its minimal budget and absence of stars, its open and almost fragmentary narrative structure with multiple parallel stories, and an obvious improvisational spirit that derives from the fact that the play and stories originated in a theater workshop whose members included both professional actors and amateurs.

Purely in terms of production technicalities, and circumventing the usual laws and protesting state censorship, El-Batout set a precedent with *Ain Shams* by producing his movie without a film permit. However, before its commercial screening he had to reach a compromise with the authorities and obtain a formal permit. The controversy pertained not to the film's content per se but rather to its challenging of standard procedures. Yet the kaleidoscopic, fragmentary narrative style shown by El-Batout's early film proved to be very pioneering. Tending toward a collective orientation, other postrevolt films emulated this narrative form as well, such as Maggie Morgan's *Asham: A Man Called Hope* (2012), which features actors improvising various episodes linked by only one thing—namely, an encounter with a cheerful casual worker called Asham (hope). The author's attempt to use improvisation to escape a strict dramatic narrative generates a shift from the large, meaningful narration to the small detail, while the concentration on individual episodes creates a kaleidoscopic perspective that approximates MacCabe's subversive text. We can expect to find a similar polyphony in *In the Last Days of the City (akhir ayam al-madina)* by Tamer Said. Being completed as of this writing, this film groups improvised narrative components and video letters from different cities—among others, Berlin, Beirut, and Baghdad—around the personal memories of the filmmaker-protagonist (and alter ego of the filmmaker himself).

As already mentioned, El-Batout and Abdalla, who began by using this form, have tended to abandon it in their new films, moving into the progressive camp, to which we must also assign Yousry Nasrallah's *After the Battle (bad al-mawqia)* (2012). These are, in Bakhtin's terms, classic dialogical works in which the old regime and democratically oriented ideas collide, cleanly divided into protagonists and antagonists. At the same time, the plots of these films elucidate a system of oppression. *Winter of Discontent*, for example, deals with the anguish of a former political prisoner, his ex-girlfriend—a state-television journalist who shows her colors during the revolution and again draws close to him—and their antagonist, a calculating state security officer. *After the Battle* looks at the ambivalent relationship of a young bourgeois woman attracted to a horseman at the pyramids who was purportedly involved in the attack in Tahrir Square during the so-called "Battle of the Camel." Through him, she and the viewers obtain an insight into the machinations of the orchestrators behind the scenes and, above all, the economic pressure faced by horsemen reliant on a tourism sector in crisis.

Tunisia also witnessed the production of progressive films, such as *The Professor (alustath)* (2012) by Mahmoud Ben Mahmoud (Mahmud b. Mahmud), which follows the efforts of a well-known jurist under Ben Ali who is appointed to the national human rights commission but then, after the arrest of his student and lover, finds himself in a dilemma between his feelings and the regime's demands. This kind of antagonism—sometimes downright sloganistic—also animates the documentary films created in the wake of the first uprisings that predominantly showed solidarity with the insurgents. From today's perspective, three films above all—*Red Word (Rouge Parole)* (2012), by Elyes Baccar (Ilyas Bakkar), *No More Fear (Plus Jamais peur)* (2011) by Mourad Ben Cheikh (Murad b. Shaykh), and *Dégage!* (i.e. *Get Lost!;* 2012) by Mohammed (Muhammad) Zran—look like chronologies of the revolt's eighteen days and the subsequent struggles between the old system on the one hand and the desire for liberation and democracy on the other.

The focus on events on the streets and the mass protests—even though *No More Fear*, for example, repeatedly returns to a few select contemporary witnesses—produces a leveling effect comparable to the television images broadcast during the protest. The same can be said of Tamer Ezzat's (Tamir Izzat) documentary episode in *Tahrir 2011: The Good, the Bad, and the Politician* (2011), which was screened jointly with two other contributions by Ayten Amin and `Amr Salama at the 2011 Leipzig Film Festival. Despite individual portraits, such as that of a photojournalist and an activist, this work, too, offers little to counter the inflationary deluge of images from the new media and satellite television. Ayten Amin offers a somewhat different approach in an episode where she interviews policemen from her own personal environment and circle of acquaintances to thereby scrutinize their professional ethics. Although an obvious antagonism underlies this episode as well, the director's subjective perspective tends to undermine the hierarchy-creating discourse.

We also frequently find this penchant for the personal or attempts by filmmakers to introduce themselves—as filmmakers—as subjective and thus also partisan witnesses in other works, such as in Ahmad Rashwan's *Born on the 25th of January (mawlud fi 25 yanayir)*, a painstaking chronicle of the first phase of the revolt. However, the film's subjective—yet nonetheless extremely stringent—narration substantially limits its polyphony, quite in contrast to *Forbidden (Mamnu)* (2011), made by Amal Ramsis prior to the revolt. Ramsis—a political activist—shaped her film essay through a strongly associative approach by using conversations with friends and acquaintances, enriched by general observations from her social environment, to pursue questions regarding the numerous taboos—political, social, and cultural in nature—that she and others grew up with. But the film's technical quality leaves something to be desired.

The Tunisian Nadia El-Fani's *Laïcité Inchallah* (2011), which likewise can be categorized as a personal film essay, boasts a much higher cinematic quality than its Egyptian counterparts, probably because the French production was far better equipped and El-Fani can look back on a long filmography. She undertakes during Ramadan to scrutinize Islamic ideology and the double moral standard of many of her compatriots from an aesthetic perspective, keeping an eye on the ideal of the separation of religion and state. Similar to *Dégage!*, this film—which was originally supposed to be called *Neither Allah nor Master*—clearly illustrates the hardening front between the secular and Islamic camps, a front first noticeable in Egypt primarily in the streets and in the media during the revolt's second year, but not in film.

Presented exclusively from the perspective of extremely socially marginalized characters, Hind Boujemaa's (Bu-Jumua) Tunisian documentary film *It was Better Tomorrow (ya man ash)* (2012) comes across as radically progressive; so does *Living Skin (jild hay)* (2010), a documentary by the Egyptian director Fawzi Saleh (Salih). Boujemaa's film in particular is a classic "direct cinema" contribution, in which, without commentary, the camera follows a homeless Tunisian woman for several months, depicting the violence and abuse of her everyday life. The revolt decisively shaped the bourgeois director's cinematic observations, for she confesses to having lived in the clouds under Ben Ali's government. The unrest gave her the opportunity to get to know a side of the country and its people that she had never known before.[11] Saleh, whose film deals with a group of young people and their harmful—even life-threatening—working conditions in the Cairo commercial district, likewise keeps his camera close to his characters and their everyday life. The film's subjective voice provides stories and commentary recited off-camera by the protagonists.

Another observational "direct cinema" film is *Revolution under 5' (thawra taht daraj)* (2011), in which, without commentary, the Tunisian filmmaker Ridha Tlili gazes over the shoulders of a group of graffiti artists called *Ahl al-Kahf* (literally, cave people; metaphorical for "underground") who conceive of themselves as aesthetic guerillas. (See Chapter 16.) But in contrast with Boujemaa and Saleh, Tlili, when recording and montage editing, heavily fragments and disregards the unity of time and space. The film therefore relinquishes any kind of narrative stringency and becomes a subversive cinematic intervention, a sort of associative cinematic manifesto. It forms a kind of counterpart to Tlili's 2011 prerevolutionary film essay *Jiha (Region)*, a kaleidoscope of endangered traditional arts from the filmmaker's home region. Tlili had already pursued a similar disruption of narrative continuity in a short film created prior to the revolt entitled *Anyone (Ayan Kan)* (2007), about a couple's unsuccessful suicide attempt and the man's subsequent arbitrary arrest. As accurately noticed by the Tunisian blogger and filmmaker Ismaël, Tlili organizes his material concentrically: like the ripples of stone thrown into water, a circle forms around the center, then another, and then the next one. In addition, mute faces—indeed, silence as such—play a large role in this as in other Tunisian films made by younger Tunisian *cinéastes* prior to the revolt, as if someone had "killed their language."[12]

As mentioned earlier, decentralization and collectivism played a major role for artistic activities after the revolt. This also applies to the film industry, an area where the ATAC (*Association tunisienne d'action pour le cinéma*)—which chiefly organizes workshops and traveling performances in the provinces—as well as the film group Exit have since excelled. Along with Ismaël (Isma'il), the group includes Youssef Chebi (Yusuf Shabbi) and Ala Eddine Slim (Ala al-Din Salim). Stylistically, their jointly made film *Babylon* (2012) can be categorized as "direct cinema," particularly since the filmmakers document the construction and later dismantling of a Tunisian refugee camp near the Libyan border without commentary and through long, observational shots. In the process, they depict the major and minor adversities and pleasures of the refugees, as well those of their supervisors from countries throughout the world from Bangladesh to West Africa, situating them in relation to the harsh natural environment of the surrounding desert. The film deliberately avoids rendering the camp's prevailing linguistic chaos accessible through subtitles so that the viewer, too, remains helplessly exposed to the camp's babel effect.

This collective work unmistakably features the same distance from the spoken word that, as mentioned above, Ismaël identified in Tlili's films. We also find a similar orientation in an earlier work by one of the trio's directors, namely Ala Eddine Slim's short film *The Stadium (al-stad)* (2010), produced back in the period of the dictatorship. In endlessly long tracking shots, this film follows a man through the city on the evening of a soccer game. He sits for a long time in a café before making his way through a dark, hostile urban setting. He gets randomly beaten, and then the film moves on through deserted streets and abandoned factory halls while the game's official commentary acoustically counteracts—indeed, almost parodies—the picture. The latter, however, slowly consolidates into a capricious and terrifying landscape that leaves the individual wordlessly exposed.

For the film theorist André Bazin, the long take, in combination with the specific framing of the long shot and the renunciation of rapidly changing close-ups—today commonly featured, of course, above all in action films—is the quintessence of realism.[13] In actual fact, this renders the individual's social embeddedness, his interaction with the environment, all the more apparent. The long shot leaves viewers—who especially today are accustomed to sequences of rapid cuts in varied distances—to their own devices, thereby producing a strong effect of alienation and estrangement. We find something similar in Hala Lotfi's (Lutfi) Egyptian drama *Coming Forth by Day (al-khuruj illa al-nahar)* (2012), which, compared to other Egyptian productions, enters completely new terrain. Lotfi uses this stylistic device to such an extent that her film's individual shots usually correspond to an entire scene. Produced by the collective *al-Hasala* (the money box), *Coming Forth by Day* was a work in progress already years prior to the revolt, but could only be completed in 2012. With a steady hand, the filmmaker follows a young woman for a day and a night while—between the healthcare needs of her bedridden, dying father and the moods of her exhausted mother—she tries to inject a little joy and dignity into her own daily routines. As its title suggests, the film builds on the ancient Egyptian idea of the soul's journey after death, and thus is also intended as a meditative confrontation with the experience of parting and death.

With respect to subversive cinematic work, we should mention, last but not least, the films by Kaouther Ben Hania (Kawthar b. Hania) and Muhammad Ben Attia, who have both dedicated themselves to the genre of the so-called fake documentary or mockumentary. The alternating use of both designations as terms for the genre still causes confusion. The "fake documentary" employs the stylistic device of the documentary form but consists wholly or partially of fictional material. This does not mean, however, that it loses sight of the dissection of real circumstances. The "mockumentary," in contrast, goes perhaps one step further, poking fun at reality by means of its fictional content or even parodying the entire documentary form.

The latter also applies to Ben Hania's *Challat Tunis* (2012), a film about a fictional criminal (the director does not reveal just how fictional), Challat Tunis, who was supposedly arrested and sentenced for using a razor blade to slice open the back sides of girls wearing tight pants. The film's interviews are real, as is the filmmaker's search on the streets of Tunis for her title character, until she in fact finds someone claiming to be him. And thus instead of deconstructing a masculine mythos, the film moves in precisely the opposite direction by participating in its construction—and in doing so naturally pokes fun at Tunisia's macho culture. This is contrasted sharply by Ben Attia's *Law 76 (Loi 76)* (2011), a short film that consists exclusively of fictional interviews and observations from a fictive future in the year 2017. The film illustrates the consequences of an imagined Islamic government whose legislation mandates the closure of all cafés and bars and makes the secretive visitation of bars a punishable offense.

As evident in all of the aforementioned examples of films, the revolt has clearly resonated in the film productions of both Egypt and Tunisia. It is just as obvious, however, that this "resonance" already began prior to the actual outbreak of the uprisings, much like in the political sphere, where signs of mobilization and resistance to the respective regimes had appeared years earlier, in the uprising in Tunisia's Gafsa mining basin in 2008, for example, and the workers' uprising in al-Mahala al-Kubra in Egypt, also in 2008. The new film culture that has been unfolding for a few years in the alternative, independent—whether self-financed or subsidized—art sector, and which is reflected in cyberspace as well, flourishes in large part because of the increasing affordability of digital technology and efforts by nongovernment initiatives to provide training workshops and performances. They constitute the breeding grounds that will also contain the future of "revolutionary" film. The extent to which political antagonism proves to be a stumbling block for this radical change remains to be seen. But the mobilization of Tunisian and Egyptian society—and thus also of its artists—has just begun.

NOTES

1   Viola Shafik, "*Genug – Kifaya – Game over! Die arabische Welt im Aufbruch (2012) Kultur im Umbruch? Ägyptens "revolutionäre" Filmlandschaft*, LISAN 13/14.

2   Larbi Sadiki, "Tunisia: Portrait One of a Revolution." www.aljazeera.com/indepth/opinion/2012/01/2012114121925380575.html

3   Mélissa Leclézio, "Fighting for Democracy: Street Art in Tunisia," theculturetrip.

com/africa/tunisia/articles/fighting-for-democracy-street-art-in-tunisia

4   Naceur Sardi, "Ridha Tlili, à l'image d'un cinéma tunisien nouveau," www.
     africine.org/?menu=art&no=10763

5   Narjès Torchani, "Tunisie: Centre national du cinéma et de l'image – Du retard à
     rattraper," fr.allafrica.com/stories/201211201588.html

6   Daniel Defert, ed., *Schriften in vier Bänden. Dits et Ecrits*, Frankfurt: Suhrkamp,
     2003.

7   Julia Kristeva, "Ein neuer Intellektuellen-Typ: der Dissident," in *Die schwarze
     Botin. Frauenhefte,* Nr. 7, Berlin, 1978: 5–10

8   See Stuart Hall, "Notes on Deconstructing the 'Popular'," in *People's History and
     Socialist Theory*, ed. Raphael Samuel, London: Routledge, 1981, pp. 227–240.

9   Robert Lapsley & Michael Westlake, *Film Theory: An Introduction*, Manchester:
     Manchester University Press, 1988, p. 172

10   Robert Lapsley & Michael Westlake, *Film Theory,* pp. 172–173.

11   Personal conversation with the author, Dubai, December 13, 2012.

12   Ismaël, "Films, *Jiha' et Thawra ghir draj'* de Ridha Tlili: *Deux
     mondes autour d'une révolution*," nawaat.org/portail/2012/02/01/
     films-jiha-et-thawra-ghir-draj-de-ridha-tlili-deux-ondes-autour-dune-revolution

13   André Bazin, *Was ist Film*, Berlin: Alexanderverlag, 2004.

Just as Chapter 15 demonstrated, cinema and street art suffered from censorship anew under the post revolt Tunisian regime dominated by the Islamists, challenging creative artists to find new means of expression to escape state vigilance and Salafist wrath. As had been the case under the French protectorate (1881–1956), when graffiti and broadsides illegally painted or posted on walls were either removed or whited out, the new authorities acted similarly and viewed street art as subversive. This time, however, much like the equally subversive graffiti pop artist, Keith Haring (1956–1990), who posted his creations in the New York City subway over paid advertisements and had a photographer-friend take pictures of them before the authorities removed them, so Tunisian street artists have begun to photograph their works before the authorities remove them or paint over them. The artists then immediately post images of their creations online, leaving a permanent record of their art. The streets may now "be cleaned up," but the Internet is filled with Tunisian street artists' creations.

IIIIIIIIIIIIIIIIIIIIIIIIIIIIIIIIIIIIIIIIIIIIIIIIIIIIIIIIIIIIIIIIIIIIIIIIIIIIIIIIIIIIIIII

CHAPTER 16
STREET ART AND THE TUNISIAN REVOLT*
CAROL SOLOMON

One of the most immediate and strikingly visible changes that took place in Tunisia as a result of the revolt was the physical transformation of public space. Displacing the silence of empty walls—a testament to decades of censorship, fear, and oppression—the language of graffiti and street art took hold of the popular imagination in the streets of Tunis and other cities across the country. The uncommon presence of images like Zoo Project's wall-size mural showing dissident fists rising from the earth, nourished by the seeds of revolt, invigorated public space (Fig. 1). The fall of Zine al-Abidine Ben Ali gave rise to an efflorescence of freedom of speech manifest in all forms of cultural expression. In the visual arts, it was reflected not only in the widespread appearance of street art but also in the proliferation of painting, sculpture, video, installation, and especially photography, which gained significantly in practice and popularity through exhibitions and the diffusion in the media of photographic images of the uprising.

IIIIIIIIIIIIIIIIIIIIIIIIIIIIIIIIIIIIIIIIIIIIIIIIIIIIIIIIIIIIIIIIIIIIIIIIIIIIIIIIIIIIIIIIIIIIIIIIIIII

*Research for this chapter was conducted with the generous support of a 2012–2013 Middle East and North Africa Regional Fulbright Scholar Award. Artwork cited appears at the end of the chapter, and is reproduced with permission of the artists.

224

Other art-related changes also occurred in the wake of the revolt. The number of exhibitions increased, many of them, not surprisingly, focusing on the revolt.[1] This period likewise saw the establishment of several new associations for the promotion and protection of the visual arts—groups that organized special events devoted to the discussion of the arts and the role of culture in a society in transition. There were calls for the integration of state and privately sponsored arts organizations, for more art periodicals, and for a museum of modern and contemporary art.[2] The pervasiveness of this nascent political-aesthetic activism, characterized by the Tunisian art critic Rachida Triki as "*un art citoyen*," or an art of civic engagement, signaled the collective commitment of artists and others involved in the arts to participate in the post revolt construction of a new Tunisian social and political order.[3]

Having witnessed the revolt as it happened—and now being ostensibly free of censorship—artists, filmmakers, writers, and journalists engaged in an ongoing project to create a unique visual and historical archive of the socio-political transition unfolding in their midst. They memorialized martyrs, and they documented and commented upon both the daily progress and the setbacks of the revolt. They recorded and responded to the revolt's extraordinary details, including the profound spectacle of the self-immolation of a desperate man (Mohamed Bouazizi, the revolt's first martyr). They memorialized the communal euphoria of people gathered to protest en masse, as well as the assassination of an outspoken opposition party leader.

Since the revolt, free speech has flourished, but not without significant challenges. On several occasions, art has been a target in the battle over free expression—that is, the target of violence by Islamist extremists acting, from their perspective, to protect religion. Incidents include the screening of Marjane Satrapi's graphic-novel-turned-film, *Persepolis,* which was shown before the revolt without drawing much attention. However, when screened in October 2011, radical Muslims denounced the film as blasphemous for including a scene depicting Allah, and the owner of the private TV station where it was broadcast was fined. The film was, in short, now considered by many to represent a threat to public morals and public order.[4] In June 2012, a Salafist attack on the *Printemps des Arts* (Springtime of the Arts) exhibit in the Tunis suburb of La Marsa—which showed works the Salafists saw as religiously offensive—resulted in riots that led to the death of one person and injuries to more than a hundred others. Death threats were made against artists. Nadia Jelassi and Mohamed Ben Salem were threatened with prison for their works in the exhibit, which were considered immoral and harmful to public order.[2] And in November 2012 two members of the activist graffiti art group Zwewla were arrested in the southeastern town of Gabès, charged with defacing government property and disrupting public order. Their "inflammatory" slogan on a university wall had read: "The people want rights for the poor." Devoted to the cause of the poor—hence the group's name, which means "the Poor" in Tunisian Arabic—Zwewla slogans were tagged with a large black "Z," like the mark of Zorro, who championed the poor and disadvantaged (Fig. 2). Public outrage over the arrests, which, in effect, made street art a criminal offense, prompted an online campaign in support of the artists with the slogan "Graffiti is Not a Crime."[5] Most artists remain undaunted by these and other events, but they have had a destabilizing effect on society and throw into question the final fate of the hard-won right to free expression in post revolt Tunisia.

Visibly at play from the beginning of the overthrow of Ben Ali's oppressive regime was the control of public space, the most vital arena for the staging of the revolt. It is here that street art made its courageous entry and flourished, reflecting a newly established dynamic in the relationship of power and control in the public sphere and assigning new symbolic meaning to places associated with governmental and political authority. Revolutionary by nature, this popular art of resistance claimed a presence in the Tunisian urban landscape, turning public space into a living museum of the street. Providing an effective visual rhetoric for the voicing of sociopolitical issues and the concerns of the people, street artists helped to bring about changes in societal behavior and to activate a reappropriation of public space. Their works served an emancipatory function, encouraging solidarity, public discourse, and dissent in a population denied these civil liberties for decades. Street art events and interventions brought individuals and the community together in public spaces. They inspired a "taking back" of the streets and, in so doing, engendered a sense of collective ownership of public space. The graffiti, stencils, and painted murals produced by these artists depicted the lived experience of the revolt—its memories, its martyrs, its hopes, its fears. The activity of street artists reinforced a new found sense of personal dignity and collective identity in the Tunisian people. In this context, street art constitutes what the philosopher Jacques Rancière has described in *The Politics of Aesthetics* as "aesthetic acts as configurations of experience that create new modes of sense perception and induce novel forms of subjectivity."[6]

The Tunisian revolt provided a unique set of conjoined circumstances, bringing together art and politics to effect societal change. With the overthrow of Ben Ali's authoritarian regime, people were no longer forbidden to congregate and now had the right to express themselves freely, to engage in public discourse and dissent. Before the uprising, street art, while prevalent in other Arab countries, especially Egypt and the wider Middle East, was less common and slow to develop in Tunisia, where there was strict enforcement of censorship and a heavy-handed control of public space. This is not to say there were no street artists in Tunisia before the revolt. SK-One and MEEN-One, two celebrated Tunisian graffiti artists, have been known since 2009, when, at the Arty Show gallery in La Marsa, they participated in *Evasion Urbaine*, the first Tunsian exhibition devoted exclusively to graffiti artists (Fig. 3).[7] However, the most common type of graffiti seen on Tunisian streets before the revolt was the soccer team tag; and its occurrences were invariably covered or washed away soon after they appeared. Thus, graffiti and street art were relatively little known to the Tunisian public before the uprising. Because of their novelty in Tunisia, these alternative art forms were all the more conspicuous and powerful in their impact. These combined circumstances created a perfect storm for their explosive emergence.

As the following discussion of selected works will make clear, the varied visual rhetoric of graffiti and street art in Tunisia at the time of the revolt fueled public action, thus establishing art as a conceptual basis for the reorientation of societal behavior. Intentionally ephemeral and often anonymously produced, the works of graffiti and street artists took many forms—simple tags or slogans, such as the ubiquitous *Dégage!* (Get Out!); small stenciled images; huge, photo-based murals; and the highly elaborate designs of calligraffiti, mixing elements of graffiti and Arabic calligraphy. Sometimes the works seemed to appear spontaneously out of nowhere; in other instances they were carefully orchestrated events/happenings/performances involving the active participation of the public. On yet other occasions, they were singular creations by well-known artists whose distinct styles, once repeated, were easily recognized. By name as in practice, the many graffiti and street artists active in Tunisia since the revolt constitute a lively, heterogeneous lot, displaying a wide variety of styles and expressive means. Variously identified by their original names or by an alias, a project's name, or the name of a collective, this pantheon features Zoo Project, eL Seed, SK-One, MEEN-One, and Willis from Tunis, with the latter three making up the artist collective Z.I.T. (Zombie Intervention Tunisie). Other collectives include Ahl al-Khaf (People of the Cave), Zwewla (the Poor), and projects such as Faten Rouissi's Art dans la rue – Art dans le quartier (Street Art in the Neighborhood) and INSIDE OUT: Artocracy in Tunisia.

Seen throughout Tunis and its suburbs, the sprayed, stenciled, or painted works of these artists invaded the country's historical, political, and economic heart. They could be seen in the city center on the Porte de France, the principal entrance to the Medina, and the old city, in the streets and alleys of the ancient Medina, and along the city's main artery, Avenue Habib Bourguiba. They also appeared in the ruins of presidential family homes, in ransacked government buildings, and in long-abandoned buildings, on billboards, and on burnt-out cars. The reach of graffiti and street art extended beyond the capital to cities throughout the country—including Sfax, Sidi Bouzid, Kayrawan, and Gabès, home to the tallest minaret in Tunisia, at the Jara Mosque, which is adorned with the largest calligraffiti mural.

ART DANS LA RUE – ART DANS LE QUARTIER (STREET ART IN THE NEIGHBORHOOD)

In the early days of the revolt, Tunisians unleashed their anger through destructive acts of rebellion, ransacking presidential family homes and burning hundreds of cars belonging to Ben Ali's family and his entourage. The charred and mangled remains of these vehicles filled empty lots around the country, including one in a suburb north of Tunis. This caught the attention of the Tunisian artist Faten Rouissi, who saw in the wreckage the potential for a creative collective intervention in a public space, her *Art dans la rue – Art dans le quartier* (Street Art in the Neighborhood) project. Seeking "to create new artistic and aesthetic forces that promote the collective dynamics in our daily lives, at a time when Tunisia is in real need of such forces,"[8] Rouissi sent a Facebook invitation to artists, photographers, designers, students, and a variety of young people to join her in transforming the burned-out cars into "blooming objects in bright colors, adorned with political graffiti."[9] Emblazoned with familiar phrases and iconic emblems of the revolt (Figs. 4 and 5), the painted cars represent hope for the future rebuilding of the country and the desire of "young Tunisians to live with dignity and freedom."[10] Street Art in the Neighborhood engendered a spirit of solidarity and public action in contrast to the once prevalent mood of passive resignation. With it, one Tunisian artist had successfully established a site in the public realm for the practice of art as a creative collective.

AHL AL-KAHF (PEOPLE OF THE CAVE)

One of the most provocative Tunisian street art collectives to emerge in the early days of the revolt was Ahl al-Kahf (People of the Cave). The antipolice and antigovernment graffiti and stencils of this dissident, underground, student-run movement were seen throughout the streets of Tunis during the days of continuous demonstrations and occupation of the sit-ins at the Kasbah from mid-January to early March 2011, which brought down the interim government after the fall of Ben Ali (Fig. 6). Emblematic of the political awakening of the Tunisian people after years of oppression, the collective's symbolic name, Ahl al-Kahf, is based on the well-known story of the "People of the Cave," narrated in surah 18 of the Koran (verses 9–26), and also recounted in its Christian/

Western variant as the "Seven Sleepers of Ephesus," most notably in Jacobus de Voragine's *The Golden Legend*. It is the story about keeping one's faith, in which a small group of persecuted people flee to a cave and fall asleep only to awake after a period of 300 years. For the members of Ahl al-Kahf, the story of the cave also "symbolizes the spirit of underground culture."[11] As an activist art movement, Ahl al-Kahf was conceived "not as an art of the revolution but as a revolutionary art … against global capitalism and orientalism," and was "truly devoted to the people."[12] Through its street art Ahl al-Kahf explicitly intended to foster individual and community dialogue, to raise consciousness, and to effect social change; a deliberate and performative political act of resistance against the controlling authority of the state, that is. Through street art, this collective challenged established boundaries, reclaiming and redefining urban space, reconfiguring it in the newly imagined political order as a space not of alienation but of empowerment and liberation.[13]

The group counts among its theoretical sources Gilles Deleuze, Michel Foucault, Toni Negri, and Edward W. Said. They specifically mention the influence of ideas from Deleuze and Guattari's *A Thousand Plateaus* (1980), on "forms of resistance beyond our capitalist times" to create what the group calls "alternative communication" or simply "résistance."[14] Among its artistic influences, Ahl al-Kahf identifies the Dadaists; the well-known British street artist Banksy; and the Situationist and Fluxus artist Ernest Pignon-Ernest—the original street artist, who started pasting images in urban spaces in the 1960s with the aim of transforming those places into artistic spaces.[15] Ahl al-Kahf has similarly taken over large wall spaces in highly visible public locations as well as places identified with the margins of society—abandoned buildings and warehouses in central Tunis. Here, its members have paid tribute to their heroes in complex murals combining portraits, quotes, and other images in the formation of a virtual museum of the street, free to all and open to interpretation (Fig. 7).

INSIDE OUT: ARTOCRACY IN TUNISIA

In a country where for a half century the only photographic images prominently displayed in public places were those of presidential figures, the sight, over a period of several weeks in March 2011, of 100 larger-than-life-size photographic murals of ordinary citizens in these same, often very symbolic, places was met with mixed reactions. Described as "one of the most ambitious contemporary street art projects to vibrate the Arab world,"[16] INSIDE OUT: Artocracy in Tunisia was a participatory project involving the collaboration of the French street artist JR; the Tunisians Slim Zeghal and Marc Berrebi, who initiated the project; and a group of six Tunisian photographers (Sophie

Baraket, Rania Dourai, Wissal Dargueche, Aziz Tnani, Hichem Driss, and Héla Ammar). The photographers traveled throughout the country taking pictures of ordinary Tunisians, which were then enlarged as posters and mounted in public locations in several cities (Sidi Bouzid, Sfax, Le Kram, and Tunis)—on former government buildings, including the headquarters of the RCD (Ben Ali's political party) in Le Kram (a suburb of Tunis) (Fig. 8); in the police station in La Goulette (another suburb of Tunis adjacent to Le Kram), which had been burned during the revolt (Fig. 9); on the Porte de France in the center of Tunis (Fig. 10); in the ruins of presidential family houses, on billboards, and on burnt-out cars. The goal of the Artocracy in Tunisia project was to elicit conversations, "to challenge their compatriots to see the familiar in a new, post-revolutionary, light."[17]

Ubiquitous pictures of Ben Ali had long been the required adornment of store windows, offices, schools, and even entire buildings. These were universally destroyed as symbolic acts of revenge against the hated autocrat. So intense was this act of symbolic denunciation and destruction that, for example, one man reportedly took such a picture of Ben Ali, tore it up, and ate it.[18] But, while the pictures might be gone, Ben Ali's repressive hold on the people had a residual psychological effect; it was not so immediately or so easily renounced. This was illustrated by an experimental media campaign launched in La Goulette to encourage voting prior to the elections of October 23, 2011, in which a huge portrait of Ben Ali was installed in a public space where his picture could be seen months before. Upon sight of the image, the citizens of La Goulette first reacted with bewilderment; this was followed by anger, until finally they tore down the poster under which a warning was revealed: "Beware, dictatorship can return. Vote."[19]

At the first locations of the Artocracy in Tunisia project, in La Goulette and central Tunis, the artists encountered opposition. The images pasted during the night on the Porte de France were torn down early the next morning. Aziz Tnani, one of the photographers, recounted that some people were uncomfortable with the very presence of the pictures, saying, "We saw so many pictures for so many years, we don't want anyone to impose their pictures anymore."[20] At other locations—in Sfax, Sidi Bouzid, and Le Kram—they were more successful, having consulted with the community in advance and solicited local participation, but even then there was not always universal approval of the project. Some opposed it for religious reasons; one man said it was "a needless provocation" and another said "all artistic projects belonged in galleries, or official spaces, not on the street."[21] Summarily commenting on the experience, the artist JR remarked, "There is nothing better to understand the weight of traditions and the willingness to change than to post big portraits in the symbolic places of the popular districts and try to explain the concept to people nearby."[22] By adding a new layer to the existent palimpsest of historical layers on these buildings, the Artocracy project was attempting to initiate a resymbolization of Tunisian urban space. The new images of ordinary citizens would replace old images of Ben Ali to form new symbolic associations of civic identity and agency while destroying old associations of corruption and subservience to autocratic control. But, as the initial resistance to the project showed, after so many years of Ben Ali the process of resymbolization was best achieved not through an abrupt, imposed transposition of images in the space but rather through an active process of civil engagement, knowledge, and collaboration.

The looting and ransacking of houses belonging to Ben Ali family members and of government buildings, the burning of cars, and the destruction of Ben Ali's images were actions of displaced anger, revenge, and a symbolic reclamation of property. These places and objects of destruction, as already indicated with regard to the cars in the discussion of the Street Art in the Neighborhood project, were sites of significant artistic activity. The exterior and the interior walls of these ruined structures became the canvases of graffiti and street artists who, in covering these surfaces, were performing yet another gesture in the symbolic, even ritualistic, transference of ownership of these properties to the people. Becoming sites for collective viewing, as in a museum, the public flocked to see the embellished ruins of these spaces of once protected opulence.[23]

ZOO PROJECT

The Algerian French street artist known as Zoo Project arrived in Tunis from Paris in March 2011 intent on making his own modest contribution in celebration of the revolt, this "*unique événement*" in Tunisian history. He created several large and distinctive murals, drawn in a simple linear style with clear forms and subjects conveying the energy and the youthful dynamism of the uprising; works such as the image of the emblematic clenched fists sprouting from the earth to represent the groundswell of resistance (Fig. 1), or the image of a motorbike piled high with young Tunisians waving a banner emblazoned with the phrase "*Vive le Peuple*," as the bike races in the direction of a sign pointing the way to "Freedom" (Fig. 11). These are among the best known and most frequently reproduced images of the Tunisian revolt, but the most important work Zoo Project produced over the course of his two-month stay in Tunis was the series of life-size silhouettes painted with thick black lines on cardboard entitled *The Martyrs – Tunis*. Realistically rendered, they are the portraits of approximately forty of the 236 ordinary people who lost their lives in clashes between the demonstrators and the police. When Zoo Project arrived in Tunis, he did not have a predetermined subject. Before painting, he talked to people and learned of the lives of those who became his subjects by listening to their friends, families, and neighbors. Encouraging him, they provided photos or Internet images so that he could recreate their actual likenesses. In a statement on the artist's website explaining why he painted *The Martyrs,* Zoo Project acknowledged that it was the people he met who determined the choice of his subject, that each of them, in their own way, had expressed the sentiment that these victims of the revolt "must not disappear, that to forget them would be to kill them a second time."[24] Well received by the public, the individual memorials he created honored ordinary people—men and women, young and old, from all walks of life—rendered as they appeared in life in casual poses and dress. Once completed, the silhouettes were placed at carefully selected locations in the streets of Tunis, the martyrs eerily integrated back into the life of the city in groups, along the walls of the Porte de France (Fig. 12), at night, like sentinels posted at intervals along a vaulted alley in the Medina (Fig. 13), or isolated and alone, on a rooftop (Fig. 14), in a store window, or against a wall in a quiet street in the Medina, as in the case of the portrait of Mohamed Hanchi, a yong man of nineteen who was killed by a sniper on February 25, 2011 (Fig. 15).

EL SEED

In December 2011, to mark the first anniversary of the Tunisian uprising, the French Tunisian artist eL Seed was invited by the Tunis-based cultural group El Khaldūnia to oversee the production of a commemorative mural in the historic city of Kayrawan, a UNESCO world heritage site, renowned as a center of cultural and artistic innovation since the seventh century (Fig. 16). eL Seed is one of the best known of a rising number of calligraffiti artists, who have created a new and uniquely non-Western variant of graffiti through the expressive use of Arab calligraphy in this modern, urban art form. Of Tunisian descent, eL Seed (an artistic pseudonym based on the Spanish hero El Cid, which means "The Master") was born and raised in Paris and now lives in Montreal. Having never been recognized as French, eL Seed was drawn to the use of Arab calligraphy as a means of affirming his Tunisian identity. As the artist's celebrity has grown, his calligraffiti works have provided a highly visible platform for the contemporary popularization of an aesthetic rooted in Islamic art and design. A self-proclaimed activist artist, eL Seed uses the power and beauty of Arabic calligraphy placed in prominent public places as an instrument of social and political change. Through his work, he seeks to promote a vibrant Arab identity, tolerance, and the undoing of negative cultural stereotypes. Acknowledging the explosion of street art and graffiti in Tunisia and its role in the democratization process taking place since the fall of Ben Ali, eL Seed has commented:

> Before the revolution, art was reserved for the bourgeoisie and the elite and to a large extent it still is today. But the fact that street art was appropriated and is associated with a grassroots movement has brought a new dimension to the role of art in mainstream Tunisian society.[25] ... The revolution pushed people to be more creative because before they were scared—and now they have more freedom."[26]

In the production of the Kayrawan mural, the artist recognized a participatory opportunity for the community and successfully collaborated with local government officials, organizations, the young people of El Khaldūnia, and the general public in his orchestration of a "mini cultural revolution" with the end result of "bringing back some form of self-confidence."[27] eL Seed encountered only one major problem in the execution of the mural. His proposal to use purple as the predominant color for the work was met with great opposition. Purple was the official color of the Ben Ali regime. The artist was intent on reclaiming this color for the people and to begin to wipe away the fear, corruption, and oppression for which it stood, thus giving it new and positive associations. However, so firmly rooted was the former regime's claim on the color purple that the people of Kayrawan were incapable of seeing it afresh at this time; so el Seed capitulated. Months later, he fulfilled his intention to liberate the color with a work entitled *Take Back the Purple,* which he created at Harvard University in March 2012.

In form and scale, the monumental Kayrawan mural, measuring forty meters by seven meters (approximately 22 x 130 feet), is the first of its kind in Tunisia. Entitled *A New Revolution,* the work is a permanent artistic stamp located just beyond the wall of the old city of Kayrawan, a site where people had painted comments of protest and dissent during the revolt. The mural now stands, in the words of el Seed, "as a celebration of the unity of the Tunisian people, who managed to change the course of their own history, and the histories of many others around the globe."[28] A community-building project based on active engagement, *A New Revolution* offers "a message of hope and reminds Tunisians that tyranny does not prevail."[29]

In August 2012, eL Seed created another monumental mural in Tunisia. The outbreak of violence at the Printemps des Arts exhibition in La Marsa by Salafist extremists, in June 2012, and other events that pitted religion against freedom of creative expression prompted eL Seed's most ambitious calligraffiti project to date.[30] It is a virtuoso painting representing a verse from the

233

Koran on the tallest minaret in Tunisia, which is at the Jara Mosque in Gabès, the artist's ancestral home (Figs. 17 and 18). An excerpt from surah 16 of the Koran, measuring forty-seven meters tall and ten meters wide (about 152 x 33 feet) and appearing on two sides of the minaret, reads: "Oh Mankind, we have created you from a male and a female and made people and tribes so you may know one another." Painted during the month of Ramadan, with the support of the mosque's imam, the mural provided a conciliatory message of tolerance on one of the most prominent of Tunisia's religious buildings.

WILLIS FROM TUNIS

This brief overview of Tunisian graffiti and street art concludes with an introduction to a cat, Willis from Tunis, whose cartoon image has become an icon of the Tunisian revolt. His graphic silhouette made its way onto walls in buildings and in the streets of Tunis in the early days of the uprising (Fig. 19), but the real celebrity of this wry and comic cat was created through his daily pictorial presence and sarcastic political/social commentary on the Facebook blog of his creator, the artist Nadia Khiari (Figs. 20 and 21). Willis from Tunis was born of the revolt. He came into being, as told by the artist, on the night of January 13, 2011, when, in his last speech, President Zine al-Abidine Ben Ali declared freedom of expression. As the visual voice of Khiari's thoughts and comments, Willis from Tunis had a fan base that quickly numbered more than 20,000, so eager was the Tunisian public to follow the daily chatter of this witty little cat. Thanks to the revolt, the forbidden art of political caricature and satire was once again alive in Tunisia. Willis from Tunis, availed of free speech, became yet another voice in the aesthetic arm of the revolt in Tunisia.

CONCLUSION

The confluence of art and politics was at the heart of the cultural reawakening that took place in Tunisia. Freedom of speech, however threatened it has become, unleashed a wave of creative expression in all media and types of art, but its greatest flourishing and most profound effect was in the art of the street. In all its richness and variety of expression, this ephemeral, alternative art form, previously almost nonexistent in Tunisia, was embraced by the people as it harnessed their hopes and dreams and became an active agent in the process of democratization and the campaign to regain control of the public sphere.

Fig. 1. Zoo Project, *Resistance Grows,* Tunis, 2011.

Fig. 2. Zwewla, *The Employed and the Unemployed are Against Injustice.* Sousse, 2012.
Photo credit: Free Zwewla.

Fig. 3. SK-One and MEEN-One, TounsiMothaFucka, Kasbah, Tunis. April 16, 2011.

Fig. 4. Faten Rouissi, Art dans la rue – Art dans le quartier (Street Art in the Neighborhood), Tunis, 2011 © Ulrich Münstermann, with permission.

Fig. 5. FatenRouissi, Art dans la rue – Art dans le quartier (Street Art in the Neighborhood), Tunis, 2011 © Ulrich Münstermann, with permission.

Fig. 6. Ahl al-Kahf, *Police Attacking Protester,* Tunis, 2011. With permission.

Fig. 7. Ahl al-Kahf, untitled mural with image of Gilles Deleuze, Tunis, 2011. With permission.

Fig. 8. INSIDE OUT: Artocracy in Tunisia, Headquarters of RCD (Ben Ali's political party), Le Kram (suburb of Tunis), March 2011 © JR/Aurora Photos. Used with permission.

Fig. 9. INSIDE OUT: Artocracy in Tunisia, police station in La Goulette (suburb of Tunis), March 2011 © JR/Aurora Photos. Used with permission.

Fig. 10. INSIDE OUT: Artocracy in Tunisia, Porte de France, Tunis, March 2011 © JR/ Aurora Photos. Used with permission.

Fig. 11. Villa of Imed Trabelsi, nephew of Leila Trabelsi, the wife of Ben Ali, La Marsa, 2011 © Michael Caster. Used with permission.

Fig. 12. Zoo Project, *Motorbike Ride to Freedom,* Tunis, 2011.

Fig. 13. Zoo Project, The Martyrs –Tunis, Porte de France, Tunis, 2011.

Fig. 14. Zoo Project, The Martyrs –Tunis, Quartier Hafisa, Medina at night, Tunis, 2011.

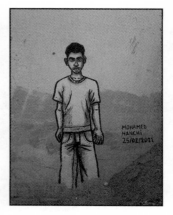

Fig. 15. Zoo Project, The Martyrs –Tunis, Hatem B. (died December 1, 2011), Tunis, 2011.

Fig. 16. Zoo Project, The Martyrs –Tunis, Mohamed Hanchi (died February 25 2011), Tunis, 2011.

Fig. 17. eLSeed, *A New Revolution,* Kayrawan, Dec. 2011.

Fig. 18. eL Seed painting calligraffiti on minaret of Jara Mosque, Gabès, Aug. 2012.

Fig. 19. eL Seed, Calligraffiti, minaret of Jara Mosque, Gabès, Aug. 2012.

Fig. 20. Nadia Khiari, Willis from Tunis, Tunis, 2011.

Fig. 21. Nadia Khiari, Willis from Tunis, 2012.

Fig. 22. Nadia Khiari, Willis from Tunis, "Debatpolitiquetunisien," January 4, 2013.

NOTES

1   For example, in 2011, the exhibitions *Le parfum du jasmin: chronique de la révolution tunisienne*, Galerie de la Fondation Sophia Antipolis, Sophia Antipolis, and *Dégage! Une revolution*, Paris: Institut du Monde Arabe, and in 2012, *Chroniques d'une révolution* (L'Espace KEN, Bouficha) and *Dégagement ... la Tunisie un an après* Paris: Institut du Monde Arabe.

2   These exhibitions, associations, and events are discussed in Rachida Triki, "Tunisia: A Dynamic and Vigilant Art Scene," *Nafas Art Magazine*, February 2012, universes-in-universe.org/eng/nafas/articles/2012/tunisia_art_scene.

3   Rachida Triki, "Une Scene Artistique en Mutation," in Institut du Monde Arabe, *Dégagements ... La Tunisie un an après*, exhibition catalog, Paris, 2012, p. 24.

4   On the *Printemps des Arts* exhibition with illustrations of the targeted works, see Rachida Triki, "Freedom to Express: The Abdellia Affair," IBRAAZ, 23 Aug. 2012, www.ibraaz.org/news/30.

5   Two activists of the Zwewla Graffitti collectivwe were aquitted of disturbing public order on April 10, 2013. If convicted, the two could have faced imprison-ment for up to five years. See Eric Davis, "'Zwewla': The Tunisian Graffiti Rebels," *New Middle East*, February 23, 2013, new-middle-east.blogspot.com/2013/02/zwewla-tunisian-graffiti-rebels.html.

6   Jacques Rancière, *The Politics of Aesthetics*, London and New York: Continuum Press, 2006, p. 9. For a fuller discussion of the ideas of Rancière in relation to the political transformations in Tunisia and the Middle East, see the essays by Anthony Downey, "Beyond the Former Middle East: Aesthetics, Civil Society, and the Politics of Representation," *IBRAAZ,* June 1, 2011, www.ibraaz.org/es-says/8 and "For the Common Good: Aesthetic Practices, Collective Action, and Civil Society in Tunisia," *IBRAAZ*, February 28, 2013, www.ibraaz.org/essays/55.

7   Both Hafedh Khediri, alias SK-One, and Mouin Gharbi, alias Meen-One, also exhibited at the annual *Printemps des Arts* Fair in Tunis in 2010 and 2011.

8   Faten Rouissi, "Emancipated Art, Tunis," *Nafas Art Magazine*, April 2011, universes-in-universe.org/eng/nafas/articles/2011/emancipated_art.

9   Faten Rouissi, "Emancipated Art, Tunis."

10 Faten Rouissi, "Emancipated Art, Tunis."

11 As explained by member Elyès Mejri, quoted in Betty Wood, "Take the Power Back," September 6, 2011, www.themotiononline.co.uk/2011/09/power.

12 As quoted in the interview in *Cahier de Tunisie*, #6, "Ahl Al-Kahf: Le Peuple Souterrain," *AUTAUT*, October 27, 2011, www.autautpisa.it/modules/news/article.php?storyid=1212#.USZRMigxArl.email.

13 As explained by an Ahl al-Kahf member in an interview in *Cahier de Tunisie*, #6, "Ahl Al-Kahf." See also the discussion of Ahl al-Kahf in Nicholas Korody, "The Revolutionary Art: Street Art Before and After the Tunisian Revolution," *Independent Study Project (ISP) Collection*, 2001, Paper 1134: 16.

14 As quoted in the interview in *Cahier de Tunisie*, #6, "Ahl Al-Kahf," *AUTAUT*, October 27, 2011; Gilles Deleuze and Félix Guattari, *A Thousand Plateaus, 1980*, Minneapolis: University of Miinnesota Press, 1987. See also the discussion of

these influences in Nicholas Korody, "The Revolutionary Art: Street Art Before and After the Tunisian Revolution": 33–36.

15   *Cahier de Tunisie* #6, "Ahl Al-Kahf," *AUTAUT*, October 27, 2011.

16   Yasmine Ryan, "Art Challenges Tunisian Revolutionaries," Al Jazeera, March 26, 2011, www.aljazeera.com/indepth/features/2011/3/201132223217876176.html.

17   Yasmine Ryan, "Art Challenges Tunisian Revolutionaries."

18   Brandon Letsinger, "Reclaiming Ben Ali: Symbols of Fear, Repression, Freedom," November 4, 2011, Letzingerwrites.com/2011/11/04/reclaiming-ben-ali-symbols-of-fear-repression-freedom.

19   Brandon Letsinger, "Reclaiming Ben Ali: Symbols of Fear."

20   Yasmine Ryan, "Art Challenges Tunisian Revolutionaries."

21   Yasmine Ryan, "Art Challenges Tunisian Revolutionaries."

22   As quoted in Adriana MacPherson, "Artocracy in Tunisia," March 30, 2011, encounteringurbanization.wordpress.com/2011/03/30/artocracy-in-tunisia.

23   Brandon Letsinger, "Reclaiming Ben Ali: Symbols of Fear."

24   Zoo Project, "*Pourquoi je peins Les Martyrs*," zoo-project.com/tunis.

25   Megan Bénéart Donald, "Graffiti, Meet Arabic Calligraphy," *Fair Observer*, December 17, 2012, www.fairobserver.com/article/graffiti-meet-arabic-calligraphy-O.

26   Catriona Davis, "Tunisian Artist Graffitis Minaret, Fights Intolerance," *Inside the Middle East*, September 20, 2012, www.cnn.com/2012/09/19/world/meast/el-seed-graffiti-minaret.

27   Megan Bénéart Donald, Graffiti, Meet Arabic Calligraphy."

28   eL Seed, as quoted in Amaka M. Onyioha, "el SEED Bridges Cultures Through Calligraphic Street Art," www.afrostylemag.com/elseed.html.

29   eL Seed, as quoted in Amaka M. Onyioha, "el SEED Bridges Cultures."

30   On the *Printemps des Arts* exhibition with illustrations of the targeted works, see Rachida Triki, "Freedom to Express: The Abdellia Affair," *IBRAAZ*, August 23, 2012, www.ibraaz.org/news/30.

New forms of music in the Arab world such as rap, hip hop, and heavy metal—all imports from the West, either straight from the US or through the filters of French or British artists, or Arabs and Berbers growing up overseas—have taken root among the young generations through the Internet, satellite TV, or pirated CDs that are sold everywhere at low cost. Local rap artists, writing and reciting their songs in Arabic, have gained large followings, especially those of them who, like poets of old, have challenged dictators and unabashedly declaimed their disgust with the system as it stood, either before or after the Arab revolts. They have done so just like the great political poets—such as the Syrians Nizar Qabbani and Adonis, the Palestinian Mahmoud Darwish, and Faiz Ahmad Faiz of Pakistan, all of whom had their poems set to music and chanted in the streets—confronted the evils of dictatorship, illiteracy, poverty, and gender inequality, speaking truth to power and often got in trouble for doing so. Before, during, and after the Arab revolts a number of songwriters and singers in the affected countries have been arrested and spent time in jail only to gain greater notoriety and international acclaim. Other singers—those with political agendas—have galvanized the masses and contributed to the élan of revolt starting in 2011. This chapter highlights some of these brave young women and men.

CHAPTER 17
MUSIC AND REVOLT*
FARID EL ASRI

The boundaries between art and politics have always overlapped. Clearly, during the recent uprisings in the Arab world, most cultural creations, including popular music, merged with politics. Recording studios, in entirely new ways, reflected the radical transformations taking place throughout the MENA region. Songs became vehicles for contestation and part and parcel of political struggles. Musical production during the revolts reflected myriads of songs written and sung by twenty-first century Arab musicians responding to the wider uprisings. The fall of a regime is always fodder for the creative artist, who necessarily becomes politicized.

The flight of the Tunisian dictator, Zine al-Abidine Ben Ali, on January 14, 2011, recalls the audacity of a twenty-two-year-old Tunisian rap artist who

*Translated from the French by Radia Benabbou and Stuart Schaar.

called for the departure of the president just weeks earlier. Hamada "El General" Ben Amor recited his song, "President, Your People are Dying," in Arabic and placed it on Facebook, where it became a sensation. El General spoke directly to Ben Ali about unemployment and hunger ravaging the country at the same time that Ben Ali and his family were living in the lap of luxury and were filthy rich. He captured the resentment felt throughout the country about rampant poverty, police brutality, and the first family's corruption, so that when he was arrested, popular reactions were furious and led to mass protests.

The subversive nature of such lyrics entails risks, and in so acting artists lead with messages that can provoke radical action. The daring provocation, which was welcomed by and energized Internet users, while destabilizing the state's Internet police. Musical expressions can thus act as tools for militant action and as a mobilizing force. In fact, music is above all a means of effective communication in the context of moments of political gravity. The creative artist often reflects the reality of the moment and therefore can help us understand what a protest movement is all about. This ability to write and produce songs in tune with events unfolding on the streets have made these singers into experienced and appreciated commentators of the news. The artist, by her/his textual presence or direct involvement in the events, becomes a journalist in rhyme. It is in this sense that music acts as complementary media coverage of sociopolitical events in progress. The effect of such songs or journalistic musical expressions can speed up change and galvanize participation in a movement.

Music certainly functions as entertainment, but it also can become a vehicle of political expression, with musicians helping to shape the course of uprisings and even, at times, anticipating them. Tunisia's El General is one of these pioneering voices.

The best collective expressions of musical production had sizeable transnational echoes. In this way a mass audience shared similar experiences across national frontiers and challenged neighboring dictators. One example is the mixtape *Khalas* (enough), a collaborative effort of Egyptians, Algerians, Tunisians, including El General, and Libyan rappers *uich Baⴲid* (It is close). This was the first attempt to bring together local rap icons from various countries, performers who already had established renown and legitimacy.

The star behind the Syrian song "Asalah Nasri" has also spoken against the regime of her country, or rather against the chaotic humanitarian situation in Syria. Her song clearly benefited the humanitarian response. Critics have called such expressions of protest through rap or traditional song "resistance of the twenty-fifth hour." Odes to a revolt completed or underway, their impact can be global and they can provide potent political symbols even though the artists associated with them might aim to avoid politics as they seek to push people more generally, poetically, to look with hope to a brighter future.

Arab music stars have set the pace. One such famous piece is the *Bokra*[1] (Tomorrow), a joyous ballad for the new Arab generations that has become a popular music video. Though its naively light content is somewhat wanting in quality, the song is important nonetheless for bringing together various celebrities and symbols of resistance in a single production. Other genres of music beyond the traditional Arab that performers in the region have excelled in include Andalusian, as well as jazz, soul, reggae, and even classical from Mozart to Chopin.

Beyond making its way into catchy slogans voiced during mass gatherings and at times of decisive political discourse, the popular language of the Arab uprisings bears witness to the commitment of a youthful Arab generation to a brighter future—and much of it has been expressed through music. With textual content that accompanies the melodies, the artists behind this music have sought to tell us how the societies of the Arab world—and of the Maghreb, too—should now be built.

RHYTHM OF POLITICAL UPHEAVAL

Arabic music can be understood through both the sociology of protest and the conventional analysis of cultural practices. The logic of protest through music can be understood in the socioanthropological contexts of musical expressions. The impact of music on politics is not, of course, exclusive to recent events. Creating and performing new music in the Arab world—whether rap, hip hop, or heavy metal—has carried risks, for it has been seen by many in the region as a threat to social stability.

In the past, under the old regimes of the Arab world, the conditioned reflexes of most people against the voicing of politically critical opinions comprised the dominant tool to silence those who expressed discontent and to avoid sensitive issues. A dense network of censorship monitored the streets, while religious and/or political authorities acted as moral police—in the case of music, monitoring and prohibiting a wide range of lyrics. In this climate, musicians had to be cautious. Only a brave few pushed the limits, and at times they ended up in jail. A turn of phrase—an explicitly negative reference to a regime, for example, whether deliberate or inadvertent—was enough to trigger censorship or, at the least, fear on the part of the artist. This led to lyrics filled with allusions and irony, producing vagueness and a variety of interpretations of a single song. Singers and songwriters were expected to promote boundless patriotism and enhance the standing of those in power, and those who fell short faced censorship and repression.

Syria in revolt produced some courageous examples of rebellious music. One was the voice of a fireman in the city of Hama, Ibrahim Qashoush, who harangued the crowd with his texts to the frenetic rhythm of the *Dabqa* of *Shams*. His famous call, "Come on, Bashar, time to leave!" reappropriated in unison by Hama townspeople, quickly became the voice of the Syrian protest. On July 4, 2011, his body was found floating in the Orontes River, with his throat cut and his vocal chords ripped out, demonstrating the high risks taken by those who openly opposed the Assad regime.

Another example was the Tunisian singer and songwriter Amel Mathlouthi, who had been a finalist in the Middle East Music Competition in 2006 and later sang spontaneously among protesters. She had returned from Paris, where she had lived in exile since 2008, after the Tunisian government had banned her songs from radio and television. Mathlouthi's recordings of live performances in France and elsewhere were accessible on the Internet in Tunisia before the revolt and she had developed an underground fan base in the country. Her protest songs "Ya Tunis," "Ya Meskina" (Poor Tunisia), and "Kalmti Hurra" (My Word is Freedom) became anthems for both the Tunisian and Egyptian revolts. She recorded the latter song on an album (her first) by the same name in January 2012, demonstrating the influence on her work of internationally renowned stars including Bob Dylan, Joan Baez, and John Lennon. After the death by self-immolation of Mohamed Bouazizi, Mathlouthi recorded a Joan Baez song, "Here's to You," which she sang in Arabic and dedicated to him. Her international concerts are now sold-out events.

On May 31, 2013, Mathlouthi published *Ma Katlou Had – Who Killed Him?*, a tribute to Chokri Belaid, a secular activist assassinated three months earlier by Salafists in front of his apartment building near Tunis. The shock of his death mobilized large segments of the population, who demonstrated en masse in response, leading to the reshuffle of the first Islamist government in the country. The songwriter based her lyrics on a real event that had happened in 2008 during an uprising in the town of Redayef. A young unemployed man, Ali Ben Jeddou El Aleimi, was electrocuted during those events. His mother, when interrogated, responded, "Nobody killed my son, only the mayor and the governor," code words understood by Tunisians to stand for the terror under which the population lived during the Ben Ali years.

Amal Mathlouthi picked up the same refrain and chanted an ode to the newly slaughtered secular activist, Chokri Belaid:

Nobody killed Chokri, only the mayor and the governor
Nobody killed my son, only the mayor and the governor
Nobody killed Lotfi, only the mayor and the governor
Nobody killed my son, only the mayor and the governor

Oh dear country, you have nothing but your sore
Oh my dear people, wake up and get up for your country

Nobody killed Chokri, only the mayor and the governor
Nobody stole my bread, only the mayor and the governor
Nobody has betrayed my people, only the mayor and the governor
Nobody has strangled my country, only the mayor and the governor
Nobody killed Chokri, only the mayor and the governor

Oh dear country, you have nothing but your sore
Oh my dear people, wake up and get up for your country
Oh my dear Chokri, your blood flows in my veins
Oh my dear Chokri, I give you my art, my voice, and my songs.[2]

The Moroccan rapper Moad Belghouat aka Al-Haqed or L7a9e, an active militant in the F20 Movement (see Chapter 9) whose bluntly worded lyrics push the limits of freedom of expression, was arrested on September 10, 2011, for allegedly participating in scuffles during a demonstration. After four months of detention the artist was released, only to be sentenced in March 2012 to a year in prison for a song he wrote and sang that denounced police corruption. Human Rights Watch intervened on his behalf to stop legal proceedings against him, and he was released while awaiting the outcome of his appeal.[3] After being awarded Transparency Morocco's "integrity" prize in 2012, he told the press: "I will continue to rap. I am committed to the people and to echoing their problems."

The Egyptian artist Ramy Essam, in his early twenties, strolled along in Tahrir Square with his guitar in hand singing the famous catchphrase: "Get out!" In 2011 the song was chosen by *Time Out* magazine as the third-most world-changing song of all time. He also produced the Arabic music video *Voices of Freedom,* which received more than a million hits on the Internet. A collection of photographs of people that gives a face to Liberation Square in Cairo, this homage to the Egyptian mobilization against the Mubarak regime lasts approximately four minutes.

Essam's notoriety, however, did not protect him on March 9, 2011, when soldiers raided Tahrir Square, intent on clearing it out. He was arrested and dragged to the Egyptian National Museum, which had become a security headquarters. There he was beaten and tortured with electric shocks. When the authorities had finished with him, he could scarcely walk.

Here is an example of a self-made man. Born in 1987 in Al-Mansura, a small Egyptian town where he later attended the university to study engineering, Essam taught himself the guitar and started writing songs at the age of seventeen, inspired by dissident Arab poets. In 2009 he established the band Mushakil (Problems), and wrote songs calling for freedom while detailing the daily travails of living under the Mubarak regime. After the revolt, his notoriety led to concert tours in Britain, South Africa, Sweden, and Germany. In 2011 he was the second runner up for that year's Freedom to Create Award. In November 2011 he won Sweden's Freemuse Award. His international touring and place in the pantheon of rebellious Egyptian artists has established him as a major figure on the Egyptian and Arab musical scene.

Especially in the Maghreb but elsewhere across the Arab world as well, rappers have drawn attention to a host of issues—including corruption (Mister Bigg, in Casablanca), the bombardment of Gaza in December 2008 and January 2009 (Balti, in Tunis), the horrors of arbitrary imprisonment and humiliations suffered at the hands of the police (Muslim, in Tangier), military occupation (DAM, in the West Bank), and heightened Islamophobia (Lotfi Double Kanoun, Algeria). DAM, which pioneered Palestinian rap, was founded in 1999 and was the subject of a documentary film by Jackie Salkūm, *Slingshot Hip Hop*, dealing with the emergence of Palestinian Rap. In 2001 this group became notorious after the release of a clip called *Min Irhābī?* (*Who is the Terrorist?*) seen by more than a million viewers on its website. The group's success lies in the emergence of a new Palestinian youth culture that began to use previously unexplored nonviolent methods, including intifada "through the microphone," as a way to resist Israeli occupation (see Chapter 6) and was a precursor to the wider Arab revolts.

CONCLUSION

The eruption of the Arab uprisings moved Arab music from self-censorship to radical protest. The new political discourse became virulent and explicit, and used lyrics defiantly, breaking with the rules set down by the old regimes. The shock produced by the political breaks affected aesthetics as well. Artists have melded the traditional Arabic forms and language with new genres of music, producing a new dynamic that appeals to young people who have grown attached to new sounds through digital experiences. Poetry, the art form par excellence of the Arab world, has worked its way into song, and the best artists are also the most creative poets. Numerous rappers, including El General in Tunisia—who calls his music "Revolutionary Rap" and invites Tunisians to join him—have followed this ancient tradition. Indeed, when post revolt elections in Tunisia brought the Islamists to power for a time, El General was active in creating a new revolution. As a result, he reported that the Ennhada-dominated government asked him to moderate his position.[4] If music as a field of study in the Arab revolts was initially neglected in the fury of contestations that took place, today we realize just how important songs were for galvanizing crowds and providing frameworks for contestation.

NOTES

1 A website was dedicated to this initiative: www.tomorrowbokra.org.
2 www.youtube.com/watch?v-mECSs-a1Hxk (accessed June 10, 2013)
3 www.en.wikipedia.org/wiki/Ramy_Essam - cite_note-2
4 www.youtube.com/watch?v=QIPOf96_XtM

II

Suicide in any form—including self-immolation (a term used in this chapter in its broadest, historical sense, meaning the taking of one's own life for a common cause whether by fire or otherwise)—is anathema to Islam, making the act a secular one. Obscuring the issue in the Muslim world is the fact that Kurdish women have been subject to significant numbers of honor killings (burning a prominent method), some of which are masked as supposed suicides. Jihadists have meanwhile adopted suicide as a preferred political act. The ulema, like the wider Muslim society, are divided on how to view the practice. Islam, as a living religion, has to take into account the feelings and reactions of the masses, whose perspectives often shape the reactions of the ulema, some of whom thus ride the mainstream bandwagon and celebrate martyrdom by suicide despite its theological prohibition. These contradictions are at the heart of the debate regarding the worthiness of suicide as a political act and form the theme of this chapter. When the Tunisian fruit vendor Mohamed Bouazizi committed suicide by torching himself, he had no idea that his act would set in motion wide-scale revolts throughout the MENA region and beyond.

IIIIIIIIIIIIIIIIIIIIIIIIIIIIIIIIIIIIIIIIIIIIIIIIIIIIIIIIIIIIIIIIIIIIIIIIIIIIIIIIIIIIIIIIIII

CHAPTER 18*
THE ARAB REVOLTS AND SELF-IMMOLATION
FARHAD KHOSROKHAVAR

IDEOLOGICAL PATTERNS OF PROTEST IN THE MUSLIM WORLD

At least since the nineteenth century, the dominant model of resistance, uprising, or social protest in the Muslim world has been martyrdom, expressed either in the Islamic or the nationalist fashion—whether against an imperialist Europe (from the nineteenth century up to the end of World War II), a domineering America (from the 1950s onward), an occupying Russia (at the beginning of the nineteenth century, with the conquest of the Caucasus), or the Soviet Union (in Afghanistan, from 1979 to 1989). The Islamic Revolution in Iran promoted martyrdom in the name of Shiism, jihad being played down. In contrast, the Sunni Islamist movements from the 1990s onward have privileged jihad, martyrdom being the means to achieve it. Self-immolation has no Islamic credentials and was practiced on a large scale neither in the Arab World nor in Iran. The Kurds in various countries of the Middle East—in Iran,

IIIIIIIIIIIIIIIIIIIIIIIIIIIIIIIIIIIIIIIIIIIIIIIIIIIIIIIIIIIIIIIIIIIIIIIIIIIIIIIIIIIIIIIIIIIIII

*Adapted from Farhad Khosrokhavar, "The Arab Revolutions and Self-immolation," *Revue d'Etudes Tibétaines*, no. 25 (Décembre 2012), 170: 169-179. Used by permission.

Iraq, and Turkey—were the exception, self-immolation (by fire) developing there as a strategy by their political parties. This type of suicide also developed among Muslim women protesting their social conditions, although some fire-induced "suicides" among Muslim women have in fact been honor killings (or other killings that qualify legally as murder) committed by their relatives. Between 2000 and 2007, available figures indicate 3,039 such cases across the Muslim world, though the true figure is presumably considerably higher, as family members were pressured by the authorities to avoid publicly declaring honor killings or else failed to confirm suicides on account of Islamic norms religiously prohibiting that manner of death.[1]

PREVIOUS CASES IN THE MUSLIM WORLD

As regards self-immolation by fire, one can find in the Muslim world two major models before Mohamed Bouazizi's suicide in Tunisia on January 4, 2011. Self-immolation by politically minded Kurds constitutes one of these; that by women (including Kurdish women)—or honor killings of women—owing to domestic violence, social injustice, and suspicion of adultery constitutes the other.[2] In Iran's Western Azerbaijan province, more than 150 Kurdish women committed suicide within a few months up to February 2006, the majority setting themselves on fire. This happened also in some other Western provinces in Iran with large Kurdish populations, such as Ilam, Kermanshah, and Kurdistan. Between March and May 2012, eleven Kurdish women were recorded as having committed self-immolation in the Kurdish provinces of Iran.[3] In Iraqi Kurdistan, one finds women having committed suicide or been put to death through strangulation or beating, as well as burning. The cases are often difficult to assess: suicide, or homicide by relatives seeking to preserve their honor (a woman can easily be suspected of adultery or indecent relations with a man or, more simply, she may be punished for refusing an arranged marriage).

According to Hataw, a women's rights advocacy group in Iraqi Kurdistan, the number of Kurdish women killed by others increased from 349 cases in 2003 to 812 in 2006.[4] In 2007, local sources reported, around 400 women there met their deaths by burning. More generally, in Iraq, after the fall of Saddam Hussein in 2003, honor killings increased, in part due to the lack of state authority in the wake of the US intervention. In a single month, December 2007, 130 unclaimed bodies of women were found in the Baghdad morgue.[5]

Self-immolation through prolonged hunger strikes and fire has been part of the strategy of the Workers' Party of Kurdistan (PKK). During its struggle against the Turkish army, the PKK combined a three-pronged strategy based on martyrdom in guerilla actions, self-immolation by fire, and hunger strikes. Up to 2006, two cases of self-immolation by fire mentioned, against seventeen suicide attacks (and nine other attempts).[6] Out of the seventeen suicide attacks, eleven were by women.

Women in the region are indeed the main victims of deaths ascribed to self-immolation. Many such instances are in fact either unreported honor killings ensuing from real or imagined adultery, for example, or suicide in order to escape opprobrium or to end intolerable situations. Women are often also political actors, willingly accepting self-immolation as martyrs in the fight against the enemy or by setting themselves alight, as PKK members, male activists in particular, have done.

THE CHANGE OF THE DOMINANT PARADIGM: FROM MARTYRDOM TO SELF-IMMOLATION

The major transformation in the last few years has been the challenge presented by self-immolation by fire to the model of martyrdom, particularly during the Arab revolts, beginning at the end of 2010 in Tunisia—the trigger point being the case of Mohamed Bouazizi, who doused himself with gasoline on December 17, 2010, and set himself on fire, dying in a hospital on January 4, 2011. The impact of his death was immense, launching as it did the Tunisian revolt that overthrew the Ben Ali regime twenty-eight days later.

A comparison with the 1979 Islamic Revolution in Iran throws light on the change of paradigm. The Islamic Revolution in Iran and then, in the following decades, the jihadist movements in the Sunni world, were based on the idea of martyrdom as self-sacrifice in a ruthless struggle against the enemy. Martyrdom was the weapon of the weak against the strong[7] in a merciless war against a foe far stronger: either the government or the West. In both cases, the path to perceived success was self-sacrifice; that is, fighting the enemy to (one's own) death; and indeed being ready, even eager, to die in the effort to kill heathen adversaries. From this perspective, violence is directed toward the other and the religious justification is that one should fight him or her in order to restore Islamic order worldwide.

This paradigm reached its peak during the jihadist movement that swept across the Muslim world in the 1990s and 2000s. The September 11, 2001, terrorist attack, the American invasions of Afghanistan in 2002 (with the assistance of Western allies) and Iraq in 2003 (with the help of Great Britain) resulted in a deep sense of indignation on the part of the Muslim world. Jihadist groups thrived over this wave of humiliation, amplified by America's unwavering support for Israel. Violence was the rule in a ruthless war in which no other solution seemed imaginable. As a major social and political phenomenon, martyrdom, in the service of jihad, became the leitmotiv of the radical movements that swept across the Muslim world, seeking to respond to humiliation by defiance and self-sacrifice. In a world in which Muslims are technologically inferior, endangering one's life became a sign of moral superiority against a foe that was militarily superior but fearful for his/her life and, therefore, spiritually inferior.

This paradigm ruled supreme (and is still prominent in jihadist circles) until the self- immolation of Mohamed Bouazizi in Tunisia. Through his example, the dominant style of protest changed radically: instead of directing the violence against the enemy in a crescendo that resulted in an endless fight, self-immolation entirely changed the meaning of sacrifice. The new model is based on putting oneself to death in a manner that can leave no one indifferent, on self-suppression with the aim of denouncing the illegitimacy of the political order.

This model spread all over the Arab world and indeed also to some predominantly non-Muslim countries. In July and August 2012 even Israel witnessed two self-immolations (likewise by fire) in protest against economic injustice. In the six months following Bouazizi's self-immolation, at least 107 Tunisians tried to follow suit.

SELF-IMMOLATION AS A NEW PARADIGM IN THE ARAB WORLD

In the Arab world, self-immolation by fire is a daring act, denoting a rupture with Islamist rhetoric and a high level of secularization, and inducing a rupture with Islamic orthodoxy. Mohamed Bouazizi's setting himself ablaze set the tone for this new style of "sacred death." The general public called it martyrdom, but the ulema, with few exceptions, regarded the act as an infringement on God's commandment.[8]

According to that commandment, no one should take his or her own life, and one's death can be decided only by God. From the dominant Islamic perspective, Bouazizi's act could not be qualified as martyrdom but as a desecration of God's commandment stipulated in the third chapter, or surah, of the Koran: "No person can ever die except by Allah's Leave at an appointed term" (Surah Al-Imran, verse 145); or, more explicitly, "Don't kill yourself" (Surah The Women, verse 29) or "Don't throw yourself into destruction" (surah The Cow, verse 195). In spite of the misgivings and even condemnation by some of the ulema, people across the Muslim world celebrated Bouazizi's death as a heroic act, and indeed songs and videos were created in his honor, calling him a martyr. This situation points to a widening divide between the religious meaning of martyrdom and its secular, popular signification, the latter having become largely autonomous from the strictly religious idiom.

Yusuf al-Qaradawi, the only major alim (relgious scholar; singular form of "ulema") who deplored Bouazizi's death with commiseration, said in an interview with Al Jazeera that he would not issue a fatwa but would content himself with a commentary on his TV program on Al Jazeera, *al sharia wa al hayat* (*Religious Law and Life*), concerning Bouazizi's self-immolation and death: "I implore Allah the Almighty, and pray Him to pardon this young man [Bouazizi] and forgive him and go over his action [self-immolation by fire] that was against the religious law, which forbids killing oneself."[9]

Under the pressure of Arab public opinion, largely created by Al Jazeera, which viewed Bouazizi's action as that of a martyr's and therefore laudable, al-Qaradawi softened his former position, explaining on his website that Bouazizi's self-immolation was justifiable (and not having to be pardoned by God), since it was in rejection of humiliation and hunger.[10]

Still, as already mentioned, the ulema of Cairo's al-Azhar, the most prestigious Sunni mosque university in the world, issued a fatwa condemning self-immolation.[11] In Saudi Arabia, the Grand Mufti Abdul-Aziz ibn Abdullah Al ash Sheikh condemned suicide even in response to harsh economic conditions.[12]

Killing oneself is not traditionally regarded as martyrdom, the more so as Bouazizi's act was not preceded by any call to jihad or fight against the unbelievers or un-Islamic rulers. Bouazizi's self-immolation had no reference to religion, being a pure act of protest against social injustice and humiliation, with no religious undertone or justification. The secular aspect of his act was paramount. Two decades earlier, the trend had been toward adherence to the religious meaning of martyrdom, with Islamist would-be martyrs proud to claim the title and show their willingness to be categorized as Islamic heroes by sacrificing their lives for the sake of religion. Now, what is regarded by public opinion as "martyrdom" has become wholly secular, an act of protest subsequently characterized by others as martyrdom, not by the one who committed suicide, perhaps out of anger and a sense of intolerable social iniquity.

In defiance of the ulema, the Progressive Democratic Party (PDF) in Tunisia declared that it considered Bouazizi a martyr.[13] His glorification by the Arab world and the world's celebration of his act overshadowed the ulema's reluctance to condemn his act. On February 8, 2011, a square in Paris was named Place Mohamed Bouazizi.[14] On February 17 of that year, the main square in Tunis was renamed after Bouazizi.[15] He was posthumously awarded the 2011 Sakharov Prize.[16] On December 17, 2011, a statue of him was unveiled in Sidi Bouzid, Bouazizi's hometown. Tunisia's first elected president, Monçef Marzouki, attended the ceremony, saying, "Thank you to this land, which has been marginalized for centuries, for bringing dignity to the entire Tunisian people."[17] In Britain, the *Times* named Bouazizi person of the year for 2011.[18] Bouazizi's self-immolation triggered a series of imitations in the

Arab countries and even in Europe and, as previously mentioned, Israel. In all those cases, the reasons cited were desperate personal situations and despondency, not the will to die for Islam—which, from an orthodox perspective, is the necessary condition for martyrdom. In Sidi Bouzid, soon after Bouazizi's act, a second young, unemployed man, Houcine Nejii, jumped to his death on December 22, 2010. A young Moroccan set himself on fire during a teachers' sit-in in front of the Ministry of Education in Rabat. The demonstration was being held to demand secure jobs for those teachers who had been granted only insecure work contracts. The police intervened and saved his and a bystander's lives.

THE ARAB REVOLTS AND SELF-IMMOLATION

Between January 22 and February 2, 2011, Morocco witnessed four suicide attempts by fire. None of them succeded.[19] Fadoua Laouri, a twenty-five-year-old unmarried mother of two, set herself alight after being refused housing by the state after the authorities demolished the adobe house made of dried mud in which she had previously lived with her parents and children. She committed her act in front of the municipal building in Souk Sebt, in central Morocco, and died of her wounds in a Casablanca hospital. She was the first woman to commit suicide in the new Arab revolts.[20] Here too, the act had no religious content, but since the protest movement in Morocco did not then gather pace, her death was not widely characterized as martyrdom. This model was imitated in other countries, as was the case in Mauritania. There, a forty-three-year-old man tried to burn himself on January 17. In Egypt, Abdou Abdel-Moneim Gaafar, a forty-nine-year-old owner of a small restaurant in the town of Qantara close to Ismailiya, attempted to take his own life by setting himself on fire in front of the Egyptian parliament in Cairo on January 17, 2011.[21] Apparently he had not received vouchers to buy bread for his restaurant.[22] Two others attempted suicides in Egypt around the same time achieved prominence, that of a twenty-five-year-old jobless man with mental problems in Alexandria and another one in Cairo.[23] Similar incidents occurred in Algeria: In Algiers, a jobless thirty-four-year-old attempted suicide on January 15 in front of the city's security headquarters. Another man, Mohsen Bouterfif, a thirty-seven-year-old father of two, committed suicide by fire.[24] He died on January 24. Maamir Lotfi, a thirty-six-year-old unemployed father of six who had been denied a meeting with the governor, set himself ablaze in front of El Wad town hall on January 17. He died on February 12.[25] Abdelhafid Boudechicha, a twenty-nine-year-old day laborer who lived with his parents and five siblings, did the same in Medjana on January 28 after the mayor refused his request to provide him with a job and housing.[26] He died the following day.[27] In Saudi Arabia, in perhaps the first such incident in the history of that country, a sixty-five-year-old man died on January 21, 2011, after setting himself on fire in the town of Samtah, Jizan.[28]

Nor did Europe remain immune to the wave of copycat suicides by fire. On February 11, 2011, Noureddine Adnane, a twenty-seven-year-old street vendor from Morocco, set himself ablaze in Palermo, Sicily, in protest against the confiscation of his property and harassment by municipal officials. He died five days later.[29] Sub-Saharan Africa and Israel were affected too: in the same year, Yenesew Gebre, a high school teacher in Ethiopia, committed suicide by fire in protest against the Zenawe regime's oppression. On July 14, 2012, during a rally in Tel-Aviv, a man set himself on fire in protest against the government, which, in his words, "constantly humiliates the citizens of Israel who have to endure humiliation on a day-to-day basis. They take from the poor and give to the rich." On July 20, 2012, Akiva Mafi, a disabled Israeli Defense Forces veteran, set himself on fire in Yehud Israel, in protest against economic injustice.[30]

THE ARAB REVOLTS AND SELF-IMMOLATION

The effect of Bouazizi's act was tremendous in the Arab world, but also beyond. It made a horrendous suicide an accessible model for others who thought such acts might initiate social protest on parity with the Tunisian revolt. Consideration of the pain to be endured before death almost disappeared before the earthshaking consequences of such an act, bringing postmortem fame to modest individuals who became national heroes and thereby wreaked revenge on repressive power holders. Of course, the copycat effect did not have the same impact in other countries. The surprise effect had waned, as police forces were now ready to confront demonstrators, and the "trigger element" of the protest movement had to change in order to succeed.

In Egypt, protestors came up with the innovation of tying the project to a place, Tahrir Square. Notwithstanding, Egyptians had their own "martyrs": the equivalent of Bouazizi was the Egyptian restaurant owner Abdou Abdel-Moneim, who died after suicide by fire on January 17, 2011.

Bouazizi's act made him a national hero in Tunisia and a hero for those Arab nations that followed suit in their own protest movements. One YouTube declaration in French called him "the hero of the Tunisian nation and the founder of democracy in Tunisia."[31] In that video, Bouazizi's photo is accompanied with the chanting of a man in Tunisian Arab dialect set to traditional guitar, together with a French translation of the song and words attributed to Bouazizi. Then follows the statement, "The uproar spreads. With clamor, the warships of the barbarous soldiers are thrust. Everywhere floats death.

And the homicidal sword pierces at the threshold of the altars. ... Mohamed Bouazizi, the eagle who carries fire, the benefactor of humanity, the bird whose omen is happiness!"

Before Bouazizi, self-immolation in the Muslim world was a phenomenon largely confined to women (although men were also present, especially in the ranks of the Kurdish PKK). The Arab revolts opened up a new style of self-sacrifice, this time almost exclusively male. Indeed, as of this writing there had been but a single case of a woman associated with those revolts—namely, that of Fadoua Laouri.[32]

CONCLUSIONS

"Self-immolation" by fire can mean different things. It can be an act perpetrated by an individual himself or herself, but it can be a homicide disguised in suicide, a sheer killing—mainly tied to honor killings of women. It can also be an act of despair, traditionally by women—and even in a more marked manner, by predominantly Kurdish women, With the exception of male members of the PKK before the Arab Revolts, this was generally practiced by women. In the Muslim world, mainly among Kurdish activists, self-immolation by fire existed side by side with the other sort of martyrdom, committed in the course of violent action against an enemy. Martyrdom was the dominant model through which protest movements, mostly political in nature, expressed their content, either in religious terms (martyrdom in the strictly Islamic idiom) or in a metaphoric one (in nationalist movements).

The Arab revolts introduced a rupture in the dominant model of martyrdom. Incidents of self-immolation by fire spread across the Arab world, at least in the months following the suicide of Mohamed Bouazizi in Tunisia—replacing, perhaps momentarily, martyrdom based on an attempt to fight the enemy, on getting killed while seeking to kill. The self-immolation pattern underlines the new content of the social movements in the Muslim world, in which violence is denounced and the peaceful activist refuses to engage in that variation of martyrdom. However, the efficacy of the nonviolent model—self-immolation—has been cast into doubt by the long civil wars in Libya, Yemen, and Syria. In those countries, autocratic governments refused to retreat, and the result was military violence that could not be halted through nonviolent action symbolized by self-immolation. Instead, a new type of social action has surfaced that neither avoids violence nor espouses the legitimacy of the ideology of violence as such, as was the case with the jihadist or the authoritarian nationalist ideologies in the past.

For the first time in the Arab world, a model of action based on non-violence toward the enemy has been inaugurated with considerable success.

Self-immolation in the Muslim world in recent years has indeed pointed to the secularization of many Arab societies. Bouazizi's act was not grounded in or motivated by Islam, nor did those cases that followed—and there were more than a hundred across the Arab world—claim religious justification.

It is not that those people in the region who in recent years have committed self-immolation by fire have been professed atheists or have declared anti-Islamic sentiments. Rather, they were simply secularized enough to restrict the realm of religion to their spiritual needs, leaving the social sphere to the freedom of human volition. In this respect, too, such suicides denote a distance toward religion. The case of the Kurds confirms this view, since many of them espoused Marxist ideologies that were not congenial to religion. In its new fashion, free of any explicit ideology, Marxist or otherwise, this type of secularization marks a step toward a new society where the civil sphere is subjectively grounded in the mindset of the new generations.

NOTES

1   See Olivier Grojean, "Self Immolation and Murder Cases of Kurdish Women," Hataw organization, April 10, 2007, www.kmewo.org/documents/Assignment. pdf.

2   Golnaz Esfandiari,"Iran: Self-Immolation Of Kurdish Women Brings Concern," Radio Free Europe Radio Liberty, February 8 2006, www.rferl.org/ articleprintview/1065567.

3   "A young Kurdish girl sets herself ablaze in Iranian Kurdistan," May 14, 2012. www. ekurd. net/mismas/articles/misc2012/5/irankurd852.htm.

4   Olivier Grojean,"Self Immolation and Murder Cases of Kurdish Women."

5   Mark Lattimer, "Burning and Women's Self-immolation in Iraqi Kurdistan," *Guardian*, December 13, 2007, www.guardian.co.uk/world/2007/dec/13/gender. iraq.

6   See Olivier Grojean, "*Investissement militant et violence contre soi au sein du Parti des travailleurs du Kurdistan*," *Cultures & Conflits* 63, Automne 2006, conflits.revues.org/index2108.html.

7   Diego Gambetta (ed.), *Making Sense of Suicide Missions*, Oxford: Oxford University Press, 2006.

8   The notable exception was Yusuf al-Qaradawi, head of the World Union of the Islamic ulema (*rais al itihad al alami li ulama' al muslimin*) and one of the most prominent ulema in the Sunni world, known for his contributions to IslamOnline.net and his hosting Al Jazeera's weekly TV program *Sharia and Life,* attracting tens of millions of Muslims. He refused to condemn the act of Bouazizi as being against Islamic law.

9   For the Arabic text, see www.radiojektiss.com/qaradawi-explique-sa position- sur-bouazizi.

10 "Tunisian Uprising: the Other Martyrs," *New American Media*, January 22, 2011,

newamericamedia.org/2011/01/tunisian-uprising-the-othermartyrs.php.

11   "*Al-Azhar*: Self-immolation is a 'sin'," *Al-Ahram* Online, January 19, 2011, english.ahram.org.eg/News/4310.aspx.

12   "Man Dies after Setting Himself on Fire," *Gulf News*, January 23, 2011, gulfnews. com/news/gulf/saudi-arabia/man-dies-after-setting-himself-on-fire-1.750, 642.

13   Yasmine Ryan, "The tragic life of a street vendor," Al Jazeera English, January 16, 2011, www.aljazeera.com/indepth/features/2011/01/2011116842425188 39.html.

14   Agence France-Presse, "*Delanoë veut donner le nom du jeune Tunisien immolé à un lieu parisien,*" February 4, 2011.

15   "Tunis renames square after man who sparked protest," Reuters, February 17, 2011.

16   "Sakharov Prize for Freedom of Thought 2011," www.Euro parl. europa.eu/news/en/headlines/content/20111014FCS29297/html/ Sakharov-Prize-forFreedom-of-Thought-2011.

17   BBC News, "Tunisia Unveils Bouazizi Art Statue in Sidi Bouzid," December 17, 2011.

18   *Al-Arabiya*, "UK's *Times* newspaper names Bouazizi person of the year 2011," December 28, 2011.

19   "A Moroccan Set Himself Afire," Al Jazeera English, February 2, 2011.

20   "*Une jeune mère célibataire s'immole par le feu,*" *France 24*, February 23, 2011, www.france24.com/fr/20110223-maroc-jeune-femme-celibataire-immole-feu suicide-logement-social-souk-sebt-fadoua-laroui.

21   "In Egypt, Man Sets Himself on Fire, Driven by Economic Woes," *Ahram Online*, January 17, 2011, english.ahram.org.eg/NewsContent/1/2/4115/Egypt/Society/ In-Egypt,-man-sets-himself-on-fire,-driven-by-econ.aspx.

22   "*Trois hommes se sont immolés par le feu,*" *France 2*, January 18, 2011, info. france2.fr/ monde/trois-hommes-se-sont-immoles-par-le-feu-668857 54.html.

23   "*Trois hommes se sont immolés par le feu,*" *France 2*, January 18, 2011.

24   Mehdi Benslimane and Slim Badaoui, "*Le maire à Mohcin Bouterfif: 'Si tu as du courage, fais comme Bouazizi, immole-toi par le feu,*'" *DNA-Algérie*, January 242011, www.dna-algerie.com /interieure/le-maire-a-mohcin-bouterfif-si-tu-as-ducourage-fais-comme-bouazizi-immole-toi-par-le-feu-2.

25   "*Quatrième décès par immolation en Algérie, à la veille de la marche du 12 février,*" *Jeune Afrique*, February 12, 2011, www.jeuneafrique.com/Article/ ARTJAWEB20110212105526.

26   "*L'immolation, ultime acte de désespoir des laissés pour compte,*" *Le Monde*, January 17, 2011.

27   "*Un jeune décède après s'être immolé par le feu à Bordj Bou Arréridj,*" *El Watan* (Algiers), January 29, 2011.

28   "Man Dies in Possible First Self-Immolation in Saudi," *Sunday Times* (Sri Lanka), January 22, 2011, www.sundaytimes.lk/world-news/4231-man-dies-inpossible-first-self-immolation-insaudi? tmpl=component&layout=default&page=.

29   "Palermo, Moroccan Street Vendor Dies after Setting Himself on Fire," *Ahora Italia*, February 22, 2011, www.ahoraitalia.com/giornale//117595/

palermo-diesafter-setting-himself-fire.htm.

30   See "Man Sets Himself on Fire During TA Rally," ynetnews, July 14, 2012; "Man self-immolates in Israel over cost of living," Reuters, July 15, 2012.

31   "YouTube Mohamed Bouazizi *Héros Tunisian Révolution Tunisie Túnez,*" www. youtube.com /watch?v=5Nir6FcXDM8.

32   See Farhad Khosrokhavar, *The New Arab Revolutions that Shook the World,* especially the chapter "Self-Immolation: Bouazizi's Paradigm of Martyrdom." Boulder, CO: Paradigm Publishers, 2012.

Belonging to a group of US graduate students from multiple nationalities living in Cairo during the revolt, Alex Winder and his friends, starting in March 2011, began collecting, archiving, and translating from Arabic into English activist papers from Cairo's Tahrir Square. These can be found at TahrirDocuments.org. The group is not affiliated with any political organization, Egyptian or non-Egyptian, and was organized and executed entirely by volunteers. The complete archive of documents collected by TahrirDocuments.org is currently housed at UCLA's Charles E. Young Research Library. This chapter was developed out of a paper delivered for a panel based around TahrirDocuments.org at the November 2012 Middle Eastern Studies Association annual meeting in Denver, Colorado.

CHAPTER 19
RUMOR AND CONSPIRACY THEORY IN TAHRIR SQUARE
ALEX WINDER[1]

On July 17, 2011, the Union of Egyptian Socialist Youth, a self-described "non-party leftist youth organization" whose members were both members of other leftist parties and individuals unaffiliated with any party, distributed the sixth issue of its newsletter *al-Midan al-Yawm* (The Square Today) in Tahrir Square. In addition to articles on the appointment of new ministers to Issam Sharaf's cabinet, statements issued by the Supreme Council of the Armed Forces (SCAF), and tensions within the Muslim Brotherhood, the newsletter commented on rumors circulating in Tahrir Square that beverages being distributed to demonstrators there had been poisoned:

Rumors have spread daily throughout the square since the beginning of the sit-ins, with the latest of these being that there were cases of poisoning from the tea that is sold by street vendors in Tahrir. In response, people have passed by every tent to caution those present against drinking tea from the vendors on the square. This has angered the vendors, because it is their livelihood. Doctors at the field hospital in Tahrir denied the occurrence of any cases of poisoning on the square and confirmed the rumor's falseness.[2]

With the passage of time, it is not difficult to imagine a historian of this critical period in Egyptian history turning to such a newsletter to reconstruct the attempts of the SCAF to install a civilian government under Sharaf and its attempts to cow demonstrators in Tahrir Square. Certainly the dynamics within the Muslim Brotherhood and its relationship with other opposition groups would be of interest to anybody trying to understand the events unfolding in Egypt since January 2011. But what of this short notice denying any validity to rumors of poisoning? Why did the Union of Egyptian Socialist Youth feel the need to publish it, and what value does it hold for historians or contemporary observers seeking to better understand the January 25 revolt and its aftermath?

As I will discuss below, rumors and conspiracy theories that circulated in this period can illuminate the anxieties and concerns of Egyptians during a period of both intense turmoil and fantastic possibility. More than this, though, I will argue that the failure to give adequate attention to these forms of information and their transmission significantly limits our ability to make sense of the January 25 revolt and the momentous political changes that preceded it and followed it in the region.

As one of the many Egyptian, American, and international volunteers who worked to collect and translate Arabic documents published by TahrirDocuments.org,[3] I found myself drawn to the traces of rumors that appeared in the various pamphlets, broadsheets, fliers, poems, and other items distributed in Tahrir Square in the weeks and months following Hosni Mubarak's dramatic departure as president of Egypt. What follows will draw primarily, though not exclusively, on these documents and their role in both reporting on or disseminating rumors and commenting on the phenomenon of rumors and their impact on Egypt during this period. I will begin by outlining the conditions within which rumors were produced and circulated. I will then look at how certain themes—in this case, sexual harassment and violence against women—illustrate the continuity of particular concerns and anxieties through the political developments in Egypt since January 2011. I will conclude with a discussion of the revolutionary potential of rumors as well as the critiques of rumor that were voiced by insurgents.

QUESTIONING OFFICIAL MEDIA

Dan Miller, in his discussion of the groundbreaking work of Tom Shibutani, notes that "rumor processes are most likely to occur when institutionalized channels of communications (e.g. print and electronic media) are not available to a population, or when those sources of information are not trusted by the people."[4] As numerous demonstrations against the Egyptian state-run media[5] and complaints voiced in the documents collected by TahrirDocuments.org attest, Egyptians were alienated from the official media outlets.

The first issue of the revolutionary newsletter *Gurnal* ("Journal," as pronounced in Egyptian colloquial Arabic) excoriated the media, writing, "After the events of January 25, however, [the Egyptian media] lost what credibility it had. What was shown on television, the radio, and the national papers from the period of January 25 to February 11 was a deception to the people and a distortion of the popular revolution."[6] It was not only the media's treatment of the turbulent moment but its imbrication throughout the Mubarak era with the ruling National Democratic Party and the state security services that further served to discredit it.

The lack of change within media circles even after Mubarak's departure was the subject of another piece, which asked readers, "Has the regime fallen?"

We still have the editors-in-chief of the newspapers and television chairs, who exulted the tyrant, justified his actions, lied to the people for many long years, accused the Egyptian people of treason and brokerage throughout this noble revolution, and played a central role in the protection of the tyrant and his entourage, just as they spread corruption in the press organizations of our country. ... Usama Saraya (*al-Ahram* newspaper)–Mumtaz al-Qatt (*al-Akhbar* newspaper)–Abdullah Kamal (*Rose al-Yusuf* newspaper)–Muhammad Ali Ibrahim (*al-Gumhuriyya* newspaper)–Usama al-Shaykh and Abd al-Latif al-Manawi (Radio and Television Union)–have they been tried? Have they even been removed from their positions to prevent the continuation of corruption and lying and fabrication and what we all know about them?[7]

The proliferation of alternative media sources following Mubarak's departure and the expanded use of "new media" outlets such as Facebook and Twitter were part of a larger rejection of state-run media. However, the conditions that gave added credence to rumor as a form of information were not just tied to the absence of trusted institutionalized media, but also to the unprecedented political changes taking place inside Egypt and elsewhere. What only months before had been unthinkable had suddenly become a reality, momentarily opening up a world of possibility and allowing Egyptian popular imaginations to contemplate myriad scenarios. Further, the uncertainty of unfolding events—in contrast to the monotonous certainty that had characterized the previous thirty years and that had only a few years earlier seemed poised to extend uninterrupted into the foreseeable future—lent itself to attempts to formulate overarching narratives that could impose a logic and an order on the chaotic present.

That is, unsubstantiated information not only circulated as discrete (if fluid) rumors, but was gathered together and ordered as holistic narratives, as what might be termed "conspiracy theories." Drawing on Foucault, Paul Silverstein writes that conspiracy theory in Algeria and among Algerians outside of Algeria during the Algerian civil war constituted "a form of 'vernacular' knowledge production—contrasting with overlapping 'official' modes of media and scholarly knowledge production—that outlines an alternative 'truth regime' with its own discursive rules, institutions, and diffusion networks."[8] Indeed, the diffuse and polyvocal Egyptian scene—as participants in the revolt became increasingly fractured and an increasing number of people grew frustrated with what was happening—led to alternative truth regimes rather than an alternative truth regime. However, rumors or particular facts could be mobilized and remobilized at different times and with different aims, thus giving a sense of how particular issues and anxieties were shared across political factions or affiliations. Two anxieties that featured prominently across varying political discourses were foreign interference and the safety and dignity of women.

FOREIGN MEDDLING

A document distributed in Tahrir Square and subtitled "The Conspiracy Exposed and Demands for Salvation" opened as follows: "It may seem like the many events that took place in the last few days were a coincidence." It went on to list twenty "events"—ranging from a birthday celebration for Hosni Mubarak in the Maspero television building to the orchestration of criminal waves by the state security services—that it described as a full-blown conspiracy between domestic enemies of the revolution (members of the former regime, religious authorities, and opportunists among the liberal, leftist, and radical factions) and its external enemies (Arab reactionaries led by Saudi Arabia, Israel and the Mossad, and the United States).[9]

This triumvirate of Saudi Arabia, Israel, and the United States was cited frequently in the newsletters and pamphlets as posing the greatest threat to Egypt. In July 2011, the Egyptian Communist Party warned: "The forces hostile to the revolution from outside, at their head the United States of America, Israel, Saudi Arabia, and their allies, lie in ambush with the internal counterrevolutionary forces, which still nest in every corner of the organs and institutions of governance and the state and especially in the Ministry of the Interior."[10] A flier from November 2011 urged Egyptians to go come together to form a revolutionary government that "can overcome … [the] will of [Field Marshall] Tantawi and his army of billionaire thieves, his businessmen, his parties and his Saudi Arabia, his Israel, and his America."[11]

Other documents point to rumors of foreign interference directed against those who revolted. One critique of the Egyptian media accused it of having "fired off various rumors … for example the exaggerated [claims] about our being led by foreign agents. In this way they hurled the rumor of 'infiltrators' at us."[12] Another source decried rumors claiming that protesters in Tahrir Square were receiving money or food, asking readers to "come to the square and look at our situation. … You surely see that no one is paying us and there's no KFC [Kentucky Fried Chicken] or any other of the media's lies."[13]

Accusations of foreign interference leveled at both revolutionary and counterrevolutionary forces were not totally without merit. Certainly, regional and international powers were not neutral bystanders in the unfolding events of Egypt. Nor were they in other Arab states that witnessed widespread political protest or violence in 2011 and 2012. In fact, it is the general veracity of claims of foreign interference that gave momentum to complex theories that placed Mossad snipers around Tahrir Square[14] or had America funding the distribution of Kentucky Fried Chicken to demonstrators in the square. Similarly, the question of violence against women in Tahrir Square has been the subject of rumor in part because of incidences of sexual assault. Let us take a closer look, then, at how these incidents fueled rumors that were placed into larger narratives about the state of Egypt pre- and post-Mubarak.

VIOLENCE AGAINST WOMEN

In December 2012, pictures of Egyptian actresses Laila Elwi and Yousra amid a scrum of young men began to circulate on the Internet. Allegations that the two were being harassed by the crowd set the Internet "abuzz with rumors."[15] The actresses ultimately denied being harassed, explaining that the photographs merely captured the attempts of fans to get closer to the screen stars. Yet such rumors clearly represented a larger concern regarding the sexual harassment in Tahrir Square and in Egypt more generally.

In the early months of the revolt, the treatment of women emerged as a prime concern in documents distributed in Tahrir Square. A March 7, 2011, handout entitled "Start with Yourself First," implored Egyptians to commit to a number of changes, among them: "I will not harass girls or even flirt with them."[16] Similarly, a handbill distributed on March 18, 2011, exhorted its readers: "We must stop harassing women.… Respect the freedom of women and girls walking on the street and make them feel as if they are among family."[17] A poem distributed in Tahrir Square on April 19, 2011, began: "Don't ask me not to get angry. Don't empty my body of blood. Don't make me watch as my women's honor is publicly violated in the streets."[18] These are only a few examples of numerous exhortations to respect women in Egyptian society.

An implicit link is thus made between the Mubarak regime and the degradation of Egyptian women. Although different factions (Islamist and secularists, for example) may have seen this degradation and what kinds of steps needed to be taken to redeem female honor quite differently, they agreed that this was a priority that had to be dealt with. When, in December 2011, Egyptian soldiers attacked a woman whose blue brassiere was exposed during their assault, this became an iconic image among many Egyptians and internationally, symbolizing Egypt's military rulers' complicity in the continued violence against Egyptian women and, by extension, SCAF's counterrevolutionary nature.

An even more explicitly political rumor of sexual harassment and violence against women was subsequently reported by Ruth Whitehead of Britain's *Daily Mail* and quickly picked up by right-wing American media outlets online. In the wake of massive protests against President Mohamed Morsi's controversial November 22, 2012 decree, granting him immunity from judicial review until the drafting of a new constitution and authorizing the retrial of Hosni Mubarak and other regime figures, Whitehead reported: "Egypt's ruling party is paying gangs of thugs to sexually assault women protesting in Cairo's Tahrir Square against President Mohamad Morsi, activists said."[19] Disturbing instances of group sexual assault against women in Tahrir Square are not in dispute. Nor is it unlikely that young men affiliated with the Muslim Brotherhood received material support to attend gatherings in Tahrir Square or elsewhere and disrupt the activities of rival factions. Little supporting evidence, though, emerged to support the accusation that the Brotherhood was organizing groups for the express purpose of harassing and assaulting women.

This rumor does, however, serve to link anxieties about the safety of women in Tahrir Square to anxieties about the role of women in an Egypt run by the Muslim Brothers and to draw a continuity between the Muslim Brotherhood and the Mubarak regime, which was accused of similar tactics. Indeed, Magda Adly, director of the Nadeem Center for Human Rights, explicitly makes this connection in the article: "I believe thugs are being paid money to do this. ... The Muslim Brotherhood have the same political approaches as Mubarak."[20]

Such rumors take particular facts—the assaults of women in Tahrir Square, the clashes between protestors of various factions—and fit them into narrative that allows a window into the kinds of anxieties felt by actors on the ground and the kinds of linkages that these actors made. These rumors sought to draw a distinction between the purity of the young male "revolutionaries" in Tahrir Square, who presumably uphold the revolutionary ethos of respect and dignity for women, and "counterrevolutionary" forces of the Muslim Brotherhood, who revert to Mubarak-era norms of harassment. We can read in them anxieties about the practices, having taken hold of certain positions of power, of Morsi and the Muslim Brotherhood. We should also read anxieties about the behavior of men in Tahrir Square, about anonymity within crowded public spaces, and about the potential brutality of such crowds in the absence of certain forms of authoritarian control.

Clearly, rumors lend themselves to complex and multiple interpretations. They are fluid and open to change. They can contain seemingly contradictory threads—anxiety about Muslim Brotherhood rule and anxiety about the congregation of large groups of anonymous young male anti-Brotherhood protestors, for example. In the following section, I will look at the various degrees to which rumors could be seen as a contributing factor to the revolt in Egypt.

RUMORS: AGENTS OF REVOLT?

One of the contributions of the subaltern studies movement has been the willingness to approach rumor seriously as a counter hegemonic form of communication. In this view, rumors by their very nature challenge power. Giyatri Chakravorty Spivak writes, "Rumor evokes comradeship because it belongs to every 'reader' or 'transmitter.' No one is its origin or source. Thus, rumor is not error but primordially (originally) errant, always in circulation with no assignable source. This illegitimacy makes it accessible to insurgency."[21] Certainly, in the early weeks and months of the revolt, it is possible to see how rumors gave momentum to insurgents and brought them together.

Rumors ranging from the health and wealth of Hosni Mubarak and his family to the retrograde influence of foreign powers, to Egypt's personal status laws (one flyer asserted that the government had "raised the marriage age to over thirty and discouraged men from getting married, especially to Egyptian women")[22] certainly motivated protesters, adding a sense of urgency to the demonstrations and demands. Their power can be seen in such documents as *al-Midan al-Yawm*, which in July noted that in Suez, "some of the protesters … attempted to hold a sit-in and storm the harbor at Port Tawfiq in response to a rumor that one of the protesters was being detained within."[23]

Rumors and conspiracy theories that focused on global and regional counterrevolutionary forces—like those discussed above—also deflected attention from the disorganization or incoherence of the insurgents and their various demands, creating an alternative truth regime wherein those who revolted remained united and failure was attributable to external intervention rather than internal frictions.

But if Spivak stresses rumor's affinity with insurgency, it is important to note the repeated concern that rumor was working against those who revolted. A group calling itself The United announced its formation in a flier distributed in Tahrir Square, and listed among its goals: "Combating conspiracies" and "Combating deceptive rumors."[24] Another group, calling itself the Try-to-Understand Movement, advocated the publication and distribution of "true and useful information" in order to produce "a generation that can advance sound opinions based on knowledge, not on rumors and information received from superficial sources."[25]

Rumors could lead to panic and chaos, embarrassing protesters or playing into the hands of counterrevolutionary forces. State security forces, "with the help of its clients among the Wahhabis and the remnants of the dissolved party," were accused of spreading rumors "to create new sectarian strife."[26] An online attempt to trace the spread of rumors that nerve gas was being used by the military against demonstrators in November 2011 illustrates how panic and fear based on unverified information led to confusion from the ground level to such figures as Mohamed ElBaradei and Queen Noor of Jordan.[27]

It may be possible to distinguish between various phases of the revolt in Egypt: an early period within which rumor can be seen as serving the insurgents' interests by undermining the power and authority of the regime; and a later period, following Mubarak's departure, when rumors undermined the protesters' struggles to cohere. This is ultimately too simple a view, however. Rumors certainly have the potential to disrupt hegemonic narratives, but this power is not always productive. On a psychological level it can lead to confusion or disenchantment, and on a much more physical level it can lead to injury and even death.

The power of rumors should not be dismissed or minimized. As I have tried to demonstrate here, the particularity of rumors and their impact can help us understand the movement of ideas and bodies. Returning briefly to the rumor with which I opened, the distribution of poisoned tea in Tahrir Square, note how it gives a sense of space and of the circulation of people in that space: "people passed by every tent to caution those present against drinking tea from the vendors in the square." Without movement, fundamental transformation is impossible. It is important to remember rumor not only as being facilitated by such movement, spreading through crowds more easily and more quickly than through individual contacts, but also as motivating such movement.

CONCLUSION

The documents drawn on here give some sense of how rumors operated within Tahrir Square and in Egypt more generally, but it is important to recall that these sources cannot fully illuminate the transmission and impact of rumors. Social media sources, though their significance in the events of January 2011 and the following months may have been overstated, are probably more useful in that they record data that can provide clues regarding the speed and routes with which certain information, both accurate and inaccurate, spread among certain communities of activists and observers. But as Ranajit Guha has noted, "rumor is spoken utterance par excellence."[28] As such, the documentation of rumor is something quite distinct from rumor itself and it is difficult from a distance—now both physically and temporally—to recreate or get a firm grip on the way rumors spread, the particular forms they took, and the reactions of individuals to them.

This should not, however, dissuade observers or historians from investigating rumors. In his work on the transmission of information in prerevolutionary eighteenth-century France, Robert Darnton argues that the preponderance of venues for the exchange of information have distorted our ability to think about the transmission of information before television, the Internet, and widespread literacy: "The marvels of communication technology in the present have produced a false consciousness about the past."[29] I would argue that they may have produced an equally false consciousness of the present, a period in which orality remains a significant element of information transmission. Historians increasingly have noted the impact of rumors on past events. Commentators on current events too often dismiss them because they are "not true." Yet this does not diminish their impact. Rumors of Mubarak's imminent departure encouraged demonstrators to join the crowds in Tahrir Square. Rumors of police or military presence or actions in one location drew some demonstrators toward that location and others away from it. Rumors of poison gas spread panic among protesters, while those of poison tea spawned tensions between vendors and activists. On a basic level, rumors put bodies in motion. Without acknowledging this basic fact, it would be impossible to understand the events of 2011 and 2012 in Egypt. Rumors also gave expression to shared anxieties, pitted factions against one another, or sought to salvage a sense of unity as the months of political turmoil produced increasing tension. As such, they may be just as important as official statements, elections, cabinet selections, or presidential decrees, and should be taken just as seriously. This chapter has been a limited attempt to do so, one I hope encourages further investigation into the rich and vivid arena of rumor, innuendo, and conspiracy theory.

NOTES

1   Alex would like to thank the other participants on the Middle East Studies Association panel dealing with Tahrir Documents (2012): Emily Drumsta, Cameron Hu, Murad Idris, Elias Saba, and Levi Thompson—as well as Professor Stuart Schaar for his interest and encouragement.

2   "The Revolution's Doctors Deny Tea Poisoning Rumor," *al-Midan al-Yawm* vol. 6: 3. Translated and posted on TahrirDocuments.org, August 11, 2011 (accessed June 17, 2011), www.tahrirdocuments.org/2011/08/the-square-today-6-17-june.

3   Dan E. Miller, "Rumor: An Examination of Some Stereotypes," *Symbolic Interaction*, vol. 28, no. 4 (Fall 2005): 508.

4   See, for example, "The Egyptian Media Coalition," TahrirDocuments.org, March 21, 2011 (accessed March 11, 2011), www.tahrirdocuments.org/2011/03/the-egyptian-media-coalition.

5   Ziiyad Tariq Hasan, "Egyptian Media, Symbol of Hypocrisy," *Gurnal* vol. 1: 12. Translated and posted on TahrirDocuments.org, July 22, 2011 (accessed March 11, 2011), www.tahrirdocuments.org/2011/07/the-legitimate-demands-of-the-revolution.

6   "Has the Regime Fallen?" *Gurnal* vol. 1: 7. Translated and posted on TahrirDocuments.org, July 22, 2011 (dated February 24, 2011, accessed March 11, 2011), www.tahrirdocuments.org/2011/03/has-the-regime-fallen.

7   Paul A. Silverstein, "An Excess of Truth: Violence, Conspiracy Theorizing, and the Algerian Civil War," *Anthropology Quarterly* vol. 76, no. 4 (Autumn 2002): 646.

8   "Third Statement of the People's Revolution," TahrirDocuments.org, June 16, 2011 (accessed May 13, 2011), www.tahrirdocuments.org/2011/06/third-statement-of-the-peoples-revolution.

9   Egyptian Communist Party, "The Revolution First: Friday of Purification, Retribution, and Social Justice," TahrirDocuments.org, August 2, 2011 (accessed 1July 15, 2011), www.tahrirdocuments.org/2011/08/the-egyptian-communist-party-the-revolution-first-friday-of-purification-retribution-and-social-justice.

10   "Go Forward, Revolutionary Egypt, and Complete Your Revolution!" TahrirDocuments.org, February 2, 2012 (accessed November 5, 2011), www.tahrirdocuments.org/2012/02/go-forward-revolutionary-egypt-and-complete-your-revolution.

11   Hasan, "Egyptian Media, Symbol of Hypocrisy."

12   "Why a Sit-In at Tahrir Square," TahrirDocuments.org, March 13, 2011 (accessed March 13, 2011), www.tahrirdocuments.org/2011/03/document-1.

13   "Why a Sit-In at Tahrir Square," TahrirDocuments.org, March 13, 2011 (accessed March 9, 2011), www.tahrirdocuments.org/2011/03/document-1.

14   See "Yousra Denies Harassment in Tahrir Despite Shocking Photos of Pal, Laila Elwi," *Albawaba*, December 2, 2012, www.albawaba.com/entertainment/yousra-tahrir-45359.

15   "Start with Yourself First," TahrirDocuments.org, March 14, 2011, www.tahrir-documents.org/2011/03/start-with-yourself-first.

16   "Egypt of Change," TahrirDocuments.org, April 12, 2011, www.tahrirdocuments.org/2011/04/egypt-of-change.

17   "My Father's Pride," TahrirDocuments.org, May 20, 2011, www.tahrirdocuments.org/2011/05/my-fathers-pride.

18   Ruth Whitehead, "Muslim Brotherhood 'Paying Gangs To Go Out and Rape Women and Beat Men Protesting in Egypt' as Thousands of Demonstrators Pour on to the Streets," *Daily Mail Online*, December 1, 2012, www.dailymail.co.uk/news/article-2241374/Muslim-Brotherhood-paying-gangs-rape-women-beat-men-protesting-Egypt-thousands-demonstrators-pour-streets.html.

19   Whitehead, "Muslim Brotherhood 'Paying Gangs'" (emphasis added), December 2012, www.dailymail.co.uk/news/article-2241374/Muslim-Brotherhood-paying-gangs-rape-women-beat-men-protesting-Egypt-thousands-demonstrators-pour-streets.html.

20 Whitehead, "Muslim Brotherhood 'Paying Gangs'" (emphasis added).

21 Gayatri Chakravorty Spivak, "Subaltern Studies: Deconstructing Historiography," in Spivak and Ranajit Guha, eds., *Selected Subaltern Studies*, Oxford: Oxford University Press, 1988, p. 23.

22 "Save Egyptian Families," TahrirDocuments.org, June 16, 2011 (acquired May 15, 2011), www.tahrirdocuments.org/2011/06/save-egyptian-families.

23 "Fifteen Injured in Arba`in Square," *al-Midan al-Yawm*, vol. 8, p. 3. Translated and published on TahrirDocuments.org, October 28, 2011 (acquired July 22, 2011), www.tahrirdocuments.org/2011/10/fifteen-injured-in-arbain-square.

24 "The United," TahrirDocuments.org, April 15, 2011, www.tahrirdocuments.org/2011/04/1392.

25 "The Try-to-Understand Movement," TahrirDocuments.org, September 2, 2011 (acquired July 29, 2011), www.tahrirdocuments.org/2011/09/the-try-to-understand-movement.

26 "Third Statement of the People's Revolution."

27 Dave LaFontaine, "Real-Time Coverage of Nerve Gas Rumors (via Storify)," Sips from the Firehose (blog), November 22, 2011, www.artesianmedia.com/blog/2011/11/22/real-time-coverage-of-nerve-gas-rumors-via-storify.

28 Ranajit Guha, *Elementary Aspects of Peasant Insurgency in Colonial India*, Durham: Duke University Press, 1999, p. 256.

29 Robert Darnton, *Poetry and the Police: Communication Networks in Eighteenth-Century Paris*, Cambridge, MA: Belknap Press of Harvard University Press, 2010, p. 1. I thank Juan Cole for suggesting Darnton's work as a rich source dealing with the circulation of rumors and rumor's complex relationship with authority. In addition to Guha and Darnton, see, for example, C. A. Bayly, *Empire and Information: Intelligence Gathering and Social Communication in India, 1780–1870*, Cambridge: Cambridge University Press, 1996; and Arlette Farge and Jacques Revel, *The Vanishing Children of Paris: Rumor and Politics before the French Revolution*, trans. Claudia Mieville, Cambridge: Harvard University Press, 1993.

II

Israeli/Scottish/British novelist Simon Louvish writes in the first person about the parallel Israeli and Arab searches for identity in a fast-changing Middle East. His personal narrative differs from many of the contributions in this book and adds an important cultural dimension only an accomplished author can offer. Louvish has published more than twenty-seven books including The Blok novels, six in all, filled with magic realism and wonderfully zany humor.

IIIIIIIIIIIIIIIIIIIIIIIIIIIIIIIIIIIIIIIIIIIIIIIIIIIIIIIIIIIIIIIIIIIIIIIIIIIIIIIIIIIIIIIIIIII

CHAPTER 20
SPRING, SUMMER, WINTER—ISRAEL AND THE REST OF THE MIDDLE EAST— A POLITICS OF IDENTITY
SIMON LOUVISH

My father, who was a lifelong Zionist, devoted to the "Mapai" Labor Party, shared with the fellow believers of his generation, those who straddled the eras before and after the founding of the State of Israel, a certain opinion about the nature of the conflict over the future of Palestine—namely, that the issue was essentially insoluble until the Arab states surrounding Israel evolved in their structures from dictatorships to democratic societies. Not that it was futile to try to "explode" the Middle East from its stalemate; indeed, this position, cemented by the Zionist right and later coalesced around what became known as the "neo-Con" outlook, presumed physical action, such as the war in Iraq. But it was based on the mantra, still echoed by politicians in the West, that "democracies do not go to war with each other."

The conceptual difficulties with this would seem fairly clear to anyone whose life is not invested in the absolute priority of Israel's state interests, not the least the question of the precise form in which Israel can be seen as a democracy, particularly after 1967, when the long occupation of the West Bank and Gaza began. But it was part and parcel of a certain vision of the Zionist project in Palestine, a view that was hegemonic among those who saw themselves as Socialist Zionists, whose hold over the governments of Israel was paramount until the Likud Party's election victory in 1977. This can be seen by accessing the archival records of the "Histadrut" trade-union newspaper *Davar*, founded in 1925, and available online in great detail from the website of the Historical Jewish Press (www.jpress.org.il, in Hebrew.) I have found it very difficult to convince my Palestinian friends that the mainstream view of left-wing Zionists, particularly those of the kibbutz movement, was that their own efforts—i.e. Jewish immigration and settlement in Palestine from the turn of the twentieth century—was essentially benign, and that the more Jews (of the correct political outlook) who settled in Palestine, the more they would challenge the feudal land ownership of the soil of Palestine, and thereby benefit the subservient *fellaheen*. This view was challenged, in their own ranks, by their fellow immigrants of the rival right-wing "Revisionist" movement, led by Vladimir Ze'ev Jabotinsky, who told them they were deluded, and that Palestine would only be won by the establishment of a distinctly nationalistic entity that would have to be imposed by force. Thus the Zionist left always defined its own militia forces as a "Haganah" – Defense, as against the proactive force of the right, which was already forming underground militias to combat both Arab Palestinians and the British Mandate's regime.

At its root, this was not an argument over tactics or even strategy, but over the very issue of identity, which still dominates the agenda of the current leadership of the State of Israel, the direct descendants of the "Revisionism" of the early 1920s. Jewish immigration to Palestine—after the earlier nineteenth-century trickle of pre-Zionist idealists asserting a newfound Hebrew revival that grew among Eastern European Jewish intellectuals from the 1860s—was from the first decade of the twentieth century overtly and decisively ideological. "A land without people for a people without land" is an oft-quoted line, attributed to writer Israel Zangwill, but it was fairly clear to everyone who actually set foot in Jaffa after crossing the Mediterranean that this was not the case. The challenge of communicating with the local Arab population was the subject of endless discourse among the Jewish "pioneers" from the minute they stepped off the boat, literally carried ashore on the arms of Arab longshoremen. Why have we come here? What is our claim? Are we to supplant the "native" population? Can we communicate with their concerns? This was a constant and ongoing discourse.[1] It was after all a world of flux, only a few years after the collapse of the Ottoman Empire, with almost all the new Jewish immigrants cadres of one branch or another of the revolutionary movements that toppled the Empire of the Tsar. On the one hand, there were those who saw the challenge of creating a New Society in the "Land of our Fathers"; and on the other, those who seized on the new kind of militant nationalism that was already rising in parts of Europe—first in Italy, and then in Germany. The pages of *Davar*, in the early 1930s, as Hitler rose to power, are full of fulminations by devout socialists against some of the most fanatic among the Revisionists, who saw nothing wrong with Hitler's formulas for Germany apart from the small fact that he didn't like Jews.[2] As a German, they expected him to side with the Germans. As Jews, they would naturally side with the Jews, mutated by the rise of secular nations into a nation like any other, with its own state and borders, preferably way across the Jordan. "Democracy," in this sense, was an unfortunate necessity among the fellow brethren, as the schismatic nature of Jewish village life required endless debate and argument. The heirs to this debate were the Zionist Socialists, in their already fracturing subparties and conclaves. Religion was nowhere in this equation; it was a separate issue, of relevance only to those communities, mostly Hassidic Jews who had trickled into the Holy Land over centuries, that had their own fiefdoms in places like Jerusalem and Safad. Some were part of the Zionist movement, some indifferent to it, some vehemently opposed.

The big question was, however, "Who are we?" The theorists of the left-wing movements met in marathon sessions at their kibbutz venues, chattering, over weeklong debates, about the nature of society, the esoteric "stychian" processes of human development, types of organization, the nature of Man (and Woman), much as student groups would debate endlessly in the halcyon days of 1960s Europe. The "Brotherhood of Man" did not exclude Arabs, who were, however—and this was the only problem—seen as being sunk in their own feudal and backward mentality, and the "objective" situation rendered them foot-soldiers of the most reactionary elements that formed the "Levantine" mode of life: the few, the landowners, the feudal sheikhs, the enemies of progress. Dehumanization, as we know, or should know, from the twentieth century's dismal record, can proceed as easily from a base of "socialist" dogma as it can from ultranationalist zealotry.

My father wrote the following about his own parents in an unpublished autobiography, in a chapter titled "WHAT IS A JEW?": "My parents had no identity problems. They were Jews, and that was that. They had both come from religious families: my mother told us how particular her mother had been that not a grain of *hometz* [a fermented grain] should come into the house once it had been scrubbed clean for Passover: she even tied little socks onto the cat's feet in case it should bring in some breadcrumbs on its paws." There was no sense in which they would define themselves as Russians, let alone Ukrainians (my grandfather was born in the Ukraine) or Austrian (my grandmother was born in Bukovina, which is now Romania), and British nationality, which they eventually took, was a matter of refuge. One's passport is not one's identity. And an Israeli one? That is citizenship, which is still distinct from identity. (My grandparents only came to Israel once my parents were settled, in the early 1950s.)

One becomes caught here in words, which change their meaning from language to language. The standard English idea of "nation," as a bunch of people living in the same place, cannot define the Hebrew "*am*," as it cannot define the equivalent Arabic "*umma*," which encompasses an entire community, wherever it may reside. In this sense, my grandfather's generation would have no problem speaking of a Jewish "nation," however dispersed it might be. Zionism's project of a "return" is resolutely secular, despite its appropriation of the daily Jewish prayer for a return to Jerusalem, a symbolic and Messianic yearning that led to a mere trickle of actual "returnees" over two millennia of daily devotion. (The Jews who were seduced by the prophecies of the "false Messiah" Sabbatai Zevi in the 1660s confined their preparations for a miraculous return to climbing on the rooftops of their homes to await the angels who would appear to conduct them to the Holy Land. Sabbatai himself was expelled by the rabbis of Jerusalem as a fake.) In historical terms, one might compare the Jews of the postbiblical "diaspora" to another people, the Greeks, who spread out from an origin nation and settled throughout the world.

This issue of identity as "*am*," "*umma*," "nation," and "people" returns to haunt us when looking at the upheavals that are shaking the Middle East in our own moment. The standard analysis defines the events that spread from Tunisia to Egypt, Yemen, and Libya, and then to Syria in terms of political tyranny, economic despair, and the global crisis that piles on the pressure in countries least able to withstand the financial meltdown. One can brandish various slogans, and point to the counterforces of new mechanisms of communication that appear to empower the previously silenced. Who could not be moved by the courage of the demonstrators in Tunis, the cross-section of poor and middle classes, men and women, who poured into the streets, the youth who took down Mubarak in Egypt? Who can forget Mubarak's last forlorn speeches, appealing finally as the ultimate patriarch, the "Father of his People," calling for his "children" to go home, to stop worrying their parents? How could they doubt his caring paternal destiny? Then there was Gaddafi, explaining patiently to assemblies of journalists that "my people love me," ergo those who did not were not his people, not sons and daughters of their own soil but a conglomeration of rats, vermin, and external invaders. And Bashar al-Assad and his tame media, unable to explain why hordes of terrorists suddenly descended on the good people of Syria—tragically, one of the Middle East's worst examples of self-fulfilled prophecy. But to what are they appealing, these blood-stained oppressors, if not to some imagined identity, which has suddenly, inexplicably in their own eyes, disappeared, like the wisp of a genie released from a smashed bottle?

As in all revolutions, a primary spasm shakes the entire population, both those who participate and those who stand by and watch, as the old order totters, as a king, a tsar, a despot falls. The crowd in Tahrir Square, throwing its shoes at the image of Mubarak on screen as he makes his last, lost bid for power. Gadaffi's terrible and blood-stained end. The world watches in wonder.

Rulers ponder in their own halls of power. Then the long hangover: the realization that not all was Facebook and YouTube; that other, intact forces made their own play, or stood back, biding their time. The realization that large swathes of the population remained fearful of the day after. That the old order not only had crucial forces that remained unbroken, in the shadows, in tactical retreat, but also a deeper sediment within the population than appeared at the first blast of fury and joy. And above all, the realization that old, manufactured, or false identities that were now broken had to be replaced by new answers to the same old questions: Who are we? What do we want?

Questions can also be asked of those states of the Arab Maghreb and Mashraq that did not, in that first spasm, blow open: the Gulf States, Saudi Arabia, Jordan, and Morocco. Algeria—the case of a regime hardened by previous conflicts, quick to nip protest in the bud; massacres and deadly civil conflict too fresh in recent memory, the fear of chaos and national collapse. Jordan and Morocco, two "kingdoms" with rulers claiming an ancient legitimacy based on religious-historical precedent. The Arabian sheikhdoms, with their skein of clan and family embedded deeply in every sphere of power, political and financial, their cushion of oil alleviating the worst aspects of the global crisis, despite sectarian schisms coupled with economic disparities that in Bahrain threatened a new precedent. But in all the upheavals, and in all those regions where upheaval has yet to make its mark, identity emerges as an unavoidable issue.

In both Tunisia and Egypt, as unprecedentedly democratic elections brought the previously banned Islamic movements to power, both parties professed to represent the essential religious impulse in a society where secularism had been identified with dictatorial power: in Tunisia, Ben-Ali's usurpation of Bourguiba's anticolonial revolution, and in Egypt, the Nasserist legacy, army rule in the apparent name of "the people." Both Tunisia's Ennahda Movement and Egypt's Muslim Brotherhood presented themselves as arbiters and protectors of the majority's primary identification as Muslims. As both also promised to answer the two popular cries of the street protests that toppled the two dictatorships—freedom and bread, a solution to poverty and unemployment—events now show how difficult it is to make even modest gains in this respect. The answer, particularly in Egypt, was to tighten, rather than relax, the new ruling parties' emphasis on the traditional, inalienable identity of their supporters—Islam is, after all a doctrine of submission to the will of God, a trope that trumps all other requirements—until, in the summer of 2013, the pressures burst open in the anti-Brotherhood protests that called on the army to rescue Egypt's new-born democracy by abolishing it, returning (for how long?) to the old order.

In Tunisia, Rashid Gannouchi, long the leader in exile of the country's Islamists, gave copious interviews explaining his own interpretation of religion as a matter of personal choice. A precarious balance between religious and secular parties endures, for the moment. The aftermath has shown that religious identity politics alone cannot answer to the popular will for greater freedoms—freedom from want, certainly, but also the more secular freedoms of speech, expression, organization, and women's rights. In both Tunisia and Egypt, sitting on the maw of a volcano proved to be an uncomfortable perch for new rulers. Modern society, East and West, teems with a range of identities, thrown up both by history and the flux of ever-evolving modernity.

Meanwhile, back in Israel-Palestine, how has the great upheaval played to a region consumed by its own long-term impossibilities: squaring the circle between the Israeli state's self-preservation in its own image, and Palestine's cry for an end to occupation and the establishment of its own freedom? After all, my Zionist father's long expressed cry for democracies to flourish among the neighboring states of the confrontation has been answered, at least in intention: The people want freedom. The cry of one middle-aged man interviewed by CNN in a Cairo café in January 2011 echoed in Tahrir Square: "I feel that I have been choked to death for forty-five years." The explosion of free speech, the banners, the posters, the graffiti, the impassioned speeches, the songs. The force of unarmed masses physically pushing back police wagons across the Nile bridges. These were relayed in Israel as elsewhere. The same events were watched in the West Bank and Gaza. There were some scattered demonstrations of Palestinian support. There were trenchant analyses on Israeli TV. But, apart from this, nothing happened. The Israeli army tightened its grip around the occupied areas. The Israeli people went about their business as usual. The occupied areas did not rise up. Why?

While the world's attention was on Arab uprisings, would not the addition of a renewed reminder of the quintessentially repressed Arab people by the last colonial power in the region add renewed force to their seven-decades-old cry for freedom? Was this not the moment long awaited? But there were several crucial discouragements. The obvious deterrence of brute force: the ring of steel and close surveillance of practically every inhabitant of the West Bank, available on Israeli security databanks for swift arrest or retribution, a machine of state terror built over many years. But a vital part was also played by the reluctance of local forces, primarily the Palestine National Authority—long locked in a syndrome of "will we/won't we" return to a facade of peace talks, but constrained, as the leaked "Palestine Papers" revealed in their nakedness, to futile pleas for fairness—to move to a mode of all-out resistance. Possibly for good reason, perhaps not. It is easy to judge others when one is not in their place. For the leadership, the long trek around the councils of the established Arab states and their apparently immoveable leaders—the Mubaraks,

Ben Alis, the Gulf sheikhs, and Syria's Assad—was inevitably disturbed by the sudden disappearance of some of their major interlocutors. And in Gaza, besieged in its own peculiar syndrome of unofficially self-governing status under the fiefdom of Hamas—elected, but unrecognized by Western powers, and professing absolute resistance to Zionist rule in any part of Palestine while in effect holding down the populace in its own semimafia honeycomb of self-serving militias and allied gangs—the people themselves exercised no power whatsoever, reduced to objects of charity, a focus for well-wishing groups from Western Europe, Turkey, and elsewhere to vent their moral anger at their plight. Amid the upheaval there was a poignant Palestinian plea in the shape of a "fuck everybody" statement from a group of young people fed to the teeth with their lock-down emerged over Internet media[3], but was quickly sidelined by all the usual rhetoric of solidarity.

The sudden eruptions in Tunisia and Egypt, and the tragic collapse of Syria, took the Palestinians by surprise, and had the inevitable side-effect of militating against the essential mantra of all Palestinian leaders since 1948—that the Palestine issue, the "last European colony," was, ipso facto, the fulcrum of the ongoing crisis of the Arab world; by definition the reason why the State of Israel could not be accepted as part of the region, and by extension the reason why Western powers struggled to gain support in the Arab world. The wars between Israel and the Arabs—from Suez Crisis in 1956 through the Six-Day War in 1967, the 1973 Arab-Israeli War, and the 1982 Lebanon War—all threatened global stability in a Cold War context, and all (more or less) focused upon the running sore of Palestine, the Arab world's gaping wound. But suddenly this was not the case.

In Israel, this was not unwelcome to the Likud government. Obviously there were strategic shifts, potentially looming, particularly over the Egypt-Israel Peace Treaty in 1979 ensuing from President Carter's Camp David coup of 1978. Would a Muslim Brotherhood government in Cairo abrogate the deal, bringing the immensely powerful Egyptian army into a renewed confrontation? In Egypt's first spasm, the army had played its crucial part in refusing to back Mubarak's survival, keeping its tanks in abeyance at Tahrir Square. Policies of collaboration over Hamas in Gaza were changeable, but not the strategic issue, underpinned by American support. Jordan was as yet unaffected. The Syrian apocalypse had not yet materialized. In Israel's population, among those who paid any attention to politics—apart from the rat race of tribal elbow-thrusting among the leaders of competing political parties, leaders long recognized even by their supporters as self-serving and corrupt—the Arab Spring inspired some hope. This became expressed, unexpectedly to everyone outside Israel, in the summer of 2011, in massive middle-class protests in the streets of all Israel's big cities and in many smaller centers. About one-tenth of Israel's total population, several hundred thousand people, took part in rallies in Tel Aviv, Jerusalem, Haifa, and elsewhere against the government of "Bibi" Netanyahu, focusing on the issue of high taxation and the inability of ordinary, hard-working citizens to make a living. What began as the derided "cottage cheese" rebellion became a rallying call of discontent, led by both men and women—mainly young, and overwhelmingly secular—who made a conscious decision to maximize their support by omitting from their slogans the main reason for the state's wasting budget—the Occupation, and the subsidization of settlements.

This was very much a politics of identity. We are Israel, was the essential message. We are not fanatics, zealots, religious maniacs, or even heroes—we are just ordinary people who want to live a decent life in this land. Many of them represented a strand of society that had appeared to have vanished—more akin to my father's image of a people at peace above all with themselves, and secondarily, with their "neighbors." In Haifa, the demonstrations took on an overt Jewish-Arab solidarity: tens of thousands marched with slogans proclaiming "Jews and Arabs Refuse to be Enemies." Even in Jerusalem, which had appeared, since the 1960s, to have become an ultrareligious fiefdom twinned with Iran's holy city of Qom, tens of thousands marched for secular freedoms. The religious communities were conspicuously absent, though in actual fact they remain the most socially deprived and poorest sector of the Israeli Jewish population.

My father did not live to see this upheaval. In his old age he sat at home and wrote letters to the newspapers advocating progress to Israeli-Palestinian peace. In his working life he served the "Mapai" political structure, as one-time head of the Government Press Office, and official interpreter from Hebrew to English of the first prime minister, David Ben-Gurion. After Ben-Gurion he became involved with the short-lived internal party rebellion named "Rafi," led by ex-general Moshe Dayan and the then young Shimon Peres. I once asked my father why all these people around him, given that they knew a Palestinian state was the only practical way out of the morass of the unending conflict, did not come out and say so in public? (This was long before the Oslo process.) His answer was that they knew their constituents were not ready for this, and the politicians were biding their time. When, in 1977, his own "Mapai" party was routed by Menachem Begin's Likud, he was mortified, as Begin represented for him all the destructive forces of the Zionist Movement, which he had always regarded—just as his predecessors had in the 1930s—as "fascists." It was during the 1982 Lebanon War, he told me, that he had realized for the first time that his leaders had been lying to him. He had been seventy-three years old at the time.

My father's essential identification of himself was first of all as a Jew. He was an Israeli citizen from 1949 to his death in 2001. The generation that demonstrated in 2011 demonstrated primarily as Israelis. Its members would not be too hot and bothered about Prime Minister Netanyahu's latest ploy to keep the danger of peace at a distance by insisting that the Palestinians—and the rest of the world—sign on to the formal recognition of Israel as an ethnically Jewish state. In this, "Bibi" remains the son of his father, the Herut zealot, the last gasp of the old "Revisionists" whose nationalism was more akin to Mussolini's blackshirts than to anything else. The song of their youth movement, "Beitar," retains the refrain: "With blood and with sweat we will build us a race [*geza* in Hebrew] that is proud, generous, and cruel [*gaon ve'nadiv ve'akhzar*]." Party leaders still sing it at their conventions. Their identity is of militant rebels, fighting in shadows, no matter how long they have now been in government, making deals with mafiosi and billionaires.

The demonstrators in Tel Aviv often unfurled a slogan—"We are also Tahrir." This may well appear bizarre, as the revolutionaries in Tahrir emphatically rejected Mubarak's collaboration with Israel and the Camp David Accords. I recall a young man interviewed wielding a broom at the square during the Egyptian Revolution of 2011. He told the interviewer: "I am sweeping Egypt, because it is my country now."

Identities are important, and are not just a label. They have no expiry date. Israelis are Israelis now, in their fifth generation, and their identities as Jews, in secularity, are coupled to their identities as Israelis but are not necessarily predominant. My elder brother, on the other hand, son of a self-proclaimed socialist, "rediscovered" religion at his Bar Mitzvah and became devout, siring a now extensive tribe of ultrareligious Louvishes, by now, I am afraid to tell you, populating swathes of the "settlements," in which the religious have primary vested interests, since their large families—averaging more than five children per couple—require ever expanding living quarters, which they cannot afford short of millionaire status in the main cities of "green line" Israel. Their core beliefs and their economic interests are entwined. They pray to God daily and raise families within sight of the Israeli West Bank barrier, the concrete excrescence that walls in the Palestinian villages just a few hundred yards from their windows.

In Cairo, in Tunis, in Lybia, and in Syria, the culture wars of identity were being waged ever more fiercely alongside the calls for freedom and bread. In Palestine, the Palestinians are sustained essentially and primarily by their identity, by not letting go. In both Palestine and Israel, the regional swathe of rebellion and change reinforced not a sense of some global solidarity but the sense of identity itself, the core expression of each community, a reiteration of self, when imposed structures begin cracking. And this sense of identity is fluid, not fixed. It adapts itself to circumstances; it is nurtured, not natural; it is both self-expression and its own empowerment.

In Israel, the summer's "minirevolution" waned, the democratic safety valve enabling a new political party to emerge that, in the fullness of time, as ever in Israel, betrayed its promise. Joining "Bibi" Netanyahu's new coalition government in 2013, it was absorbed into the power play of elites. Israel's version of "Occupy" appeared to be short-lived, but its legacy remains a shade in the background.

We can apply old prescriptions, mutter about world power plays, conspiracies ("The Plot"), defunct theories, wishful thinking about how other people should by necessity conform to our own inherited prejudice. But people will push, and nothing remains the same, except perhaps our own capacity to look back to the false comfort of how things used to be, or should have been.

NOTES

1 See Moshe Smilansky's novel *Ba'Arava*, published in Hebrew in the 1930s (MAssada Books), in which new Jewish immigrants arriving in Palestine in the 1890s argue with established colonists who inform them that the land is already occupied:
"Is there a scarcity of space here, in Judea and Galilee?"
"In Judea and Galilee the land is occupied by Arabs."
"So what? We have to inherit their place."
"How?" a voice came from the side.
"Revolutionaries do not ask innocent questions."

2 *Davar*, May 12, 1932 (Commentary column against the revisionist right wing: "I have read that ..." ["*karati* ..."]): (in the context of comments on the Palestine mufti communicating with the German Nazi party): "But what do we hear? Attorney Cohen, who has just been elected to the central committee of the Revisionist party, proclaimed before the Jerusalem court: "If the Hitlerists took out of their program their hatred for the Jews, so we too would stand by the Hitlerists, as the German Hitlerists, to say, Yes, Hitler saved Germany."

3 Gaza Youth Breaks Out, manifesto, www.gazaybo.wordpress.com (January 2011): "Fuck Hamas. Fuck Israel. Fuck Fatah. Fuck UN. Fuck UNWRA. Fuck USA! We, the youth in Gaza, are so fed up with Israel, Hamas, the occupation, the violations of human rights and the indifference of the international community! We want to scream and break this wall of silence. ... We want to be free. We want to be able to live a normal life. ... We are a peace movement consist[ing] of young people in Gaza and supporters elsewhere that will not rest until the truth about Gaza is known by everybody in the whole world."

The Arab revolts, which began in Tunisia in December 2010, spread rapidly through several countries of the Middle East and North Africa, and also overseas among young people who were inspired to rise up by events taking place in the MENA region. Several commentators spoke of a global phenomenon of revolt, with protestors taking over public spaces in many cities throughout the world. Wall Street, with its narrow hallowed streets, became the focal point of one protest as the Occupy Movement settled into a nearby private park, acknowledging its debt to the Arab precedents. The occupiers claimed to represent the 99 percent of Americans struggling to make their livings while 1 percent of the population, symbolized by the Wall Street elite, lived in luxury. For the first time in decades the concept of inequality was reintroduced into American popular culture. Professor John Hammond joined the protesters and became one of the occupiers.

CHAPTER 21
THE ARAB (AND EUROPEAN) REVOLTS AND OCCUPY WALL STREET
JOHN L. HAMMOND

In 2011, *Time* magazine named the Protester as Person of the Year.[1] In a time of economic stress and political uncertainty, protests had broken out that year, first across the Arab world—in a series of events that came to be known as the "Arab Spring"—and then in southern Europe, followed by the United States. Foreshadowed by the abortive Green Movement of 2009 in Iran, a wave of protest spread from Tunisia to Egypt, Libya, Bahrain, Syria, and elsewhere; then demonstrators occupied the state legislature in Wisconsin to protest the curtailment of public employee unions' collective bargaining rights; the *indignados* made their voices heard in Spain, while Greek protesters revolted against austerity; and a heterogeneous group of activists camped out in Zuccotti Park in lower Manhattan under the banner "Occupy Wall Street" (OWS).

In all these places, protesters used an innovative tactic: the occupation. They filled an outdoor public space (except in Wisconsin) and proposed to remain indefinitely, day and night, until some demands were met. Young people, facing grim or (at best) uncertain economic prospects, took prominent roles, and electronic social networking media were used to recruit participants. Occupying a common space for several days or weeks, the occupations developed at least incipient organizational structures that were nonhierarchical and promoted an egalitarian, nonalienated form of interaction. (This chapter will later refer to these characteristics as "horizontality" and "prefiguration.") Observers in each country were astonished by the size and duration of these occupations and the way they spread out from a central node across their respective countries and beyond.

But each occupation had its peculiarities as well. Notably, each had different political objectives and confronted different types of regimes. This chapter will compare three occupations: that of Tahrir Square, Cairo, beginning on January 25; of the Puerta del Sol, Madrid, beginning on May 15; and of Zuccotti Park in New York City, beginning on September 17. Tahrir Square was not the first. Massive protests began in Tunisia in December 2010, and some analysts trace antecedents further back, to the Green Movement in Iran in 2009. These three locations were central, however; and each became the epicenter of a wave of protest that spread out within and beyond its respective country. I will mainly discuss New York, based on my direct experience there.

THE OCCUPATION AND THE NINETY-NINE PERCENT

The New York movement (and by extension the movement in the US as a whole) was known as Occupy Wall Street (OWS). The initial call to occupy, in a two-page spread in the July issue of the Canadian magazine *Adbusters*, cited Tahrir Square as its inspiration. It read (in its entirety):

OCCUPY WALL STREET

Are you ready for a Tahrir moment?
On Sept. 17, flood into lower Manhattan, set up tents,
kitchens, peaceful barricades and occupy Wall Street.

Not knowing exactly what to expect, groups of people started meeting in general assemblies in New York through the summer to lay plans, communicate them through the media, and prepare logistical support for what was intended to be a long-term occupation. Then, on September 17, a few hundred demonstrators gathered in lower Manhattan. Because they had made no secret of their intention, Wall Street was heavily guarded, so they proceeded to a nearby privately owned public space called Zuccotti Park, which they rebaptized Liberty Plaza, and set up camp.

Protesters chose Wall Street rather than a governmental target to express their view that major problems in American society stem from the stranglehold of capitalist corporations, particularly financial corporations, on US politics and social life. Corporate greed and corporate power were a major force in the drastically increased concentration of wealth and income in a tiny fraction of the population. There are many ways to measure inequality, but all of them show the same trend in the United States during the last three decades: a very small layer at the top of the distribution has experienced dramatic increases in its share of the nation's income and wealth. To take a representative example, a 2011 report by the US Congressional Budget Office shows that between 1979 and 2007, the real after-tax household income of the top one percent of the population grew by 275 percent, while that of the rest of the population grew much more modestly: for the top 20 percent (excluding the top 1 percent), the growth was 65 percent; for the bottom fifth of the population, it was 18 percent.[2]

The increasing concentration of wealth is both a result of the increasing political power of corporations and the enabler of further concentration of wealth and power. Thanks to the rising profitability of capitalist corporations, business executives, often paid in stocks as well as cash, captured the lion's share of this increased income at the highest levels.[3]–At the same time, thanks to what Nobel prize–winning economist Joseph Stiglitz called "an increasingly dysfunctional form of capitalism,"[4] ordinary Americans suffer stagnant wages and long-term unemployment, and millions of families have lost their homes to mortgage foreclosures.

Some of the increased riches of the top tier is due to market forces—technology and changing international trade, for example—but much of it is due to government policies adopted in response to corporate influence, including regressive taxes and deregulated financial institutions. Three policies of the preceding decade stand out: the George W. Bush administration's tax cuts, especially for the highest-earning taxpayers; the bailout of major banks after the 2008 financial crisis, with no punishment and little change in regulation of the (often fraudulent) practices that produced the crisis;[5] and the Supreme Court's ruling in the Citizens United case, allowing unlimited corporate contributions in electoral campaigns. All these measures exacerbate both the unequal distribution of wealth and its growing power to influence political outcomes through campaign contributions in the millions of dollars and the more direct purchase of political influence through lobbying.

This emphasis sets the US protests apart from those in the Old World. The protests in the Arab world were against authoritarian governments. Those in Europe, especially Spain, rejected government austerity policies. Both targeted the state. Occupy Wall Street, on the other hand, targeted corporations as economic actors, especially (but not only) financial corporations. While the Occupy protesters objected to government policies that favored those corporations, it was the private financial sector that OWS identified as the main source of problems. The target, accordingly, was Wall Street, the heart of the nation's financial district, and not the national capital. On September 29, 2011, a general assembly of Occupy Wall Street adopted a declaration (the closest thing there is to an authoritative statement of the occupation's platform) presenting a catalogue of grievances that echoed the Declaration of Independence. They were addressed not to the king, however, or even to the president or some other branch of government, but to "corporations, which place profit over people, self-interest over justice, and oppression over equality, [and] run our governments" (Declaration, 2011).

While condemning concentrated wealth and government subservience to economic interests, the occupiers deliberately refrained from making any demands, unlike the Arab and European occupiers. They argued that it was not their role to offer concrete proposals; rather, they wanted to avoid entanglement with the political system and remain free to use direct action to call attention to these issues.

The quintessential slogan of Occupy Wall Street is "We are the 99%," dramatizing the gap between the wealthy and the great majority of the population. The slogan implicitly claims that 99 percent of the population is suffering, has common interests, and should make common cause against the wealthiest one percent. Though the movement hoped that the vast majority would identify with an undifferentiated 99 percent, most activists came from a particular segment of society whose growth itself reflected the polarization of the economy. The growing inequality of wealth and income consigns many to working harder and for longer hours but for stagnating wages. It has also spawned a growing "precariat," a class of people, mostly young and many well educated, without access to stable employment. Global shifts in capitalism have driven large numbers into this class around the world; its members have populated the protests in North Africa and southern Europe as well as the United States.[6] Many such young people in the US experience sporadic employment or long-term unemployment despite educational credentials acquired at great cost and, often, crushing personal debt. Many of them have postindustrial skills in media and information technology, but opportunities in these fields are increasingly rare and often available only for a short-term or freelance basis. Young people have often been the main recruits to social movements in the past—their attachments to family and economy are weak, and they are more likely to embrace ideals that call for social change. But they are even more susceptible to joining protests today than in more ordinary times, because economic crisis has swelled their numbers and magnified their grievances. They are the people who have filled the Occupy camps.

Even though the protest did not enlist the whole 99 percent, the slogan "We are the 99%" entered common discourse as a way of denouncing inequality. (It was chosen as "quotation of the year" by Fred Shapiro, editor of *The Yale Book of Quotations*, who compiles a list of the ten best quotes of each year.[7] The rhetoric of opposition to economic inequality is strikingly different from the discourse that has prevailed in the US left in recent decades, which has emphasized issues of group identity over class issues. Progressive politics has worked to assert the claims of particular groups defined by race, gender, sexual orientation, or other specific categories more than to combat economic injustice and class differences. The Occupy movement has not used the language of class, but with "99%" it has found a new vocabulary to assert the centrality of economic issues, both inequality and the corporate structures that are held responsible for it.

The occupation struck a responsive chord. Echoing a widespread discontent, an electronically networked movement with no formal leadership spread quickly to over 1,500 cities and towns in the US and around the world. Tens of thousands joined in the protest against escalating inequality. The movement was decentralized and took pride in being leaderless (or "leaderful," according to some, since everyone is deemed a leader). Each occupation was independent of the others, but all were in constant contact using modern communications. Beyond the occupations, the movement's issues permeated popular culture, coming rapidly into the public consciousness and provoking widespread discussion of topics that had been long ignored.

The protest was not just about the corporations or economic inequality. Beyond the political issues, occupiers shared a general rejection of the materialism and alienation they found in contemporary culture and strove to overcome them within their movement itself. The tactic of indefinite occupation encourages a unique internal process: the creation of a community. As protesters remained on a site around the clock for days or weeks, the occupation became more than a protest site; it became a space for living. In the US as well as in the Arab world and Europe, the occupations became an occasion for communication and organization considerably more intense than occurs in more ephemeral or sporadic protest movements.

INTERACTION, VIRTUAL AND REAL

One of the most surprising aspects of the Occupy Wall Street movement was the restoration of face-to-face interaction, in real time and real space, to political life. (I write from my experience in New York City, but according to reports something similar has occurred in other occupations.) Young, articulate, and well-informed protesters at any occupation spent a large part of their day in intense discussions of political issues, personal troubles, the structure of the economy and the polity, and the future. Groups formed and dissolved in the course of a day as people switched back and forth from concrete tasks to deliberation and discussion.

Full-time occupiers and others who just dropped in took part and found the experience of these conversations energizing and liberating. Anyone on the occupation site in New York, occupier or visitor, could feel the sense of pulsating, vibrant energy—and indeed many visitors showed up, as the occupation became a major public attraction. People milled about, peddled their causes, and talked and debated in informal groups and more formal working groups. They met in the daily general assembly to make collective decisions. They performed the tasks that kept the occupation going. They interacted in the public space where each person's actions were visible to everyone else. These interactions constituted the basis of democratic participation: they reinforced the sense of equality and joint ownership because everyone took part, everyone shared the experience. In talking to each other, people rehearsed their commitment to social justice at the macro level and personal empowerment at the micro level. Occupation presents this opportunity because it demarcates a specific physical space where a Habermasian public sphere can come into existence, a liberated space where deliberation about goals and future plans can take place.[8]

This intense personal interaction marked quite a departure for progressive political activity. For the last decade or more, many people's "activism" has been limited to reading emails and signing online petitions, a practice that has been criticized as "slacktivism."[9] Click a mouse, sign a petition; you have done your duty. In striking contrast, the Occupy movement recognized that electronic communication is no substitute for direct participation.

The Occupy movement depended heavily on the Internet for initial and ongoing organizing, to be sure, especially the new electronic social networking media: Facebook, Twitter, YouTube, and Livestream. Their use comes naturally to a generation that grew up with computers and can do anything with the phone they carry in their pockets. For live streaming in particular, the technical capacity has improved and the costs have come down, making it readily accessible. The new media embody occupiers' cultural commitment to open access because they allow anyone both to produce and to distribute ideas.

But occupiers recognized the Internet's limitations. They understood that as important as electronic communication is, it achieves little unless it leads to face-to-face interaction in which people do more than respond passively and reflexively. It is when people come together visibly in physical space, debate and discuss, march and demonstrate, and live a community life that social movements can empower them and prefigure future social relations.

Thus the electronic media were not used in isolation but to promote nonhierarchical, egalitarian, and above all active participation in the movement's activities, interaction in real time and real space. They drew protesters into the heart of these contemporary protest movements, in public spaces where people interacted in multitudes. As an editor of the *Occupied Wall Street Journal* (who requested anonymity because he also works for a mainstream publication) told me in an interview, social media "became a tool for action as opposed to a reason to stay on the couch."

While many observers have drawn attention to the role of social media in convoking the demonstrations of the Arab revolts and protests since then, its limits have rarely been noted. However much Facebook and Twitter can be important for mobilizing, it should be evident that by themselves they do not constitute political protest. Slacktivism is fully compatible with the extensive use of such electronic media. Rather, social media outlets contributed to the protests of 2011 only because they fed into live action.

A lot of that action consisted of talk—in small group conversations and in larger meetings. An Occupy Wall Street general assembly met daily; anyone could attend and take part in its collective decisions. It was the definitive voice of the occupation and the expression of direct democracy. Facilitators of the meeting trained the public in procedures designed to reach consensus, though when there was no consensus votes were taken. The principle of "step up – step back" was meant to equalize participation: the more reticent were urged to speak out, the more vocal to restrain themselves. This principle was sometimes enforced by a facilitator responsible for the "stack," determining the order in which people would speak, who was charged with giving priority to the more reticent, and preventing a few louder voices from dominating.

In large assemblies, people communicated via the "people's microphone," the most innovative medium enlisted to support face-to-face communication (apparently adopted from the demonstrations in the spring of 2011 in Spain). It is prohibited to use bullhorns in public in New York City without a police permit. To circumvent the ban, someone addressing a mass meeting paused after each phrase and the people nearby repeated it in unison to the crowd; if the crowd was big, a second circle of shouters repeated it. If it was even bigger than that, people on the periphery listened on their phones and shouted it to the crowd.

The people's microphone did not lend itself to long or complicated presentations, a limitation that carried both advantages and disadvantages. A speaker had to talk in short, Twitterlike sound bites. Nevertheless it provided a sense of power: I can personally attest that if you say something and dozens of people repeat it, you have the feeling of really being listened to. And for those playing the role of the mic amplifying a speaker's voice, the call and response was physically energizing and provided a strong sense of participation. If the people's mic was initially adopted as a form of resistance against regulations that occupiers regard as imposed to silence them, it could become a source of joy: people took so much pleasure in using it that sometimes a small group that could hear perfectly well nevertheless went through the ritual of repeating each speaker's words.

The occupation was not all talk. Organizing several hundred people on a site required work. Occupiers divided themselves up to perform a variety of tasks, some focused on the community at the site itself, some on addressing the outside world in political mobilization and in media of communication. Using their postindustrial skills in writing, the arts, the media, and information technology, they spread the occupation's message in word and image, on paper and electronically. A spectacular outpouring of creative talent emerged to illustrate the plight that they were protesting and the transformations they were seeking.

Some occupiers managed logistics: keeping the place clean, receiving and distributing donations of food and supplies, and providing medical care. Many who were homeless or poor showed up asking for help, and they were provided for. (They were also incorporated into the occupation's activities. Some caused problems; others made important contributions.) Others prepared the seemingly daily demonstrations or chatted up the local merchants who allowed the people camping out to use their facilities.

There was a people's library with donated books. Groups spent time drumming or preparing artwork. Since full-time political discussion did not appeal to everyone, many immersed themselves in these tasks to express their membership in and commitment to the occupation. Participation in the occupation entitled each group to speak up in the sometimes heated debates in general assembly meetings to make claims on a share of the money donated to the occupation.

HORIZONTALITY AND PREFIGURATION

The ideal of community that these occupations strove to realize is based on the principles of horizontality and prefiguration. A horizontal movement is one with no permanent leadership; everyone has equal standing. A prefigurative movement tries to create, within the movement itself, social relations without alienation or exploitation, anticipating (or "prefiguring") the social relations of the new society the movement hopes to bring into existence.[10]

These principles emerged in part organically, from practice, but they are not new. The occupations of 2011 drew on prior models developed by movements that rejected the top-down leadership of traditional left movements. Among the predecessors were the US women's movement of the 1960s and

1970s, the antinuclear movements in the US and Europe of the 1970s, and the antiglobalization movement of the 1990s and early years of the twenty-first century, preceded by the Zapatista uprising and movements in solidarity with it.[11]

While many movements have been called prefigurative and attempted to innovate new patterns of interaction, the occupation site provided more fruitful ground because it became the home of the occupiers twenty-four hours a day for an indefinite time. So OWS also built on the developments in Tahrir Square, the Puerta del Sol, and the other occupations that preceded it. In Egypt, when the demonstrations in January 2011 drove the police off the streets, protesters stepped in to maintain public order in cities and towns all over the country.[12] Spanish occupiers created modes of participation that later became the hallmark of the Zuccotti Park occupation, with the emphasis on extended meetings to reach consensus and new processes to facilitate that consensus.[13]

These principles found direct expression in an occupation's organization, from the processes for reaching consensus in meetings to the provision of food, medical care, and security. They permeated every activity. Among many noteworthy practices, I will mention two. First is the pedagogy of participation, based on the conviction that everyone should take an active part and develop new capacities in the process. In performing tasks as in recognizing speakers at meetings, the more reticent or less experienced were encouraged to take leading roles, and those who were accustomed to leadership to relinquish it. As already discussed, many occupiers had highly developed communication and media skills. But they shared their skills with novices. They regarded themselves as "citizen journalists" and believed that everyone was entitled to a voice regardless of prior training or experience. The beginners were systematically incorporated and trained, assumed responsibility, and put their new skills into practice. For such tasks as consensus facilitation and media production, people who were trained in workshops were immediately put to work.

The second example was the use of handwritten signs in the Occupy demonstrations. It may seem trivial, but this expressed the principle of horizontality and offered an opportunity for creativity. In other demonstrations, more formally structured organizations (such as unions and political groups) often decide on the permitted slogans, print signs in advance, and distribute them to members to carry. Occupiers, in contrast, created their own slogans and painted them on cardboard. Many of these signs showed a touch of humor.[14] They created an atmosphere very different from one dominated by uniform, printed signs. By exercising individual creativity, protesters rejected subservience to a hierarchical organization.

The antihierarchical and prefigurative ideals were just that—ideals. In practice, of course, they did not work perfectly. The fact that participation was open to all comers brought many who wanted to take advantage of the free services and donated goods. Some were suspected of being infiltrators.

Other problems arose despite participants' good faith. The consensus process can be very cumbersome. It requires that everyone be committed to participate and to restrain any impulses to exert control. All must be willing to subordinate their particular goals at times to the larger goal of maintaining harmony. It is very difficult to run something as big and complex as an occupation with a horizontal structure. Though measures were taken to overcome the temptation of hierarchy, the lack of formal leadership can leave space for dominant personalities to impose themselves. The expectation of intense interaction among participants on the scene, as well as anxiety that the occupation would be evicted led to burnout. After the eviction did then come to pass, major conflicts caused rifts in the general assembly, including disputes over the disposition of donated money.

But participants were deeply committed to creating a new form of social interaction, with a vision of a new society. Many of them found that the experience was truly liberating despite its limitations, and offered a model on which they could build in future experiments.

OCCUPATION IN REAL SPACE

The development of community is possible only because an occupation takes place in a defined physical space.[15] Because of the importance of specific places, I have chosen to focus on the protests in three cities and not on the countries as a whole (or other countries) even though the protests all spread quickly. Not only the city but the location within the city became important. Tahrir Square and the Puerta del Sol, located in the heart of Cairo and Madrid, respectively, are traditional gathering places and hubs of social activity.

Zuccotti Park is not such a central or widely recognized location, though it is a few short blocks from the intended occupation site, Wall Street itself. It is safe to say that few people in the US or even New York City had heard of Zuccotti Park before the occupation. It is a particular kind of social space, a "privately owned public space." Real estate developers can get exemptions from zoning requirements, for example, allowing them to build taller buildings than zoning regulations would otherwise allow, in exchange for some sort of public amenity like an outdoor or indoor open space which would be open to the public. Though there are several privately owned public spaces in New York City, it is also safe to say that few people, even those who frequented them (and even the occupiers of Zuccotti Park when they arrived) knew just what a privately owned public space is. Brookfield Properties, the real estate company led by former deputy mayor John Zuccotti, agreed to maintain the small area that came to be called Zuccotti Park for a zoning concession.

As days of occupation turned into weeks and as public support appeared to be growing, public officials watched warily. Because of Zuccotti Park's legal status as a privately owned public space, the rules that govern its use are different from those that apply to city parks. Most important, it did not close at midnight but was accessible around the clock. For weeks the mayor's office, Brookfield Properties, and the occupiers engaged in a complicated tug of war over whether the occupiers had the right to camp out and whether it was up to the city or the company to order them out. At first the city adopted a policy of toleration and made no move to dislodge them.

Meanwhile, the occupiers organized or participated in almost daily demonstrations and marches. If public officials were wary of intervening in the occupied park, that was not the case for the marches. Generally without permits, these marches were legal as long as they remained on sidewalks, but because they attracted large crowds they often spilled out onto the streets.

Police responded with force. On September 24, 2011, a week after the occupation began, police intervened in a march, arresting about eighty people, and an officer used pepper spray on a woman demonstrator who was sitting down. This attack, which appeared to be unprovoked, was captured on video. Posted to the Internet, the pepper spray video quickly went viral. It produced a tremendous outpouring of sympathy for the protest and repudiation of police brutality. Another pepper spray incident against an October 5 demonstration in New York, and yet another at the University of California at Davis on November 19, were also filmed and posted to the Internet, showing quite graphically the police intervention and the victims' agonized reactions. Among many further incidents of police aggression against occupations across the country, two stood out: the arrest of 700 OWS demonstrators on the Brooklyn Bridge on October 1, and the attack on Occupy Oakland (California) in which military veteran Scott Olsen was critically injured on October 25. These incidents showed that the movement was spreading; gave evidence of the harsh police tactics deployed against peaceful, if deliberately provocative, protesters; and reinforced public opinion in the protesters' favor.

The New York City administration was meanwhile increasingly wary of the occupation's apparent staying power, of the movement's strengthening internal organization and the community that emerged on the site, promising (or threatening) to stay put for a long time. Mayor Michael Bloomberg, having decided that the time had come to end the occupation, announced that the police would evict it on October 14. In response, thousands showed up at 6 AM that day to defend the park. Their presence persuaded the police to call off the eviction. On November 15, a month later, however, the police returned, this time unannounced, in the middle of the night. After a heated battle, the police cleared the park and ended the occupation.

Since then a legal tug of war has ensued. For several weeks the police barricaded the park and kept occupiers out; then activities began to be permitted again, but a court had ordered that occupiers could not sleep there overnight. This ended the momentum of the occupation per se. Occupiers continued to meet, in small, issue-oriented groups (such as those around schools and housing foreclosures), general assemblies, and groups to maintain the movement's presence on the Internet. The movement called or joined demonstrations of specific groups acting under the umbrella name of Occupy Wall Street. Activists built toward a large demonstration on May Day, 2012, in collaboration with sympathetic unions. Despite these eruptions, however, the movement clearly lost momentum with the loss of its central focus, the occupation of Zuccotti Park.

THE IMPACT OF THE OCCUPY MOVEMENT

Gauging the impact of a social movement is difficult, because it is often diffuse, and often more successful at preventing undesired outcomes than at imposing its own solutions. Sometimes, however, the effect is clear: The Tahrir Square movement evidently succeeded in its first objective, the ouster of President Hosni Mubarak, which could hardly have happened without it. On the other hand, though the movement regularly called out major mobilizations to protest actions by the Supreme Council of the Armed Forces, these were not so successful. Though the SCAF recognized Mohamed Morsi, the Muslim Brotherhood's candidate, as the winner of the presidential elections, it was still the SCAF that ruled the country, and not only did protests not succeed in reversing any of its previous dictates, but indeed, after less than a year in office, in July 2013 Morsi and the Muslim Brotherhood were overthrown in a military coup, and in June 2014 it was none other than former armed forces chief Abdel Fattah el-Sisi who ran for and was elected to the country's highest political office.

The effect of Occupy Wall Street has been less direct and less consequential, but I would argue that it has in fact had a significant impact on the political process even though the movement has not attempted to influence that process directly. It has had important effects in three areas: public discourse, the activity of institutionalized movements, and (still mostly potentially) policy.

First, it has affected public discourse. The occupation was a spectacular demonstration of the power of transgression to move people's minds. Violating public order is a mind-altering experience. By the very act of defiance protest-ers deny the power of authorities that is normally taken for granted. In the case of Occupy Wall Street, occupiers and supporters learned that they could stand up to authorities in defense of a cause they felt deeply about.

News coverage was extensive. Wall Street, "99 percent," and criticism of financial institutions became part of everyday political and journalistic discourse. Sometimes they were used in specific connection to the issues of income distribution and financial control that the movement had raised; sometimes they were used humorously to criticize the inequality implicit in a situation with no direct connection,[16] showing that the ideas are now taken for granted—itself an important demonstration that the movement's ideas have filtered into public consciousness.

In particular, public discourse around the federal budget and spending priorities changed significantly in the fall of 2011 and the winter of 2012. It became possible to criticize economic inequality and to call for government intervention in the economy, contravening the previously prevailing discourse that demanded austerity and a reduction in the federal budget deficit. News stories appeared in print and on television exposing economic inequality, and commentators calling on government to adopt reforms in taxation or bank regulation referred to Occupy protesters as a source of legitimacy for their proposals.[17]

At the level of movement politics, many social-movement–based non-profits and other organizations in the United States have adopted the language and positions of Occupy, likewise invoking the movement to legitimize their causes. These moderately progressive political organizations mainly work to exert pressure on Democratic legislators. Among them are MoveOn and the AFL-CIO, which together offered workshops for activists in 2012 called "spring training for the 99 percent." (Most OWS activists, however, believe that the Democratic Party is just as beholden to Wall Street as the Republican Party and offers no greater hope for reform. They are therefore suspicious of any organizations that collaborate with the Democrats and believe that those organizations are trying to co-opt OWS.)

Finally, there has been a notable shift at the level of policy, sometimes in proposals and sometimes in actual legislation. Several state legislatures have passed or are debating laws to raise the minimum wage above the federal level. President Obama's State of the Union speech in 2012 and his demand for the "[Warren] Buffett tax," a 30 percent tax on incomes over one million dollars, while not giving credit to OWS, nevertheless can be understood as a response to its pressure. United States Senator Bernie Sanders and Representative Ted Deutsch proposed "OCCUPIED," a constitutional amendment that would address campaign finance reform in the wake of the Supreme Court's controversial decision in the Citizens United case. The name stands for "Outlawing Corporate Cash Undermining the Public Interest in our Elections and Democracy"—evidently a contrived acronym chosen to absorb the aura of the Occupy movement (Occupied Amendment, 2011).

The impact of OWS on US politics in the medium and long term remains uncertain with regard to both the survival of the movement itself and the possibility of major policy changes to benefit the 99 percent. As a movement, OWS is presently becalmed. There was a lot of activity going on in New York City and elsewhere in its name. Subgroups promoted specific political goals and worked to maintain the movement's own presence. But these activities were not very visible. Further massive occupations are unlikely in the wake of police repression and (in many places) court injunctions. The lack of a physical center in Zuccotti Park and in other occupation sites across the country deprived the movement of its specific character and made it hard to maintain momentum. It is in the nature of social movements that they are ephemeral; the spectacular early success of OWS will be hard to repeat.

The possibility of major policy changes is also uncertain, especially since OWS declines to pursue change through institutional politics. But its effect has already been felt. OWS has changed the agenda of political discussion. Turning discourse into tangible outcomes may depend on the more moderate organizations directly engaged in influencing elections and legislation rather than on the Occupy movement itself. Some within the movement believe that those organizations are illegitimately co-opting the spirit and rhetoric of OWS, but the position of the moderates has been strengthened by the impetus of OWS. Even though occupiers reject collaboration with them, the Occupy movement can claim a substantial share of the credit for pushing the envelope to promote those issues and legitimizing the efforts of others to bring them into the institutional arena.

NOTES

1   Isham Tharoor, "Occupy Wall Street Protests Spread," TIME. com, December 7, 2011. www.time.com/time/specials/packages/article/0,28804,2101344_2101369_2101667,00.html.

2   Congressional Budget Office, 2011. Income concentration can be measured by comparing the top layer (which might be defined as the to 1 percent, the top 0.1 percent, or something else) to the rest of the population, by a more general measure of inequality like the Gini index or some other measure. Taking wealth instead of income, the concentration is even greater. But by whatever measure is chosen, the concentration has increased dramatically since approximately 1980, after having fallen during the postwar period.

3   Paul Krugman, *End This Depression Now!* New York: Norton, 2012, pp. 74–76.

4   Joseph E. Stiglitz, *The Price of Inequality*, New York: Norton, 2012, p. 1.

5   Though no officer of any bank or financial corporation has been prosecuted for any misdeed leading up to the fiscal crisis, at least one mortgage holder was jailed for misreporting his income on a mortgage application, though the loan he was applying for was of a type widely known among bankers as "liars' loans" because banks and loan originators encouraged applicants to falsify the records to appear qualified for loans. Joe Nocera, "The Mortgage Fraud Fraud," *New York Times* (June 2, 2012): 21.

6   Gilbert Achcar, "Roots and Dynamics of Arab Revolt." Paper presented at a conference titled "The Arab Revolt: Causes, Dynamics, Effects." Columbia University, April 13, 2012.

7   John Christofferson, "'We Are The 99 Percent' Chosen As Year's Top Quote," *Huffington Post*, December 20, 2011. www.huffingtonpost.com/2011/12/20/ we-are-the-99-percent-chosen-quote_n_1160171.html.

8   Jurgen Habermas, *The Structural Transformation of the Public Sphere: An Inquiry into a Category of Bourgeois Society*, Cambridge, MA: MIT Press, 1989.

9   Evgeny Morozov, *The Net Delusion: The Dark Side of Internet Freedom*, New York: Public Affairs, 2011, pp. 189–191.

10   Carl Boggs, "Marxism, Prefigurative Communism, and the Problem of Workers' Control," *Radical America*, 11 (November 1977): 99–122; John L. Hammond, "Social Movements and Struggles for Socialism," in *Taking Socialism Seriously*, edited by Anatole Anton and Richard Schmidt, Lanham: Lexington Books, 2012, pp. 213–247; Luis Moreno-Caballud and Marina Sitrin. "Occupy Wall Street, Beyond Encampments," yesmagazine.org, November 21, 2011, www.yesmagazine.org/people-power/occupy-wall-street-beyond-encampments; Marina Sitrin, ed., *Horizontalism: Voices of Popular Power in Argentina*, Oakland, CA: AK Press, 2006.

11   Barbara Epstein, *Political Protest and Cultural Revolution: Nonviolent Direct Action in the 1970s and 1980s*, Berkeley, CA: University of California Press, 1991; Marianne Maeckelbergh, "Horizontal Democracy Now: From Alterglobalization to Occupation." *Interface: a journal for and about social movements*, 4, No. 1 (May 2012): 207–224; Francesca Polletta, *Freedom is an Endless Meeting: Democracy in American Social Movements*, Chicago: University of Chicago Press, 2002; Marina Sitrin, ed., *Horizontalism*.

12   Gilbert Achcar, "Roots and Dynamics of Arab Revolt"; Lisa Anderson, "Demystifying the Arab Spring," *Foreign Affairs*, 90, No. 3 (May/June 2011): 2–7; Mohammed Bamyeh, "The Egyptian Revolution: First Impressions from the Field. "*Jadaliyya*, February 11, 2011, www.jadaliyya.com/pages/index/561/ the-egyptian-revolution_first-impressions-from-the-field.

13   Tomás Alberich Nistal, "Antecedents, Achievements and Challenges of the Spanish 15M Movement," in *From Social to Political: New Forms of Mobilization and Democratization*, ed. by Benjamín Tejerina and Ignacia Perugorría, Bilbao: Universidad del País Vasco, 2012, pp. 78–92; Center for Group Dynamics, 2011;

Marianne Maeckelbergh, "Horizontal Democracy Now"; Luis Moreno-Caballud and Marina Sitrin, "Occupy Wall Street."

14   A sampling can be seen at www.damncoolpictures.com/2011/10/best-signs-from-occupy-wall-street.html.

15   Puneet Dahliwal, "Public squares and resistance: the politics of space in the Indignados movement," *Interface: a journal for and about social movements*, 4, No. 1 (May, 2012): 251–273.

16   For example, Adam Gopnik, in a short article in the *New Yorker*, reported that Benjamin Franklin wanted to reject the bald eagle as the American national bird because of its "bad moral character," since it regularly stole fish that other birds had caught. Gopnik comments, "Truly, a one-per-cent kind of bird." Adam Gopnik, "The First Served," *New Yorker*, 87, No. 37 (November 21, 2011): 45.

17   Fran Hawthorne, "Color the 1 Percent 99 Percent Conflicted," *New York Times* (February 9, 2012); Paul Krugman, "Money And Morals," *New York Times* (February 10, 2012).

ADDITIONAL REFERENCES

Commission for Group Dynamics in Assemblies of the Puerta del Sol Protest Cam, 2011. Quick guide on group dynamics in people's assemblies. July 31, 2011, www.takethesquare.net/2011/07/31/quick-guide-on-group-dynamics-in-peoples-assemblies.

Declaration of the Occupation of New York City. 2011. New York City General Assembly, September 29, 2011, www.nycga.net/resources/declaration.

Paul Krugman, *End This Depression Now!* New York: Norton, 2012.

Joe Nocera, "The Mortgage Fraud Fraud," *New York Times* (June 2, 2012): 21.

Occupied Amendment. 2011. The Occupied Amendment, www.TheOccupiedAmendment.org.

Jennifer Preston, "Occupy Video Showcases Live Streaming," *New York Times*, December 12, 2011: B1.

CONCLUSIONS:
POST-ARAB UPRISINGS: HOPES AND FEARS
MOHSINE EL AHMADI

More than four years have passed since massive Arab uprisings toppled several long-lasting autocrats. Reverberations were felt from Morocco to Yemen and beyond. Since that defining winter day in December 2010 when Mohamed Bouazizi set himself on fire in Tunisia, much has been said and written about the process and outcomes of these revolts. Pessimists wrung their hands in despair, while those favoring the new direction of change in the MENA region celebrated the coming to power of several Islamist movements—until that ended, whether by way of a coup (as in Egypt) or the electoral process (as in Tunisia). What can we now expect?

In several Arab countries social movements succeeded in destabilizing and overthrowing long-established regimes. Although the Islamists were not in the vanguard of these revolts, they fairly quickly exploited the new environment to organize for and win free elections, sometimes in coalition with secular parties. How can we explain this unexpected result?

Under the authoritarian old regimes ruling over the MENA region, Islamists were for years the most significant opponents to the status quo, since mainstream parties and associations and those on the left, where they existed, had largely lost their social base and grip on civil society. Members of non-Islamist political parties were seen by voters as opportunists. Also dictators restricted what these parties could do. The weakening of the left was part of a worldwide trend that saw the fall of the Soviet Union in the early 1990s and the transformation of communist China into a capitalist giant. Within a local context, far more than other opponents of the old order, the Islamists suffered the most at the hands of fierce dictatorial regimes. They were the most cruelly persecuted.

At the same time, following a long Muslim tradition dating back centuries, affiliated Muslim underground organizations helped the needy, providing income in the informal economy for many without jobs; selling food at discounted prices, and subsidizing families of imprisoned activists regardless of their party affiliations. At the same time, some dictators demonized men sporting beards and women in hijabs, who seemed to fellow citizens just like ordinary folk. No wonder then that free and fair elections initially gave the Islamists all the space they had been denied in the past. We also have to remember that many secularists who voted for them voted for change and not necessarily for establishing an Islamic state.

The global financial crisis that began in 2008 also took its toll. Private investments diminished in the region's non-oil-rich states. Foreign tourists thought twice before traveling abroad on holidays. External investment in real estate, which accompanied the previous Western boom, dried up, leaving some massive projects unfinished in several parts of the MENA region, as was the case in the West. Simultaneously Western financial lenders, led by the International Monetary Fund and the World Bank, backed by the United States, pressured heavily indebted states to privatize both industries and government employment and to end subsidies on gasoline used for personal automobiles (thereby giving largesse to the middle classes) and for making staple food products more affordable. As China developed into the world's center of cheap production, pressures rose globally to keep wages down so as to remain competitive. The cost of living rose while wages stagnated.

Health care, education, and social services suffered cuts as governments introduced austerity measures to curb rising debt. The youth bulge, a product of past prosperity, produced a mass of young people who were both underserved and badly trained for the new, modern economy. Nationalists had promised free mass education through the doctorate and affordable or free health care for all. Yet resources were not available to fulfill these promises because of heavy defense and security budgets and kleptocracies in the form of ruling families who creamed off and stored billions overseas, which they siphoned out of their respective economies. In the Maghreb, the Arabization of education added to disarray, because few trained teachers were available to take over classrooms. Those who did were often badly qualified. Economic constraints produced very large classes. This, combined with poor teaching, left university graduates with few job opportunities. Mainly the rich and well connected, often possessing private family resources, attended the top public and private schools and found good permanent jobs in the private sector. Most others, if employed, ended up working on short-term contracts and received no or paltry benefits. The informal economic sector grew apace. When Tunisia's Mohamed Bouazizi immolated himself, many others throughout the MENA region empathized with his plight.

Past political stagnation in the Arab world may also help explain the initial victories of the Islamist parties. Authoritarian regimes often sponsored a state-controlled Islam, which denatured the religion and robbed it of its spiritual and moral core. In addition, in Egypt the state under Hosni Mubarak sanctioned Islamic charitable activities as the state debt mounted, making it difficult for the public sector to subsidize health care, education, food, and other staples. It likewise provided space for Islamists to win elections in civil society organizations, such as lawyer's and judge's associations and other important professional groups, with the country's leadership thinking that as long as they controlled the national electoral process and rigged results, the state could tolerate an apparently active civil society influenced by Islamist elements. Many of those associations, free to function for more than a decade in Egypt, joined the revolt and mobilized their members and other secular, allied groups.

Economically, too, the Islamists proved little threat to the economic system and capitalism already in place. They made known their intention to retain the unequal class structures of their respective societies, and indeed they moved quickly to protect private property through sharia or Islamic law. They had no intention of disturbing class relations and redistributing wealth from the rich to the poor; hence they assured for themselves the loyalty of large segments of the middle classes. Apart from advocating Islamic finance and banking, Islamists did not call for the overthrow of the existing economic order. Moreover, they were able to attract mass support by promising to remedy the deficiencies of the prior, failing states without challenging capitalism. By so doing, Islamists were unifiers, and played the role of bringing together people from different social classes, therefore reinforcing the Islamic notion of solidarity within the Ummah (community of Muslim believers).

A classic example is the Justice and Development Party (AKP) in Turkey, which is often cited as a model Islamic party in having adapted to modernity. Its major constituencies are the subordinate elites of provincial origin, who have prospered in the decentralized economy promoted by the AKP. (See the end of Chapter 2.) Their amazing past success, allowing Turkey's economy to grow by 8-10 percent yearly despite the downturn of the world economy beginning in 2008, allowed them to take their revenge on Kamal Atatürk's statist economic model, which since the 1920s favored state enterprises and the elites of the coastal cities to the detriment of the private entrepreneurs and provincial agriculturists who now determine Turkey's future.

Yet there are problems with the Islamist model in the Arab and wider Muslim world. In the face of large-scale mass poverty, the solution offered by the Islamists has been charity, not sustainable economic development. Moreover, the AKP's record on human rights leaves much to be desired. Also, once in power, the Islamists have had to navigate between their generous donors (Qatar, Kuwait, and Saudi Arabia), and the growing social pressures coming from the Arab masses. It is on this front of the society and economy—not on slogans in favor of morality, or the establishment of an Islamic state—that the new holders of power will be evaluated very soon. It will take Islamists more than just the Islamization of mores to meet the expectations of those who elected them.

Secular women, especially, are fearful about the turn of events. Several feminist leaders have been threatened in Egypt and Tunisia. Other women have been molested by police officers, often with impunity. A few have found themselves victimized because of their sex. In Tunisia, the moderate Islamist party that held power for a time, the Ennahda Movement, tried to introduce a constitutional amendment changing the status of women from men's equals to their "compliments." An uproar ensued, forcing party leaders to withdraw the proposal, but the process was enough to frighten many women who had taken their legal status as men's equals for granted. In Egypt, meanwhile, constitutional proposals by the Muslim Brotherhood while it held the reins of government there likewise attempted to downgrade women's status, making the minority of modern women nervous and fearful for their future.

The increased role of Salafists, who claim a return to the Islam of the well-guided caliphs' period, complicates the situation even more. They have been present for several years in countries such as Egypt, Syria, and Morocco, to name a few. But they were unable to occupy the political field on their own. They acted mainly within the private sphere, stressing mores and morals. They were also more or less legalistic vis-à-vis the regimes, which saw in them a means of weakening the more powerful Egyptian Muslim Brotherhood or its offshoots outside of Egypt. Yet the partial success of Salafism, especially in Egypt—where they won nineteen seats in Parliament with Saudi and perhaps other Gulf states' financial backing—can partly be explained by the disappointment people experienced with the moderation of the Muslim Brotherhood and other Muslim-influenced parties. In fact, such frustration is in part attributable to the failure of the "moderate" Islamist groups to win large majorities or seize power in Arab states.

The year 2011 ushered in new forms of debate, controversy, and pluralism. The question then was this: From what values would social and moral standards be defined, and who would decide? Some would say that sharia (the law of Allah), the Ummah (the Muslim community), and the caliphate (an Islamic state) must prevail, while others reply that individuals and citizens are the origin of all authority and law. This is the core of the actual debate on secularism and Islamism in the present post–Arab Spring revolts.

ISLAMISTS AND SECULARISM

Electoral successes brought Islamists to power in several Arab states, including Morocco, Tunisia, Egypt, and Libya. But the military coup in Egypt in the summer of 2013 forced the Brotherhood to give up power. In Tunisia, Ennahda, under mass pressure, negotiated its way out of power as well. In Morocco, the Party of Justice and Development (PJD) is under political pressure since its implication in many moral debates and struggles with other secular parties and civil society organizations. In reality, this question of relinquishing power through the ballot box raises the issue of what Anglo-Saxon sociologists and historians call secularism and francophone commentators call *laïcité*.[1] Secularism is a public policy pertaining to the administrative organization of the religious and political spheres. Secularization is a social process of dissociation between worldly affairs and religious beliefs.

Some parties claim their legitimacy through their immediate closeness with Islam. Some are conservative and neoliberal, others state-bound and/or revolutionary, and all are nationalistic, giving the interests of the nation state priority over those of the Ummah. Similarly, secularism does not rule out the possibility of an Islamist party assuming power through the ballot box, as happened in Turkey, Egypt, Morocco, and Tunisia provided that party does not challenge the secular nature of state institutions or the acceptance of the right to adhere to a secular society. Secularism presupposes a steady relationship with both the political and the religious.

The 2011 mobilizations provided both the secular and Islamist militant youth with the opportunity to struggle together, to share public space at the cost of mutual compromise, and to impose new visions on the seniors of their respective camps. This led to debates about not only the relationship between religion and politics but also the relation of Islamic parties to democracy and human rights.

In the Muslim world, most countries have not experienced any meaningful "secular break" leading to a strict split between religion and politics. The few countries that have tried doing so quickly saw Islamic elements use the political scene for social and cultural proselytizing. In few other countries, meanwhile, rulers kept tight reins on both the political and religious leadership.

In Turkey, Atatürk's break with the Ottoman sultan's dual religious and worldly power in the 1920s and 1930s and after was made possible by the existence there of an autocratic military power opposed to the democrats whom it accused of the Islamization of Turkish society. Victory in the heroic war for independence, which followed the Ottoman defeat in World War I, gave the Turkish military special legitimacy to act as the arbiter of Turkish secularism. The AKP—as a moderate wing of the Muslim Brothers, which split from the Welfare Party established in 1983 and dissolved by the Constitutional Court in 1998—regained power during the 2002 legislative elections, only to be again accused by the secularists of attempting to re-Islamize society.

Some Arab countries have also tried to establish secular regimes, generally based on a nationalist, more or less socialist ideology embodied by leaders relying on powerful mass parties or movements, as was the case with Hafez al-Assad in Syria, Gamal Abdel Nasser in Egypt, Ali Abdullah Saleh in Yemen, and Muammar Gaddafi in Libya.

However, no autocratic secular states have been successful in burying Islamic movements and parties. Over the long haul and after having faced persecution, they have often prospered—including Ennahda in Tunisia; the Muslim Brotherhood in Egypt and Syria; and, in Iraq, the Islamic Dawa Party and the Supreme Council for Islamic Revolution in Iraq (SCIRI). They found ways to put increasing pressure on regimes whose legitimacy they constantly contested.

In Algeria and Yemen, regimes based their legitimacy on the fight against Islamist movements. This was followed by a radicalization of these movements, even though the Islamic Salvation Front (FIS) was on the verge of being brought to power through democratic elections in Algeria in January 1992. However, after the military regime cancelled the election results, the FIS jettisoned politics in favor of violent confrontation and morphed into the Armed Islamic Movement (MIA), the Islamic Army of Salvation (AIS), and the Armed Islamic Group (GIA), from which derived the Salafi Group for Preaching and Combat (GSPC). The latter has, in turn, become al-Qaeda in the Islamic Maghreb (AQIM), a jihadist transnational mutation of an originally political movement. During these three last years a significant number of its members joined the Islamic State in Iraq and Syria (ISIS). As for Yemen, autocracy and secessionist unrest have only encouraged the emergence of an armed Zaydi movement (a branch of Shiite Islam, where its eighth-century imam assumed both worldly and religious power) of Young Believers and the creation of al-Qaeda in the Arabian Peninsula (AQAP).

Both in Morocco and Jordan, as well as in the Gulf monarchies, statesmen protect monarchical regimes from extremist political Islam through religious references and symbols held by the monarchs themselves. Thus Mohammed VI in Morocco is *Amir Al Mu'minin* (Commander of the Faithful). He is also a *Sharif*, or descendant of the Prophet, and Abdullah II of Jordan is the forty-third in the Hashemite dynasty, and likewise a descendant of the Prophet. As for Saudi King Salman bin Abdulaziz Al Saud, he holds the title of Custodian of the Two Holy Mosques by virtue of being their protector. Finally, after trying many contortions of nationalism, Arabism, and Islamism, Libya accumulated all these trends and eventually resorted to its long-lasting statelessness by Gaddafi declaring the death of politics after symbolically turning governance over to the people who in theory, but not in practice, led the late *Jamahiriya* (republic).

THE NEW VARIETIES OF ISLAMIST MOVEMENTS

In recent history, no Arab country has been able to keep religion out of politics. But, more often, Islam has emerged as an oppositional force. Four chief trends have developed within the Islamist movement in recent years. The first is the tendency of mainstream Muslim parties to moderate their demands, engage in political processes, and try to win power through elections, which are more and more difficult to rig. The old days when Muslim Brotherhood leaders Hassan al-Banna and Sayyid Qutb preached the violent overthrow of the secular state in order to gain power have long disappeared. Other Islamist parties, some of whom have flirted with violence in the past and even engaged in it against established states, have now joined the mainstream and have learned to compromise with other forces to make their presence felt politically. The exception, of course, is the Islamic State in Syria and Iraq.

The second trend—aided by considerable sums of money bestowed on them by some Gulf states led by the Saudis—is represented by the Salafists, already discussed above, who are tolerated and perhaps encouraged by the mainstream Muslim parties as a mechanism to keep the issues of Islamic morality alive and in people's consciousness. The third trend is represented by the radicalization of armed fighters, also discussed above, morphing into variants of the al-Qaeda brand, who are ready to wield violence against all who oppose their jihadist vision. They include the well-organized fighters who overturned the Malian state in alliance with Tuareg warriors. French military intervention momentarily slowed down their advance and also led to splits between the jihadists and the Tuareg, but the Saharan zone is now a center for intervention of the great powers, including the US, which has small military bases in the Maghrebian Sahara to monitor jihadist movements there. What is new with this second trend is that all disappointed Islamists of the Maghreb gathered their efforts to form Jihadist groups in big cities such as Tunis, Algiers, and Tripoli for instance and gave allegiance to self invested caliph Abu Bakr Al Baghdadi also known as al-Husseini al-Qurashi in June 2014. Many theologians debated across the Muslim world on the subject of the legitimacy of this claim while officially authorized religious scholars denounced the ISIS caliphhood which they consider as being self declared governments with no relation to Islamic texts of Sunna and Koran. To be a caliph, al-Baghdadi is supposed to base his power on the Islamic consultation (Shura) among the community of believers. According to Islamic tradition, if a caliph cannot meet any of these obligations, he is legally asked to renounce his position and the Islamic Ummah should appoint another caliph among the most pious individuals.

Finally, there remain tiny groups of individuals, or sleeper cells, of al-Qaeda—or what is left of it after the assassination of its leader, Osama Bin Laden—mainly in Yeman and Libya, that crop up periodically and stage bombings. Ministers of interior of the varied Arab states are tracking such groups, but some people slip pass police grids and succeed in igniting their bombs, killing people in their vicinity. What seems significant is that mainstream Islamists, even before gaining power, renounced violence and were willing to engage in electoral politics. This was certainly a big plus, but is changing in the wake of the military coup against the Muslim Brotherhood government in Egypt. In fact, radical Islamist discourse is gaining terrain in the MENA region and even in Africa with Boko Haram (which means "Western education is forbidden"), as a consequence of aggressive Western policies in this part of the world plus the return of authoritarianism. In comparison with other "Islamist" organizations in the Middle East and North Africa, Boko Haram, along with Somalia's Al-Shabaab, have not been getting the closer attention from the international community. In reality, Boko Haram—born out of the teachings of the Nigerian preacher Mohammed Marwa—and Al-Shabaab are seen as being outside of the MENA region, and as such they are often regarded as independent groups and not thought of as within the same type of organizations such as ISIS and al-Qaeda in the Arab World.

With hindsight it now seems clear that the Iranian Revolution of 1979 legitimized bringing Islamist movements to power. That upheaval represented the first time in the Third World that a mass revolution occurred in an urban setting rather than in the countryside. Contributing to that trend was the fact that by 1979 more than 50 percent of the Iranian population lived in cities, beginning a movement that has since spread through the MENA region. The revolution in Iran reflected that new reality. Secondly, when the Ayatollah Ruhollah Khomeini took over power, he established a theocracy, which he controlled with autocratic efficiency, although it had some superficial democratic trappings, such as an elected parliament and presidency. It then spread to the Arab world, notwithstanding the fact that it was basically a Shiite revolution. Other victories of Islamist movements include the electoral success of Hamas in the Palestinian territories in 2006. Likewise, in the Iranian presidential elections of 2009, the green movement, which lost, nevertheless challenged the theocratic basis of the Iranian regime.[3]

THE FAILURE OF THE JIHADIST MODEL DURING THE ARAB REVOLTS

The successful Iranian revolution has opened the possibility of having Islamic regimes prevail everywhere. The failure of such an eventuality has been seen by Islamists in the Arab world in conspiratorial terms. Many of them think that Western powers, especially France and the United States, backed up by Israel, and authoritarian regimes subservient to the West—have stood in the way of achieving this goal. The ideological basis for spreading the Iranian model was the theological reality that Muslims were part of the Ummah and should be united under a single caliphate (replicating the political organizations in previously existing MENA states). This urge for a new unity left unspecified whether the caliphate would be created under a Sunni or Shiite ruler. No matter how diverse and complex the variety of Muslim dogmas are, the geopolitical realities on the ground have proven somewhat different from the expected goals. Sharp differences prevented some strategic alliances: Hezbollah is deeply anti-Saudi, and al-Qaeda considers the Palestinian Hamas movement more nationalistic than religious. In Iran and Saudi Arabia, two countries where the ulema have an official role, the rulers totally oppose each other. The 2003 US invasion of Iraq gave a fatal blow to the utopian idea of a homogenous Ummah, for it deepened the cleavages between the Iraqi Shiite and Sunni communities.

JUSTICE, THE FAVORITE THEME OF POLITICAL ISLAM

Certain concepts already unite the Ummah. That of social solidarity is most visible in Muslim societies, some of which are still currently living below the poverty line. The idea of social justice is probably the one with the strongest appeal, namely in political contexts where authoritarian regimes could be sustained only through bureaucratic pyramids of power based on widespread corruption. By spreading wealth at the top of the pyramid, this prevented widespread socioeconomic development. The quest for social justice undoubtedly remains the main reason for the emergence of Arab uprisings. It is the idea of justice, omnipresent in "political Islam" during decades of authoritarianism, upon which public anger grew and eventually found its expression in 2011 in Tunisia, Egypt, and elsewhere.

THE MOSQUES, A SPACE FOR PRAYER, HOPE, AND SOCIAL RECONSTRUCTION

It is almost a cliché to say that Islam as a practice was and still is very important to Muslims. Mosques have always been a gathering space for reflection on virtues that are rarely brought into practice. The faithful regularly listen, think, pray, and hope within them, and so too they exchange ideas in the courtyard, engaging in a process of social construction that often has come at a lesser cost than expressing the same ideas politically. Growing social anger and the Islamic principle of justice have thus transformed the mosque into a reflexive free-flow movement from the religious into the political sphere, in which ideas can be expressed overtly any time.

When protest movements of a sociopolitical nature have roots in a religious background their potency increases exponentially. Besides being a permanent source of intellectual and moral inspiration, hope, and social construction, Islam also remains present in the interpretation of political and military phenomena in the post–Arab uprisings, specifically with the Salafists, who occupy more room since the coming of moderate Islamists to power.

The manifestation of Allah was so omnipresent for the protesters with respect to the incessant *Allahu Akbar* ("God is Great") repeated during the demonstrations in Egypt and Tunisia and during military confrontations in Libya and Syria. The actors ultimately appeared as a realization of the divine will and therefore constituted a clear theophanic interpretation, or a manifestation or appearance of God to the protesters. In this regard, it is no surprise that Islam would be granted a special position after the fall of the authoritarian states. That is why parties claiming a connection to "political Islam," either radical or moderate, won votes in the first free and fair elections after the revolts subsided. Islam played a clear role in the fall of autocratic regimes because it provided a yardstick of social justice, which the autocrats continuously violated. For all these reasons it seems natural that those who revolted gave a prominent place to Islam in the new political environment.

WHAT "POLITICAL ISLAM" AFTER THE REVOLTS?

The question then is not whether the accession to power of movements of "political Islam" is "normal" in the course of events. We have seen Islam integrated into the political sphere as a factor of inspiration and support, and credited with the establishment of a seemingly virtuous democratic system that the defunct autocratic rulers could not provide. If one assumes that politics is also about collective morality, this morality, in the case of Arab countries, draws heavily on Islam. But despite the common dogmas shared by the community of believers, Islam as a religion is anything but homogeneous. The same applies to "political Islam," which also has many varieties. By actively helping societies transform themselves politically, Islam shapes its own practice to the same degree. The living religion reflects praxis.

Surely it is too early to tell what type of governance parties of "political Islam" will implement. Yet one cannot ignore the fact that a dynamic developed in prison and on the torture rack. What does it mean to spend thirteen years in solitary confinement, as did Hamadi Jebali, the first Tunisian prime minister after the October 2012 elections? The same thing can be said abour Mohamed Morsi of Egypt. Is it just that you become radicalized? If you survive, do you kiss the ground outside the prison and celebrate life, or do you turn inward and distort all reality? Do you become more humane, more human in how you deal with daily problems? Does such persecution force you to fight for democracy as a daily chore or disbelieve in it as a consequence of deception and disillusion?

Whether they realize it yet or not, Islamist movements have entered into a process of "political secularization." Whatever the radical nature of the collective moral ethos they are practicing once in power, they have had to give up power and will have to respect the results of future elections, which might hand the government to political parties that make little or no reference to Islam. Unless this happens, the emergence of a truly democratic and pluralistic "political Islam" will be nothing more than a vain pursuit. If it does happen, it will distinguish and transform Arab societies and states, and become an example of a struggle for democracy inspired by Islam, producing a genuine theology of a democratic age. If not the door will be open on unknown and unprecedented events. The Islamic state is poised to take advantage of this last trend.

On coming to power in the wake of that country's revolution, Egypt's Muslim Brotherhood did not officially abandon its primary objective—the restoration of the caliphate—although in practice it relinquished the goal. Its leaders were quite happy to reap the benefits of the Arab revolt and accede to power. But then they never got the chance to follow through with the democratic process in full recognition of the right and the principle of pluralism; that is, respecting an opponent's right to take power away from you after free elections, all this under a constitution without a strict reference to religion.

Unlike Egypt, Tunisia does not have the same demographic and social problems. It has a tradition of secularism. The situation of women may prove to be better than that in Egypt. Minorities may be able to articulate their religious freedom. Many questions remain about the future as the country undergoes a transitional phase.

Even if the desire for freedom in these countries is widespread and strong, people are not quite familiar with the democratic process, which is more often than not alien to their culture. Islamists meanwhile have long histories—almost a century for Egypt's Muslim Brotherhood, which was then outlawed in September 2013 by court order, its future uncertain as thousands of its supporters—and its leadership—languish in prison as of this writing. Equipped with logistical skills, experience in mass organization, and strong financial assets, Islamist movements have, notwithstanding such setbacks, demonstrated that they know how to mobilize. Facing them, secular movements are recent, poorly organized, and lack resources.

Secularism does not resonate with the Arab population. It is perceived as something opposed to religion, and therefore anathema. On the other hand, the Islamists are populists. Many voters choose them less for their ideology than for the simplicity of their discourse. They promise democracy and social justice. People voted for parties legitimized by the ordeals they have been through, less for Islam per se.

What will happen, then after the brutal dismissal of first democratically elected president in Egypt? Three scenarios are possible in the region.

Pessimistic, the first is a status quo: almost five years after the uprisings, Arab societies would switch back to what they were, mismanaged and poorly organized. The second scenario is even more pessimistic, as it describes the arrival to power of radical and jihadist Islamist forces that threaten in varying proportions the future of these countries and the peace in the world. Forces that would establish ultraconservative regimes such as ongoing policies in Libya and Syria or even Iraq under ISIS authority. The third scenario is an optimistic one which visualizes an orderly transition toward democracy and political and religious pluralism. This political transition would be made possible by the adoption of an Islamic democracy not Islamist based on sharia, a bit like the Christian Democrats in post–World War II Europe. This would be a new trend of democracy inspired by Islamic scripture and favorable to a multiparty system. Though this scenario is less probable, the Turkish AKP may help to understand that Islam may give birth to democracy if some textual efforts are made to adapt Islamic discourse to modern times.

However, some dangers threaten the last of these possibilities. First, old autocratic regimes may recover from their ashes. Second, these countries are not immune from economic failure that would heighten social tensions and create new social conflicts if not civil wars. Third, radical Salafist groups are not only openly against democracy, but they are firmly and violently against any political system which may be based on democracy, since they consider this valueto be western and, as such, against Islamic perception of political life and principles.

Breaking with the autocratic past cannot be achieved overnight. This will require a clear vision, hard work, patience, and abnegation. The Arab revolts have initiated the process of a profound social and political change. The end of despots in Tunisia, Libya, Egypt, and Yemen represented the first stage in this long and complex process. The path of the political, social and economic renewal that lies ahead is even longer and has only just begun.

NOTES

1   In France, this means the pragmatic separation of church and state on behalf of a universalistic conception of citizenship. Conversely, in Turkey it means the political and bureaucratic subordination of the religious to the state, in the context of an ethnoconfessional definition of citizenship.

2   The Ummah is a community of faith. It does not mutate into civil society or state.

3   Farhad Khosrokhavar, "The Green movement in Iran, Democratization and Secularization from Below," in *Society and Democracy in Iran*, Ramin Jahanbeloo, ed., New York & Toronto: Lexington Books, 2012, pp. 39–77.

4   It is worth recalling that the concept of jihad is divided into a macro jihad, or

struggle against the self to become better, and a micro jihad, defending religion against external threats of destruction.

5 See Mohsine El Ahmadi, *Political Islam in Morocco* (in French), Mohamadia, Morocco: Ittissalat Sabou, 2006.

ABOUT THE CONTRIBUTORS

EDITORS

Stuart Schaar, Professor Emeritus Department of History, Brooklyn College, lives in Rabat, Morocco. He is the coeditor and a coauthor of *The Middle East and Islamic World Reader* (New York: Grove Press, 3rd ed. 2012) and *Eqbal Ahmad, Critical Outsider in a Turbulent Age* (New York: Columbia University Press, 2015; published the same year in Karachi by Oxford University Press as *Eqbal Ahmad: Critical Outsider and Witness in a Turbulent Age*). His coauthored collection with Odile Moreau, *Subversives and Mavericks in the Muslim Mediterranean: A Subaltern History (Late 19th Century–Early 20th Century)* is forthcoming in 2016 with University of Texas Press.

Mohsine El Ahmadi, based in Morocco, is Associate Professor of Political Sociology at Cadi Ayyad University of Marrakesh, an associate researcher at the International University of Rabat and the Centre d'Analyse et d'Intervention Sociologiques (Center for Research and Sociological Intervention), and an international visiting scholar at the École des Hautes Etudes en Sciences Sociales (School for Advanced Studies in the Social Sciences). He is the author of three books in French on the Islamist movements in Morocco, and the coauthor (with Fatima Mernissi) of *Rêves des Jeunes* (Dreams of Youth). He was a recipient of a 2009–2010 Fulbright Fellowship at Georgetown University in Washington, D.C. He is currently a program director at the European Inter-University Center on Democratic Governance and Human Rights in the MENA Region, Venice (Italy) in association with Cadi Ayyad University.

CONTRIBUTORS

Farid El Asri is Doctor of Anthropology, Catholic University of Louvain, Belgium. He teaches and conducts research in political science at the International University of Rabat, Morocco, and is a Research Associate at the Jacque Berque Institute for Social and Human Sciences, Rabat.

Karim Amellal, a French-Algerian author and lecturer at the Paris Institute of Political Studies (Science Po), is a founder and CEO of Stand Alone Media (SAM). He is the author of *Discriminez-moi! Enquête sur nos inégalités* (Paris: Flammarion) and the novel *Cités à comparaître* (Paris: Stock). In 2013 he founded www.chouf-chouf, the first participatory video platform for Algeria.

Prashant Bhatt is a medical doctor, specializing in radiology, who has lived and worked in Tripoli since 2003. He stayed in Libya throughout the conflict of 2011 and wrote anonymously and openly about developments there. Using oral history and ethnographic techniques, he seeks to map the everyday history of working people who have experienced decades of life in a dictatorship.

Seth W. Binder is the program associate for the Security Assistance Monitor program at the Center for International Policy in Washington, D.C. He has an MA in international relations from Syracuse University's Maxwell School of Citizenship and Public Affairs and a BA in history from Oberlin College, where he served as Associate Director for the American Democratic Culture Partnership from 2010 to 2012.

Christopher Davidson is a reader in Middle East Politics and a fellow at Durham University (UK). He studied modern history at King's College, University of Cambridge, before earning a master of letters and PhD in political science at the University of St. Andrews. He was previously an assistant professor at Zayed University in the United Arab Emirates, first on the Abu Dhabi campus, then in Dubai. He has also lived in Beirut. In 2009 he was a visiting associate professor at Kyoto University in Japan. Davidson is the author of After *the Sheikhs: The Coming Collapse of the Gulf Monarchies* (Hurst & Co).

Abaher El-Sakka is Chairperson of the Department of Sociology and Anthropology, Birzeit University in the West Bank, Palestine. He received his doctorate in sociology from the University of Nantes, France, and is the author of many scholarly papers and articles on Palestinian society.

Omar Foda is a PhD candidate in the Department of Near Eastern Languages and Civilizations at the University of Pennsylvania, where he is writing a dissertation on modern Egyptian economic history. He has published work in the journal *Arab Media and Society* and on TahrirDocuments.org, a compilation of Arabic documents, translated into English, tracing the developments of the 2011 Egyptian uprising and its aftermath.

John Hammond has studied social movements in the United States, Europe, and Latin America and is the author of *Fighting to Learn: Popular Education and Guerrilla War in El Salvador* (Rutgers University Press) and *Building Popular Power: Workers' and Neighborhood Movements in the Portuguese Revolution* (Monthly Review Press). He is professor of sociology at Hunter College and the Graduate Center, City University of New York.

Clement Moore Henry is Visiting Research Professor at the Middle East Institute of the National University of Singapore and Professor Emeritus of Political Science at the University of Texas, Austin. He has written, coauthored, or edited eleven books and numerous articles on the MENA region, including *Globalization and the Politics of Development in the Middle East* (coauthored with Robert Springborg), *The Mediterranean Debt Crescent*, *The Politics of Islamic Finance* (coedited with Kate Gillespie), and *Oil in the New World Order*. His coedited collection *The Arab Spring: Will It Lead to Democratic Transitions?* appeared in 2013 (Palgrave MacMillan, UK).

Dr. Sahar Khamis is Assistant Professor of Communication and Affiliate Faculty of Women's Studies and Race, Gender, and Ethnicity at the University of Maryland, College Park. She is an expert on Arab and Muslim media and the former head of the Mass Communication and Information Science Department at Qatar University. Khamis holds a PhD in mass media and cultural studies from the University of Manchester in England. She is the coauthor of *Islam Dot Com: Contemporary Islamic Discourses in Cyberspace* and *Egyptian Revolution 2.0: Political Blogging, Civic Engagement, and Citizen Journalism* (both Palgrave Macmillan, UK). She has published articles in international and regional academic journals in both English and Arabic. She is the recipient of a number of prestigious academic and professional awards.

Farhad Khosrokhavar is a professor at the Ecole des Hautes Etudes en Sciences Sociales in Paris, France, specializing in the social movements of Iran after the Islamic Revolution; radical Islamist movements; and the Arab Spring revolts. He has published eighteen books in French, English, and Persian, three of which have been translated into at least eight different languages, and more than seventy articles. He has been a Rockefeller Fellow (1990), a Yale Visiting Scholar (2008), and a Harvard Visiting Scholar (2009). His latest book is *The New Arab Revolutions that Shook the World* (Boulder, CO: Paradigm).

Joshua Landis is Director of the Center for Middle East Studies and Associate Professor at the University of Oklahoma's College of international Studies. He is also President of the Syrian Studies Association. He writes *Syria Comment*, a daily newsletter on Syrian politics that has some 50,000 readers a month. His publications include "The US – Syria Relationship: A Few Questions," *Middle East Policy* (17: 3 – Fall 2010): 64–74; and, with Joe Pace, "The Syrian Opposition: The Struggle for Unity and Relevance," in Fred Lawson, ed., *Demystifying Syria*. London: Saqi Books, 2009, pp. 120–143.

Simon Louvish is the author of almost thirty books including novels and film biographies of Laurel and Hardy, the Marx Brothers, Cecil B. DeMille, May West, and W.C. Fields. A film school teacher and dual Israeli-UK citizen, and a resident of London, he is also the author of the Blok Saga series of novels (vols. 1–6), which are available from the author at simonlouvish.com

Mouin Rabbani, a Dutch Palestinian, is a coeditor of *Jadaliyya* and a contributing editor of *Middle East Report*. His collection *Aborted State? The UN Initiative and New Palestinian Junctures* was coedited with Noura Erakat (Washington, D.C. and Beirut: Arab Studies Institute, Forum on Arab and Muslim Affairs, 2013). He has written and commented widely on Middle East affairs and currently lives in Jordan.

Abdelaziz Radi, who received his PhD from Marc Bloch Humanities University in Strasbourg, France, is currently a professor of business management at the Faculty of Law at Cadi Ayyad University in Marrakesh. He was previously a research fellow and guest lecturer at the Refugee Studies Centre, Oxford University and a fellow of the Maxwell School of Citizenship, Syracuse University, where he researched such issues as citizenship, civic engagement, and civil society.

Curtis R. Ryan is a professor of international relations and comparative politics at Appalachian State University, with a particular interests in Middle East politics, Islam and politics, and international terrorism. He holds a PhD from the University of North Carolina, Chapel Hill. He has been a Fulbright Scholar in Jordan and the author of *Jordan in Transition: From Husayn to Abdullah, Boulder* (Lynne Reinner Publishers) and *Inter-Arab Alliances: Regime Security and Jordanian Foreign Policy* (University Press of Florida).

Eve Sandberg, Associate Professor of Politics Oberlin College, received her Ph.D. from Yale University. Her research centers on comparative democratization, political party systems, non governmental organizations, and gender studies. Most recently she has written on South Africa, Morocco and Zambia. Her teaching focuses on international relations, Third World political-economies, African Studies, and U.S. foreign policy. She received the Distinguished Teaching Award from Oberlin College in 1999 and in 2005 the Outstanding Teacher Community-Based Learning Practitioner Award.

Viola Shakir, who grew up in both Germany and Egypt, is a freelance filmmaker, film curator, and movie critic. She studied arts, Middle Eastern studies, and cinema at universities in Stuttgart and Hamburg. Between 1998 and 2005 she lectured on cinema at the American University in Cairo, her subjects including the history of Arabic films. Her books include *Arab Cinema: History and Cultural Identity* and *Popular Egyptian Cinema: Gender, Class and Nation* (both American University in Cairo Press).

Carol Soloman is Visiting Associate Professor of Art History at Haverford College. She is also a curator specializing in nineteenth-century French art and the contemporary art of the Arab world. She received a 2012–13 Fulbright Fellowship for research on contemporary art and identity in the Maghreb. From 2002 to 2008 she was Curator of European Art at the Mead Art Museum at Amherst College. She has published and lectured widely on topics ranging from Napoleon and Josephine to Cézanne and issues of diaspora and transnational identity in contemporary art, especially during the Arab Spring revolts.

Alex Winder is a PhD candidate in the departments of History and Middle Eastern and Islamic Studies at New York University, where his work focuses on police and crime in Mandate Palestine. He received a master's degree in Middle Eastern Studies from Harvard University in 2009. In 2010 and 2011 he was a fellow of the Center for Arabic Study Abroad Program in Damascus, Syria and Cairo, Egypt.

INDEX